Understanding Human Motivation

Understanding Human Motivation
What Makes People Tick?

Donald Laming

Blackwell Publishing

© 2004 by Donald Laming

350 Main Street, Malden, MA 02148-5020, USA
108 Cowley Road, Oxford OX4 1JF, UK
550 Swanston Street, Carlton, Victoria 3053, Australia

The right of Donald Laming to be identified as the Author of this Work has been
asserted in accordance with the UK Copyright, Designs, and Patents Act 1988.

First published 2004 by Blackwell Publishing Ltd.

Library of Congress Cataloging-in-Publication Data

Laming, D. R. J. (Donald Richard John)
Understanding human motivation : what makes people tick? / Donald Laming.
p. cm.
Includes bibliographical references and index.
ISBN 0-631-21982-X (alk. paper) — ISBN 0-631-21983-8 (pbk. : alk. paper)
1. Motivation (Psychology)   I. Title.

BF503.L36 2003
153.8—dc21
2002154555

A catalogue record for this title is available from the British Library.

Set in 10/12$^{1}/_{2}$pt Sabon
by Graphicraft Limited, Hong Kong
Printed and bound in the United Kingdom
by MPG Books Ltd, Bodmin, Cornwall

For further information on
Blackwell Publishing, visit our website:
http://www.blackwellpublishing.com

CONTENTS

Preface and Acknowledgments   xii

INTRODUCTION: THREE FUNDAMENTAL IDEAS   1
What is "Motivation"?   2

How Can We Study Human Motivation?   3
The use of anecdotal material   3

Three Fundamental Ideas   6
Quasi-mechanical behavior   6
Personal view and camera view   6
Social extrusion   7
Some omissions   8

The Plan of this Book   9
Questions for discussion   10

1 DETERMINISM AND FREE WILL   11
Determinism   12
Psychological theory treats behavior as determinate   13

Free Will   14
Questions for discussion   20

2 TERROR   21
The Origins of Fear   23

Components of Fear   25
Two stages in the genesis of fear   27

Fear as Instinct   30
   Pathological fear   32

The Experience of Fear   33
   Companionship   33
   Military combat   34
   Being in control   34
   Training and skill   35

The Persistence of Fear   35
   The persistence of memory   35
   Recurrence of fear   36
   Questions for discussion   37

3 SEX   38
  Personal View and Camera View   40
   Which view — personal view or camera view?   42
   Lay psychology   43

  Sexual Behavior is Quasi-Mechanical   45
   "Mechanical"   45
   "Substantially mechanical"   46
   Acquisition of patterns of sexual behavior   47
   The pleasure principle   49

  Some Questions about Sexual Behavior   51
   1 What are the extraneous signals which trigger sexual behavior?   51
   2 What other signals or social constraints act to modify sexual behavior? 52
   3 What about the intense feelings that accompany sexual activity?   53
   4 What has this to do with the survival of the species?   54
   5 What about the variation in sexual behavior from one adult to another?   56
   6 Does sexual behavior have to match between male and female?   56
   7 How much of our sexual behavior is innate and how much acquired?   57
   Questions for discussion   59

4 CONSCIOUSNESS   60
  Two Views of What People Do   61

  The Meaning of "Consciousness"   62
   Philosophical inquiry into consciousness   64
   The neural signature of consciousness   65
   Personal view and camera view   67

The Relationship of Subjective Experience to Objective Observation   69
The split brain   75
Why is consciousness important to the study of motivation?   79
Questions for discussion   80

5 BOREDOM   81
The Political Background   82
"Brainwashing"   83

Sensory Deprivation   84
Hallucinations   85
Disturbances of perception   92
Cognitive deficits   94
What does it all signify?   96

Boredom   96
Boredom at work   97
Leisure activities   97
Questions for discussion   102

6 SOCIAL CONVENTIONS   103
Milgram's Experiments   104
Proximity of teacher and pupil   104
What is going on?   106
Relaxation of the conflict   108
The importance of social structure   109

Social Conventions   111
Social conventions are different in different societies   113
Social conventions also differ between subgroups within the one society 116

Understanding Milgram's Results   117
Military obedience   119

The Stanford County Prison Experiment   120
Questions for discussion   123

7 THE RATE FOR THE JOB   124
How Much Do Different People Earn?   124
*1 People doing the same job get paid the same (irrespective of how well they
do it), unless, sometimes, they happen to be women*   125
2 Those people closest to the money are paid the most   125
*3 If someone can earn more by negotiating a private deal, well, good luck
to her or him*   128

Boardroom pay   130
MPs' financial interests   134
What has this chapter really been about?   137
Questions for discussion   139

8 LONELINESS   140
The Experience of Being Alone   140
Applications of research into social isolation   143
"Brainwashing"   144

Feral Children   147
What may we conclude from the attempted rehabilitation of these three children? 151

Conclusions on Social Isolation   153
Questions for discussion   155

9 THE MORAL SANCTION   156
The Moral Sanction   157
An experimental study of extrusion   157
Whistleblowers   159
Examples from the wider society   162

Some Interim Conclusions on Extrusion   167
1 Extrusion is spontaneous   167
2 Moral constraints are subconscious   169
3 The sanction of extrusion is powerful   171
4 The underclass   171
Questions for discussion   173

10 PEER PRESSURE   174
Social Conformity   174

Informational and Normative Influences   177
Informational influence   178
Normative influence   179
Group cohesiveness   180

What Happens if the Majority is Not Unanimous?   181
Inversion of majority and minority   184

How Large Does the Majority Have to Be?   185
Individual differences between participants   186
Interrogation by the police   188

Summary   192
Questions for discussion   194

11 THE CROWD   195
The Problem   195
The flashpoint   196
"Group mind"   197
The random evolution of crowd behavior   197

1 Social Attitudes, Standards, Conventions Evolve   197

2 Social Conventions Can Evolve Rapidly   198

3 The Evolution of Social Conventions is Essentially Random   202
Rumor   202
Public protest   203

4 The Likelihood of Disorder, of Riot, Depends on the Crowd's
Reason for Being   205

5 The Likelihood of Disorder, of Riot, also Depends on the Social Setting   207

Summary   209
Questions for discussion   209

12 RAGE . . .   210
Why Are People Aggressive?   211
Frustration   212
Negative affect   212
Retaliation   213

Aggression as Instinct   213
The "terrible twos"   213

Instrumental and Emotional Aggression   214

Experimental Methods   215
The Buss aggression apparatus   216
The effects of alcohol   218

Aggression in Everyday Life   220
Domestic violence   220
Road rage   222
Social cognition   223
Crowding   225
Three principal factors   226

Summary   228
Questions for discussion   229

13 ... AND ARE WE PROVOKED TO VIOLENCE BY THE MEDIA?   230
    Video Nasties   230

    "Copycat" Murders   231

    Boxing   234
        The effect of watching a boxing match   235

    Neighbor Disputes   236
        Sympathetic motivation   237

    Suicides   238

    The Long-Term Effect of Television Violence   239

    Summary   243
        Questions for discussion   244

14 MONEY   245
        Two ways to become rich   246
    The Psychopathic Personality   247

    Machiavellianism   248
        The $10 game   249
        The con game   250
        Pawnbroking   252
        Eye contact   253
        Credibility when lying   253
        Pyramid selling   256
        Commissions for financial services   257
        Questions for discussion   261

15 GAMBLING   262
    The Prevalence of Gambling   262
        Rationality   264
        The estimation of probabilities   265

    Blackjack   268
        How gamblers play blackjack   269

    Roulette   270
        Betting systems   271

    Luck   272
        Personal view and camera view   274

    Sales Promotions   276
        Questions for discussion   277

16 HUMAN MOTIVATION: HOW DOES IT WORK? 278

Three Fundamental Ideas 278

Personal view and camera view 278

Quasi-mechanical behavior 279

Social conventions 280

How Does it All Work? 281

Hormones 282

References 284

Index 302

PREFACE AND ACKNOWLEDGMENTS

What makes people tick? Why do people do what they do? I set out to write a book on human motivation and found that those questions could not be satisfactorily answered by themselves. *Homo sapiens* is the most advanced, the most complex, most adaptable, and most intelligent of all biological species, but is still a biological species. One must therefore expect people to display instinctive patterns of behavior like those which ensure the continuing survival of all subhuman species. But we do not feel as if our behavior is instinctive, mechanical, switched on by circumstances outside of us; we feel, instead, that we are *choosing* what to do. So I am immediately involved with the apparent irreconcilability of determinism and free will.

I have also to be concerned with the nature of consciousness. We sometimes feel angry or afraid or excited and those feelings color what we do, even to the point of sometimes doing things we did not intend. Do other people feel emotions in the same way as I do? and how are those internal feelings related to what I see them do? Boredom, for example, we know as a subjective malaise, but that feeling has much in common with the frustration of other, more obvious, motivations. So we have, on the one hand, what people *say* they feel and, on the other, what they are actually seen to do, such as injecting drugs. We need to trace a relationship between these two accounts.

There is also the notion of *responsibility*. Except for those who are certified insane, each of us is responsible at law for our actions and, more immediately, we have moral obligations to those around us, especially our close families. So why is it that we do not routinely cheat and defraud and rob each other? Indeed, there are a few people who do just that! That is a profound problem and the pronouncements of religious leaders and philosophers do not provide the answer. The standards of behavior which obtain in our society and the way in which those standards are enforced are of great importance to what people do, and do not do, and I cannot but be concerned with the psychological foundations of ethical behavior. An enquiry into human motivation must therefore involve itself with many derivative questions and becomes, like it or not, a study of the entire human condition.

By *motivation* I mean the initiation of quasi-mechanical behavior, and it needs to be emphasized straight away that this is the antithesis of the meaning of "motivation" in a detective story. The detective – Hercule Poirot, or Miss Marple, or Adam Dalgleish, or whoever – asks who would profit from this murder, the underlying idea being that the murder has been carefully planned (it has indeed, so that the reader can have the enjoyment of puzzling out who did it and how it was done) and carried out with only one small slip. Real-life murders are seldom like that, and neither is real-life motivation. If you suppose that the things people do are the carefully considered actions of rational men and women, then there is a long catalog of stupid actions which defy explanation. Norman (1999) lists a succession of men (and one or two women) in recent public life who have made fools of themselves with indiscretions of various kinds, mostly of a sexual nature. The prince, of course, is the President of the United States of America playing with Monica Lewinsky in a windowless corridor off the Oval Office. How could they be so silly?

If you continue to think of motivation in detective-story terms, there is no getting beyond that question: How could they be so silly? To understand actions such as Bill Clinton's seduction of, it seems, a series of women, that internalized, reason-for-action, calculated-outcome, rational notion of motivation has to be abandoned. Bill Clinton and the other public figures did what they did because they were "switched on." Switch someone on and their actions follow almost like clockwork. What we have to study is the innate patterns of behavior stored inside individuals, the signals that switch them on and those other circumstances which modulate the expression of their innate patterns. That represents quite a different view of motivation. It does not accord with personal experience – and we must ask why it does not accord – but it is nevertheless the view that ultimately makes sense.

Chapters 1 to 15 are based rather closely on a series of lectures that I have given to third-year undergraduates here in Cambridge for the past six years. Giving those lectures has meant working out what ideas about motivation especially need to be put across and how best to do it. I have endeavored to transpose those explanations into text. My lectures are also illustrated with video examples of the kinds of thing people actually do, but unfortunately those examples cannot be reproduced here.

Nevertheless, I emphasize that this is the subject above all others in which the student should observe what people around him or her do, and video is much the best way to accomplish that. At present there is a substantial volume of broadcasting on UK terrestrial television of some relevance to understanding human behavior. There is quite a bit of sex (of a serious, what-do-people-do-and-why? rather than a purely prurient kind), there are programs on drugs, and crime, and a surprising amount of "aggro" – *Neighbours at War* and *Workers at War* (BBC1), *Neighbours from Hell, Garages from Hell, Nannies from Hell, Parking Wars*, and *Police, Camera, Action!* (ITV) – to say nothing of other documentaries on more diverse topics. I emphasize that this material is broadcast as entertainment; it entertains by informing, but it is still entertainment. Moreover, in most cases a television journalist can do no more than interview the participants after the event. Nevertheless, when two well-heeled neighbors spend tens of thousands of pounds each at law contesting the ownership of a three-inch strip of land (Gibb, 1999), what is going on? That is the kind of episode to make one think. The springs of human behavior are not what we suppose them to be.

It should cause no surprise if, *viewed as material for the social psychologist,* I say that these programs generally are of a low grade only. I repeat that they are made for entertainment, not for academic study. Only a tiny fraction of the material I record off-air makes it into my lectures as illustration. But what also needs to be emphasized is that seeing people doing their "thing" without thought of being recorded and later mulled over by a social psychologist is, in spite of the defects and the difficulties of capturing valid material in the first place, immensely more informative than merely reading about it in a book or newspaper. Again, on-the-spot home video footage of young men squaring up to fight (Woodford, 1998) is very much an exception, but it should not be missed. It does not have the quality of wildlife filming (it is only home video, filmed through a window), but it does have the objectivity, and it reminds me of nothing so much as two tigers fighting over vacant territory (Birkhead, 1997). I find that comparison a source of inspiration.

I emphasize that this book does not present a complete survey of human motivation. There is, for example, nothing about hunger or thirst. At the physiological level of investigation hunger and thirst have been much explored. It has happened so because these have been the principal manipulations to make rats run mazes and press levers in Skinner boxes. Current knowledge about the substrates of hunger and thirst are well covered in texts on physiological psychology (e.g., Rolls, 1999) and nothing is achieved by reiterating that material, less authoritatively, here. But in human society the meals that we take, when we eat, where, and what we eat, are very much a matter of convention, different in different cultures. So the physiological substrate is far from being the total of human hunger and thirst; though, frankly, I have little to add to it. But in a society where people generally are as well nourished as we are in Britain today, the social psychology of eating and drinking does not have much to tell us about the nature of human motivation. I may be wrong here; there may be a treasure-trove of exciting information that I have yet to discover. But according to my present knowledge, hunger and thirst do not tell us much.

But one serious omission from this book is maternal care. A baby cries in the middle of the night. Mother wakes and gets up to feed her infant. It happens night after night, notwithstanding that the mother is tired and short of sleep. Why? If mothers did not routinely get up to feed their babies when they cried in the night, we should (probably) none of us be here. But what is the psychological mechanism that wakes the mother up and gets her out of bed? My intuition is that maternal care could tell us much about human instinct, and there is an enormous existing literature. My only excuse is that I just do not know that literature and must leave this domain of motivated behavior to someone who knows much more about it than I.

Finally, I should like to say thank you to Colin Fraser, Anthony Marcel, and Trevor Robbins with whom I have enjoyed a number of especially illuminating discussions during the seven years in which my understanding of human motivation has been maturing. In addition, Trevor Robbins read the first draft of this book and I am grateful to him for his critical comments. I also thank my editors at Blackwell, Phyllis Wentworth and Sarah Coleman, for their patience in nudging me toward this final version of my text.

The author and publishers gratefully acknowledge the following for permission to reproduce copyright material:

Extract from *Panorama: First Sex*, producer S. Powell. BBC1, March 8, 1999. © 1999 The British Broadcasting Corporation.

Extracts from "Mental effects of reduction of ordinary levels of physical stimuli on intact, healthy persons" by J. C. Lilly. *Psychiatric Research Reports*, vol. 5, pp. 3, 6–7. © 1956 American Psychiatric Publishing Inc. Reprinted with permission.

Extract from *Walk On The Wild Side: Firebugs*, producer S. Cosgrove. Channel 4, January 19, 1994. © 1994 Channel 4. Reproduced with permission.

Extracts from *World in Action: An MP's Business*, producer N. Hayes. ITV, March 26, 1992. © 1992 Granada Television Ltd. Reproduced with permission.

Extract from *Wolf Children* by L. Malson, pp. 71–3. © 1972 Verso. Reprinted with permission.

Extracts from *The Wild Boy of Aveyron* by J. Itard, pp. 103–4, 175–6, 177–8. © 1972 Verso. Reprinted with permission.

Extracts from *Error of Judgement* by C. Mullin, pp. 220–1, 222. © 1986 C. Mullin. Reprinted with permission.

Extracts from *TV Eye: Scab*, producer J. Lewis. Thames Television, May 25, 1985. © 1985 FremantleMedia Ltd.

Extract from *Public Eye: Serial Rapists*, producer J. Burge. BBC2, March 19, 1996. © 1996 The British Broadcasting Corporation.

Extract from *Hartlepool Mini Driver*, Network North, February 10, 1993. © 1993 Tyne Tees Television Ltd. Reproduced with permission.

Extract from *First Tuesday: Free to Talk*, producers R. Franey and G. McKee. Yorkshire TV, November 7, 1989. © 1989 Granada Media Group Ltd. Reproduced with permission.

Extract from *Panorama: Bridgewater – a Miscarriage of Justice*, producers M. Dowd, K. Sutcliffe, D. Lord, and M. Renn. BBC1, February 24, 1997. © 1997 The British Broadcasting Corporation.

Extracts from *Cutting Edge: Casino*, producer M. Nelson. Channel 4, February 15, 1998. © 1998 Channel 4. Reproduced with permission.

The publishers apologize for any errors or omissions in the above list and would be grateful to be notified of any corrections that should be incorporated in the next edition or reprint of this book.

INTRODUCTION: THREE FUNDAMENTAL IDEAS

A, B, C,
tumble down dee.
The cat's in the cupboard,
and can't see me.

(Cited by Opie & Opie, 1997, from Halliwell, 1842)

But *why* is the cat in the cupboard?

Archy and Bella are just 2 years old as I write this. They cannot actually say why the cat is in the cupboard, but, if ever my wife or I open a cupboard door, one of them or the other or both immediately jump in. If I try to lift them out, they retreat behind the hot water cylinder or the wine rack. To Archy and Bella "cupboard" includes any compartment big enough to take a cat but ordinarily closed to them – the toilet, the bathroom, the garage, and the spare bedroom, the opened drawer of a dressing table or an umbrella opened up indoors to dry, even the wheel arch of a car, perching on top of the tire! If they hear the bedroom door open and shut, they will queue outside and, when I come out, they are in, often without my noticing. In that way it happens from time to time that they get shut in a cupboard for hours on end. Nevertheless, they seem not to learn. They do not want to stay in the cupboard – they will come out of their own accord after perhaps 10 minutes – but their fascination with entry into a cupboard continues unabated. With Archy and Bella it appears to be a near-mechanical response.

That some biological responses are mechanical is shown especially well by the begging response of herring gull chicks described by Tinbergen (1951): "Newly hatched chicks of the herring gull beg for food by pecking at the tip of the parent's bill. The latter regurgitates the food on to the ground, picks up a small morsel and, keeping it between the tips of the beak, presents it to the young. After some incorrect aiming the young gets hold of the food and swallows it" (p. 29). The bill of the herring gull is yellow, with a red spot at the end of the lower mandible; that stimulus can be easily simulated with a cardboard model in the laboratory.

Experiment shows the red spot to be critical. Spots of other colors will also produce a begging response, but less freely, while a plain yellow bill is the worst of all. In fact, the color of the bill makes no difference at all, nor does the color of the head.

This begging response is clearly instrumental in the nurture of the young, and it is easy to imagine that evolution has shaped it and the color of the parent's bill to match perfectly. But the truth of the matter is actually simpler than that. In the laboratory it was found that a red pencil-shaped model with three white roundels near the tip proved even more effective than an accurate three-dimensional model of the parent's head (Tinbergen & Perdeck, 1951). The begging response is simply a mechanical reaction (Tinbergen's term is *innate releasing mechanism*) to a specific stimulus (a *sign stimulus*) and the red spot on the parent's lower mandible merely triggers that reaction sufficiently well to ensure that the young get fed. There is no biological adaptation; there is no necessity even for an innate releasing mechanism to be biologically useful (though this one clearly is). It is just that if the begging response were not triggered by the parent's bill, or did not exist at all, neither would the herring gull.

WHAT IS "MOTIVATION"?

For this book, motivation means the switching on of some pattern of behavior, of a program of action specified within the individual. That program might be innate or it might have been modified by experience. But each biological species has to have a repertoire of instinctive, "hardwired," patterns of behavior; humankind is no exception. If we, and all other animal species, were not equipped with such patterns of behavior, we should none of us be here. Given an appropriate stimulus, the corresponding pattern is triggered. Although the word "motive" suggests a source of energy, the trigger stimulus is not itself that source; rather, it releases an internal source of energy, somewhat like switching on a television set. We are therefore set to look for instinctive patterns – I shall use the phrase "quasi-mechanical" – in human behavior.

Eating food when hungry is instinctive. Laboratory training can tack another sequence of behavior – traversing a maze or pressing a lever – on to the front end of that instinctive pattern, a procedure known as "conditioning." When the augmented pattern which results has been well learned, it is executed pretty much as one single pattern, as though it were all instinctive. When a rat has thoroughly learned its way through a maze, its performance on repeated trials is fast and accurate. Carr and Watson (1908) examined the effects of shortening or lengthening certain of the alleys in such a well-learned maze. When an alley was shortened, rats tended to run into the end wall instead of turning as required. When an alley was lengthened, rats tended to turn (into what was now a blind) at the place where they had formerly been accustomed to turn and then to continue at full speed to the end of the cul-de-sac.

Placing a rat in a familiar Skinner box provides the stimulus that triggers the augmented behavior pattern. Once that augmented pattern is reliably acquired, a further sequence can be tacked on to its front end, and animals can, in some cases, be trained to execute remarkably elaborate sequences of behavior (Skinner, 1951). But if the stimulus that triggers that elaborate pattern approximates a stimulus that triggers some other instinctive pattern, the sequence breaks down or, at the least, becomes unstable. Breland and Breland (1961, p. 683) found that though their pig had been properly trained to put a (wooden) penny in a piggy bank, he would, after a matter of weeks, "repeatedly drop it, root it, drop it again, root it along the way, pick it up, toss it up in the air, drop it, root it some more, and so on." Any stimulus which engages some instinctive (or augmented) behavior pattern will cause the animal to do something. The wrong social stimulus at the wrong time and place can throw a child into a tantrum or cause an adult to turn to violence.

HOW CAN WE STUDY HUMAN MOTIVATION?

On February 12, 1993, James Bulger, aged 2, was led away by two 10-year-olds from the Strand shopping precinct in Bootle, Merseyside, and brutally murdered. Everyone asks: "Why did they do it?"

When an experimental scientist is faced with an empirical question, he or she devises an experiment to provide the answer. But there is not going to be any experiment in which a child of 2 gets killed, or even runs a risk of being killed, or gets hurt in any way, or is even scared or subject to any other kind of trauma. And there is not going to be an experiment in which 10-year-olds are invited to do any of these things, even in simulation. Experimental manipulations in which motivational states are induced, even in volunteer participants, are potentially unethical. To put the matter succinctly, no experimenter (in our society) is going to be allowed to wind anyone up over something which actually matters. So how then can we study human motivation?

The Use of Anecdotal Material

We must use whatever material evidence comes to hand – experiment where experiment is feasible (but frequently experiment is not feasible), survey evidence (but often it is not possible to record a sufficient number of like cases), and elsewhere anecdote. Anecdotal material does not have the reliability of controlled experimental observation, nor even the lesser reliability of survey data. So, does it tell us anything of value? And let not the fact that "human interest" stories make attractive reading delude us into thinking that they therefore convey a balanced picture. Anecdotal material fulfills three functions.

1 Illustration of experimental findings

Particular well-chosen episodes are cited as illustrations of the kind of behavior to which experimental findings relate. This may sound needless to the professional who is *au fait* with the history and direction of the investigation. But leave that illustration out, and the reader has to supply a substitute from his or her own experience and that substitute may be lacking. So, one very important function of anecdote, which I believe psychologists use too infrequently, is to illustrate what the experimental findings mean for ordinary everyday behavior. Psychopathologists have long used case histories to illustrate their discourse and social psychologists need something similar. In fact, mere verbal description of what someone did is often inadequate – the reader needs to see them doing it and, in these days, that is feasible with video recordings.

2 Confirmation of the validity of experimental findings

Surprising though it may seem, anecdote is also needed to check on the applicability of experimental results. Laboratory experiments on aggression are a particular case in point. The laboratory procedure (e.g., Lang, Goeckner, Adesso, & Marlatt, 1975; see p. 216) is contrived. Two strangers meet in a laboratory and carry out some task together. One of them (a confederate of the experimenter) is abusive to the other. The other (the real participant) subsequently gets a chance to administer "electric shocks" to the confederate. What level of shock, or how many shocks, will he administer? The results of such an exercise are, of course, valid for that particular laboratory milieu, but what do they tell us about spontaneous violence in the real world outside? Do they extrapolate to violence on the football terraces?

The participant in a laboratory experiment enters into a social relationship with the experimenter, a factor which proves material in understanding the results from Milgram's (1974) experiments in chapter 6. If the experiment provides knowledge of results at the end of every trial, that social relationship hardly affects the outcome, but when the experiment involves a choice of response for which there is no "right" or "wrong," implicit indication from the experimenter of what kind of response would appear plausible can have material effects on the data. Magnitude estimation (Stevens, 1956) is a case in point. The experimenter nearly always illustrates his instructions with numerical examples and the values of the numbers in those examples are taken by the participants as an indication of how widely they should spread their numbers. Preplanned manipulation of the numbers in the illustrative examples has fed through into the spread of the numerical estimates (see Laming, 1997).

In experiments with confederates and electric shock there are two additional hazards. Some of the participants might suspect (1) that the confederate is a confederate, not a real partner, and react differently in consequence, and (2) that the confederate does not really get shocked anyway. So experiments on aggression, especially, need to be validated by comparisons with real aggressive behavior from the world outside, and that means anecdote. Berkowitz (1993, chap. 13) addresses this question and is able to confirm that the results of laboratory experiments hold up when extrapolated to the real world outside the laboratory; but – that question very much needed to be answered.

3 Identification of questions for further study

There are some areas of human social behavior which are not amenable to specifically experimental manipulation; for example, the influence of the media on violent crime and suicide or the evolution of social conventions. Some of these topics can be studied by sociological survey (e.g., Phillips, 1983), but there are others which, seemingly, cannot – extrusion from society; allocation of very large rewards in any context; the effects of bringing up a child in isolation from human society. In addition, the experiments which Asch and Milgram performed would probably not be permitted according to the ethical standards prevailing today. In these cases, anecdote is all that we have left. The question therefore arises: What use can we make of anecdote? Does it have any usable reliability?

The design of an experiment or a survey first requires the formulation of a question to put. While the correlations in survey data can often be reanalyzed from a different point of view, experimental data usually cannot because control observations, essential from that different point of view, are commonly lacking. So an important preliminary concerns the choice of hypothesis around which to design the experiment. *The function of anecdote in the absence of experimental or survey data is to identify useful questions to put.* If there is no opportunity to answer those questions – the experiments cannot be carried out, or insufficient cases are available for statistical analysis – that is as far as the inquiry can proceed. There is no reason why the inquiry should not proceed that far, but the conclusions are necessarily tentative and their fallible basis must always be borne in mind.

To sum up, anecdote provides an invaluable source of ideas and hypotheses in areas of human behavior where experiment is lacking. Anecdote does not supersede experiment – quite the contrary. Its most important function is to provide the inspiration for experimental investigation, where such investigation is feasible. But anecdote can also inform us about the extremes of human motivation, especially terror and rage. By looking at those extremes we can see the most clearly what motivation is and how it works. Moreover, those extremes are where experiment is most frequently infeasible.

THREE FUNDAMENTAL IDEAS

It is in the nature of scientists to propose theories and to use those theories both to guide further research and to systematize the material to be taught. But in the field of human motivation I, personally, think that "theory" is premature. In our present state of understanding, "theory" amounts to no more than "perspective." But perspectives are important. They assist the student to assimilate the material and to relate different observations to each other. This book is written around three particular perspectives that complement each other. The examples I have already cited introduce the first.

Quasi-Mechanical Behavior

Some part of human (and animal) behavior consists of instinctive patterns of response. Some larger part consists of instinctive patterns which have been augmented by acquired sequences of behavior; these might be due to specific learning or to cultural constraints. These augmented behavior patterns are initiated sometimes by quite specific stimuli – the sight of one's girl- or boyfriend.

Archy and Bella will jump into any small compartment, and some not so small. The responses of my pet cats look quasi-mechanical, triggered by quite specific circumstances. Is there any reason why similarly mechanical responses should not be incorporated in human behavior? If that possibility sounds implausible, out of the question, that is only because we are accustomed to look at human behavior, especially our own behavior, from the inside out, as it were. Our own behavior does not *feel* mechanical at all, and that lack of a mechanical feel to it calls forth a second idea.

Personal View and Camera View

On May 26, 1999, Manchester United played Bayern Munich at Nou Camp, Barcelona, in the final of the European Cup. The football match was watched by about 500 million people worldwide (Dickinson, 1999) who all saw exactly the same video transmission. That is exactly a *camera view*, perceptible by anybody and everybody, except for those who were there at the match. One such was David Beckham. Two minutes into injury time at the end of the second half he took a corner kick on the left. This was Manchester United's last-gasp opportunity to win the match outright before going into "extra time." What was in Beckham's mind as he took that kick? Whatever it was, it constitutes a *personal view*, private to the individual. No one else can experience what David Beckham felt as he took that kick.

Now the viewer, any of the 500 million, would have seen that corner kick as fairly predictable. David Beckham is highly skilled and very well practiced at corner kicks. He routinely took them for his side throughout the game. The only uncertainty for the viewer was exactly where the kick would go. But for Beckham the kick was anything but mechanical. He had to choose where to put the ball – on whose head he should try to place it. The kick does not seem at all mechanical to the footballer because he is at one and the same time both the highly skilled and complicated biological machine kicking the ball and also the observer of that action – a machine observing itself.

Here is the crucial point: A machine cannot see itself as mechanical. Look at the clock sitting on your mantelpiece. (I envisage a clock of traditional construction driven by a mainspring.) You use it to tell the time. Now imagine yourself to be the clock, looking out into the room. What would you see from your perch on the mantelpiece? The clock itself cannot tell the time because, like you and me, it cannot see its own face (except with a mirror and then the face would be left-to-right). Nor would the clock know anything about clockwork, just as you, unless you happen to be a doctor, do not understand the internal workings of your own body. And even doctors have to speculate about what happens in the brain. But you *do* know what it is like to be "wound up," and so also does your clock. I would guess, without inquiring, that David Beckham felt immense internal tension at that crucial moment in the game.

Social Extrusion

We shall also need a third idea. When we compare social behavior in one culture with that in another it quickly becomes apparent that much of what people do, socially, is constrained by the society in which they live. To take one simple, but very common, example. Although it is practicable in these days of the welfare state for a mother to bring up children on her own, her task is much easier if she has the children's father to help her. That cooperation comes at a "price," because the management of the children, the way they are disciplined, the holidays the family takes, is now a joint decision of both parents, neither of whom has exclusive command. Marriage has been with us for as long as historians can trace the custom, and many husbands and wives find the arrangement satisfactory. But the nature of the marriage relationship is characteristically different in different societies. Compare, for example, marriage customs on the Indian subcontinent (see p. 115) with marriage between spouses of Anglo-Saxon descent in the UK; that difference is the result of social custom. Compare also "plural marriage" as practiced by some Mormons (Whitworth, 1999b). An additional idea is needed to answer the question of how different societies maintain these different institutions of marriage – how society exercises that kind of control over its members.

The analogy of the clock is again useful. The clock on the mantelpiece is there so that we can tell the time at a glance. There is, however, a "correct" time and if that is not what the clock shows, it must be put right. Once the clock has been put right, it must continue to tell the correct time, and if it runs slow or fast, it must be regulated. Ultimately, if regulation does not achieve sufficiently accurate running, the clock is thrown away and replaced by a more reliable timepiece. Individual members of society are subject to an analogous control. Our interaction with others around us seems to be instinctive. But if we, as individuals, do not respond sufficiently to the people around us, that interaction decreases and, if sufficiently deviant behavior be persisted in, ultimately ceases. Two practical examples are the incarceration of the criminal in prison and of the insane in a mental institution. But, for most of us, the resulting loneliness proves so intolerable that the patience of society is seldom pressed that far. Society maintains control over its individual members through the ultimate sanction of extrusion. That is the third idea we shall need.

These three ideas will help us to understand why people do what they do. What people do is to express innate patterns of behavior and culturally acquired patterns in ways that are constrained by the demands and conventions of the society in which they live. The same three ideas will also help in transposing what people say – why they did certain things, or the emotions they felt while doing them – into terms of what can be objectively observed.

Some Omissions

There are some topics, however, that I have omitted, even though most people will naturally look for them in a book on human motivation. Foremost are eating and drinking, because the long tradition of research into how our intake of food and water is controlled is all at a physiological level and seldom makes contact with the reasons why ordinary people eat and drink when they do. While the physiological mechanisms controlling water intake are sensitive to internal deficit, we habitually drink before any deprivation arises at that level. The internal deficit needs to be severe to promote drinking. Blood donors lose about 10 percent of their blood volume, but do not usually report thirst (Wagner, 1999, chap. 4). How then is normal drinking controlled? It seems to me that these topics are more appropriately placed in a book on physiological psychology. Sleep and arousal are two other omissions, and I suggest Wagner (1999) as a readable physiologically based account to make up this deficit.

But I see the absence of any account of maternal care as a serious omission. A mother's getting up in the middle of the night to feed her newborn baby is, surely, instinctive. But I do not know enough to write about it.

THE PLAN OF THIS BOOK

In the study of human motivation, we are still at the stage of searching for those questions that especially need to be asked. This book is therefore organized around a series of elementary propositions that may, or may not, hold true. Each chapter argues one such proposition. The plan of the whole is most succinctly set out by listing these propositions.

Chapter 1	There are two quite distinct views of what people do; there is (1) the (subjective) personal view we each have of our own behavior and (2) the (objective) camera view that everybody else has of us. In camera view behavior appears determinate, but in personal view it is characterized by free will.
Chapter 2	Terror is the circumstance in which, even in personal view, people realize that their actions are no longer under their own control.
Chapter 3	Sexual behavior is compulsive. In camera view it appears substantially mechanical; and the emotion we experience is the subjective counterpart (in personal view) of being motivated.
Chapter 4	The relation between subjective experience (in personal view) and objective behavior (in camera view) is important to the interpretation of anecdote . . .
Chapter 5	. . . and is used to put the question: Why is boredom so unpleasant? Is it because some basic motivation is being frustrated?
Chapter 6	Much of our social life is governed by the expectations of people around us. Experiments by Stanley Milgram on obedience reveal some of the ground rules.
Chapter 7	Expectations are sometimes different in different societies, and in different subgroups within the same society.
Chapter 8	Deprivation of social contact with other people is intolerable. This is important because . . .
Chapter 9	. . . the ultimate threat of extrusion provides society with the sanction by which social conventions are maintained.
Chapter 10	Social conventions evolve through interactions between individual members of society. Experiments by Solomon Asch, ostensibly on the judgment of lengths of line, reveal some of the ground rules.
Chapter 11	When a crowd is temporarily cut off from the influence of the larger society around it, those interactions can sometimes cause collective behavior to evolve rapidly.
Chapter 12	Aggressive behavior is also instinctive, but is ordinarily held in check by social convention. Sometimes that constraint proves insufficient . . .

Chapter 13   . . . but incitement by the media proves to be no more than slight.

Chapter 14   Money is technically an incentive, but proves to be a great motivator. It quickly brings out the baser side of human nature . . .

Chapter 15   . . . and drives people to gamble.

Finally, chapter 16 summarizes the entire argument and speculates how our understanding of human motivation might develop over the next 50 years.

QUESTIONS FOR DISCUSSION

1   How would you (the reader) formulate a theory of motivation, and what do you think such a theory should look like?

2   What differences (if any) are there between the motivation of humans and of subhuman animals?

1

DETERMINISM AND FREE WILL

Why should a book on human motivation be concerned with determinism and free will?

I have already described Archy and Bella's habit of entering every cupboard they can and, not infrequently, getting trapped inside. They have other near-mechanical habits as well. If I open a bottle of mineral water – sssss! – they quickly run off. When Bella stalks a pigeon, she crouches low, with her belly almost on the ground. No one taught her to do that – she left her mother at the age of 3 months – and she does it in the middle of an open lawn – she has not yet learned the advantages of cover or of dappled shade to a white and tabby cat. When she catches a bird, she brings it into the dining room to eat. The bird is promptly confiscated, so, when she next catches a bird, she brings it into the dining room to eat . . . It is not surprising that we usually think of animals as responding mechanically to stimuli and events around them and being thereby devoid of responsibility. But we do not speak about human behavior like that!

As a cultural matter, we have one way of speaking about animal behavior, why an animal does what it does – animal behavior is generally seen as determinate, though some people do anthropomorphize their pets – and quite another way of speaking about human behavior – people have free will. Why the difference? It is generally agreed that what people do and why they do it is controlled by events in the brain and central nervous system, and examination of the brains of humans and of most mammals shows them, in the first instance, to be morphologically alike. Is the organization and direction of human behavior, on the one hand, and of animal behavior, on the other, really so different?

This problem arises because we are, at one and the same time, scientists asking questions about what people do and also people about whom those questions might be asked. We can observe other people with complete objectivity and notice that they do things that we might easily be doing ourselves. At the same time, we experience our own actions from a distinctly subjective viewpoint. There are, therefore, two quite distinct viewpoints from which *our* behavior might be observed. There is the viewpoint (*personal view*) from which we experience our own actions, and that other viewpoint (*camera view*) from which every one else observes us. We typically look at what animals do in camera view, but interpret other people's behavior from a personal-view standpoint.

If we decide, on careful examination, that people and animals are motivated in much the same way, then we have to choose between these two different viewpoints. Each of us has a lifetime's experience of feeling, thinking, planning, and doing, and we view all that in terms of intention. We assume that other people have a similar fund of experience and that what they do can be understood in the same way. This is characteristic of the personal viewpoint from which we experience our own actions and all our internal thoughts, feelings, and desires.

But we do not know what it is like to be a cat and therefore take an objective camera view of what cats do. Cats are seen as somehow mechanical, their behavior as determinate. But we can also look at our fellow men and women in camera view – though, curiously, not ourselves. There are, then, these two ways of looking at what people do. Which of these is the more appropriate to a scientific study of motivation? That question has to be resolved before we can even get started. The apparent antithesis between determinism and free will is truly "Question No. 1" for the study of human motivation.

It will help to have a peek at the solution in advance. What each of us does is, at one and the same time, *both* determinate and *also* characterized by free will. If we observe someone else's behavior in camera view, their behavior appears determinate; but our own behavior in personal view is characterized by free will. Someone else looking at what we are doing will see our actions as determinate, but see themselves as having free will. The difference between determinism and free will lies not in the behavior but *in the viewpoint from which that behavior is observed*. That is the central issue in this chapter.

DETERMINISM

Philosophically, free will is "the power or capacity to choose amongst alternatives or to act . . . independently of natural, social or divine restraints" (*Encyclopaedia Britannica*, 1989b), while determinism is the "theory that all events, including moral choices, are completely determined by previously existing causes" (*Encyclopaedia Britannica*, 1989a). The philosophical idea of determinism is particularly associated with Laplace in the eighteenth century, but it has an ancient theological history as the doctrine of predestination. However, while it might appear that the theologians have been arguing some real difference of opinion, though one very difficult to resolve, the arguments to follow here will show that determinism and free will are not antitheses – they are simply the characteristics of two different ways of looking at what people do. So, in their theological incarnation, they are no more than shibboleths, serving only to distinguish between different religious societies.

Psychological Theory Treats Behavior as Determinate

In the sixteenth century astronomers discovered the motions of the planets to be precisely determinate. Could that physical determinism be extended to the sphere of human action? Could it be that human behavior is also determinate? That question led to the science of experimental psychology that emerged in the middle of the nineteenth century. "Every man has will power and is a free agent to do as he likes, but what he likes is based on causes operating within him" (Gruenberg, 1967, p. 810). Experimental psychology is the study of those causes, and treats human behavior as determinate.

The constant-ratio rule

As one example, Clarke (1957) asked four participants to listen to a sequence of consonant-vowel morphemes, selected at random from a set of six, in a background of noise. The noise was set at a level that permitted about 50 percent correct identifications. The participants then listened to further sequences of morphemes selected, again at random, from a subset of three of the original six. Could the probabilities of identification from the subset of three be predicted from the corresponding probabilities for the master set of six? An answer based on the constant-ratio rule is set out graphically in figure 1.1. The constant-ratio rule says that the probabilities of identification from a subset of three are proportional to the corresponding probabilities within that subset when it is a part of the master set of six. The filled circles compare predictions and outturns for single cells in the 3×3 confusion matrices. The open circles compare articulation scores for complete subsets of three morphemes. What this result means is that while the participants are pondering "Is it /pa/ or /ta/ or /ka/?" with no feeling whatsoever of constraint or coercion, the experimenter can predict what they will say, at the least in the long run.

As another example, manufacturers of foods and drinks maintain panels of tasters to sample new recipes and say which they prefer. It is assumed that the preferences expressed by the panel extrapolate to consumers in general, and that extrapolation presupposes that the preferences are somehow determinate, at least in aggregate. There has been a very extensive investment in statistical theory, how best to analyze data from tasting panels and from similar sources (e.g., Böckenholt, 1992). Such work raises an obvious problem.

One can rarely predict a single individual's choice reliably, predictions only work for the proportions of choices by large numbers of people. This is characteristic of much of psychological theory and one might well ask if the indeterminacy implicit in psychological prediction reflects the operation of free will on the part of the participants. In practice, it is assumed that each individual choice is entirely determinate – it is just that we do not know all the causal factors. Provided those unknown causal factors are none of them individually significant, their aggregate

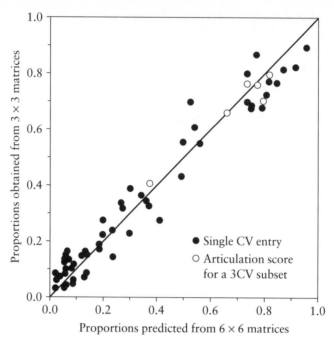

Figure 1.1 Articulation scores for morphemes in a background of noise. The ordinate shows the score obtained when the morpheme was selected at random from a subset of three, and the abscissa the score predicted from identifications when the same morpheme was selected from the master set of six. Reproduced with permission from Clarke (1957, p. 718). © 1957 American Institute of Physics.

effect can be summarized by a normal distribution in a manner that is justified by well-established mathematical theory. There is no such thing in psychological theory even remotely resembling free will.

FREE WILL

The distinction between determinism and free will is properly a distinction between the (subjective) personal view and the (objective) camera view. In the classroom, I bring that relationship out with three demonstrations.

"Paper, Scissors, Stone"

"Paper, Scissors, Stone" is a traditional children's game. It is illustrated in figure 1.2. There are three alternative configurations of the hand which the two children

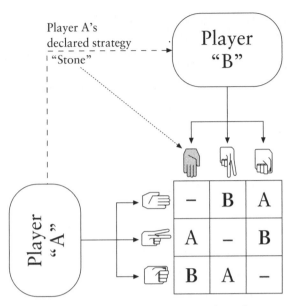

Figure 1.2 Feedforward between players in "Paper, Scissors, Stone."

produce simultaneously from behind their backs. Paper loses to Scissors (because scissors can cut paper), but wins over Stone (because paper can wrap round a stone); and Stone wins over Scissors (because scissors will blunt on a stone). If both players produce the same configuration, it is a "washout."

In my classroom demonstration, Player "B" is a student volunteer from the class, but Player "A" is a confederate who has been instructed what to do. I explain that the game is all about choice of strategy. So, after three rounds to make sure that everyone knows how the game is played, I ask my confederate what strategy she will employ next time. Knowing what configuration "A" is going to produce enables "B," of course, to win every time. If "A" says "Stone," then "B" chooses Paper.[1] Once "B" has got into this way of playing, "A" takes advantage of her foreknowledge of what "B" is going to do and wins with Scissors.

The point of my classroom demonstration is brought out by two questions. First, I ask the student volunteer whether she had a free choice of configuration or whether she felt that her choice of play was forced. Of course, the student says that she could have produced any of the three hand configurations she wished; she simply *chose* to

---

[1] Alas, students at Cambridge University are sometimes too sophisticated. As Player "B" they will typically say to themselves: "If 'A' says she is going to produce Stone, she will expect me to choose Paper; in which case 'A' will win by choosing Scissors. But I shall outsmart her by choosing Stone." If "A" does indeed produce Stone, the result is a "washout."

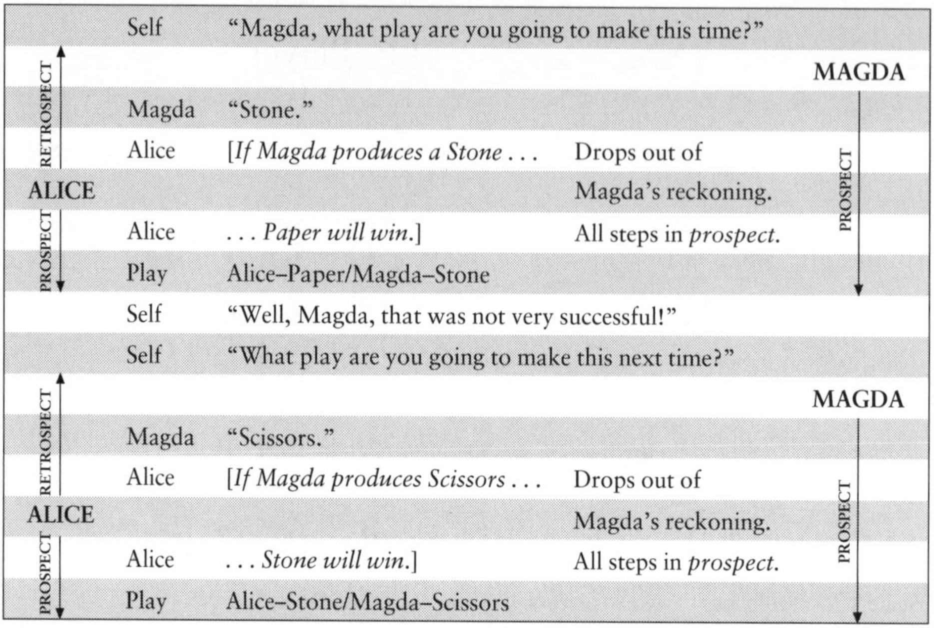

	Self	"Magda, what play are you going to make this time?"		
				MAGDA
	Magda	"Stone."		
	Alice	[If Magda produces a Stone . . .	Drops out of	
ALICE			Magda's reckoning.	
	Alice	. . . Paper will win.]	All steps in prospect.	
	Play	Alice–Paper/Magda–Stone		
	Self	"Well, Magda, that was not very successful!"		
	Self	"What play are you going to make this next time?"		
				MAGDA
	Magda	"Scissors."		
	Alice	[If Magda produces Scissors . . .	Drops out of	
ALICE			Magda's reckoning.	
	Alice	. . . Stone will win.]	All steps in prospect.	
	Play	Alice–Stone/Magda–Scissors		

(Left margins labelled RETROSPECT and PROSPECT for ALICE; right margins labelled PROSPECT for MAGDA.)

Figure 1.3   Prospect and retrospect in "Paper, Scissors, Stone."

produce Paper. The second question is to my confederate: Was she able to predict the hand configuration her opponent subsequently chose? And the answer, of course, is that once, as Player "A," she had announced what she was going to do, her opponent's choice was predictable. Those two answers pose this further question: How is it that behavior by Player "B" that "A" can predict in advance is subsequently described as "free"?

The answer is elementary. The two players view the game from different points of view. Each player has an entirely unfettered choice of play but is, at the same time, influenced by her opponent's declared (or presumed) choice. A choice which is unfettered from the player's (personal) point of view is seen as constrained from the opponent's (camera) view. Behavior which is predictable from the viewpoint of Player "A" is experienced as *free* from the viewpoint of Player "B." It is the same behavior; and the predictability attaches to the point of view, not to the behavior. This relationship, as it emerged on one occasion, is set out in figure 1.3.

The italic type indicates Alice's presumed internal thoughts which are not available to Magda and so cannot form part of Magda's basis for prediction. But those internal thoughts are entirely in Magda's *prospect* and could not, in any case, enter into her reckoning. Magda predicts Alice's play directly on the basis of her own announcement. But Alice can choose her play (in *prospect*) simultaneously with those internal thoughts (in *italic*) and with Magda's declared play in *retrospect*. This gives Alice a different basis for her choice of play and with respect to that different basis her choice is *free*.

So *free will* is characteristic of one's own behavior experienced in personal view, observed from the personal viewpoint of the actor. One cannot view other people's behavior from the vantage point of the actor and for that reason other people cannot be perceived to have free will. Of course, we commonly attribute to other people the same freedom of will that characterizes our own personal experience; but that is assumption, not perception.

Chess

The game of chess provides another demonstration. Figure 1.4 shows the position after Black's twenty-fifth move in the game between Sämisch and Nimzowitch at

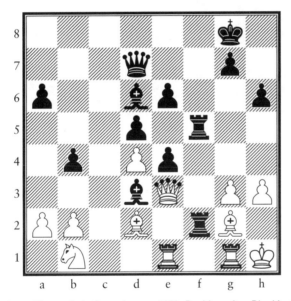

Figure 1.4   Sämisch vs. Nimzowitch, Copenhagen, 1923. Position after Black's twenty-fifth move.

- 26. Kh2, R(5)f3 wins the White Queen.
- 26. B(d2)c1 permits B(d3) × b1.
- 26. R(either)f1 or Bf1 loses a piece after R × f1ch; 27. R × f1, B × f1; 28. B × f1, R × f1ch.
- 26. Rd1, Re2; loses Queen for Rook; while
- 26. g4, R(5)f3; 27. B × R, Rh2 is mate.
- If 26. a3, then 26. . . . , a5, and the position is essentially unchanged.
- Likewise 26. h4 followed by 27. h5 is met by noncommittal moves by Black (e.g., Kh8; Kg8), again leaving the position unchanged. White quickly runs out of such moves.

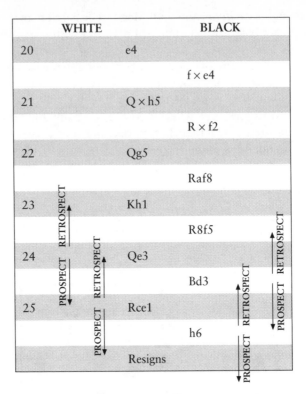

	WHITE	BLACK
20	e4	
		f × e4
21	Q × h5	
		R × f2
22	Qg5	
		Raf8
23	Kh1	
		R8f5
24	Qe3	
		Bd3
25	Rce1	
		h6
	Resigns	

Figure 1.5   Sämisch vs. Nimzowitch, Copenhagen, 1923 – prospect and retrospect.

Copenhagen in 1923. This is, perhaps, the most famous of all examples of *Zugzwang* from actual tournament play. Sämisch (White) had a free choice of several different moves, "free" in the sense that all these moves were permitted by the rules of chess. However, moving the King leads to loss of the Queen; likewise any move of the Queen or Knight leads to immediate capture. The available moves of both Rooks and both Bishops are similarly constrained. In each case Black's reply is predictable and, in the event, Sämisch resigned. Figure 1.5 shows the different prospects and retrospects of the two players interleaved. The two sets of prospects and retrospects correspond, of course, to the two sides of the board – the two points of view from which the game might be observed.

Games provide clear illustrations of the way in which free will depends on the point of observation, first, because the rules of a game constrain what each player may do to the point that the opponent's reply is quite often predictable and, second, because one can always move round to the other side of the board to see how things look from there. Chess exemplifies this possibly better than any other game. Each player chooses his move (action) after consideration of what his opponent might do

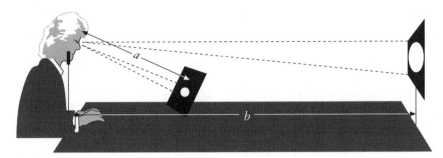

Figure 1.6 Experimental setup for the measurement of phenomenal regression to real size.

next (reaction). The game looks different according to the side from which it is viewed; if the vantage point be changed, action and reaction interchange.

Phenomenal regression to real size

A third example is provided by the measurement of phenomenal regression to real size (Thouless, 1931a, b). The experimental setup is shown in figure 1.6. The participant chooses a disc placed normal to her line of sight at a distance *a* to match as accurately as possible the *angular size* of the disc at the rather greater distance *b*. People invariably choose too large a disc, a bias toward matching the *physical* size.

In the experiment matches are obtained to discs of different sizes. After a few matches have been made, the experimenter is able to predict what match the participant will choose for other sizes of disc because the match chosen tends to be a constant fraction of the physical size of the target (though not, of course, so small a fraction as that needed to match its angular size). But, if questioned, the participant still reports having a free choice of match. The difference between the experimenter's and the participant's view of the procedure is summarized in table 1.1.

So, free will does not imply arbitrary behavior; it is simply a property of the personal point of view. The opponent's free will cannot be observed in camera

Table 1.1 Two views of phenomenal regression to real size

Experimenter's (camera) view	*Participant's (personal) view*
• Present stimulus card	• Examine stimulus card
• Record participant's choice of match	• Choose matching stimulus
• Can predict participant's choice . . .	• "Should it be this circle or that?"
• i.e., determinate	• i.e., free will

view; every play by the opponent is seen as a *reaction* to the player's prior *action* and therefore not free. All that the experimental psychologist might be aware of as observer is a limited ability to predict a participant's response.

There is, however, one qualification. A person's behavior is certainly determinate if it can be predicted accurately in advance. But if that prediction be signaled to the individual, he or she can then (if so minded) choose some different behavior; and it might appear that free will, or at least indeterminacy, is introduced into the objective record thereby. This is illusory. A participant receiving feedforward of the experimenter's prediction is a (slightly) different participant to the one who remains incommunicado, and behaves differently in consequence. The experimenter's prediction relates to the uninformed participant; it does not apply to the participant receiving feedforward. But one might, of course, develop a second prediction for a participant who has received a specific feedforward, and this is the basis of the bluff in "Paper, Scissors, Stone." It has its real-world applications.

If one counts the cards played in blackjack with sufficient accuracy, it is possible to gain an edge over the casino and casinos will bar players who demonstrate too much skill. Black (1993, pp. 67–75) recounts the success of a "little dark-haired guy from California" who challenged certain Nevada casinos in the 1960s to a private "no-limits" game of blackjack. For the first few evenings the advantage appeared to fluctuate between the player and the house. But once the casino had got accustomed to the swings of this particular gambler's play, "the little dark-haired guy from California" turned on the heat and the casino was stung before it realized what was happening. Since a casino does not willingly reveal that it has been stung, the coup was repeated in different Nevada casinos to yield a total profit estimated at $250,000.

The important conclusion for this chapter is that a scientific study of motivation must proceed in camera view, from a wholly objective vantage point. But perhaps that conclusion is not yet sufficiently obvious. So, imagine a situation in which people find themselves doing things without choosing to do them – doing things whether they wish to or not. That kind of compulsion would sit uneasily with free will and show a study conducted in personal view to be inadequate for our purposes. The most compelling circumstance of that kind is terror, to which I turn next.

QUESTIONS FOR DISCUSSION

1 How can you choose what you will do if a psychologist can, at the same time, predict what you will choose?

2 Why do we attribute free will to other people while regarding subhuman animals as (more or less) stimulus-response machines?

2

TERROR

Ordinarily people talk about what someone else does by imagining themselves in that other person's shoes, in a pseudo-personal view. They do not do that with animals because they cannot imagine what it would be like to be, say, a cat. For this reason human and animal behavior are typically viewed from two quite different vantage points, from personal view and from camera view respectively. In principle, an account of human motivation might be formulated from either point of view – though we must be careful not to mix the two. But if there are circumstances in which people find themselves doing things without choosing – doing things whether they wish to or not – consciously unable to control their own behavior, then a purely personal-view account becomes inadequate. Here is an example.

British Airtours Flight KT328

At 7.13 a.m. on Thursday August 22, 1985, British Airtours Flight KT328 to Corfu lined up to take off from Ringway Airport, Manchester. As the aircraft was gathering speed along the runway, seconds before actually leaving the ground, the port engine exploded, puncturing the fuel pipe, wing tanks, and fuselage, and setting the aircraft on fire. The takeoff was immediately aborted. But the fire spread to the interior of the aircraft within a matter of seconds, producing dense smoke and panic. Notwithstanding that the emergency services were alongside the aircraft within seconds of the explosion, 55 passengers were burnt beyond recognition; 82 escaped (Davenport et al., 1985).

Among those who escaped were Ellis Wardle, his girlfriend Deborah Wilson, and two of their friends. The following year, in August 1986, these four took a holiday together in the south of France. But they did not, of course, travel by air – they took a coach tour instead. During their tour their coach passed a forest fire.

> A forest fire created much excitement for a coachload of holidaymakers speeding through the south of France last month. Amid the laughter some took pictures but at the rear of the coach four young people sat petrified.

Ellis Wardle, Deborah Wilson, Alison Hughes and Mark Tatlock were on their first holiday since August last year when 55 people died in the fire after an engine exploded on the British Airtours Boeing 737 as it prepared to take off at Manchester.

. . . for Wardle, a 21-year-old joiner, last month's forest fire revived unbearable memories: "I remembered the black smoke, the pitch darkness and I thought I was going to die again."

His girlfriend, Deborah Wilson, 20, a trainee chartered accountant, said: "When the coach stopped moving because of a traffic jam I felt trapped. There were bushes on either side of the road and I kept thinking that if the fire got closer there would be nowhere to run."

The coach passed by safely but the four were so upset by the experience that they cut short their holiday and returned to their home in Northwich near Manchester.

. . . for survivors like Wardle and Wilson, not a single day goes by without them reliving what happened.

"It didn't sink in for days," said Wardle. "Then I started turning the whole thing over and over again in my mind. Some nights I couldn't sleep and when I did I dreamt about the plane and the fire. I was moody and I became irritable for no reason."

The smell of any sort of smoke reminds them of the pungent fumes from the burning aircraft. The bad dreams and fits of irritability are triggered off by sounds, pictures and last week by the coroner's inquest into the disaster. (Krushelnycky, 1986)

Ellis Wardle and his friends cutting short their holiday and returning home is a patent example of compulsive behavior. People do not terminate their holidays because they want to; they do so because they cannot help themselves. If people cannot help themselves, then a personal-view account of their inability will not be able to explain why. The reevocation of terror in a situation which is reminiscent of some previous trauma is the occasion above all others in which people realize that they are no longer in control of their actions. It provides an especially clear example of the substantially mechanical nature of what people sometimes do, and why we have to look at human behavior in the same way as we look at animals.

Lisa Potts

Here is another example. Lisa Potts was formerly a nursery nurse at St Luke's School, Wolverhampton. On July 8, 1996, Horrett Campbell, a paranoid schizophrenic, took a machete to a group of 3- and 4-year-old children who were enjoying a teddy-bears' picnic.

Miss Potts, 21, who suffered deep wounds to her back, chest and hands, a broken arm and severed tendons on her hands, had grabbed the children, hidden some in a school storeroom and some beneath her skirt as the blows rained down. Stafford Crown Court heard that she had shown "astonishing courage" and completely disregarded her own safety to save the children's lives. (Midgley, 1996)

To the school, to the staff, to the parents and the children, to the nation as a whole, Lisa is a heroine. But, notwithstanding all that goodwill and sympathy, Lisa has been unable to resume her job at St Luke's. She suffers "vivid daytime flashbacks of the incident" which make continuing to work at St Luke's intolerable (Duce, 1997). Indeed, she has been unable to maintain any permanent employment since that episode (Coates, 2001b); it has devastated her life. One might naively think that the brave, the courageous, are those who feel no fear. Not at all! They are afraid just as much as you or I. It is just that, at the moment of trial, they subordinate their fear to the needs of other people: "for me it feels like on that day I hadn't really done anything out of bravery. [Of course not!] I was in a position to run back for the children and that's what I did. It was out of instinct [thinking only of the children] really more than bravery" (Midgley, 1996). But the suffering afterwards, the emotional trauma, is not any the less on that account.

THE ORIGINS OF FEAR

There are two distinct elements in each of these episodes. First comes the initial traumatic experience, the being trapped inside the burning aircraft with its associated terror, or the machete blows from Horrett Campbell. Then some subsequent episode – the forest fire in the south of France, or a return to the scene of the attack – elicits recall of the original traumatic experience which, in turn, reinstates the terrified state of mind. Ellis Wardle and his friends found that second-hand terror more than they could bear and had to abandon the rest of their holiday. Lisa Potts's experience was no different.

It is an old idea that fear and anxiety result from the reactivation of some previous trauma. It figured in the early days of psychoanalysis.

> In the book which Freud published jointly with Breuer – the well-known *Studies on Hysteria* (1895) – *real* traumatic events were thought to lie behind the symptoms of the neurotic patient. Such traumatic experiences were postulated as having given rise to a "charge of affect." This, together with the memories of the traumatic event, was actively dissociated from consciousness, and could find expression by being converted into symptoms. Based on this view, treatment consisted of a variety of attempts to force the forgotten memories into consciousness, simultaneously bringing about a discharge of affect in the form of catharsis or abreaction.

This idea

> lasted till 1897, when Freud discovered that many of the "memories" of traumatic experiences, especially seductions, given to him by his hysterical patients were not in fact memories of real events at all, but rather accounts of fantasies (Freud, 1887–1902). (Sandler, Dare, & Holder, 1973, p. 14)

But this idea which Freud at first espoused, and then rejected, has recently been resurrected in the alleged recovery of memories of sexual abuse. The present-day version says that many of the psychological difficulties which people experience as adults originate in sexual abuse as a child. People have suddenly "remembered" sexual abuse by their parents, often after undergoing psychotherapy.

> The lives of Joe and Sheila Skitt have been shattered by an accusation they consider to be . . . false . . . , an accusation all the more painful since it comes from their only daughter. Suffering post-natal depression after the birth of her second child, and hoping for advice on how to cope with tensions in her marriage, she sought help from a counsellor. Her father says that counselling changed her. "At the end of this therapy, when she was 29, she suddenly accused me and her mother and various other people of abusing her as a child, not just once but over and over again." (Lambert, 1995)

The charges of childhood sexual abuse have been named "false memory syndrome" by parents thus accused.

The merits of this and of most other similar cases are unclear. Certain it is that some children are sexually abused by parents or other adult relatives or by carers. It is equally certain that many of those children are profoundly disturbed by the abuse and, at the same time, unable to talk about it, either because they cannot bring themselves to do so or because there is no sufficiently sympathetic ear to listen to them. When the child becomes an adult, especially an adult undergoing therapy, that situation may change. But it would be too much to suppose on that basis that all such allegations were true. Each recollection is a construction from past experience, often from past experiences, drawing on several different sources. And frequently the individuals who make allegations of past sexual abuse come from dysfunctional families within which the "recovered memories," real or imagined, serve a psychological purpose.

Irrespective of the general validity of "recovered memories," it is unlikely that *all* fears originate from some previous psychological trauma.

1   First, the end product of psychoanalysis often turned out to be no more than childhood fantasy.
2   Second, some fears, most notably the fear of going outside (agoraphobia), often have a gradual onset (though not always). Marks (1978, pp. 79–82) describes two such cases.
3   Third, there is the clinical syndrome of "free-floating anxiety." This is a state of anxiety of pathological intensity, characterized by excessive irritability and other bodily symptoms, but not attributable to any external source.

It is more likely that some people are naturally anxious and develop pathological fears and anxieties following much, much slighter episodes than being trapped inside a burning aircraft or suffering a machete attack.

Under the heading of *fear* I include normal reactions to perceived danger, together with *phobias* which are irrational reactions to specific situations or objects, reactions out of proportion to any danger which those situations might bring, and *anxiety*, a general condition of unease. Fear becomes "pathological" when the emotional reaction that accompanies it interferes with the individual's everyday life.

COMPONENTS OF FEAR

Looking at the signs and symptoms which are grouped together under the heading of *fear*, there are four components that need to be distinguished (cf. Lang, 1970).

1   First, there is the subjective apprehension of danger, the internal emotion itself.
2   Second comes the activation of the sympathetic nervous system. This activation generates the physiological symptoms of fear which include an increased pulse; palpitations; muscular tremor; sweating, especially on the palms of the hands and the soles of the feet; the hairs of the skin standing on end; pallor; dilation of the pupils; a rise in systolic blood pressure; dryness of the mouth; constriction of the chest, the feeling of choking, and rapid breathing; nervous dyspepsia, the "butterflies in the stomach"; frequent micturition and defecation; and weakness in the limbs, "India-rubber knees."
3   The third component is the cognitive object of the fear, what one is afraid of – snakes, spiders, cats, birds, heights and fear of falling, flying, darkness, thunderstorms, specific noises, enclosed spaces, going out-of-doors, blood, and more besides.
4   Fourthly, there are attempts to escape the object of fear by, for example, staying at home, or abandoning one's holiday.

But these four components of fear do not correlate well with one another.

Infantrymen going into battle feel intense fear – but they do not (usually) run away! Here, however, is one exception "to prove the rule." Four days after the D-Day landings in Normandy,

> a sergeant in the First Battalion, 502d Infantry, was hit through an artery during the Carentan Causeway fight on June 12, 1944. It happened in a flash. One second he was hit and the next he was running for a first-aid station without telling his own squad why he was getting out. They took after him and then the line broke. Others who hadn't seen the sergeant make his dash saw someone else in flight. They too ran. Someone said: "The order is to withdraw." Others picked up the word and cried it along the line: "Withdraw! Withdraw!" It happened just as simply as that. (Marshall, 1947, p. 146)

Panic is always latent in battle.

The "free-floating anxiety" mentioned above is a kind of fear devoid of any cognitive object. The notion sounds bizarre, but analogous "free-floating" emotional states can be created artificially, in an experiment – in this example, euphoria and anger. Schachter and Singer (1962) engaged volunteer participants ostensibly for an experiment on the effect of a vitamin compound on vision. In fact, the participants were injected with 0.5 cc of either adrenaline (adrenaline bitartrate) or saline. Now adrenaline is released into the bloodstream by sympathetic nervous activity (which mediates the physiological concomitants of fear), and adrenaline itself produces the very same physiological effects. So here is the critical question which Schachter and Singer addressed: What kind of emotion would the participants experience, fear (in the absence of any reason to be afraid) or something else?

Some of the participants were told, while the injection was being given, that it was mild and harmless with no side-effects. Others were told to expect side-effects such as numbness of the feet, an itching sensation over parts of the body, or a slight headache, side-effects other than those which normally occur from adrenaline. Yet other participants were told, correctly, to expect hand tremor, palpitations, and flushing. And a fourth group of participants received only a placebo (saline) with the advice that it was totally harmless and without side-effects. There was, therefore, a four-way comparison between three groups who had received an injection of adrenaline but had been variously (mis)informed about its effects and a control group who had received only a placebo.

The injection of adrenaline had the effect on purely physiological measures – on pulse rate, and on palpitation and tremor as assessed by self-report – that one would expect. But while the participants in this experiment were filling out their self-report questionnaires, they were joined by another participant (a confederate of the experimenters) who filled out the same questionnaire, either in a happy, carefree frame of mind (euphoria) or in an abusive, contemptuous mood (anger), both moods being clearly exhibited to the real participant. This introduced a third factor, induced mood, to compare with (1) the actual injection (adrenaline or saline) and (2) what the participant was told about its effects.

Those participants who had been correctly informed about the side-effects attributed their internal bodily sensations to the injection, and were relatively unmoved by the antics of the confederate. But those who had been misinformed were more labile, so that what the participants had been told to expect was rather more influential in determining their reaction to the injection than the adrenaline they had actually been given. Even more to the point, the polarity of each participant's reported mood (euphoria or anger) depended on the interaction with the confederate. This makes that interaction the most influential factor of all; that is to say, in the generation of emotional reactions, it is social factors that matter the most. All this suggests that fear is not a single concept with a fixed pattern of signs and symptoms but, rather, a collection of loosely related phenomena which we just find it convenient to group together.

Two Stages in the Genesis of Fear

It is helpful to distinguish two stages in the genesis of the initial traumatic experience. These are (1) an innate fear reaction to certain kinds of *stimuli* and (2) the transference of that reaction to other situations that are not, of themselves, intrinsically fearful. I emphasize that the innate reaction is not a reaction to danger *per se*, but to certain kinds of stimuli which may be associated with danger. The idea of innate fear reactions possibly explains why people who develop irrational phobias develop them in relation to certain categories of objects and situations – snakes, spiders, cats, birds, heights and fear of falling, flying, darkness, thunderstorms, specific noises, enclosed spaces, going out-of-doors, blood – but not to other situations, equally dangerous – cars, machinery, bombs, and gunfire. The suggestion is that people are biologically prone to develop fear reactions to certain kinds of stimuli and these stimuli only. These hypothetical reactions have been called *prepared* fears (Seligman, 1970, 1971). Marks (1978, pp. 31–4) suggests that we innately react with fear to certain kinds of movement (characteristic of snakes and spiders, but not to the snakes and spiders themselves), to being stared at by others, to heights, and separation from parents among other possibilities.

This idea of "prepared fears" is still no more than conjecture. But if it accurately describes the state of nature, one would expect to see these innate fears in individuals who have had no opportunity to acquire them by training, that is, in the very young.

The visual cliff

The visual cliff (figure 2.1) is an apparatus for testing whether young infants, too young to tell us what they can distinguish, can nevertheless judge differences in depth. There is a central platform with strong plate glass at about the same level on either side. All surfaces are covered with a checkerboard pattern of black and white squares, both the central platform and the surfaces *under* the plate glass on each side. On one side the checkerboard is placed just under the plate glass so that the surface on that side appears only just below the glass. But on the other side the checkerboard pattern is placed much further below the glass, to give an impression of depth. So, assuming that the infant – about 9 months old, just beginning to crawl – does not yet know about the properties of plate glass, one side puts the infant only a little above the surface he can see, but the other suspends him over what appears to be a substantial drop. What is commonly found is that a 9-month-old infant will crawl to his mother over the shallow side, but not over the deep side, notwithstanding that mother is calling him. The inference is that at 9 months old babies can distinguish deep from shallow depths.

But does the infant refuse to go to his mother because he is actually afraid of the depth, and could he nevertheless have learned that reaction during 9 months of

Figure 2.1 The visual cliff. The baby will crawl to his mother over the shallow side (left), but not over the deep side (right) (Gibson & Walk, 1960).

being carried around in his mother's arms? Suppose we take a much younger infant – 2 months old and not yet able to crawl – and place him on the deep and on the shallow sides in turn. When placed on the glass over the deep side, infants as young as 2 months show an increased heart rate, which is one of the physiological signs of fear (Schwartz, Campos, & Baisel, 1973). This does indeed look to be an innate response to depth.

"Looming"

Another reaction which looks innate is the response to "looming." The infant is seated in a baby chair (figure 2.2). In front of him is a large object which can be moved either toward the infant or away on a rack. When the object looms toward him, the infant shows a characteristic reaction; his body stiffens, but relaxes when the object recedes. Infants aged from 2 to 11 weeks have been shown to react in this way to objects coming straight at them, but not to objects which, though approaching, can be seen to be passing to one side, nor to objects receding (Ball & Tronick, 1971). This reaction has been observed both when the infant can see the moving object directly (as in figure 2.2) and also when he sees only the shadow it casts on a screen. One study (Bower, Broughton, & Moore, 1970) has reported that infants are visibly upset and cry during the "looming" phase of the object's motion. This again looks like an innate fear reaction.

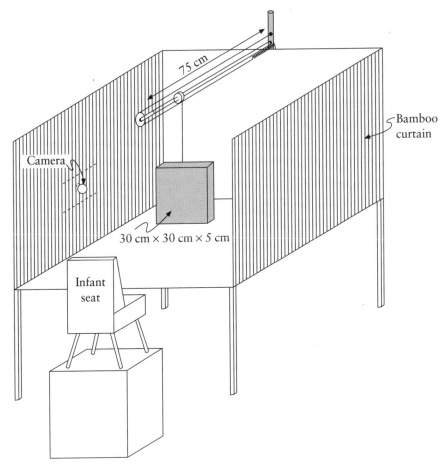

Figure 2.2 Apparatus used to study infants' reaction to "looming." Reproduced with permission from Ball & Tronick (1971, p. 819). © 1971 American Association for the Advancement of Science.

"Looming" has its adult counterpart. "Sue Fox is paralysed with fear every time she drives on a busy road" (Fox, 1999).

Snakes

Young children have also been tested with snakes, though the observations here are less convincing. Children from an orphanage aged 1.5 to 3.5 years (Prechtl, 1950) were shown a grass snake. First, the snake was held in the hand in front of the child who could see its vigorous wriggling movements. Then the snake was laid on the ground in front of the child. Finally, the snake was shut in a box while the child watched, and the child was invited to pick the snake up and take it out of the box.

The youngest children, 1.5 to about 2 or 2.5 years old, immediately reached for the snake. At about age 2.5 these reactions became muted. Children of 3 years and upwards would touch the snake tentatively when it was held in the tester's hand, but drew back as soon as the snake was put on the ground. If the snake crawled to the child and over the child's foot, the child pulled its foot away and wiped it on the ground. Finally, the invitation to open the box with the snake in it was refused with varying degrees of vehemence. The fact that this reaction does not really appear until age 3 is no bar to its being innate, but the reactions sound more like disgust than fear.

FEAR AS INSTINCT

The results of these studies with infants suggest that fear reactions may be instinctive and, as such, entirely normal. Fear is somewhat like pain. There is a component of our nervous system that serves to protect the body surface and certain internal organs from damage. If I put my hand on a hot coal, I withdraw it immediately, minimizing the burning to my skin and superficial tissues. I do not withdraw my hand because the hot coal is painful, notwithstanding that that is how the sequence of events seems to me. I withdraw my hand much quicker than that, before I have time to be aware of the pain. The withdrawal is a spinal reflex and a truly mechanical action. The pain that I feel is simply the subjective experience accompanying that hand withdrawal.

So, pain is the internal experience arising from the activation of a component of our nervous system which protects our bodies against superficial damage. Although that pain is unpleasant, we would not wish to be without it. Fear seems to be the internal sensation we get from a similar instinctive system that protects us against remote threats. The initial response to particular kinds of stimuli, which *happen* to be commonly associated with danger, helps to preserve the integrity of the individual. And that fear response is also compulsive, mechanical. But fear is not a response to danger *per se*, because the initial response is immediate; it happens before one is aware of the danger, like withdrawing one's hand from a hot coal. Fear is simply a response to certain stimuli that are associated with danger.

The "Blitz"

The heavy German air attacks on British civilians in September 1940 provide an episode which emphasizes this distinction. Philip Vernon, an eminent social psychologist of that time, wrote:

In the summer of 1940 when raids on a large scale seemed imminent in Britain, many of us were apprehensive lest they should lead to widespread panic and hysteria. Many trained and disciplined soldiers had broken down under bombardment in the war of 1914–18 and at Dunkirk. Was it likely that civilians would be any less prone to "shell shock"?

Fortunately we were wrong. Doubtless newspaper reports are often very incomplete and unduly optimistic, but the data I have collected generally confirm their accounts of the imperturbability of the majority of the population.

All observers seem to agree that raids have even less effect upon children than adults. One might have supposed that they would be more susceptible to the operation of a "fear instinct" which is stimulated by loud noises. Though sometimes frightened by the sirens or explosions when they wake up, those that I and others have observed got to sleep again remarkably easily. The novelty and the social activities of shelter life greatly appeal to them, for a time at least. Even when bombed out of their homes they have frequently been found playing happily next day, regarding it all as a great adventure. (Vernon, 1941, pp. 457, 471)

I lived through those German air raids as a small child and Philip Vernon is quite correct.

Contrary to what one might expect, an explosion is not one of the stimuli for which there exists a "prepared" fear reaction. A fear reaction to explosions has to be acquired. Soldiers acquire that reaction during their training; children have not received that training.

Fear is biologically useful because the kinds of stimuli which excite it often signal danger, heights, for example – people *naturally* draw back from the edge of a cliff. But our environment has changed so much and so recently that there are now many dangers against which fear provides no protection. One such is industrial machinery and another is driving a car too fast, especially in adverse driving conditions. People are often unaware of such dangers or, at least, of how serious they are, and protection has to be enforced by legislation. In the UK we have the Highway Code, the MOT test on cars, Health and Safety at Work Acts, and other laws besides.

Given an instinctive fear reaction, the ordinary processes of learning can transfer that reaction to other stimuli associated with danger, but stimuli which do not themselves trigger an instinctive reaction. This happens during training for active military service and for parachuting, in examinations, and while learning to drive a car. Here again the analogy with pain is helpful. The experience of pain also transfers into fear. Many people, though not everyone, are apprehensive about surgical operations and about dental treatment. Once I have put my hand on a hot coal, I am much more careful next time. So while pain and fear are *physiologically* quite distinct, the *psychological* distinction seems to be little more than a matter of context.

Pathological Fear

It sometimes happens that a fear acquired in this way is inappropriate to the circumstances – it does not protect the individual against any danger at all. When that
fear grows to a pathological intensity, when it develops to the point of interfering
with the individual's daily life, we speak of neurosis. Here is an example.

> Mima Guy's fear of spiders was so extreme that at the sight of one she would
> leap on a chair – and stay there until her husband came home.
>   "If the spider was still in the room I simply could not come down," she
> explains. "And then, if my husband refused to kill it, I would become hysterical."
>   Even pictures of the creatures made Mrs Guy turn hot, nauseous and panicky.
> "My hands would be dripping with perspiration [one of the well-known physi-
> ological symptoms of fear]." (Wooley, 1990)

Isaac Marks (1978) describes a self-help treatment for phobias, and Mima Guy
started going to the meetings of a self-help group. She kept a diary.

16 November:	Touched a picture of a giant spider. Very anxious, very hot.
23 December:	Opened an envelope containing a plastic spider in a box, with caution. Slight panic.
2 January:	Have lived with plastic spider in a box since 23 December. Can not bear to take it out or allow others to do so in case they drop it on me. Quite anxious.
7 January:	Took plastic spider out of its box. Touched it most days for a week. Even held it in my hand. Took it to the self-help group meeting in my hand. Quite relaxed.
14 January:	Small, real spider brought to the meeting. Box was opened and I did not mind. I felt I could have squashed the spider. Quite relaxed.
28 January:	Unable to look at larger real spider in a box. Looked at a spider in its web and left it there. Quite relaxed. Did not want it killed.
4 February:	Looked at three live spiders. Was completely unaffected by artificial spiders and pictures. Took three spiders home, in- cluding one quite big one (Horace). Felt quite relaxed.
10 February:	Took large, live spider back to meeting after keeping it for a week and looking at it. Let it go at meeting. Felt completely relaxed. Became a counsellor. (Wooley, 1990)

The transference of fear from some instinctive source to spiders, or any other object or situation, can be reversed – allegedly in an afternoon (Marks, 1978). But it should also be noted that some spiders are actually deadly.

THE EXPERIENCE OF FEAR

Mima Guy's diary shows that the experience of fear can be diminished, in advance of the therapy actually completing its effect. There are several ways in which this can happen.

Companionship

The experience of fear can be reduced by the presence of a companion. Here is an early case history of agoraphobia in which a companion (a prostitute picked up on the street) regularly provided reassurance (in 1871 prostitutes were viewed in a very different light to the way they are seen today).

> He is overcome by this anxiety when he is obliged to walk alongside walls or large buildings (the drill hall in the Carlstrasse [in Berlin] and the artillery school in Unter den Linden) or when he has to walk through streets on Sundays and holidays or late evenings and nights when the shops are closed. Late in the evening – he usually eats in restaurants in the evenings – he solves his problem in a curious way. Either he waits until he sees someone setting out in the direction of his home and follows close behind him, or he picks up a prostitute, gets into conversation with her and takes her part of the way home with him, until he finds another and so gradually he gets home. Even the red lights of the brothels give him some support. As soon as he sees one, his fear is lifted. (Westphal, 1871, pp. 139–40)

Kim Basinger, the film actress, is an agoraphobic. In an interview she gave to *Vanity Fair* (Bennetts, 2000), she comes across as a "bundle of nerves." "Over-whelming fears have ruled her life ever since she was a child . . . [she] was once housebound for six months." She appears to be dependent on the companionship of a husband of extraordinary patience and understanding. However, when on set, she can immerse herself in her acting role and the fears disappear.

Being alone, of course, has the opposite effect, allowing fears that are ordinarily under control to escape. This account from the Korean War is by the late Samuel Marshall, a veteran war historian who specialized in providing a worm's eye view of battles at some personal danger to himself.

> So I took off afoot across the stretch with not another person in sight. Half way, three mortar shells came in, exploding within fifty or so yards of me. The terror I knew was almost overwhelming. I ran until I was exhausted. It always

happens that way. Be a man ever so accustomed to fire, experiencing it when he is alone and unobserved produces shock that is indescribable. (Marshall, 1964, p. 72; cited by Rachman, 1990, p. 59)

Military Combat

The control of fear is of great importance in military combat. With this in mind, the attitudes and reactions of American servicemen were intensively studied during World War II by the Research Branch, Information and Education Division, of the US War Department (Stouffer et al., 1949). In one study, veteran infantrymen who had fought in North Africa and Sicily were asked to think of one of the best combat soldiers they had known and then to say what they admired in him. If the combat soldier in mind was an officer, then leadership (helping other men, leading by personal example; 56 percent) was the most salient quality of admiration, but overall it was courage (fearlessness, disregard of personal safety; 40 percent) that mattered most, especially if the respondent was thinking of another private soldier (59 percent) (Stouffer et al., 1949, chart V, p. 133).

The complement to this finding is that what unnerves a soldier more than anything else is seeing a comrade "crack." The story cited above (p. 25; Marshall, 1947, p. 146) from the Carentan Causeway battle is a case in point. For this reason, it may be better for the fighting unit as a unit that men who cannot tolerate the anxiety of frontline warfare are left behind. To discover whether this was so, some 1,766 American soldiers fighting in Italy in April 1944 were questioned about their reactions to seeing a comrade break down in battle under extreme fear. Of the 83 percent who said they had witnessed "A man's nerves 'crack up' at the front," 70 percent reported negative reactions, especially "Made me nervous, jittery, or feel like 'cracking up' myself" (49 percent) (Stouffer et al., 1949, table 4, p. 209).

Being in Control

Another factor which helps people to withstand fear is being in control. The front-seat passenger in a car, for example, is usually more anxious than the driver. In the studies of American servicemen this was shown up when aircrew in the European theater of operations were asked in June 1944: "If you were doing it over again, do you think you would choose to sign up for combat flying?" Pilots were always more willing to answer "Yes, I'm pretty sure I would" (51–84 percent) than other enlisted men (39–51 percent), and fighter pilots flying their planes single-handed (84 percent) more so than bomber pilots (51–74 percent) (Stouffer et al., 1949, charts XVIII, XIX, pp. 404, 406). Heavy bomber crews showed increasing reluctance the more missions they had flown (Stouffer et al., 1949, chart V, p. 368), and the reason is not hard to discover. The casualty rates (over 70 percent killed or missing in action after six months and 17.5 percent wounded or injured in action; Stouffer et al., 1949, table 4, p. 407) were horrendous.

Training and Skill

Another factor that helps people to cope with fear is training in carrying out exceedingly dangerous tasks. This has been studied with training courses on bomb disposal in Northern Ireland (Hallam & Rachman, 1983). Soldiers undergoing bomb-disposal training were asked to rate both their skill and their willingness to undertake seven different tasks involving different risks, ranging from a suspicious parcel in a post office to a bomb on the fifth floor of a building; they were asked for these ratings both before the commencement of their training and after they had finished their course. There were very large increases in both self-rated skill and expressions of willingness. Initially there were substantial differences between those men who had undertaken bomb-disposal duties in Northern Ireland before and those who were new to the task, but these differences had disappeared by the end of the course. An actual tour of duty, in comparison, showed rather small effects on both skill and willingness. One might suppose that the increase in willingness was consequent on seeing the dangers as less than they appeared before training. While there was some reassessment of the danger in dealing with a bomb on the fifth floor of a building, the most risky of all the tasks, the ratings of danger for the lesser tasks were unchanged. It is not that trained bomb-disposal personnel see the risks as less, but that they are simply more confident in their own ability to deal with them.

THE PERSISTENCE OF FEAR

One final question remains: Why is fear so persistent? In the story with which I began, Ellis Wardle and his friends, one year after their traumatic experience at Ringway airport, Manchester, could not bear to continue their holiday in the south of France after being reminded of that disaster by a forest fire. People seem unable to forget traumatic experiences by themselves.

The Persistence of Memory

The answer is simple: Fear is persistent because memory is persistent. And we know about the persistence of memory from some remarkable experiments published by Ebbinghaus in 1885.

Contrary to what one might suppose, memories do not decay. In nature decay is characterized by a negative exponential loss. The voltage across a capacitor, say the capacitor in a photoflash unit, decreases by some constant proportion for each unit of time that passes. After a certain period of time, the photoflash has to be recharged before it will work properly. More complex decay processes, like the decay of garden rubbish in a compost heap, are concatenations of simple processes, proceeding in sequence and at different rates. But ultimately any decay process is characterized as some quantity decreasing by a constant proportion per unit of time. It is quite clear from Ebbinghaus's data that the accessibility of the memory of some previous event decreases much more slowly than that. So memories and acquired fears persist forever. Once you have been trapped inside a burning aircraft, that experience cannot be taken away.

When recall fails, it does not fail because the memory has disappeared; it fails, if it fails at all, because one recalls a different memory (the wrong memory), or does not recall any memory at all that can possibly be correct. Therein lies the possibility of therapy.

Suppose there is some other memory, more recent than the trauma, with the potential for being recalled in place of the trauma. Suppose that second memory to have a lesser emotional affect. Therapy subsists in creating such another memory to be recalled in place of the original trauma. Because that interfering memory has a lesser affective force, so the evoked fear is weaker.

Recurrence of Fear

Let us suppose that someone suffers a traumatic experience and visits a therapist on the following day for treatment. The accessibility of a memory decreases very rapidly at first, but proportionately much slower after a lapse of time. This means that therapy that is entirely effective in the consulting room, with respect to a trauma one day old, will lose its relative dominance with the passage of time. On the following day its effectiveness will be less and the memory of original trauma may well return. This is the relationship known as Jost's law (Jost, 1897; see also Woodworth & Schlosberg, 1955, p. 730). It means that the effect of a therapeutic session should decrease with the passage of time.

It is commonly found that the effects of therapy do indeed decrease with time, and that fear recovers in part from one session to the next. According to Rachman (1989, p. 148), fear has never been reported to return with its full original force, but it returns sufficiently much to require a series of sessions for its treatment. Agras (1965) found that 50 percent of the anxiety-provoking items presented to particip-ants during systematic desensitization showed "relapse" when tested at the next therapeutic session. After these items had been re-treated in a second session, fewer of them showed repeated relapse at the next session, and so on. Philips (1985) studied seven patients with a fear of vomiting and found that short-term between-sessions recurrences of fear gradually declined with further treatment, suggesting that if treatment were continued for a sufficient time, the fear would be completely eliminated. There is experimental reason to expect this to be so.

In one of his experiments Ebbinghaus (1885/1964) learned six stanzas from Byron's "Don Juan." After 24 hours he relearned them, and again 24 hours later, and so on. After four days he was able to recite the six stanzas without error. That is to say, a sufficient number of therapeutic sessions will create a corpus of interfering memories that will last. Twenty-two years later Ebbinghaus relearned the six stanzas yet again, not having looked at them in the interim, and relearned them with 7 percent fewer recitations than in his original learning (Ebbinghaus, 1911, p. 685; cited by McGeoch, 1942, p. 329).

Returning now to the story of Flight KT328, the memory of being trapped in a burning aircraft will persist because memories persist. It is moreover very distinctive and therefore readily recalled – indeed, it tends to recur spontaneously, to the distress of the survivor. Memories that will readily be recalled in its place, competing with the memory of the original trauma, tend not to occur by chance and therapeutic help is needed. The interposition of a similar memory, but of lesser affective intensity, will dilute the emotional distress caused by recall of the original traumatic memory. That is the psychological function of therapy. The effect of a single therapeutic session will wear off, because memories created during therapeutic sessions lose accessibility like all other memories and, because the therapy is the more recent, it will lose accessibility at a faster rate than the memory of the original trauma. But a series of therapeutic sessions will build up a corpus of memories to give possibly a permanent suppression of recall of the traumatic affect. It does not matter how those competing memories are created, so that many different therapeutic techniques might work; though some methods are likely to be more effective than others.

Terror is one category of experience for which a personal-view account proves inadequate. But mild fear, even moderate fear for some people we shall meet in chapter 5, might still seem rational from a personal point of view, and terror of a paralyzing magnitude might be regarded as exceptional, the experience of only a few. So the next chapter focuses on a category of behavior, no less compulsive, but a component of nearly everybody's experience – sex.

QUESTIONS FOR DISCUSSION

1 Why do people – Ellis Wardle and his friends – feel that they cannot control what they do when they are seized with fear?

2 Why are people afraid of heights, of "looming," and of snakes, but frequently not of automobiles or machinery? And why do heights, "looming," and snakes (among other terrors) feature in phobias?

3 What can be done to counter fear in those who have to face it as part of their occupation?

3

SEX

Everybody's doing it – but *why*?

I know that *sounds* a stupid question; but the attempt to answer it leads to a profound insight into the human condition. We eat because we are hungry and we drink because we are thirsty. Our bodies suffer if they are short of food or water, and eating and drinking can be viewed as instinctive behaviors calculated to supply the body's needs. But sex? The feeling of sexual arousal is, subjectively, of similar kind to hunger and thirst in the sense that there is an internal compulsion. But what bodily deficiency does sex supply? Sexual behavior takes us to the heart of the matter of motivation.

Economists have the notion of a *rational man*. Rational Man is actuated always by profit and loss. He calculates the expected profit on any deal. He will take a bet, but only if the expected winnings exceed the stake he has to pay. I want to introduce *rational woman*. Rational Woman is just like her husband, always calculating the likely outcome and never taking stupid chances. But that is the limit of the rational family. There are no rational children because Rational Man and Rational Woman never have sex. So why do *we* have sex? That is the big question for this chapter.

Venereal disease

Consider, there are a number of unpleasant diseases that Rational Man might catch, of which two (AIDS and herpes) are at present incurable. In the UK it is estimated that 1 in 30 men and 1 in 8 women have genital herpes. That estimate is based on an analysis of the antibodies in blood donated for transfusion (Stepney, 1995). AIDS is widely known to lead to a nasty and premature death. If the risk of AIDS seems remote, what about syphilis?

Syphilis is highly contagious and could not be cured before the discovery of penicillin. It spreads especially rapidly when there are large movements of population, as happened after World War I, which mix infected individuals with other subpopulations with lesser resistance to the disease. Although penicillin was discovered in 1943, it did not become widely available until the 1950s. In the 1920s France had a population of about 40 million.

> In 1925 the Ministry of Health's commission for Prophylaxis against Venereal Diseases [this is a French author writing about the incidence of syphilis in France] issued figures which are astounding today: four million Frenchmen infected (one-tenth of the population), 20,000 children killed each year (and twice the number of abortions), 80,000 deaths, not to mention the indirect consequences of syphilis. In 1929 the number of syphilitics in France was put at eight million, and it was calculated that syphilis had killed 1,500,000 Frenchmen in ten years, "as many as the war in four years." (Quétel, 1990, p. 199)

Rational Man would never accept a risk of that magnitude.

Childbirth

Rational Woman fares even worse because she runs the additional risk of pregnancy. Pregnancy imposes a severe physiological load on her body and interferes with her lifestyle, and in former times childbirth was sometimes fatal. In rural France in the eighteenth century more than 1 percent of mothers died in childbirth. An analysis of the ruling families of Europe from 1500 to 1850 shows a mortality in childbirth of about 2 percent (Gutierrez & Houdaille, 1983), while in England today it is about 8 in 100,000 (AbouZahr & Royston, 1991, p. 597). Even so, it is not without its anxieties even today (Steyn, 2000). In former centuries expectant mothers approached their time with fear and trembling and it is estimated that 1 birth in 10 presented a problem (Carter & Duriez, 1986, pp. 31–2; Shorter, 1982, pp. 71–2). Rational Woman will never bear any children.

Let us now look at a real contemporary man. Tim Yeo used to be UK Minister of State for the Environment. At Christmas 1993, the *News of the World* broke the news that Tim Yeo had recently fathered an illegitimate child. South Suffolk Conservative Association promptly demanded that he resign as a minister. They would also have demanded his resignation as a Member of Parliament (MP) except that they expected to lose the resulting by-election (Cohen & Routledge, 1994). Why did he do it? Tim Yeo is far from being the only one. "There's lots of sex in the House. Tons of it. You know straight away which MPs are getting up to it and which aren't. They chat you up, and try to impress. It's all flattering stuff, and if you're tempted you go for it" (Caroline, former Commons secretary; cited by Rocco, 1992).

The intuitive answer, of course, is that sexual intercourse leading to orgasm is exceedingly pleasurable. That immediate pleasure outweighs all other considerations and for that reason, possibly, even Rational Man and Rational Woman might get together in bed. That answer seems very compelling because the intense pleasure of sexual intercourse is a part of so many people's experience. But let us look at sexual behavior from a different point of view.

PERSONAL VIEW AND CAMERA VIEW

A pretty fair-haired girl wearing a clinging gray shift dress and Doc Martens boots is walking down Great Western Road, Paddington, London, on a hot summer afternoon. As the camera follows her it repeatedly swings round to catch the many other people in Great Western Road, mostly young men, who turn round to watch the girl as she walks by. Two workmen look out of an upstairs window and one draws the other's attention to the girl. Four young men seated at a pavement café turn round in their seats as she passes. Another young man coming the other way turns round as he passes the girl and visibly says "Wow!" The girl smiles back. The head-turning is almost mechanical, as if the bystanders were so many rod puppets.

This is the title sequence to the first program in a TV series entitled *The Sexual Imperative* (Bromhall, 1994). It was intended to demonstrate that, "I suppose, when it comes down to it, they all are obsessed with sex." But I show it to my students to demonstrate a more subtle point.

I imagine (I do not inquire) that about half my class spend their time watching the girl. She is a very attractive young woman and, if you are a heterosexual male, it is entirely normal behavior to focus on her image. If that half of my class had been present in Great Western Road when this film sequence was shot, they would have been amongst the bystanders caught by the camera turning round to watch the girl as she walked by. This creates *two* views of young heterosexual men watching a girl walking down the street. There is the personal view which each has of his own reaction ("She's a very nice girl. I'd like to date her!") and there is the camera view that everyone else, especially the camera, has of that young man's head-turning to watch the girl as she walks by. Two views of the same behavior – but very different in character. Nevertheless, they go together in point of time and place. That relationship is expressed in figure 3.1.

In case this should seem a sexist way of introducing the matter, I comment that women do it too. Early in the fourth episode of the BBC's production of Jane Austen's *Pride and Prejudice*, Colin Firth as Mr Darcy is seen returning to his Derbyshire estate on another hot summer's afternoon. Sweating after his ride from London, he takes a dip, fully clothed, in a lake on his estate.

> The ladies of Fleet Street were, to a woman, won over. "If the BBC were to run off a poster of Colin Firth in his wet T-shirt, it would probably sell enough to halve the licence fee – that tousled brown hair and those deep-set eyes . . ."
>
> Pictures of Darcy, lovingly cut out, appeared like a rash on office pin boards and suburban fridge doors. . . . Fascination with his breeches knew no bounds. (Aitkenhead, 1995)

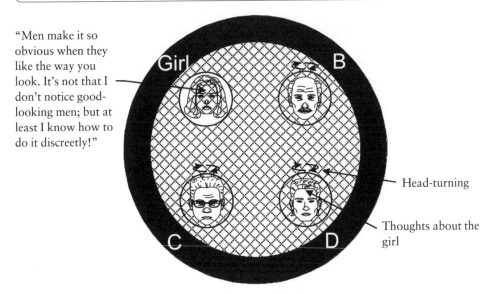

"Men make it so obvious when they like the way you look. It's not that I don't notice good-looking men; but at least I know how to do it discreetly!"

Girl

B

Head-turning

Thoughts about the girl

C

D

Figure 3.1 The social situation in Great Western Road, Paddington.

When we observe someone else's courtship behavior, it presents a completely different view to that which we have when courting ourselves. If you see some other fellow taking a girl out for the evening, that is a completely different experience from taking a girl out yourself and I presume (I am unable to vouch for this personally) that women experience a similar distinction. Nevertheless, internal musing over the person of Colin Firth as Mr Darcy, available only to personal view, goes together with the action of cutting out his portrait, observable in camera view, in point of time and place, notwithstanding that they are two very different kinds of observation.

These are two quite different views of the selfsame behavior, two views which need to be carefully distinguished. A crude physical analogy will help. Many restaurants and other establishments serving the public use Venetian half-silvered glass to segregate serving staff from their clientele. The glass is fully silvered, but only in stripes, perhaps 1 inch in width, separated by narrower gaps of plain glass. The waiters can look out from the kitchen through the narrow gaps of plain glass and see which diners require service; that is analogous to the view recorded by the video camera. But the diners see only their own reflections (personal view) in the broader silvered stripes. That view is analogous to the uniquely privileged view each of us has of his or her own behavior, with awareness of all the internal feelings – thoughts, hopes, pleasures, disappointments – which accompany it. Everybody else's romance is much the same; one's own is completely different, unique – unique because it is experienced from a privileged viewpoint not accessible to anyone else. The relationship between these two views of what people do is summarized in table 3.1.

Table 3.1   Two views of people's behavior

Personal view	*Camera view*
• One's own behavior; e.g., internal thoughts and desires: "She's a pretty girl. I'd like to date her!"; "I love the way he talks, as if he can't be bothered."	• Other people's behavior, esp. body language: men turning their heads to look at the girl; women pinning up cutouts of Colin Firth as Mr Darcy.
• Like looking at a one-way mirror from the silvered side and seeing one's reflection.	• Looking through a one-way mirror from the observer's side.
• Observational material for lay psychology, for literature, music, and other artistic activities.	• Observational material for scientific psychology.
• Characterized by free will	• . . . determinism.

The idea that sexual behavior is supremely pleasurable belongs to personal view, while the idea that it is mechanical, that the young men in Great Western Road were just so many rod puppets, belongs to camera view. Indeed, orgasm seen in camera view does not look at all pleasurable – it looks more like a climax of agony (Beynon, 1994)!

If you are seized by terror, what you do in that terrified state is no longer under your rational control. At the same time, you have an overwhelming emotional experience. The emotion is the subjective correlate, in personal view, of your quasi-mechanical reactions to the source of the terror. In the same way, if you are entranced by a potential sexual partner, you have an overwhelming subjective experience of emotion (we call it "falling in love") and, at the same time, many of the things that lovers do are no longer under their rational control. There are, therefore, two quite distinct ways in which we might look at people falling in love, and it is not yet clear which way, personal view or camera view, will afford the deepest insights.

Which View – Personal View or Camera View?

Our internal thoughts, hopes, and pleasures are exclusive to each one of us; nobody else can experience our private mental processes. So camera view omits a great deal, especially material important to the individual. But orgasm is accompanied by a profound sequence of physiological changes in both male and female, changes which engulf the whole body, even to producing an altered state of consciousness. These changes have only recently been studied in detail, chiefly by William Masters and Virginia Johnson (see Masters, Johnson, & Kolodny, 1995, pp. 73–86; also Bancroft,

1989, pp. 77–89), and are still not adequately understood. The individual engaging in sexual intercourse is unaware of most of these physiological changes. They are largely excluded from personal view, which is also incomplete.

Camera view and personal view give access to different spectra of behavior. Many elements can be perceived in only one of these two views. The spectra of behavior which each view affords are both incomplete; they overlap only in part. There must necessarily be some relationship between the two because some events – a young man in Great Western Road turning his head to watch a pretty girl walk by – can be simultaneously observed from both, but there is no necessity for that relationship to be either simple or obvious. Camera view, of course, is the objective, scientific, view. But we cannot on that ground dismiss personal view as subjective and unscientific.

Lay Psychology

We assume that other people have internal thoughts, hopes, pleasures, and disappointments similar to those that we ourselves have. That assumption leads to a *lay psychology* on which we base our understanding of people around us. It enables us to predict what other people will do and what they expect of us, and it works pretty well in practice. We can also communicate our internal thoughts and feelings in words:

> "Look, it's up to me how I dress; and when it's hot I don't want to wear a lot of clothes."
> "I know it attracts attention – I expect it."
> "Men make it so obvious when they like the way you look. It's not that I don't notice good-looking men; but at least I know how to do it discreetly!" (words attributed to the girl walking down Great Western Road, in Bromhall, 1994)

There is an immense volume of literature, poetry, and song which expresses just such internal thoughts and feelings.

Lay psychology is the psychology of the law courts. To establish a charge of murder, it has to be shown that the defendant intended to kill. What is an "intention"? In practice, it subsists in the reasonable imputation to the defendant of some prior mental processes that imaged the consequences of actions subsequently undertaken. Those prior mental processes could not have been observed by any third person. They are imputed on the basis of lay psychology.

Lay psychology does not always work. On December 18, 1992, Christopher Clunis walked up behind Jonathan Zito on a crowded platform at Finsbury Park Underground Station and stabbed him in the eye. He then calmly boarded a train. When he was arrested for Jonathan Zito's murder: "I want to go to prison so I can play all day" (Murray, 1993).

Christopher Clunis is a paranoid schizophrenic with a fascination for knives. He pleaded guilty to manslaughter and his plea was accepted on the ground of diminished responsibility; but his plea of "not guilty by reason of insanity" was not. Nevertheless, Clunis was ordered to be detained indefinitely at Rampton Hospital.[1] The insane are not legally liable for their actions. Lay psychology does not work for the insane and that failure of our ordinary, everyday understanding of other people provides one pragmatic definition of what it means to be "insane." In this respect the insane are categorized with animals.

Another repeated failure of lay psychology arises with pornography. Many men are aroused by seeing pictures of naked women (or men) and assume that their womenfolk will be similarly aroused. But very few women, in fact, are. This was reported by Kinsey 50 years ago.

> We have histories of males who have attempted to arouse their female partners by showing them nude photographs or drawings, and most of these males could not comprehend that their female partners were not in actuality being aroused by such material. When a male does realize that his wife or girl friend fails to respond to such stimuli, he may conclude that she no longer loves him and is no longer willing to allow herself to respond in his presence. He fails to comprehend that it is a characteristic of females in general, rather than the reaction of the specific female, which is involved in this lack of response. (Kinsey, Pomeroy, Martin, & Gebhard, 1953, p. 653)

That lesson has recently been relearned, at substantial expense, by certain publishers of women's magazines.

> In the early 1990s, a flock of new, erotic magazines aimed at women came on the market. Alongside *For Women* there were *Women Only* and *Women on Top* . . . plus *Ludus* and *Bite*. Each one was launched amid a fanfare of press attention. Everyone pretended they heralded a whole new era of female sexual expression, and we wanted them to succeed . . .
>
> *For Women* soldiers on but has recently had its budget slashed. The rest of the women's porn magazines have floundered. But here's a telling fact. Women's erotic fiction has done brilliantly.
>
> Black Lace novels, unhampered by problems with models, erections . . . or being on the top shelf, started in 1993 and have sold 1.5 million copies, representing half of the total market share. (Forna, 1996)

Women do have their own pornography, but it is different in kind to that which excites men.

Celia Dodd (Dodd, 1994) reviewed "a book of photographs of naked men taken by women artists, entitled *What She Wants*" (Salaman, 1994).

---

[1] Rampton Hospital is a high-security psychiatric unit. It treats the most dangerous psychiatric patients, most of whom (though not all) are responsible for very serious crimes.

The book's editor, Naomi Salaman, . . . was not surprised that the initial reaction of most of the women I showed the book to was "Yuck."

Most of the women whose initial reaction was "Yuck" went on to say: "Well, I do quite like that picture . . ."

Another woman talked about the importance of a sense of discovery: "I think the most erotic images for men and women are slightly hidden, slightly naughty. Many of these pictures leave nothing to the imagination – it's all whack it out, let's look at it, which I don't find erotic." (Dodd, 1994, p. 22)

SEXUAL BEHAVIOR IS QUASI-MECHANICAL

Enough has now been said to show that if there is to be a scientific study of human motivation, of why people do what they do, it must take the camera's point of view. From that viewpoint, sexual behavior is substantially mechanical.

"Mechanical"

By "mechanical" I mean that sexual behavior is switched on by extraneous stimuli such as a pretty fair-haired girl walking down Great Western Road. Those stimuli modulate an intrinsic source of energy, as when one switches a television set on. The audience of BBC1's *Pride and Prejudice* (Birtwistle, 1995) were much excited by reports of an on-set, but off-camera, romance between Jennifer Ehle (Lizzie Bennet) and Colin Firth (Mr Darcy). For Jennifer Ehle it was not the first time. She first came to public attention playing a leading role in *The Camomile Lawn* in the course of which she fell in love with her co-star, Toby Stephens.

> "It's so hard to have a relationship in this business, it really is," says Jennifer – who is currently single – drily. "I don't want to do it again unless it's unavoidable. It's just not worth it.
>
> "Being on location and acting in a story opposite somebody is incredibly conducive to falling in love. If you took two people who work in a bank and who might possibly fancy each other if they thought about it, and you made them stand there saying, 'I love you' every morning, *really trying to mean it*, eventually they might, you know, start to believe it." Hell, anyone could make the same mistake. (Lane, 1996)

As part of the enactment of *Pride and Prejudice* Jennifer Ehle and Colin Firth were required to make romantic gestures toward each other, in words and in body language, in the way that real-life lovers do, and to make them sufficiently convincing to satisfy the audience. Initially the actor and actress playing hero and heroine do not feel attracted to each other. The romantic gestures have to be simulated – that is part of the actor's technical accomplishment. But the fact that these gestures are only simulated does not mean that they have no effect. Quite the contrary. Jennifer Ehle and Colin Firth appear to have taken them for real, as though they were meant in earnest. That is the consequence of human sexual response being mechanical.

Another example is this interaction between strangers in a commercial aircraft.

> Amanda Holt, 37, and David Machin, 40, a married father of three, were arrested at Manchester Airport after the pilot of their American Airlines flight from Dallas had radioed ahead complaining of "lewd and drunk behavior."
>
> The couple, who had not met before the ten-hour flight, are alleged to have cuddled under an airline blanket after consuming free alcohol in the business-class section of the Boeing 757. It was then Mrs Holt reportedly removed her outer clothes and performed a sex act, despite a warning from airline staff. (Harvey, 1999)

"Substantially Mechanical"

By "*substantially* mechanical" I mean that the actual response to a particular gesture may vary from one time to another, from one person to another, and, especially, from one culture to another. Imagine a biological machine of such complexity that we do not by any means understand all of its workings. The actual response might be constrained by other competing signals or by social conventions regarding sexual behavior. So, sexual interaction of some sort is common amongst office workers, but chiefly at the Christmas party or out of hours (White, 1999). The secrecy of the Internet provides an opportunity for (virtual) sexual encounter unencumbered by social constraints. Marion McGilvary investigated some "chat" rooms:

> ... most rooms seem to be about sex. Far from being full of nerdy sociopaths, they are overrun by married men, logging on from the privacy of their own office, looking for cybersex.
>
> They are regular blokes with working wives, steady girlfriends, a couple of kids, and a joint mortgage. They are called Clive or Gary or Paul. They are thirtysomething, middle management, with a company car, a small expense account, and they appear to spend significant parts of the working day talking dirty with virtual strangers. (McGilvary, 1999)

Some patterns of sexual behavior are copied from others. It is frequently asserted that those adults who abuse children sexually tend to be those who were themselves abused as children. Although it is known that there are many exceptions to this rule, there still seems to be some truth in the correlation, though reliable statistics are difficult to come by. Following the attempt to impeach President Clinton in Washington, using testimony from Monica Lewinsky, among others,

> Our man in the know says that there has been a big increase in demand for young ladies who bear a resemblance to Monica Lewinsky. Men have been

looking to copy the world's most powerful politician and are searching for their own Monica. Playmate Escort Services . . . has been flooded with calls from gentlemen asking for what is known as the full Lewinsky and paying £200 for an hour with a Monica doppelgänger. (Steiner, 1998)

Finally, the pleasure which accompanies sexual intercourse is, I suggest, simply the subjective, personal-view counterpart of continuing an instinctively motivated behavior to its completion. The completion of any instinctive behavior is pleasurable – eating a good meal, for example – but sex is the most compelling example.

There are two particular lines of argument to support the idea that sexual behavior is substantially mechanical. The first argument asks how such behavior might be acquired if it were not hardwired, innate, and the second shows that the "pleasure principle" does not provide an adequate explanation.

Acquisition of Patterns of Sexual Behavior

Reproduction by any mammalian species requires an extraordinary level of cooperation between adult male and female. Such behavior is not *obviously* innate in humans. These days there is sex education in schools, and in former times secret knowledge was passed on from one child to another in the playground. But what about tigers?

I concentrate on tigers because they lead solitary lives – as do most cats, except lions. Adult male and female tigers patrol separate but overlapping territories. They usually meet only to mate. When cubs are born, they remain with their mother for about two years until they are able to fend for themselves and acquire their own territories (Sunquist, 1981). There is no possibility of any sex education there. How, then, do adult tigers know what to do? It is quite clear that they do know, because their reproduction rate is high. If they are left free from poachers and other human intrusion, tigers will rapidly populate all the available jungle.

Each biological species has to be equipped with a sufficient repertoire of specific behaviors to ensure the maintenance of its population. If it were not, the species would have died out long since. A human example is the United Society of Believers in Christ's Second Coming, commonly known as the "Shakers." The Shakers were founded by Ann Lee, an illiterate textile worker from Manchester, in 1758 as an offshoot of the Quakers. Ann Lee emigrated to America in 1774 with eight disciples, and by 1826 there were 18 Shaker communities with 6,000 members. Now there are only seven Shakers left. Why? Because, as a matter of religious practice, Shakers are celibate (Whitworth, 1999a).

At the same time, factual knowledge about procreation is not necessary for the perpetuation of humankind. Malinowski (1932, pp. 154–5, 160) reported that the Trobriand islanders had not made the connection between sexual intercourse and conception. Montagu (1974, pp. 194–9) reported the same of Australian aborigines.

Actual beliefs varied somewhat from tribe to tribe, but amongst the tribes of the Eastern Kimberleys in the north of Western Australia,

> A man dreams that a spirit child approaches him, announcing that it will be incarnated through his wife. Sometime later on he brings some food, such as kangaroo, emu, snake, fish, bird, *etc.*, to camp, but it is so fat that his wife refuses to eat it. Those near by, noticing that when someone else eats a bit of it he or she becomes sick, say that it is not food, but a baby. The spirit child enters the man's wife at the time of quickening, and when born has for its totem the animal, reptile, bird, fish or vegetable that had made the taster sick. (Montagu, 1974, p. 194)

Briefly, if sexual behavior were not substantially mechanical, there would be no Trobriand islanders, nor Australian aborigines!

In recent decades teenagers have been commencing sexual activity at increasingly younger ages. It is estimated that today one-third of teenagers begin sex before they are 16 (the legal age limit in the UK). More importantly, the younger they are, the less likely they are to use a condom, and that circumstance generates a public health problem in the form of sexually transmitted disease. Here is a young couple – the girl is only 15 – at a genito-urinary clinic in Chesterfield.

Girl:	He told me "I think I've got an infection" because – you know – he had a burning sensation, he was sore.
Boy:	I've had quite a lot of infections in the past – ten or more times, I've had quite a lot of times when it's sort of like reoccurring or I've sort of got rid of it and slept with someone again and then got it back.
Sarah Powell:	Their problem could have been avoided if they'd used a condom. It's the only form of contraception which stops sexually transmitted infections from spreading. The reasons they gave doctors for not using one are familiar.
Girl:	When I first met him I think I was fifteen. I think we'd been for a drink and then we went to his place. I suppose it was more from just a kiss and a cuddle to heavy petting and then – you know – I mean, as you get carried away. It's more of a lustful moment and it basically would have broken it up if – you see – you know, our stopping to use protection.
Boy:	I don't know why, I've never been able to really use condoms. It's just I've never liked it. I'd rather not have sex at all, if it was down to really using them. So, I didn't really use condoms that much. (Powell, 1999)

They give reasons (expressed in personal view) that equate (in camera view) to the fact that condoms are not natural. There is a repertoire of adult behaviors which, in interaction between the boy and the girl, lead to intercourse and procreation. Protection against conception or against any other hazard is not a part of those innate behavior patterns. If contraception were natural, we would none of us be here!

The Pleasure Principle

My second argument rests on the fact that the pleasure principle, that people engage in sex simply because it is supremely pleasurable, is inadequate. A contemporary survey of the attitudes of a group of 16–24-year-olds reported:

> No previous generation has been so well informed, so exposed to the technicalities of sex.
> No previous generation has sounded so unexcited by sex either. After half an hour listening to a group of women talking about their sex lives, I had to remind myself most of them were not yet 21. They sounded more like disillusioned 40-year-olds.
> "I've been with my boyfriend for two and a half years. But it's not always fantastic, especially when you've been drinking. Sometimes I just can't be bothered," says one 18-year-old. (Moyes, 1995)

One reason for those attitudes is that not every woman reaches orgasm. Alfred Kinsey (Kinsey et al., 1953, p. 408) found that even after 28 years of marriage 1 woman in 10 had never reached orgasm. The data are shown in figure 3.2.

A second problem with the pleasure principle is that it does not explain the feeling of compulsion which frequently accompanies sexual activity. This is important in coming to understand the criminal activities of pedophiles. Colin Hatch was convicted of murdering a 7-year-old boy. He had lured Sean Williams to his flat, sexually assaulted him, and then strangled him whilst on parole for a previous child sex attack. His defense at his trial was that "he was driven to attack Sean by a compulsion over which he had no control." Fantasies which he had written involving the abduction, sexual abuse, and the killing of young children were found in a wardrobe in his mother's bedroom after he was arrested. Hatch already had convictions for attacks on five other boys, his first offense being in 1987 when he was aged 15 (Whitfield, 1994).

Howard Hughes is another pedophile. He was convicted of the murder of Sophie Hook, aged 7. The critical evidence at his trial appears to have been a confession made to his father. He was reported to have said: "Dad, I did it. . . . You don't know what it is like to be sexually frustrated; you don't know what it is" (Jury, 1996).

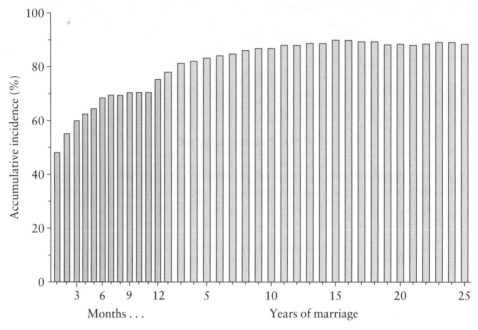

Figure 3.2 Accumulative incidence of orgasm by women in marriage (data from Kinsey et al., 1953, p. 408, table 113).

Mozart's opera *Don Giovanni* tells the story of a Spanish nobleman whose obsession was the seduction of women ("Why, they're more necessary to me than the bread I eat, than the air I breathe!"; da Ponte, 1787/1961). His servant Leporello kept a catalog of his master's conquests which numbered more than 2,000. Most people, I imagine, see such a total as pure fantasy – but not so! Johnson, Wadsworth, Wellings, and Field (1994, p. 113) recorded "The maximum reported number of lifetime partners exceeded 4,500 for men and 1,000 for women. The corresponding 5-year estimate was 500 for men and 100 for women, and in the last year 200 for men and 25 for women." Mauro Zarfanti, well known along the beach at Rimini, claims to have had more than 6,000 partners (Gumbel, 1995). The plot of *Don Giovanni* is ultimately based on real life; such characters are rare, but they do occur. Kinsey, Pomeroy, and Martin (1948, p. 557) reported:

> In some cases lower [socioeconomic] level males may have intercourse with several hundred or even a thousand or more girls in pre-marital relations. There are quite a few individuals . . . who find more interest in the pursuit and conquest, and in a variety of partners, than they do in developing long-term relations with a single girl. Some males avoid all repetitions of experience with the same girl. Sometimes the interest which such a promiscuous male has in heterosexual coitus does not involve any interest in the girls themselves. Many a lower level male

states quite frankly that he does not like girls, and that he would have nothing to do with them if it were not for the fact that they are sources of intercourse.

That circumstance also appears in the plot of *Don Giovanni*. Early in the first act Don Giovanni begins courting an unknown woman who is suddenly discovered to be Donna Elvira, a lady from Burgos, whom the Don had previously "married" and deserted after three days. Donna Elvira is passed to Leporello, the servant, for entertainment ("*Madamina, il catalogo . . .*") while Don Giovanni makes his escape.

Given that such men do exist, the common reaction, I imagine, is to envy them their skill in courtship. That also is mistaken. If a man has had 200 different partners within one year, almost all of his time must have been occupied in the pursuit. Moreover, he cannot afford to be choosy which women he beds. "Some you see are country girls, waiting maids, city beauties, some are countesses, baronesses, marchionesses, princesses: women of every rank, of every size, of every age." Don Giovanni is a character continually driven by an unsatisfied compulsion. David Milner is currently undergoing treatment for sex addiction and tells what it is like:

> No addiction is ever a pleasurable existence. Of course, the hit itself is pleasurable. That's why it's addictive, but as soon as that was over, the sadness and loneliness that I was trying to anaesthetise just returned. Then I needed another hit and another and another until I felt powerless to resist it. (Hilpern, 1999)

SOME QUESTIONS ABOUT SEXUAL BEHAVIOR

If it be now accepted, first, that any scientific study of why people do what they do has to be conducted strictly from a camera-view perspective and, second, that from that camera-view perspective sexual behavior appears substantially mechanical, some further questions arise.

1 What Are the Extraneous Signals Which Trigger Sexual Behavior?

Obviously, a potential sexual partner. A video will also do – a pretty fair-haired girl in a clinging gray shift dress and Doc Martens walking down Great Western Road on a hot summer's afternoon or Colin Firth taking a dip, fully clothed, in the pool on Mr Darcy's estate. A still picture is also effective – advertisers know this well. When writing or pictures or theatrical performances are produced as substitutes for a real sexual partner, we call it *pornography*. There is a large trade in pornography. Pornography works precisely because sexual behavior is substantially mechanical.

Within the mainstream (but tabloid) UK press the "Page Three" model has been a feature for many years. As social constraints on sexual expression have relaxed, so the "Lad Mags" – *FHM, Loaded, Maxim, Men's Health, GQ,* and *Esquire* – have evolved. *FHM,* which has the largest sales of all these magazines, exceeded 1,000,000 copies in June 1999 with its annual issue featuring the "100 sexiest women in the world" (Goodwin & Rushe, 1999). These magazines sell, not just to aficionados of pornography, but to men in general, precisely because the sexual reaction is substantially mechanical.

More recently in the UK we have had the television program *Big Brother* – 10 young adults incarcerated in a house where they cannot escape from the webcam, not even in the shower. "A teacher . . . let her towel slip twice so that she appeared naked on the voyeuristic programme *Big Brother*" (Sherwin, 2001). In France the program is called *Loft Story* ("Racy le Big Brother has France panting for more"; M. Campbell, 2001).

2 What Other Signals or Social Constraints Act to Modify Sexual Behavior?

We have social conventions to regulate the extent to which arbitrary individuals are permitted to excite each other sexually, especially with unintended gestures. Advertisers usually wait till they are advertising lingerie, or sun-tan lotion, or beauty products, or baths and showers, before using half-naked models. In the UK we have the Advertising Standards Authority to handle protests over advertisements which offend the public's sense of decency. It branded an advertisement for the film *Indecent Proposal* (featuring a photograph of a woman's body between the waist and the thighs, clad only in scanty underwear) "'tasteless and offensive' after receiving 171 complaints from the public, around half of them from men" (*Daily Mail,* 1995).

We also wear clothes, and not only for keeping warm. Here is Alfred Kinsey again:

> In many cultures, the world around, people have been much exercised by questions of propriety in the public exposure of portions or the whole of the nude body. There are few matters on which customs are more specific, and few items of sexual behavior which bring more intense reactions when the custom is transgressed. These customs vary tremendously between cultures and nations, and even between the individual communities in particular countries. The inhabitant of the Central American tropics has one custom, the Indian who comes down from his mountain home to trade in the lowland has totally different customs. There is neither rhyme nor reason to the custom – there is nothing but tradition to explain it. The mountain Indian of the warmer country of Southern Mexico is thoroughly clothed, the mountain Indian of the coldest part of Northern Mexico is more completely nude than the natives of the hottest Mexican tropics. But there are probably no groups in the world who are free of taboos of some sort on this point. The history of the origin of clothing is more often one of taboos on nudity than a story of the utility of body coverings. (Kinsey et al., 1948, p. 365)

To cite a contemporary example:

> The dean of a Cambridge University college has resigned over the lenient punishment handed out to an undergraduate who dropped his trousers at a football club dinner.
> ... a special disciplinary court banned the student from attending club dinners for a year. The student ... stripped off in front of team-mates and members of the college ladies' team. Many female students were upset and reported him to the college authorities. (*Independent*, 1994b)

Kissing in public, of which we think nothing, is offensive in many other cultures.

> The kissing which is commonplace in American films is considered most immoral in some of the foreign countries to which the films are distributed. A completely nude art production may be shown in a Latin American moving picture theatre to an audience which takes the film complacently, for its artistic value, although it will hiss the next picture off the screen because it contains a Hollywood kissing scene. (Kinsey et al., 1948, p. 365)

India is one of those other cultures.

> Until recently, girls and boys did not kiss on India's cinema screens.... Lovers would embrace, eyelashes aflutter, breath feverish, and the moment before their lips touched, the camera would cut to a wildlife scene straight out of a David Attenborough documentary, with doves cooing and bees flying in and out of flowers.
> ... before independence in 1947 a few kisses would sneak their way on to the screen. But after that, there was no kissing until the mid-1970s. Even then there was a tremendous uproar, and one didn't really see kissing again until the 1980s. (McGirk, 1991)

3 What about the Intense Feelings that Accompany Sexual Activity?

The feeling of pleasure that accompanies sexual activity is, I have already suggested, the subjective, personal-view, counterpart of some instinctive behavior continued to completion, such as sexual behavior continued to orgasm. The feeling of compulsion is similarly the counterpart of the initiation of such behavior following some external trigger. It is how a clock might feel when it has been wound up. And anger and frustration are what one feels when that instinctive behavior is interrupted before it is complete.

The pleasure and the pain and all the other private accompaniments to sexual behavior have provided the inspiration for countless poems, songs, and other writings in all cultures and idioms. Everyone has their own preferred idiom for the expression of these intense emotions. *Die Schöne Müllerin* is a cycle of 20 poems by

Wilhelm Müller (1823; Müller, 1997) set to music by Franz Schubert. It encompasses a wider range of human emotions than any other work I know of. The poet is looking for work and finds a job at a watermill, where he falls in love with the miller's daughter.

> I'd carve it in the bark of every tree,
> I'd scratch it deep in every stone she'd see,
> In every vacant plot I want it sown
> In cress whose seeds are quickly grown.
> I want to write on every scrap of paper
> "Yours is my heart;
> "Yours is my heart; and shall be yours, be yours for ever."

Four songs later, the poet is thinking he has won the girl of his heart and we have a song of pure elation.

> Mill-stream, stop the foaming brine!
> Mill-wheels, let your rumbling end!
> All you merry forest birds,
> Big and small,
> Silence all your carillon.
> Through the wood,
> In and out,
> Echo only this one line:
> The beloved miller-girl is mine!
> Mine!

But then a hunter comes out of the forest and the lady's eyes are directed elsewhere.

> Whither so fast, so rough and wild, beloved brook?
> Do you in anger for that shameless huntsman look?
> Turn back, turn back, and chasten first your miller-lass
> For all her flighty, fickle, foolish, carelessness!
> Turn back! Turn back! Turn back!

At the end of the cycle the poet drowns himself in the millstream in sorrow at the loss of his love.

4 What Has This to Do with the Survival of the Species?

For an animal species to flourish, there has to be a repertoire of complementary behavior patterns in adult males and females sufficiently effective to replenish the natural loss of numbers through death. That repertoire does not need to have any overarching organization; a collection of independent elementary responses is sufficient, each of them automatic, instinctive, triggered by some prior signal emitted by a member of the opposite sex. The game of chess provides a simple analogy.

Reuben Fine's *The Ideas behind the Chess Openings* (1989) is a classic treatise on the different ways in which a game of chess might begin. The oldest pattern of opening play is thought to be the Ruy Lopez, which dates from the sixteenth century. The game begins with the moves

	White	Black
1	e4	e5
2	Nf3	Nc6
3	Bb5	

and leads typically to subtle strategic dispositions of the pieces which may take many moves to resolve. But to get the Ruy Lopez, there has to be a certain cooperation between the players. If Black chooses 2 . . . d6 instead, we have Philidor's defense; 2 . . . Nf6 gives Petroff's defense; and 1 . . . c5 leads to the Sicilian defense. Each of these initial sequences of moves leads to a different disposition of the pieces and a game of a different character. So the kind of game that eventuates emerges from a series of moves and countermoves by each player in turn and depends on a continuing interaction between them. It is even so with human courtship.

We do not know all of the moves that a man and a woman might play in the game of courtship, but in *The Human Animal: The Biology of Love* (Beynon, 1994) Desmond Morris presents a variety of patterns of courtship behavior. Of course, these patterns vary from one culture to another, but Morris draws a sufficient number of parallels to suggest that, underlying the different cultural overlays, there is a universal repertoire of basic instinctive components.

> In fact, film of young couples shot in wildly different cultures all around the world shows remarkable similarities during this particular phase of the human life-cycle. The shy smiles and sidelong glances of the young female, the forward tilt of the body of the young male as he questions her and playfully shows off, these and a hundred other fleeting moments of human courtship are universals. They are understood across language barriers and class distinctions, and follow an almost identical pattern in the human pair-formation ritual. (Morris, 1994, p. 131)

There is a temptation, at this point, to make up for our lack of detailed knowledge of courtship behavior by assuming that all sexual (and other instinctive) behavior has some ultimate overriding purpose and to ask what that purpose might be. Dawkins (1976) sets the scene. That assumption might appear to provide a basis for identifying what is, and what is not, instinctive. But what can be reliably argued on an evolutionary basis needs to be carefully distinguished from mere speculation.

1 If a species fails to replace the numbers lost through death, it ceases to exist.
2 This is also true of an isolated subpopulation of some larger species; examples are the Tasmanian aborigines who were hunted to extinction by white settlers during the first half of the nineteenth century and, arguably, the Amerindian peoples of the Amazon basin today.
3 But it is not necessary that individual behaviors should all serve an evolutionary purpose. Homosexuality is a clear exception.

Sexual behavior merely has to work well enough. In humans, today, it works much too well. There is a widespread use of contraceptives; in 1995 there was a UN conference in Cairo on global overpopulation.

5 What about the Variation in Sexual Behavior from One Adult to Another?

There is no need for the pattern of sexual behavior to be the same in every male and the same in every female – and it is not. Homosexual intercourse does not produce children; but it is not extinguished by natural selection. Johnson et al. (1994, p. 191) found that 1.4 to 6.1 percent of their male respondents could be classified as "homosexual" depending on what criterion was applied and the context in which the questions were put; the corresponding percentages for women were 0.6 to 3.4.

What is more intriguing is that of those respondents who had ever had any homosexual contact, 90.3 percent of men and 95.8 percent of women had also engaged in heterosexual intercourse. This means that most homosexuals actually show a bisexual pattern of behavior and hetero-homosexuality varies along a continuum like right–left-handedness. As Johnson et al. (1994, p. 208) put it: "Exclusively homosexual behaviour appears to be rare." It is easy to imagine that the repertoire of sexual responses varies somewhat from one person to another and, with some people, can lead to both hetero- and homosexual interaction. Natural selection does not eliminate those behavior patterns which tend to lead to homosexual contact. Allegedly homosexual behaviors have been reported in many species including dolphins, penguins, bonobos, grizzly bears, and elephants (Farrar, 1999), which makes homosexuality appear natural. Of course, if homosexuality were the *dominant* behavior, then the population would diminish; and it is possible that the balance we observe between homo- and heterosexuality is the result of natural selection. As a species, humanity survives notwithstanding.

6 Does Sexual Behavior Have to Match Between Male and Female?

There is no biological necessity for the sexual behavior of a given male and female to match beyond a minimal level of effectiveness – and it does not. Kinsey used the

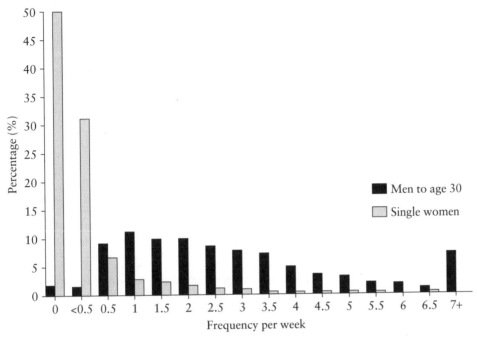

Figure 3.3   Total sexual outlet per week; men and single women to age 30 (data from Kinsey et al., 1953, p. 540, figure 116; p. 549, table 154).

word "outlet" to indicate any sexual behavior which led to orgasm and took the number of outlets per week as an indicator of the level of sexual activity of any individual. For men the number of outlets per week varies widely; but for single women – Kinsey confined his analysis to *single* women because a married woman will be responsive to her husband's demands – the spread is *much* wider. The difference between the sexes is shown in figure 3.3.

It must necessarily be that the natural level of sexual activity of husband and wife will usually not match. For this reason the sexual behavior of many husbands and of some wives becomes focused on other partners, outside of the marriage. In the UK in 1999 there were 301,000 marriages and 159,000 divorces (Insalaco, 2002, pp. 40, 42).

7 How Much of Our Sexual Behavior is Innate and How Much Acquired?

This is the difficult question. Notwithstanding that sexual behavior has ultimately to be mechanical, many details vary from culture to culture and must, at the very least, be modifiable by experience. The positions of man and woman during intercourse is one such.

> Most persons will be surprised to learn that positions in intercourse are as much a product of human cultures as languages and clothing, and that the common English-American position is rare in some other cultures. Among the several thousand portrayals of human coitus in the art left by ancient civilisations, there is hardly a single portrayal of the English-American position. It will be recalled that Malinowski (1929) records the nearly universal use of a totally different position among the Trobianders in the Southwestern Pacific; and that he notes that caricatures of the English-American position are performed around the communal campfires, to the great amusement of the natives, who refer to the position as the "missionary position."
>
> It should be emphasised that the most common variant position is the one with the female above. It is used, at least occasionally, by more than a third (34.6%) of the upper level males. The position was more nearly universal in Ancient Greece and Rome (*vide* the art objects and materials, as well as the literature from that period). It is shown in the oldest known depiction of human coitus, dating between 3200 and 3000 BC, from the Ur excavations in Mesopotamia (Legrain, 1936). The position with the female above is similarly the commonest in the ancient art of Peru, India, China, Japan, and other civilisations. In spite of its ancient history, many persons at lower social levels consider the position a considerable perversion. . . . One of the older psychiatrists goes so far as to insist that the assumption of such a dominating position by the female in coitus may lead to neurotic disturbances and, in many cases, to divorce. (Kinsey et al., 1948, pp. 373–4)

What does a man (or woman) do when he (or she) is sexually motivated? People copy what other people do. Child abusers tend to be those who were themselves abused as children. This all suggests that the cultural form of sexual expression is, in part at least, copied, but the expression itself is thereafter substantially mechanical.

There is one practical consequence of the near-mechanical nature of sexual behavior. Most cases of rape involve a man already known to the woman, and this has led to the term "date rape."

> In a poll of more than 6,000 students at 32 colleges and universities, women were asked if they had been penetrated without their consent by the use of force or the threat of it. About 15 per cent of them said they had experienced a rape and 12 per cent an attempted rape, although most did not apply that label; more than 80 per cent of them knew their assailant. Nearly 8 per cent of men admitted committing a rape or attempted rape. (Marks, 1992)

Here is one example.

> The young woman, in her second year at Durham University, had been going out with the student for a couple of weeks when he first raped her.

"We went to bed together, but I had not had sex with him. Nor did I want to have sex with him, so we just went to sleep. I woke up to find him on top of me forcing me to have sex. I know it sounds pathetic, but he was much stronger than me and I just lay there." The same scenario was repeated a week later.

"It happened once more, but this time it was on my bedroom floor. We had both been drinking and he threw me down on the floor. He thought that he was being kinky and exciting. I shouted 'No' but he carried on. Afterwards when I confronted him, he apologized and said that he never meant to hurt me and that he just had an evil streak – he kept on referring to an evil streak in him that he could not control." (Edwards-Jones, 1991)

If sexual behavior is "substantially mechanical," then, beyond a certain point, a man is not going to stop just because the woman suddenly cries "No." In Liverpool they have a phrase, "I'll get off at Edge Hill" (Edge Hill is the last station on the main line from London Euston into the terminus, Liverpool Lime Street). If a woman calculates on getting off at Edge Hill, the train might not stop; she should have left the train at Crewe. I am not concerned here with the legality of the man's actions, nor with the morality of either the man's or the woman's behavior, but simply with this – that women have been killed for trying to get off at Edge Hill ("Girl, 16, beaten to death for saying 'no'"; de Bruxelles, 2000; Wilkinson, 2000).

QUESTIONS FOR DISCUSSION

1 Why do people have sex?

2 What is the relationship between the internal thoughts of a young man as he turns his head to watch a pretty girl walk by and the view of him captured in a video recording?

3 What do we learn from the differences in courtship customs from one society to another?

4 Why do we wear clothes?

4

CONSCIOUSNESS

At the beginning of chapter 1 I explained why a book on human motivation had to be concerned with determinism and free will. But why consciousness as well? The argument stands like this.

There are two kinds of viewpoint which need to be distinguished. There is (1) the subjective "personal view" that we each have of our own actions and there is (2) the objective "camera view" that we have of everybody else's behavior and everybody else has of us. In camera view behavior appears determinate, but in personal view it is characterized by free will. So determinism and free will do not characterize the behavior itself, but the viewpoint from which it is experienced.

When someone is seized by terror, they experience (in personal view) an overwhelming (and very unpleasant) emotion, while in camera view we can observe the physiological effects of the terror and the person's attempts to escape. The physiological activation and the attempts to escape go with the internal emotion in point of time and place. When someone is entranced by a potential sexual partner, we can observe (in camera view) their courtship behavior, while their internal experience (in personal view) spans a wide range of emotions. Again, the courtship we observe goes with the internal arousal. Those two examples lead to this idea: The attempts to escape and the courtship are the motivated behavior, incorporating quasi-mechanical instinctive components, and the emotion is the subjective correlate of being motivated.

That is an important idea for the study of human motivation because it is all too frequently difficult to observe people in a truly motivated state and record (from a camera viewpoint) what they do. Much more commonly people will recount their experiences – of being trapped in a burning aircraft, for example – but recount them as experiences in personal view. How do those personal-view recollections relate to what was, in principle, observable in camera view? To the extent that such recollections can be reliably interpreted, we have an additional and much larger source of empirical material for the study of human motivation. So this chapter explores the relation between the subjective (personal) and the objective (camera) points of view in detail.

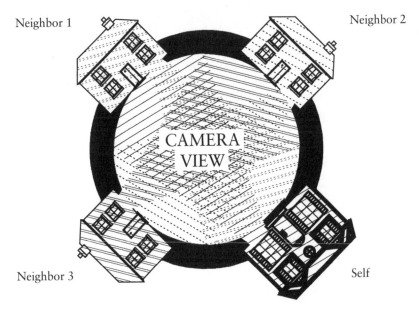

Figure 4.1 The different views from four houses on a housing estate.

TWO VIEWS OF WHAT PEOPLE DO

Personal view and camera view were illustrated in the last chapter with a video of a girl walking down a street in West London and with Colin Firth playing Mr Darcy in *Pride and Prejudice*. The relationship between those two kinds of viewpoint was related to the analogy of a Venetian-silvered mirror and summarized in table 3.1.

Figure 4.1 presents a further metaphor. Many people live in a street of similar houses or on a purpose-built housing estate. Looking out from the window of one's own house, one can see (in camera view) the *exteriors* of other houses on the estate, but cannot see inside, because the daylight reflected from the window panes obscures the very much fainter reflections from their interiors. At the same time one can see the *interior* of one's own house, but not the outside. What one's neighbors' houses are like inside is a matter of presumption. In the absence of any direct inspection, we presume those interiors to be like our own; but on those occasions when we are invited inside a neighbor's house, we typically find greater differences in decor and furnishing than we had supposed. In like manner we presume other people's personal experience to be like our own.

It needs to be emphasized, however, that there is no *perceptual* demarcation between that which is private (in personal view) and that which can be shared with others (in camera view). Camera view is simply that which is common to many different personal views (and also the camera). My view of the houses across the way is all of a piece with the interior of my own house. There is only a logical distinction, which does not even amount to separate windows on a computer screen. The neighbors can share one's view of the houses across the street (which are in camera as well as personal view), but they cannot see into one's own house (available to personal view only). But this is not perceptually apparent to the householder looking out of his or her window – the junction between the two logical categories is seamless.

THE MEANING OF "CONSCIOUSNESS"

Experience in personal view is experience of which we are conscious, and the nature of that consciousness has long been a focus of philosophical inquiry. But it is as well to be clear, first of all, what is meant by "consciousness," and that is more difficult than one might expect because conscious experience, especially the quality of conscious experience, is essentially private. It is easier to be clear about what we do *not* mean by listing the different ways in which we can be "unconscious."

"Conscious" describes the ordinary waking state of a person in camera view, and the different physiological conditions that are seen as exceptions to that state indicate that there are different states of unconsciousness. I might be asleep, or concussed (following a road accident), or under a general anesthetic (in preparation for surgery), or in a coma (following a drug overdose). In such a state I cannot attend to anything and am visibly unconscious with respect to *everything* in an experiential sense. These different states of unconsciousness are summarized in table 4.1.

Table 4.1 Meanings of the word "unconscious"

Phenomenal *(personal view)*	*Behavioral* *(camera view)*
• Failure to attend to something (e.g., this chapter) • Usual test of being conscious of an event is ability to report it . . . • . . . or to recall it (hence examinations)	• Asleep • Concussed (e.g., following a road accident) • Under general anesthetic (for surgical operation) • Coma (following drug overdose) *Altered states of consciousness* • Drunk (too much alcohol) • Cannabis • LSD • Ecstasy • Benzodiazepines

Again, I might be drunk, or I might have taken cannabis, LSD, ecstasy, or a benzodiazepine, and while not actually unconscious, am in an *altered* state of consciousness. If someone takes drugs which induce an altered state of consciousness, they may be able to report a comparison of the different states. Nicholas Pierce had been taking sodium valproate to control his epilepsy for more than 20 years. Following a change of his lifelong medication,

> At the age of 27, Nicholas Pierce has "woken up." Having suffered from epilepsy and learning difficulties since he was three, the young man had for years been the butt of production-line humour at the meat factory where he packs boxes: workmates mimicked his droning speech, ridiculed his clumsiness and mocked his slow comprehension. But now the bullying has stopped and Nicholas is the one who makes the wisecracks. Alert and confident, he is able to argue over Bosnia and the environment with the best of them. Having left school – in a unit for educationally backward children – without qualifications, he is now taking maths GCSE at evening classes and wants to study sociology. After living at home all his life, he wants a place of his own.

Nicholas describes his altered view of himself in this manner:

> I lacked confidence. I always seemed too slow at learning. I felt I couldn't try anything. Now I feel more motivated, more aware and more determined. (Moore, 1996)

On the basis of such evidence we can be confident, first, that different people do not necessarily experience the same state of consciousness – different states are possible – and, second, that Nicholas Pierce is now experiencing an altered, and much enhanced, state of consciousness. Nicholas can compare his previous and his present state and what he reports subjectively is matched by observable changes in his intellectual activity. The behavioral consequences of all these different states are observable in camera view.

But the same word, "conscious," is also used to indicate *awareness* in personal view. There are many events happening in the world around me; some of them I attend to and am conscious of (the word processor I am working with at this present moment), of others I am unaware (I go outside and am surprised to discover that it has been raining). That difference is nothing to do with drugs, or being asleep, or concussed. The most frequently accepted test of my being conscious of some present event is my ability to report it. If I am able to recall some past event, then it is presumed I was conscious of that as well. Although recall from memory is known to be affected by drugs and other physical agents – retrograde amnesia following concussion is a particularly good example – that is not the point here because I can recall and equally fail to recall, and notice and equally fail to notice, some present event under circumstances in which all known physiological and pharmacological factors are the same.

These two kinds of usage, the objective and the subjective, need to be carefully distinguished. Indeed, the connection between the two appears to be no more than this: If I have suffered concussion, or am in a coma, I would appear from external observation (camera view) to be incapable of being conscious (in the personal-view sense of the word) of anything. Nevertheless, the camera-view observer cannot always tell whether someone is conscious in this phenomenal sense and certainly cannot say anything about the quality of that consciousness.

At the age of 19 Geoffrey Wildsmith had an accident that left him with severe brain injuries, totally paralyzed and unable to communicate. Doctors believed him to be still unconscious; but two years on a way was found that enabled him to communicate at a very primitive level. Geoffrey Wildsmith had been conscious all the time: "It was awful, I was bored to tears" (Rosin, 1996). In California Robert Wendland is the subject of a suit before the Supreme Court. He also suffered a road accident, in 1993, and the doctors cannot say whether he is conscious (in any minimal sense) or not. Certainly he is kept alive only by virtue of continued medical attention and his wife wishes him to be allowed to die. But Robert Wendland's mother thinks he is able to communicate and opposes the proposal to withdraw life support. That is the case before California's Supreme Court (Bradberry, 2001).

This chapter is concerned only with the *phenomenal* notion of consciousness, as the quality of experience in personal view.

Philosophical Inquiry into Consciousness

Philosophical inquiry into the phenomenal notion of consciousness has been centered chiefly on two kinds of idea.

1 Reduction to brain function

This idea asserts that consciousness is simply another function of the brain. If it be asked why we cannot say where consciousness is to be located, this is simply because, at present, we lack the techniques to record all of a participant's internal thoughts and feelings. When recording techniques are sufficiently improved, it will be seen that all conscious experience reduces to brain function.

2 Dualism

This is the idea that conscious experience is the product of some unobservable mind-substance so that a participant's internal thoughts are essentially unobservable. It is attributed to Descartes (1596–1650), who declared that mind-substance (*res cogitans*) is wholly distinct from matter. The principal argument in support of dualism is put by Nagel (1995) in this manner:

> ... facts about the objective external world of particles and fields of force, as revealed by modern physical science, are not facts about how things appear from any particular point of view, whereas facts about subjective experience are precisely about how things are from the point of view of individual conscious subjects.

Two different kinds of substance are required to support these two different kinds of "fact," and reduction to brain function, or even the relation of subjective experience to external observation, is thereby rendered impossible. But dualism is in difficulty, because some elements of conscious experience clearly do have plausible neural correlates.

Springer's lines

If figure 4.2 be viewed from a distance of about 50 cm, faint gray diagonal lines may be seen passing through the white spaces. The discovery of these lines is attributed by Lindsay and Norman (1977, p. 40) to one Robert Springer, although this is one of several similar figures studied by Prandtl (1927). At a greater distance, about 1.5 m, bright horizontal and vertical lines, brighter than the surrounding white, may be seen in the horizontal and vertical white spaces. These lines are illusory and are not, of course, present in the printed figure; they are created internally during visual inspection. Laming (1992) has shown that the visibility of these lines, and especially the circumstances under which they become visible, may plausibly be attributed to the way in which elementary, near-threshold, stimuli are passed through the visual pathway.

There are many similar phenomena of perception showing that what people see or hear or feel is shaped by the manner in which sensory information is transmitted to and through the brain. There are therefore many points at which the contents of consciousness can be related to events at a neural level of description, and there is an empirical relationship to be investigated between the hypothetical mind-substance and the brain. For that reason, one might suppose that ultimately every aspect of consciousness will be successfully related to events at a neural level of description.

The Neural Signature of Consciousness

The fact that Springer's lines can be related to processes in the striate cortex does not mean that we can be directly aware of what is happening at so early a stage of the visual system. In fact, we appear to have conscious access only to the finished

Figure 4.2 Springer's lines. Faint gray diagonal lines running through each white space may be seen on close inspection (from about 50 cm). From a greater distance (1.5 m) bright white horizontal and vertical lines, brighter than the white surround, become apparent, again running through each white space. Reproduced with permission from Laming (1988, p. 286). © 1988 Cambridge University Press.

percept. So the question naturally arises: Where in the brain does awareness begin? That question has been addressed by Lumer, Friston, and Rees (1998) using the phenomenon of binocular rivalry.

Binocular rivalry

Ordinarily the two eyes receive two closely related images which fuse to give a three-dimensional interpretation. But it is possible to present two incompatible images to the eyes in a stereoscope. Two incompatible images do not fuse; instead, perception alternates spontaneously between the two monocular percepts. The phenomenon is called binocular rivalry. Lumer et al. (1998) used functional magnetic resonance imaging to measure the blood oxygenation level in the brain of a subject viewing two incompatible images, to identify cortical regions where activity was correlated with spontaneous perceptual transitions. Alternating activity was discovered in several extrastriate areas. Since the stimulus field in such an experiment is unchanging, this must relate to the alternation of the percept – but not necessarily to rivalry *per se*. As a control, Lumer et al. also alternated the stimulus between the two monocular fields – this forced an alternating percept, but did not give rise to any rivalry – and on that basis identified activity in the frontoparietal cortex as being specifically associated with perceptual alternation only during rivalry.

Exploration of this kind is complicated by the participant having to press a key to indicate which percept he or she is currently experiencing. The key presses themselves contribute to the recorded brain activity. Accordingly, Lumer and Rees (1999) repeated the study without asking the subjects to make any response at all, identifying relevant brain activity solely on the basis of its temporal characteristics. It appeared from this second study that binocular rivalry is associated with activity in several different areas of the cortex beyond the primary visual area – extrastriate ventral, parietal, and prefrontal areas – and this raises the question whether any one of them can be said to be the seat of awareness.

There is an alternative scenario. Suppose that phenomenal awareness is properly a function of the whole organism, though chiefly of the brain, and of certain regions of the brain more than others. Think of the individual as a personal-view observer of his or her own behavior. Then the organism that is producing the behavior is at the same time the observer of the behavior that is produced. The idea behind this scenario is not that some small "awareness" unit in the brain observes events in the rest of the central nervous system and elsewhere – not Ryle's (1949) "ghost in the machine" – but, instead, that the entire organism observes itself, the observer observing the observer. If we ask where in the brain or in the body does awareness begin, the proper answer is "everywhere."[1] Investigations such as the one described are looking not at the neural location of awareness, but at its mechanics.

Personal View and Camera View

Dualism, as an account of consciousness, fails to take cognizance of the relationship between personal view and camera view, and reduction to brain function disregards

---

[1] There are some sensations such as pain and itch and headache which we locate inside our bodies and it might appear in such cases that a part of the brain is indeed observing the rest of the body. But, in truth, these are just percepts which we refer to the interior of our bodies in the same way that most other percepts are located in the world outside, and no difference in principle arises.

the distinction between them. These failures lead to ineradicable confusion in both accounts. But if we look at the problem afresh, with that distinction clearly in mind, the most fundamental problem in understanding consciousness is resolved.

In Nagel's (1995) argument above, "facts about the objective external world of particles and fields of force, as revealed by modern physical science" are observed in camera view, while "facts about subjective experience [that] are precisely about how things are from the point of view of individual conscious subjects" are, of course, observed in personal view. We do not need two different kinds of substance to support these two different kinds of "fact"; we need only two different vantage points and, as we have already seen, this distinction – between personal view and camera view – is needed for other reasons as well. This provides an initial tie between the phenomena of consciousness and the study of human motivation.

Technically, a wholly objective camera view is a contradiction in terms. A "view" requires someone, or some device (a camera), to do the viewing, and the "view" is relative to that someone or device. But when different people view the same scene (figure 4.1 illustrates the idea), they can agree on what the state of that part of the world is, and we *approach* a genuinely objective view. The laws of physics, then, are a distillation of what is common to very many individual "personal views" and in that sense can be described as "camera view." Since everybody experiences the world from their own personal view and, in principle, cannot actually view that particular camera view, a more apt characterization, though less easily visualized, is Nagel's (1986) "view from nowhere."

The two different kinds of "fact" that Nagel distinguishes correspond to camera view and to personal view, and that correspondence immediately explains why these two kinds of "fact" are related. They are observations of the same events from two different points of view. Instead of reduction to brain function being impossible, it is actually prescribed in many cases (of which Springer's lines is one). If we replace the traditional dualism of substance by a "dualism" between personal view and camera view, the problems that have long beset dualism evaporate.

The relationship between personal view and camera view might also make it appear that, when recording and investigative techniques have been sufficiently refined, phenomenal consciousness will reduce entirely to brain function. That is not possible, for a reason I explain below. But let us first look and see where such an enterprise would lead.

If you suffer a road accident, or if you are arrested by the police in a state of intoxication, doctors have well-practiced diagnostic techniques for assessing your state of consciousness. What the doctor assesses is a purely behavioral state, observable in camera view. In fact, there are several different states of consciousness that need to be distinguished (see table 4.1), and they are all quite distinct from the phenomenal notion of consciousness of concern here. Improvements in neurological investigative techniques will never do more than refine our understanding of those different behavioral states of consciousness; they will never access the phenomenal consciousness that is exclusive to personal view. In the study by Lumer et al. (1998), participants were required to signal their changes of percept by pressing a button. So, however far that line of research might be pursued, it will never be distinct from an objective, camera-view, account of the participants' button-pressing behavior. Any assertion that it also relates to their phenomenal consciousness is pure assumption.

A complete camera-view account of personal-view awareness is impossible for this reason. Observations in camera view lead to a determinate account of behavior. Lumer and Rees (1999) might not be able to say why or when, under binocular rivalry, the percept flips from one interpretation to the other; but there is no suggestion (in camera view) that the flipping is consequent on the participant's free will. But in personal view the matter looks different. Ambiguous figures such as the Necker cube that show a similar temporal dynamics to binocular rivalry (Borsellino, De Marco, Allazetta, Rinesi, & Bartolini, 1972) can easily be influenced by a deliberate direction of attention. So, if studies of the perception of ambiguous stimuli be pursued to their ultimate conclusion, we should have a theory at the neural level of description which prescribes in a determinate manner when the interpretation will flip, an event which is at the participant's disposal and therefore *free*. To put the matter succinctly, free will will not reduce to brain function in this way without creating conflict with existing psychological theory.

In chapter 1 I explained that actions which the individual freely chooses (in personal view) appear determinate in camera view. That does not involve any contradiction because determinism and free will are not properties of the behavior itself, but of the standpoint from which it is observed, and descriptions (or theories) of behavior are also relative to that standpoint. While it appears possible to draw many plausible parallels between camera-view observations of brain function and experience in personal view, the validity of those parallels cannot proceed beyond plausible conjecture and a complete translation between the two views will never be achieved.

Nevertheless, the relationship between experience in personal view and observation in camera view is of great importance to the study of human motivation. It enables us to take introspective (personal-view) reports and descriptions of internal feelings and interpret them (so far as the relationship can be traced) in terms of camera-view correlates. Such a use of anecdotal material greatly extends the range of behavior that can be brought within the purview of this study.

THE RELATIONSHIP OF SUBJECTIVE EXPERIENCE TO OBJECTIVE OBSERVATION

The problem posed by consciousness now stands like this. There are two quite distinct viewpoints from which a person's behavior might be experienced. There is the personal view which is private to the individual, not accessible by any other observer, and there is the objective camera view from which everyone else regards that individual's actions (but not itself accessible to the individual in question). Consciousness, in the sense in which it constitutes a philosophical problem, is tied to the private, personal, view; scientific study, on the other hand, is equally firmly rooted in the objective, camera, view. What then can we say about consciousness?

The answer is "Nothing," except to the extent that we can relate the personal experience of consciousness to the camera-view regime of scientific observation. Then, and only then, might we be able to translate the phenomena of consciousness into some objectively observable correlate. That is the aspect of the problem to which experimental psychology uniquely contributes. The author of an experiment with human participants might equally be a participant in his or her own experiment, and a good professional psychologist will indeed serve as a pilot participant in his or her own experiment for the sake of whatever intuitions that experience might deliver. We must therefore inquire what parallels can justifiably be drawn between subjective experience on the one hand and scientific observation on the other, justified by correlating experience as both experimenter and as participant in the same experiment.

Without going into the details of any particular experiment here, an experimenter might record any overt behavior he or she pleases. I mention, specifically, verbal utterances such as the recall of words committed to memory; motor responses such as pressing a reaction key as fast as possible following some signal or adjusting the magnitude of one stimulus to match another; and physiological concomitants such as heart rate and galvanic skin response. All these kinds of observations, and many more besides, are raw material for experimental psychology.

The human participant in the experiment, on the other hand, may be aware of many mental events, thoughts, and desires not accessible to behavioral observation. The participant may be aware of the complete memory from which some verbal response is distilled, though *not* of the process by which that memory is recalled. She may be aware of the complete percept in which some stimulus magnitude is to be matched, though *not* of the raw sense data from which that percept is derived. She may be aware of emotion, of internal feelings which are accompanied by physiological (sympathetic) activity, but will not usually be aware of the physiological reactions themselves except in extreme cases. Nisbett and Wilson (1977) have published a variety of other experiments and circumstances in which participants are unable to report on their internal processes, or are manifestly inaccurate. These two different domains of observation are summarized in table 4.2.

The kinds of observation which a participant can make are characteristically different from those available to the experimenter. In an experiment on memory, for example, the participant may be aware of a succession of images passing through the mind of which only the last issues in any overt recall. Participants in the study by McKinney and McGeoch (1935) reported after the experiment that they had recalled certain words (from a previously studied list) but had not uttered them

Table 4.2 What experimenter and participant can separately observe

Participant	Experimenter
Many mental events, e.g.,	Any overt behavior, e.g.,
• internal thoughts and desires	• verbal utterances
• emotional feelings (but *not*, usually, physiological reactions)	• body language, esp. physiological concomitants of emotional responses
• memories (but *not* means of access)	• recalls in memory experiments
• percepts (but *not* raw sense data)	• stimulus matches in perceptual experiments

because they knew them to be incorrect. The experimenter cannot know about such intermediate recalls unless the experiment is specifically designed to reveal them. On the other hand, participants (and, even more, experimenters serving as participants) have generated in this way a wide variety of ideas about how recall is accomplished. Those ideas cannot all be correct.

Listening to speech

One demonstration to bring out the difference between personal and camera view-points consists of asking someone to record a verse of poetry on tape and then playing the recording back to them. Other people hear the same voice reading the same poem twice over and find nothing to remark; but the person reading the verse hears a *different* voice on playback. One's own voice sounds different on playback (in camera view) because the spectrum of the sounds one ordinarily hears (in personal view) is colored by transmission through the bones of the head. Only the speaker can hear that particular voice;[2] everyone else hears only the direct acoustic transmission from mouth to ear.

Again, when listening to one's native language, one is never conscious of the raw acoustic waveform and frequently not even of the accent of the speaker. The acoustic input is transposed immediately into meaning and that transposition is preconscious. Marcel (1983b) found that recognition of the meaning of a briefly presented word could be accomplished on a briefer presentation than recognition of its graphic form and even of its identification as a word at all. Compare that with listening to a language of which one has no knowledge at all. To a class of native English students, Arabic and Japanese, while recognizably speech sounds, sound like so much gabble. That is how one perceives a raw speech waveform, devoid of meaning, and if the language is sufficiently unfamiliar, one is aware of nothing

---

[2] But maybe the effect of transmission through the bones of the head can now be synthesized.

else. If, on the other hand, one has a little knowledge of the language (e.g., French and German), but not enough to be fluent, it feels as though native speakers are speaking much too fast.

The speech waveform picked up by the ears is *automatically* translated into meaning without any conscious effort on our part. (One can, of course, consciously analyze the sequence of phonemes, but not in real time.) That is the consequence of learning one's native language, and human oral communication would be much slower than it is and our intellectual life much impoverished if our understanding of our native language were not automatic in this sense. That conclusion is easily justified by listening to foreign speech. But the consequence of that automaticity is that we are unable to report on the process by which the acoustic waveform is translated into meaning. That is a process of great complexity; it takes place within our brains, but cannot enter our awareness. That interpretative process can be discovered only by painstaking scientific research; it is not a part of subjective experience, notwithstanding that it takes place within the brain.

The portrait of Cecilia Gallerani

Leonardo da Vinci's *Portrait of Cecilia Gallerani* provides another example of the automatic processing of sensory input at an elementary level. The picture shows a Renaissance lady with an ermine in the crook of her left arm. The animal is supported by the lady's right hand, which is disposed across her chest. Now that right hand is manifestly too big in relation to the rest of the figure. How could so great a painter have made so elementary an error?[3]

The outlines of the design, and therefore the relative size of the hand, are determined at an early stage in the creation of a painting, when the canvas is relatively devoid of cues to size and distance. The artist has the canvas at most at arm's length, while the model is at a rather greater distance, set for comfortable viewing. So the model's hand, seen at some greater distance in the context of all the cues to size, shape, and distance that a real scene affords, has to be transferred to an equivalent outline shape and size on the much nearer canvas. This is a circumstance where human judgment is especially fallible, even the judgment of trained artists (Thouless, 1932).

Thouless (1931a, b) studied the matching of size, shape, luminance, and color when the two stimuli to be matched were presented in different contexts. In one experiment the distances from the observer of two discs of different diameters were adjusted until they were judged to present the same *angular* size. The nearer (smaller)

---

[3] Today painters sometimes distort the human figure deliberately – e.g., Augustus John, Stanley Spencer, and especially Salvador Dali – but this minor distortion in a fifteenth-century portrait is surely not intentional?

disc was systematically moved too close (presenting too large an angle) relative to the further disc, a phenomenon Thouless named "phenomenal regression to the real object." When (in a classroom practical; see p. 19, figure 1.6) a disc, placed in a fixed position, is chosen to match another disc further away, the match is closer to the real physical size of the further disc than to its angular size. But if the two discs be viewed through cardboard tubes under subdued lighting, phenomenal regression is much less. At the same time, the observer is uncertain how far away each disc is.

Thouless (1931a, b) reported an analogous study of the matching of shape and, for that task, Taylor and Mitchell (1996; cited by Mitchell, 1997, pp. 147–9) have established securely the relationship between knowledge of object shape and phenomenal regression. The participants viewed a self-luminous disc through a peephole into an otherwise light-tight box. The disc could be rotated about a diameter so that it presented an elliptical profile to the observer and the task was to match that profile on a computer screen, viewed through a similar peephole. Matches were veridical; except that one group of participants who had been allowed to see in advance that the ellipse they were to match was, in fact, a circular disc mounted on a rod, showed a small, but reliable, bias toward a circular shape. It is clear that those participants who had not seen in advance that it was a circular disc they were to match had no idea of its shape or, therefore, of its orientation. Just as fluent knowledge of a language means that we are immediately aware of the meaning of what is said and thereby unaware of the acoustic waveform from which that meaning is distilled, so here, if the observer can perceive the orientation of the disc, it is immediately seen as a real object of a definite physical shape, and the pattern of light on the retina is not otherwise available as a basis for judgment.

Gibson (1950, pp. 176–7) has a particularly acute photographic demonstration of regression to real size. Two eye-charts, one four times the physical size of the other, are photographed in a situation particularly rich in linear perspective. The larger chart is placed at four times the distance of the smaller so that both charts contribute images of the same physical size on the photographic print. But that equality cannot be perceived (the further chart definitely *looks* larger) until the camera is positioned in such a way that the photographic images of the two charts are juxtaposed side by side. It is as though (in the absence of such a juxtaposition) the observer has to calculate the angular size mentally from each chart as it is perceived, their retinal equality being ordinarily unavailable to perception.

Auditory space

Another similar example, especially compelling, is cited by Warren (1989, p. 297):

> . . . it is impossible for us to perceive the gross spectral changes produced by head shadowing and pinna reflections when a sound source moves. These changes in peripheral stimulation (which can exceed 20 dB for particular spectral bands)

are perceived in an automatic and obligatory fashion as changes in position of the source rather than as changes in the quality of the sound or the relative intensity of spectral components. As pointed out by Helmholtz, "we are exceedingly well trained in finding out by our sensations the objective nature of the objects around us, but . . . are completely unskilled in observing these sensations *per se*; . . . the practice of associating them with things outside of us actually prevents us from being distinctly conscious of the pure sensations" (Warren & Warren, 1968).

Marcel (1983a, p. 260) writes of an analogous phenomenon in tactile space, an example he attributes to Polanyi (1967, prob. p. 12): "when we are exploring the interior of a hole with a stick we are aware of the shape of the hole not the pressures of the stick on our hand, although the former is mediated by the latter."

The expression of emotion

We distinguish a great variety of emotions (see Ekman & Davidson, 1994), but the physiological concomitant (activity of the sympathetic nervous system) is much the same in every case. The difference between different emotions lies principally in the social context in which they are generated and hardly at all in the physiology. This makes emotion a phenomenon of the internal, personal, point of view.

At the same time, the physiological expression of emotion is a phenomenon of the objective, camera, view. As a consequence the individual is not ordinarily aware of his or her body language until the physiological activity reaches a level where it generates its own sensory input – palpitations of the heart, dryness of the throat, etc. All this poses a problem for the actress who has to portray emotions she does not actually feel. The fourth episode of the BBC's *Pride and Prejudice* (Birtwistle, 1995) opens with Lizzie Bennet in acute distress following a most unwelcome proposal of marriage (at the end of the third episode) from Mr Darcy. In real life such a state of distress would persist for hours, possibly longer. But on the television screen the viewer sees only 10 seconds of Lizzie Bennet's agony. That agony has to be put across in body language, without words, and while the actress (Jennifer Ehle) will do her best to "think herself" into her part, that still does not generate (inside her) the internal distress she is required to portray.

Blindsight

These three examples show that a great deal happens in our brains of which we are unaware. An even more compelling instance is provided by blindsight.

Weiskrantz (1986) describes a patient who had the greater part of the visual cortex surgically removed from the right cerebral hemisphere. This left the patient blind over the greater part of the left hemifield, but with normal vision on the right. After the operation the patient was found to be able to locate lights in the left hemifield (by moving his eyes to fixate the light) with an accuracy better than chance, and to point to the light with a finger with an accuracy so much better than chance (though still not as accurate as in the right hemifield) that a statistical test was quite needless. The patient could also discriminate an "X" from an "O" and detect the presence of a grating.

> D.B. was questioned repeatedly about his vision in his left half-field. Most commonly he said that he saw nothing at all. If pressed, he might say in some tests, but by no means all, that he perhaps had a "feeling" that a stimulus was approaching or receding, or was "smooth" (the "O") or "jagged" (the "X"). But he always stressed that he saw nothing in the sense of "seeing," that typically he was guessing, and was at a loss for words to describe any conscious perception. (Weiskrantz, 1986, p. 31)

The study of blindsight is seen by some as a major contribution to our understanding of consciousness. But this is mistaken. Blindsight is not a conscious facility and actually tells us nothing about consciousness *per se*. What it does do is to emphasize that there is much going on in our brains of which we *cannot have* awareness. Consciousness begins with the finished percept, with the meaning of an utterance. Blindsight is simply a phenomenon of incomplete perception. The process by which the percept is derived from sensory input is not available to introspection and can be discovered (in an intact person) only from the way in which perception is degraded in impoverished situations.

The Split Brain

Although there are many neurological observations which appear to bear in some way or other on the discussion of consciousness, the study of the split brain is exceptional, being regarded, in its day, as of supreme importance. A reexamination of the evidence and the interpretation first published 30 years ago will help to clarify how little the neurological evidence actually tells us and how easy it is to read preexisting ideas into its interpretation.

The two cerebral hemispheres are connected by a large and prominent bundle of fibers, the *corpus callosum*, which enables the two to work in concert. But the *corpus callosum* also carries epileptic discharges between the hemispheres and in a small number of extremely severe cases surgical section of the *corpus callosum* has greatly ameliorated the epileptic condition. Since many cortical functions are localized in one hemisphere alone, there are effects on mental activity. But these effects are very subtle, requiring precisely focused tests to demonstrate them. When those tests are carefully administered, they appear to show the coexistence of "two

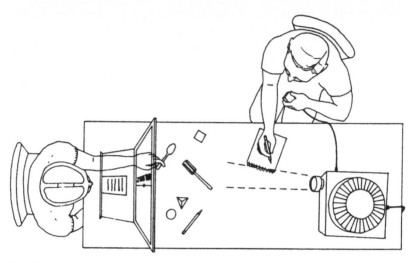

Figure 4.3 Testing setup for split-brain patients. Reproduced with permission from Gazzaniga & LeDoux (1978, p. 5). © 1978 Plenum Press.

minds in one body," interpreted by Sperry (1968) as indicative of a splitting of consciousness.

The essential feature of the testing arrangements is illustrated in figure 4.3. The split-brain patient is required to fixate on a mark so that a word flashed (for less than 100 ms – a longer exposure would give the patient time to shift his gaze) to the left of that mark is seen by the right hemisphere only, while a word flashed to the right of the mark is seen by the left hemisphere only. In most people linguistic functions are localized in the left hemisphere, so that a word seen by the right hemisphere cannot be read. Suppose then that "spoon" is flashed to the left of the fixation mark. When the patient is asked, "What did you see?" he replies (the *left*-hemisphere response), "I did not see anything." But, when asked, he can feel for and pick up a spoon (hidden from view) with his left hand (the *right*-hemisphere response). When then asked, "What do you have in your hand?" the patient replies, "I don't know" (the *left* hemisphere again). Both hemispheres are able to carry out their respective functions but they cannot "talk" to each other (Gazzaniga & LeDoux, 1978, pp. 4–5).

Another test (figure 4.4; many similar tests have been devised, based on the same principle) involves two different pictures flashed simultaneously, one to each side of the fixation mark. Suppose, to take one published example, the patient is shown a snowed-up house and car to the left of the fixation mark and a chicken's claw to the right. The patient is then asked to select a matching picture from a range of alternatives. The right hand (controlled by the *left* hemisphere) picks a picture of a chicken, while the left hand prefers a picture of a shovel. When the patient is then asked,

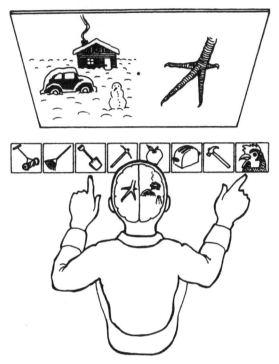

Figure 4.4 Dual task for split-brain patients. Reproduced with permission from Gazzaniga & LeDoux (1978, p. 148). © 1978 Plenum Press.

"What did you see?" he replies, "I saw a claw [with the *left* hemisphere] and I picked a chicken, and you have to clean out the chicken shed with a shovel [rationalization]" (Gazzaniga & LeDoux, 1978, p. 149).

> One of the more general and also more interesting and striking features of this syndrome may be summarized as an apparent doubling in most of the realms of conscious awareness. Instead of the normally unified single stream of consciousness, these patients behave in many ways as if they have two independent streams of conscious awareness, one in each hemisphere, each of which is cut off from and out of contact with the mental experiences of the other. In other words, each hemisphere seems to have its own separate and private sensations; its own perceptions; its own concepts; and its own impulses to act, with related volitional, cognitive, and learning experiences. Following the surgery, each hemisphere also has thereafter its own separate chain of memories that are rendered inaccessible to the recall processes of the other. (Sperry, 1968, p. 724)

But this is simply to attribute a consciousness such as the author has to each separate function by the split-brain patient.

Does sectioning of the corpus callosum also split consciousness?

There is an implicit argument here which seems (in 1968) to have run roughly as follows:

1 Only human beings have consciousness; other animals are simply stimulus-response mechanisms.
2 The chief difference between the brains of humans and those of subhuman species is the much greater development of the cerebral hemispheres in humans. Therefore human consciousness must reside in the cerebral hemispheres.
3 After sectioning of the *corpus callosum* the cerebral hemispheres function independently. Hence there are then two minds in one brain.

But there is also a counterargument:

1 Damage to the brain reduces the variety of behavior of which the human or animal is capable. The split-brain studies do no more than identify those mental tasks which depend on communication between the hemispheres.
2 The cerebral hemispheres are concerned chiefly with the analysis of sensory input (e.g., interpreting an acoustic waveform as meaningful speech; or identifying the physical size of an object seen at a distance) and with the organization of motor output (e.g., the articulatory movements required in speaking). These are not activities of which people are ordinarily conscious. They are either preconscious (sensory input) or postconscious (articulatory output). They are functionally analogous to the interfaces in a computer.
3 Damage to the cerebral hemispheres disrupts aspects of mental processing which are ordinarily subconscious. It does not alter the quality of consciousness, but merely restricts the range of real-world relationships of which the individual might be conscious.

> Starting in the eighties, major advances were made in understanding the split-brain syndrome and how it could vary from one individual to another. . . . What was so striking in these new studies was that the personal states of mind felt by the patients were similar and seemed unchanged from their preoperative feelings of mind. In other words, even though the distribution of specialized functions varied, the felt state of mind was no different. (Gazzaniga, 1995, p. 1394)

4 It follows that it is reasonable to expect subhuman animals to have a similar capacity for consciousness to us, but with respect to a much restricted range of real-world relationships. Pet cats and dogs demonstrably have dreams and presumably function in a similar manner when awake.
5 The conscious experience of a split-brain patient is simply a rationalization of his or her slightly disrupted mental function.

It is interesting to note that while the patients possess at least some under-standing of their surgery, they never say things like, "Well, I chose this because I have a split brain and the information went to the right, nonverbal hemisphere [a camera-view rationalization]." Even patients who have high IQs . . . view their responses as behaviors emanating from their own volitional selves [a personal-view conception], and as a result they incorporate these behaviors into a theory to explain why they behave as they do. (Gazzaniga, 1995, p. 1394)

The responses of a split-brain patient are, perhaps, analogous to a grandfather clock in which the chimes have become dissociated from the motion of the hour hand.

The interpretation of phenomenal reports and of behavioral deficits from persons with neurological deficits requires some care. If I, with normal vision, responded to visual stimuli as D.B. (Weiskrantz, 1986) does, then I should expect to experience (or perhaps display) at least a curious inconsistency in my conscious awareness, described as a "slippage of unity" by Marcel (1993). But the patients that Marcel was studying did not have normal vision and the experiments he reports focused on their pathology. We do not actually know what is the *content* of such patients' conscious experience. The patients can describe their experiences, but we cannot be sure that our understanding of that description is correct. Their experience may contain features for which the appropriate words do not exist. The lesson from the split-brain stud-ies is that one should at least explore the assumption that the *nature* of these patients' conscious experience with respect to their respective deficits is unchanged and ask: What content, coupled with an unchanged quality of consciousness, would yield the kinds of reports that these patients typically make?

Why is Consciousness Important to the Study of Motivation?

A layperson's view of motivation is a personal view. People plan their actions; they intend what they do. People also assume that others are conscious in the same way, and that other people's actions are directed by the same kind of intention. But exploration of the brain has not, so far, revealed any neural basis for consciousness, or for intention. There looks to be a paradox.

Let us suppose that the physical domain is closed, that brain processes are all that there is to direct behavior, and that all natural phenomena reduce ultimately to the physical domain. Scientific theory would not then have recourse to any kind of mind-substance in an explanation of behavior. In such a regime, consciousness would become simply an epiphenomenon, and our mental lives would be merely piggy-backing on some very complicated biological machinery. That is the stance I take in this book.

But such a stance does not mean that what people say from a personal viewpoint should be disregarded. On the contrary, much of my material is anecdotal; that is, it is an account of what certain people have done and said, and that account is usually expressed in personal view. It is important that such material be correctly integrated with other observations made from a camera viewpoint. Such an integration of personal view and camera view requires an understanding of their interrelationship and therefore of phenomenal consciousness.

This issue arises in the next chapter. Boredom is an unpleasant state of mind, like other unpleasant emotions. But we know about it solely from introspective report, not from camera-view observation. Are we looking here at another frustrated instinct?

QUESTIONS FOR DISCUSSION

1 "Reductionist scientists hover like vultures . . . seeking explanations through physical brain function. Daniel Dennett, with his bold title *Consciousness Explained*, and Francis Crick in *The Astonishing Hypothesis* feel that they have achieved this in all but detail. Others are not so sure. However much you correlate brain function with sensations, thought patterns and so on, all you find is brain function. You never find subjective experience in itself" (Redfern, 1995, p. 36). Why?

2 How can we tell whether someone is "conscious," in the phenomenal sense of that term, or not?

3 How much can I know of what is happening in my brain? And how much can you discover? And what common ground is there between what I can know and what you can discover?

5

BOREDOM

How would you like to spend the day in bed – not ill, just doing nothing? Your head rests in a comfortable U-shaped foam-rubber pillow. You wear translucent goggles so there is nothing you can see except for a uniform illumination, a *ganzfeld*. You can hear the hum of the airconditioner, but that is all. You wear cotton gloves and your hands and lower arms are encased in stiff cardboard cuffs, so that there is nothing to feel. This was the experimental setup used by Bexton, Heron, and Scott (1954). You would, of course, be paid handsomely for lying on this bed; even so, you would hate it! But why?

In case that should appear to be another stupid question like "Why do people have sex?" let me come to the point. If people find doing nothing, *literally* nothing, so excessively unpleasant (as they do), might there not be some instinctive pattern of behavior that is frustrated when there is nothing to do? This chapter turns the arguments of chapters 2 and 3 inside out. In those chapters I argued that terror and the emotions associated with a potential sexual partner are the subjective counterpart of being motivated – more precisely, of the initiation and fulfillment of some instinctive pattern of behavior. If that instinctive pattern is frustrated short of fulfillment, then a different kind of emotion is experienced. When we are bored, that is how we feel; so, is boredom the subjective counterpart of the frustration of some (hitherto undiscovered) motivation? Is there some instinctive pattern of behavior which is frustrated when we have nothing to do? This chapter uses subjective reports as the basis for a speculative interpretation of the results of experiments studying the effects of unvarying environments, a condition commonly called "sensory deprivation." The previous chapter, on "consciousness," was inserted to underpin the arguments of this present chapter to the extent that underpinning is possible.

THE POLITICAL BACKGROUND

Cardinal Mindszenty

There was a political background to the research on "sensory deprivation." In 1948 the communist government in Hungary took over all the church schools. Cardinal Jozsef Mindszenty, the senior Catholic archbishop and Prince-primate of Hungary, organized an uncompromising resistance to the takeover, and eventually (December 26, 1948) was arrested and charged with conspiracy against the Hungarian government. There was a "show" trial intended to destroy Mindszenty's influence with the Hungarian people. This trial opened (February 3, 1949) with a letter, written by Mindszenty in his own hand to the Minister of Justice, confessing to all the allegations against him and promising cooperation henceforward. The letter went on to suggest that there was therefore no need to continue with the trial. The trial judge disagreed; the trials went on and Cardinal Mindszenty was sentenced to life imprisonment.

At his trial Mindszenty appeared a changed man.

> A broken man psychologically and physically, the primate sat there in the dock. Like a frightened schoolboy in front of a strict master, his hands on his knees, his eyes opened wide, he did his best to give the right answers to the questions put to him. He was only a shadow of his former self; his voice trembled as he repeated that the political police had done nothing to him and had not influenced what he said in any way. (Közi-Horváth, 1979, p. 51)

That is a sympathetic description of how he appeared in the dock. Before his arrest Mindszenty had written to his cathedral chapter – a letter which had been placed in a sealed envelope to be opened in the case of his arrest.

> I have taken part in no conspiracy.
> I am not resigning from my archiepiscopal see.
> I have nothing to confess and shall sign nothing.
> If I do so, however, it will be merely as a consequence of the weakness of the human body, and I hereby declare in advance that it will be null and void. (Közi-Horváth, 1979, p. 38)

At his trial he formally declared that letter invalid. So here was the question for western political leaders: *What had the communist interrogators done to Cardinal Mindszenty?*

The war in Korea

At about the same time there was another similar event in the political background. On June 25, 1950, North Korea invaded South Korea. South Korea and the United

States were completely unprepared for this attack and some US prisoners were taken during the initial retreat. During September and October of that year United Nations forces, chiefly American, repulsed the attack and eventually forced their way deep into North Korea. Nevertheless, some US prisoners of war had collaborated with the communists. For example,

> ... at 11:55 A.M., Greenwich time, on July 9, 1950, to be precise, or only four days after our ground forces had first engaged the enemy in Korea. At that time an American Army officer of the 24th Infantry Division, taken prisoner some forty-eight hours before, made a nine-hundred-word broadcast in the enemy's behalf over the Seoul radio. Purportedly speaking for all American soldiers, this man said, among other things, "We did not know at all the cause of the war and the real state of affairs, and we were compelled to fight against the people of Korea. It was really most generous of the Democratic People's Republic of Korea to forgive us and give kind consideration for our health, for food, clothing, and habitation." Service authorities were dumfounded. Parts of the statement, of course, were actually treasonable. But a tape recording had been made of the broadcast and there was no mistaking the officer's voice. Within a few weeks, many statements of this sort were picked up by American listening posts in the Far East. (Kinkead, 1960, pp. 18–19)

But why the collaboration? Had the communists developed some technique of wiping the mind clean and reprogramming it that the West did not know about?

Western governments were alarmed. There was immediate funding for research to find out what it was that the communists knew and the West did not. But what research would you do? Donald Hebb at McGill University, Montreal, author of *The Organization of Behaviour* (1949), had an idea. The experimental chamber used by Bexton et al. (1954) was a realization of that idea.

"Brainwashing"

According to Brownfield (1972, p. 32) the term "brainwashing" was coined by Hunter (1951). The idea of "brainwashing" in the sense of wiping the mind clean and reprogramming it is science fiction. There are many people who have suffered psychological trauma (Ellis Wardle and his friends in chapter 2) who would just love to have their brains washed clean, and there are many psychotherapists who are repeatedly unable to oblige. But the experimental work by Bexton et al. (1954) and others has some profound lessons to teach us about human motivation. Here is a succinct summary of what they did and what they found.

> Their subjects were paid handsomely to do nothing, see nothing, hear or touch very little, for 24 hours a day. Primary needs were met, on the whole, very well. The subjects suffered no pain, and were fed on request. It is true that they could

not copulate, but at the risk of impugning the virility of Canadian college students I point out that most of them would not have been copulating anyway and were quite used to such long stretches of three or four days without primary sexual satisfaction. The secondary reward, on the other hand, was high: $20 a day plus room and board is more than $7,000 a year, far more than a student could earn by other means [in 1954]. The subjects then should be highly motivated to continue the experiment, cheerful and happy to be allowed to contribute to scientific knowledge so painlessly and profitably.

   In fact, the subject was well motivated for perhaps four to eight hours, and then became increasingly unhappy. He developed a need for stimulation of almost any kind. In the first preliminary exploration, for example, he was allowed to listen to recorded material on request. Some subjects were given a talk for 6-year-old children on the dangers of alcohol. This might be requested, by a grown-up male college student, 15 or 20 times in a 30-hour period. Others were offered, and asked for repeatedly, a recording of an old stockmarket report. The subjects looked forward to being tested, but paradoxically tended to find the tests fatiguing when they did arrive. It is hardly necessary to say that the whole situation was rather hard to take, and one subject, in spite of not being in a special state of primary drive arousal in the experiment but in real need of money outside it, gave up the secondary reward of $20 a day to take up a job at hard labor paying $7 or $8 a day. (Hebb, 1955, p. 247)

Boredom is unpleasant. Absence of *all* stimulation is profoundly unpleasant and can, of itself, motivate appropriate behavior; that is to say, not only is behavior, such as courtship and fear-avoidance, switched on by external stimuli, but also by the *absence* of stimulation! That realization amounted to a sea change in psychologists' thinking about motivation and is reflected in Hebb's (1955) historic paper.

SENSORY DEPRIVATION

Bexton et al. (1954, p. 71) described their experiment in this manner.

   The subjects, 22 male college students, were paid to lie on a comfortable bed in a lighted cubicle 24 hours a day, with time out for eating and going to the toilet. During the whole experimental period they wore translucent goggles which transmitted diffuse light but prevented pattern vision. Except when eating or at the toilet, the subject wore gloves and cardboard cuffs, the latter extending from below the elbow to beyond the finger tips. These permitted free joint movement but limited tactual perception. Communication between subject and experimenters was provided by a small speaker system, and was kept to a minimum. Auditory stimulation was limited by the partially sound-proof cubicle and by a U-shaped foam-rubber pillow in which the subject kept his head while in the cubicle. Moreover, the continuous hum provided by fans, airconditioner, and the amplifier leading to earphones in the pillow produced fairly efficient masking noise.

The participants initially went to sleep; but they could not sleep for ever.

Later they slept less, became bored, and appeared eager for stimulation. They would sing, whistle, talk to themselves, tap the cuffs together, or explore the cubicle with them. . . . The subjects also became very restless, displaying constant random movement, and they described the restlessness as unpleasant. Hence it was difficult to keep subjects for more than two or three days, despite the fact that the pay ($20 for a 24-hour day) was more than double what they could normally earn.

On coming out of the cubicle after the experimental session, when goggles, cuffs, and gloves had been removed, the subjects seemed at first dazed. There also appeared to be some disturbance in visual perception, usually lasting no longer than one or two minutes. Subjects reported difficulty in focusing; objects appeared fuzzy and did not stand out from their backgrounds. There was a tendency for the environment to appear two-dimensional and colours seemed more saturated than usual. The subjects also reported feelings of confusion, headaches, a mild nausea, and fatigue; these conditions persisted in some cases for 24 hours after the session. (Bexton et al., 1954, pp. 71–2)

Sensory deprivation is exceedingly unpleasant. Three of the researchers, more highly motivated than paid participants, tolerated confinement in the Bexton et al. chamber for six days (Heron, Doane, & Scott, 1956).

Experimental work was taken up in at least eight other laboratories between 1956 and 1962 (Brownfield, 1972, p. 91). It became a suddenly fashionable idea; it was seen as a new way of studying cognition. A variety of isolation chambers and different conditions of confinement were used. Shurley (1963) immersed his participant in a water tank, with the participant breathing through a mask (see figure 5.1). The tolerance of a researcher in this apparatus was 6–7 hours. Different conditions of confinement in different laboratories were tolerated for different periods of time, but all were manifestly unpleasant to the point of being intolerable. (See Zuckerman, 1964, for a review.)

Hallucinations

If the intense unpleasantness of sensory deprivation be looked upon as the most important outcome of these experiments, then the hallucinations experienced by the participants rank second. The hallucinations were chiefly visual, amounting to "perception" in the absence of perceptual input – described by one participant as "having a dream while awake" (Bexton et al., 1954, p. 73).

In the simplest form the visual field, with the eyes closed, changed from dark to light colour; next in complexity were dots of light, lines, or simple geometric patterns. All 14 subjects reported such imagery, and said it was a new experience to them. Still more complex forms consisted in "wall-paper patterns," reported by 11 subjects, and isolated figures or objects, without background (e.g., a row of little yellow men with black caps on and their mouths open;

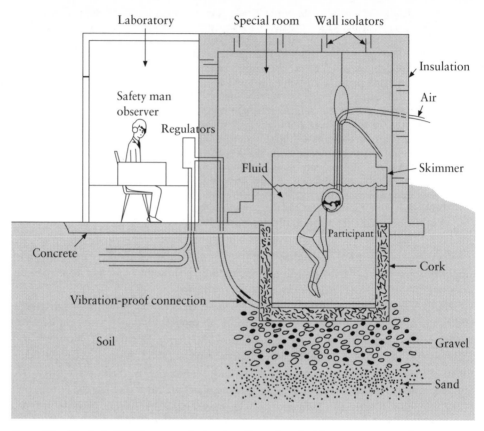

Figure 5.1 Shurley's (1963) water-tank chamber. Reproduced with permission from Shurley (1963, p. 233). © 1963 University of Toronto Press.

a German helmet), reported by seven subjects. Finally, there were integrated scenes (e.g., a procession of squirrels with sacks over their shoulders marching "purposefully" across a snow field and out of the field of "vision"; prehistoric animals walking about in a jungle). Three of the 14 subjects reported such scenes, frequently including dreamlike distortions, with the figures often being described as "like cartoons." One curious fact is that some of the hallucinations were reported as being inverted or tilted at an angle. (Bexton et al., 1954, p. 74)

Envisage that what we perceive is an interpretation of the information provided by our senses, an interpretation that is subject to internal constraints, especially constraints contributed by prior experience and by the immediate perceptual context. In principle, sensory deprivation removes all systematic changes from sensory input. Now, the study of sensory discrimination (Laming, 1986) shows that the

Table 5.1 Incidence of hallucinations in sensory deprivation experiments

Experiment	Number of participants	Confinement regime	Vision	Hallucinations
1	4	Participants eat by dim red illumination	Pattern vision for 3 short periods/day	None at all
2	9	Complete darkness	Defect in blindfold going to the toilet	6 out of 9 participants
3	11	Complete darkness	No egress for either eating or toilet	One primitive hallucination only

Source: Vernon & Hoffman (1956); Vernon et al. (1958).

brain is differentially coupled to the physical world, so that only *changes* in sensory input contribute to perception. So sensory deprivation ideally means that there is no sensory information and no perceptual context. Whatever is perceived in such circumstances can have an internal basis only and is indeed like "having a dream while awake."

But the incidence of hallucinations varies substantially from one experiment to another. Three experiments by Vernon and Hoffman (1956) and by Vernon, McGill, and Schiffman (1958), all conducted at Princeton, provide an instructive comparison (see table 5.1). These experiments used the same confinement chamber, rather like the original Bexton, Heron, and Scott chamber, but in Experiment 1 the participants were allowed to eat by dim red illumination and therefore enjoyed pattern vision for three short periods each day. In Experiment 2 the participants were kept in darkness, except for a defect in the blindfold when led to the toilet. Six out of nine participants incarcerated for 72 hours reported hallucinations, more frequently later in their confinement. In Experiment 3 11 participants were confined in complete darkness with no egress for either eating or for going to the toilet. They reported only one primitive hallucination between them.

It is clear that hallucinations occur only in conditions of exceptional poverty of sensory input, much prolonged. But the hallucinations seem to be triggered by *defects* in the sensory deprivation, defects not of themselves sufficient for perception. Complete blackout produces what one would expect – no perception at all – while adequate sensory stimulation abolishes the possibility of hallucination. This idea is supported by Doane, Mahatoo, Heron, and Scott (1959), who compared opaque and translucent masks (see table 5.2). A translucent mask led to a higher incidence of hallucinations, except that transfer from a translucent to an opaque mask led to a transient increase in vividness of hallucination, but an increase that lasted at most 2 hours.

Finally, Lilly (1956) had himself confined in slowly flowing tepid water at 94.5°F, wearing an opaque breathing mask. He reported as follows.

Table 5.2   Incidence of hallucinations with translucent and opaque masks

Type of mask	Number of participants	Number of participants reporting hallucinations
Cubicle participants in BHS chamber		
Translucent . . .	11	8
. . . transfer to complete darkness	5	Transient increase in vividness, but near-extinction after 2 hours
Opaque . . .	2	1
. . . transfer to translucent mask	2	2, with vivid hallucinations
Ambulatory participants with visual deprivation only		
Translucent . . .	4	2

Source: Doane et al. (1959).

In these experiments, the subject always has a full night's rest before entering the tank. Instructions are to inhibit all movements as far as possible. An initial set of training exposures overcomes the fears of the situation itself.

In the tank, the following stages have been experienced:

(1) For about the first three-quarters of an hour, the day's residues are predominant. One is aware of the surroundings, recent problems, etc.

(2) Gradually, one begins to relax and more or less enjoy the experience. The feeling of being isolated in space and having nothing to do is restful and relaxing at this stage.

(3) But slowly, during the next hour, a tension develops which can be called a "stimulus-action" hunger; hidden methods of self-stimulation develop: twitching muscles, slow swimming movements (which cause sensations as the water flows by the skin), stroking one finger with another, etc. If one can inhibit such maneuvers long enough, intense satisfaction is derived from later self-stimulations.

(4) If inhibition can win out, the tension may ultimately develop to the point of forcing the subject to leave the tank.

(5) Meanwhile, the attention is drawn powerfully to any residual stimulus: the mask, the suspension, each come in for their share of concentration. Such residual stimuli become the whole content of consciousness to an almost unbearable degree.

(6) If this stage is passed without leaving the tank, one notices that one's thoughts have shifted from a directed type of thinking about problems to reveries and fantasies of a highly personal and emotionally charged nature. These are too personal to relate publicly, and probably vary greatly from subject to subject. The individual reactions to such fantasy material also probably vary considerably, from complete suppression to relaxing and enjoying them.

(7) If the tension and the fantasies are withstood, one may experience the furthest stage which we have yet explored: projection of visual imagery. I

have seen this once, after a two and one-half hour period. The black curtain in front of the eyes (such as one "sees" in a dark room with eyes closed) gradually opens out into a three-dimensional, dark, empty space in front of the body. This phenomenon captures one's interest immediately, and one waits to find out what comes next. Gradually forms of the type sometimes seen in hypnogogic states [the state just before one is fully asleep] appear. In this case, they were small, strangely shaped objects with self-luminous borders. A tunnel whose inside "space" seemed to be emitting a blue light then appeared straight ahead. About this time, this experiment was terminated by a leakage of water into the mask through a faulty connector on the inspiratory tube.

In our experiments, we notice that after emersion the day apparently is started over. *i.e.,* The subject feels as if he has just arisen from bed afresh; this effect persists, and the subject finds he is out of step with the clock for the rest of that day. He also has to re-adjust to social intercourse in subtle ways. The night of the day of the exposure he finds that his bed exerts great pressure against his body. No bed is as comfortable as floating in water. (Lilly, 1956, pp. 6–7)

Hallucinations ensue rapidly. Another account of what it is like to be immersed in Lilly's tank may be found in Feynman (1985, pp. 330–7). Richard Feynman experienced about a dozen immersions of perhaps 2.5 hours. After a little accustomization, he enjoyed some quite lengthy hallucinations, including "out-of-the-body" experiences, but without any kind of alarm.

Hallucinations have also been reported in other sensory modalities.

One subject could hear the people speaking in his visual hallucinations, and another repeatedly heard the playing of a music box. Four subjects described kinesthetic and somesthetic phenomena. One reported seeing a miniature rocket ship discharging pellets that kept striking his arm, and one reported reaching out to touch a doorknob he saw before him and feeling an electric shock. The other two subjects reported a phenomenon which they found difficult to describe. They said it was as if there were two bodies side by side in the cubicle; in one case the two bodies overlapped, partly occupying the same space.

In addition, there were reports of feelings of "otherness" and bodily "strangeness" in which it was hard to know exactly what the subject meant. One subject said "my mind seemed to be a ball of cotton-wool floating above my body"; another reported that his head felt detached from his body. These are familiar phenomena in certain cases of migraine. (Bexton et al., 1954, pp. 75–6)

"Iron lungs"

There are a number of circumstances in which hallucinations occur "naturally." Severe cases of poliomyelitis lead to paralysis of the intercostal muscles and the patient will die unless breathing is maintained artificially. The patient is placed in a respirator commonly known as an "iron lung." The following case comes from an epidemic of poliomyelitis in 1955 in Boston, USA.

> A 22-year-old married white female was admitted with the diagnosis of spinal paralytic poliomyelitis with involvement of the muscles of the neck, trunk, and legs. She was placed in the respirator on the first day of hospitalization. The patient remembered being brought to the hospital and being placed in the respirator. She had good recall for all events occurring during her illness and vivid recall of the "dreams" she had during the initial phase of her respirator therapy. The patient was well oriented until her 5th day in the respirator. At this time she became disoriented to time, place and person. She had the feeling that everything in her environment was "unreal" and she asked the physicians and nurses what her name was and what place she was in. She began having "dreams" which had a more vivid quality than her real environment. During the first few days after the onset of this symptomatology she attempted to see if she were dreaming by asking the nurses and the attendants to tell her if she were awake and who she was. She said that her difficulty in knowing the real from the unreal progressed until the two became merged. During the first few days of these symptoms the "dreams" were more frequent and vivid as evening approached. She said "I was afraid of the night. When it started getting dark, I started going sort of loopy."
>
> The patient had both auditory and visual hallucinations. The visual hallucinations were three dimensional and in color. She told of travelling about the hospital in an automobile that had the shape of the respirator. She was riding in the "trunk" with her head protruding out of the rear. This automobile was driven to different places in the hospital and the patient recalled the nurses who accompanied her. She often spontaneously verbalized, "When are we going to get there?" When reassured and comforted by the nursing staff the patient again recognized her real environment and began her questions in an attempt to orient herself.
>
> The patient's symptoms gradually diminished and completely ceased by her 10th respirator day. She continued to have vivid dreams. (Mendelson, Solomon, & Lindemann, 1958, p. 422)

The involvement of the respirator in the hallucination ("riding in the 'trunk' with her head protruding out of the rear") is noteworthy. Dement and Wolpert (1958) have shown that a variety of simple stimuli may be incorporated in similar manner into a dream.

Following these observations the respirator was adopted as an experimental environment with volunteer participants confined for various periods of time. The study by Wexler et al. (1958) most closely approximates the experience of hospitalization. They confined 17 medical and graduate students in a respirator under subdued lighting. An experimenter was in the same room and fed the participants in the respirator. Even so, only six of the 17 volunteers remained after the end of the first day. Compare this with the 10 days without possibility of release suffered by the patient described above.

"Out-of-the-body" experiences

"Out-of-the-body" experiences (OBEs) are another naturally occurring disorder of orientation. They are reported most commonly between the ages of 15 and 25 and perhaps 20 percent have such an experience at some time in their lives:

> Melvyn Bragg could not bring himself to reveal his teenage OBE terrors until he was 48. In the novel *The Maid of Buttermere*, he says: "It happens to me usually when I am alone and may be associated with fear of solitude or with that greatest fear of all . . . Death. It is as if a distinct part of – is it my soul? – leaves my body entirely and completely, totally and unmistakably – hovers above it looking back on this vacated thing of flesh, bone, blood, breath, water, matter." (Burt, 1993)

Bexton et al. (1954, p. 74, figure 3) reproduce a drawing by one of their participants representing exactly that.

A related occurrence is the "near-death experience." In 1986 David Verdegaal suffered a massive heart attack, during which his heart stopped beating for 30 minutes, while on a business trip to Austria.

> "The first thing I was conscious of was the fact that I had died.
> "I was aware that there was a light all around me. It didn't seem to be coming from any particular source, it just enveloped me. And I had this impression of being transformed, both physically and mentally.
> "There was a feeling of love and warmth, as though I was a little child being cuddled by God. Everything was completely silent – no ringing in the ears, no music – and no one was with me, not my wife or my children; I wasn't even there in any recognisable form.
> "The next thing I knew, I was being led by the hand into a beautiful garden [David Verdegaal was sales director for a Lincolnshire firm growing bulbs]. I remember passing through an arch of honeysuckle and between flowering borders on either side of me. The leaves and petals had vibrant, sparkling colours, as though it was early morning and the dew was still on them.
> "At the end of the garden there was a wrought-iron gate and, as I approached, it opened for me. As soon as I passed through it, I was somehow drawn back and it was closed again. I wanted to go on but at that moment I knew that I had come back to life – and I had to accept it.
> "Then I saw a stretcher being wheeled up into a small aeroplane. I was watching from above, not really taking in that it was me. Then I was looking down again – this time on a body lying there, with massive burn marks on the chest and ribs bruised like a boxer's at the end of a fight.
> "I wasn't really concerned about the poor chap. Some doctors were standing around him, discussing the case. One looked particularly pessimistic and the others seemed to be agreeing with him. That brought me up with a jolt. It was me and somehow I knew that I had to survive this one night. I was going to hang on for dear life – if I could make it through this one night, I would make it all the way back."
> Verdegaal did make it back – blind and paralysed. (Geaves, 1994)

This case is by no means unique.

> Up to 10% of patients brought back from the dead by hospital resuscitation have reported conscious memories formed some time after all life has apparently left their body.
>
> Some patients who had been declared "brain dead" have later recounted conversations between medical staff trying to resuscitate them. Others have accurately described events or hidden objects that they had apparently observed during out-of-body experiences in the minutes following clinical death when their heart, breathing and brain activity had completely stopped. (Rogers, 2002)

David Verdegaal's "near-death experience" was his interpretation of incomplete sensory deprivation brought on by acute interruption of the blood supply to the brain. Exceptionally, perception and memory continued to function, albeit only in part, and David Verdegaal's being loaded into the air ambulance was incorporated into his account of his experience. Lesser cases of this kind would be described as "black-out"; "white-out" is a similar disruption of perception, but without interruption of the blood supply.

"White-out"

"White-out" is sometimes experienced by pilots flying at high altitude. Above 30,000 feet there is often only a circular blanket of cloud to be seen below and a nearly black sky above. The scene may not change for hours on end. Bennett (1961) has reported several cases of pilot failure under such circumstances. Here is one.

> A pilot was flying a bomber at 40,000 feet and had been continuing straight and level for about an hour. There was a haze over the ground which prevented a proper view and rendered the horizon indistinct. The other member of the crew was sitting in a separate place out of the pilot's view, and the two men did not talk to each other. Suddenly the pilot felt detached from his surroundings and then had the strong impression that the aircraft had one wing down and was turning. Without consulting his instruments he corrected the attitude, but the aircraft went into a spiral dive because it had in fact been flying straight and level. The pilot was very lucky to recover from the spiral dive, and when he landed the airframe was found to be distorted. (Bennett, 1961, p. 166)

Disturbances of Perception

Bexton et al. (1954) were investigating the effects of an entirely new kind of environment with no previous observations to guide them what to expect. Their research,

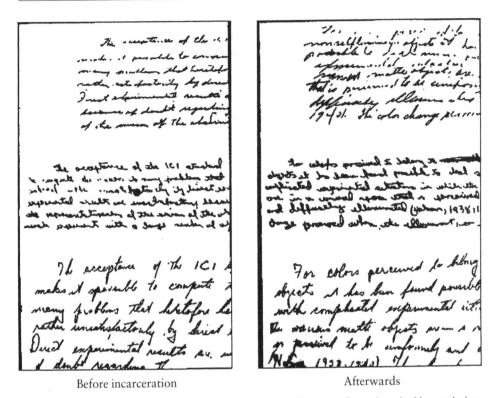

Before incarceration   Afterwards

Figure 5.2 Specimens of handwriting before and after confinement. Reproduced with permission from Bexton et al. (1954, p. 74). © 1954 Canadian Psychological Association.

very sensibly, began by simply observing their participants' behavior and interviewing them after emerging from confinement.

> After emerging from isolation, our subjects frequently reported that "things looked curved," "near things looked large and far things looked small," "things seemed to move," and so on. We therefore made some systematic tests of their visual perception. The most striking finding was that when subjects emerged after several days of isolation, the whole room appeared to be in motion. In addition there was a tendency for surfaces to appear curved, and for objects to appear to be changing their size and shape. (Heron, 1957, p. 54)

That sensory disorientation was reflected in a deterioration of handwriting consequent on confinement. Figure 5.2 reproduces an example from Bexton et al. (1954).

The interviews with the participants suggested certain formal tests of perception and cognition. Doane et al. (1959) reported the results shown in table 5.3,

Table 5.3   Results from tests of perceptual function

Effect	Method of testing	Result
Autokinetic effect	Persistence of movement against increasing luminance of background	More persistent
Color adaptation . . .	. . . to yellow disc against white field	Increased
Movement after-effect	Spiral rotated at 120 rpm	More persistent
Shape constancy	Matching triangle at different degrees of tilt	Decreased
Size constancy	Matching discs seen at different distances	Decreased
Visual acuity	Locating small gap in 3 in line	Slight improvement
Two-point limen	Distance apart on the skin of two points that can be identified as two	Reduction during incarceration

Source: Doane et al. (1959).

comparing performance before and *immediately after* incarceration – "immediately after" because the major effects seemed to wear off after an hour or two. They also tested critical flicker-fusion frequency, figural after-effect, phi phenomenon, brightness contrast, brightness constancy, Necker cube reversals, and tachistoscopic perception without detecting any systematic differences. In relation to the subjective experiences reported during interview, these test results are frankly disappointing. This suggests that whatever the perceptual deficits induced by sensory deprivation might be, they were transitory in relation to the time taken to conduct the tests.

Perception is an interpretation of what we see, hear, and feel, and the interpretative function is dependent on previous experience. We recognize without effort objects and things that we have seen before. But the subjective reports – "things looked curved," "near things looked large and far things looked small," "things seemed to move" – suggest a breakdown of perception at a primitive preconscious level. Accurate perceptual interpretation seems to depend on a continuity of the process, and that continuity, of course, is disrupted under sensory deprivation. These and other results are reviewed by Zuckerman and Cohen (1964).

Cognitive Deficits

Cognitive tests were also administered to the sensory deprivation participants, again before and *immediately after* incarceration. Table 5.4 summarizes the results from Scott, Bexton, Heron, and Doane (1959). The first two tests – Koh's Block Design Test (a test requiring the copying or reproduction of a two-color pattern of squares and triangles) and digit-symbol substitution (measuring speed

Table 5.4   Results from tests of cognitive function

Test	Method of scoring	Comparison with control group
Koh's blocks (ex WAIS)	Total time taken	Smaller improvement
Digit-symbol substitution (ex WAIS)	Number correct	Smaller improvement
Thurstone–Gottschaldt embedded figures	Number correct	Smaller improvement
Copying an unfamiliar passage	Total time taken	Increased time
Delta blocks	Number correct	Smaller improvement
Picture anomaly	Number of errors	Increased errors
Mirror drawing	Total time taken	No difference

Source: Adapted with permission from Scott et al. (1959, p. 203). © 1959 Canadian Psychological Association.

and accuracy in substitution) – were taken from the Wechsler Adult Intelligence Scale (WAIS). The Thurstone–Gottschaldt figures test consists of finding simple geometric figures embedded in a more complicated drawing. Delta blocks is copying a pattern made up from 30/60/90° triangles (Hebb, 1945, pp. 16–17) and the McGill picture anomaly series asks, "Show me what is funny or out of place [in these pictures]" (Hebb & Morton, 1943). Most of these tests show an improvement on a second administration, so that the performance of sensory deprivation participants needed to be compared to that of a control group tested at the same times. Sensory deprivation participants typically showed a lesser improvement on second testing.

Perceptual and cognitive deficits appear not to be progressive during confinement, but it is difficult to be sure. If a test is administered during confinement, the regime of sensory deprivation is thereby disrupted, and the very administration of a test provides a context that assists performance. Bexton et al. (1954) reported tests of mental arithmetic and word-making (making as many words as possible from the letters of a given word – these tests can be administered verbally) administered 12, 24, and 48 hours after the beginning of isolation. The performance of the sensorily deprived participants was worse than that of controls and recovered within three days of emerging from isolation, but that is all it is possible to say.

Perhaps the most significant finding concerned difficulties in concentration.

> The subjects reported that they were unable to concentrate on any topic for long while in the cubicle. Those who tried to review their studies or solve self-initiated intellectual problems found it difficult to do so. As a result they lapsed into day-dreaming, abandoned attempts at organized thinking, and let their thoughts wander. There were also reports of "blank periods," during which they seemed unable to think of anything at all. (Bexton et al., 1954, p. 72)

What Does it all Signify?

Sensory deprivation caught a fashion in the mid-1950s. It seemed to promise new insights into perceptual and cognitive functioning, but the results have been disappointing. The difficulty in demonstrating deficits in perceptual and cognitive functioning arises, in part, because the administration of a test interrupts the regime of sensory deprivation, providing an immediate context that assists performance. But the difficulty also signifies that the deficit was transitory in the first place.

Those deficits which do appear reliable are of a general and imprecise nature and lead to this suggestion: The maintenance of perceptual and cognitive functioning requires continuing sensory input to relate us to the world about us. Each element of sensory input is interpreted in relation to what has gone before. For example, we have detailed vision over, perhaps, the central 4° of the visual field; but the visual world that we perceive extends all around us. Continual exposure to structured input is needed to maintain contact with that world, to maintain knowledge of our immediate surroundings and a readiness to respond. Perception, as a process, takes place against the background of what is already known to be there.

Take that sensory input away, and perceptual functioning does not stop; but when sensory information is lacking, internal factors take over leading to hallucinations and dreams. Dreams are not ordinarily a problem because we are also asleep and are mostly unaware of them; but we are sometimes alarmed on awakening suddenly in the middle of the night. Hallucinations are disturbing, like nightmares, because we are aware of them. In sensory deprivation then, and also in sleep, perception performs substantially at random and anything might be perceived. External stimulation does not *drive* perception, but modulates an ongoing process. That is consistent with the view that, while a certain time in isolation is needed before the perceptual and cognitive deficits show, they are not thereafter progressive during confinement; and are reversible afterwards with apparently no long-term after-effects.

BOREDOM

This chapter has been about people who are bored – bored beyond belief. Fisher (1993) surveyed the then state of knowledge about boredom; that state of knowledge consisted principally of questions for research. Boredom is intensely unpleasant – continued long enough, more unpleasant than anyone can bear. The malaise *sounds* like the subjective counterpart of the frustration of some instinctive behavior (like sex), turning the argument of the preceding chapters on its head. It is a matter of conjecture what that instinctive behavior might be, but I suggest an instinct to keep in contact with one's surroundings, ready for action or emergencies.

Provided that contact is maintained, we are unaware of how necessary it is to us. The intriguing aspect of boredom is that it is triggered by an *absence* of stimulation. The unpleasantness of boredom is triggered at an early stage of its development (like fear) and its effect can be profound. Full-scale sensory deprivation is far from necessary – people get bored much more easily than that. Sensory deprivation is merely the most extreme form of boredom.

Boredom at Work

Boredom is common in the working environment where it has medical effects.

> Complaints of feeling bored are common. Surveys have found that up to 56 per cent of British employees report that they find their entire job boring, while up to 87 per cent say they feel bored doing their work on some occasions [Guest, Williams, & Dewe, 1978].
>
> Medical research has found that bored workers have three to five times the usual incidence of cardiovascular disease; four to seven times the incidence of neurological disorders; twice the incidence of gastrointestinal disorders; and two to three times the incidence of musculo-skeletal disorders.
>
> They are absent from work for medical reasons three to five times as often as their non-bored colleagues. Swedish research published in 1975 said that 60 per cent of mill workers doing one particularly boring task were receiving treatment for peptic ulcers. Some even complained of hallucinations during periods when they were bored. (Persaud, 1993)

It also has potential for serious accidents.

> A few years ago, an airliner flying from the East Coast overflew its destination in Los Angeles. The three-man crew of this major air carrier did not respond to radio communications until they had flown about 100 miles westward over the Pacific Ocean. Were they too busy? No, all three were asleep!
>
> "Endless hours of tedious boredom punctuated by moments of stark terror" is an oft-quoted description of an airline pilot's work. (Grose, 1989)

Leisure Activities

Boredom is also characteristic of leisure time. There is an enormous entertainment industry – books, theater, film, travel, sport, hobbies – to relieve that boredom. All this suggests that most people find their lives a bit boring and on that account seek some excitement. That is how boredom comes to have an important motivational effect.

Snake-handling cults

In the southern Appalachian Mountains of the United States there are a number of churches that practice snake-handling in the course of their worship (Hood, 1998). Sargent (1957, plates 10–17) describes the "Dolley Pond Church of God with signs following" in which the phrase "with signs following" is significant.

> And these signs shall follow them that believe: in my name shall they cast out devils; they shall speak with new tongues; they shall take up serpents; and if they drink any deadly thing, it shall not hurt them; they shall lay hands on the sick and they shall recover. (Mark 16:17–18)

Accordingly, rattlesnakes and copperheads (no, the snakes have not had their fangs drawn!) are produced in the course of their services (though only on special occasions) and there is a pitcher of water laced with strychnine to drink. "John Wayne Brown, an evangelist preacher in Alabama . . . died after being bitten by the rattlesnake he was holding while preaching. Brown's wife died from a snake bite in 1995" (Campbell, 1998). So why do these people do it?

> There is one other point on which the handlers are unanimous. No feeling on earth compares to handling snakes. "It's the best feeling you've ever had in your life. It's like being high on cocaine, pot, whiskey or whatever multiplied ten thousand times." (Fletcher, 1998, p. 39)

It is perhaps relevant that snakes are thought to be a "prepared fear" (cf. chapter 2). For that reason it might be that snake-handling is particularly effective, giving practitioners their "high" from excitement by moderate fear.

Bungee jumping

The same idea might explain why people do bungee jumping. The UK Bungee Club has a jumping platform more than 300 feet above the River Thames.

> Nearly 40 per cent of the club's customers have second thoughts about jumping once they have been winched up. . . . The club's instructors are well-versed in prompting these would-be jumpers to have the third, fourth or fifth thoughts that give them the will to pitch head-first into space. . . . Only 1 per cent of the club's customers ask to be winched down again. (Jebb, 1996)

There is a risk of injury from the sudden increase in blood pressure in the eyes, "but the elation experienced after jumping can last for several days" (*Independent*, 1994a).

Even worse, "18-stone man hurt in 200ft bungee jump" (Brown, 2002; this man had twice backed away before he finally jumped) and "Bungee jumper killed as rope fails to halt fall" (Fleck & Peek, 2000).

Skydiving

Skydiving is another "extreme" sport. "The elation wears off a little after a few days, but the dreams of floating through the air are still incredibly vivid. It was a very special experience: that feeling of flying above the clouds with absolutely no fear will live with me for ever" (Gee, 1996). That particular journalist claims to have experienced no fear whatsoever, but most people react rather differently, because skydiving is not without risk. Indeed, "Surfing skydiver falls 15,000ft to death" (Norfolk, 2000).

Parachute jumping is a popular activity for which to seek sponsorship in aid of charitable causes. So, many people take a 6-hour training course and then make one jump for charity. Of 174 patients with parachuting injuries in Tayside studied by Lee, Williams, and Hadden (1999), 94 percent were first-time charity-jumpers. The authors estimated that 11 percent of first-time charity parachutists suffered injury, mostly to the lower limbs, and 7 percent were sufficiently serious to require admission to hospital. This is very much higher than the 0.02 percent estimated for experienced parachutists in the same location and during the same period. The average cost to the NHS of treating these parachuting injuries worked out at £3,751, which in total is about 14 times the sum raised for charity after deduction of expenses (Hawkes, 1999).

Biking

"Biking" – riding high-powered motorcycles at high speeds – is an increasingly popular pastime in Britain. Bikes are used for commuting to high-level jobs in the City and there are many people, well known from television appearances and other exposure, who are, as it were, "addicted" (Foster, 1997; *The Times*, 1999b). Given that motorcycling has always had the reputation of being dangerous, why do they do it? Let Jeremy Pollack, a journalist who has just got back on a motorcycle after 10 years driving a car, explain.

> Since I stopped riding, I have sat in the car every sunny morning thinking, "Must get a bike, must get a bike." I've been back on a motorcycle just a couple of weeks, but the whole sensation – the sound, the incredible acceleration – came back to me straight away.
> There is nothing like going for a blast through the countryside, though – it's just the same thrill as before. (Jeremy Pollack cited in Naish, 1999a)

A motorcycle, of course, puts one in a much closer relation to the road than is achieved in a car. The pure sensation of speed is therefore much stronger. But, because of speed limits on the roads, still not strong enough for some. So race tracks open themselves up to amateurs:

> ... there are thousands of riders who ... are prepared to pay £100 a time to risk their roadbikes thrashing them around Britain's famous circuits such as Donnington Park and Brands Hatch.
> Track days – where street-bike owners can try the art of riding circuits at speeds that would burn their licences on public roads – are a fast-growing phenomenon in Britain. (Naish, 1999b)

Railway lines

There are other "extreme" sports as well, aerobatics, paragliding, "canyoning" (Hiley, 2000), and more beside. But these thrill-raising activities are all expensive, not least because of the safety precautions required. What do you do if you can't afford them?

> A Liverpool *Daily Post* photographer spotted a gang of up to 30 [boys] playing on the [railway] lines at Anfield ... The gang, some as young as eight, placed their heads on the tracks to see if they could feel the vibrations of any oncoming freight train.
> Youths have also been spotted playing a potentially deadly game of "chicken" with the trains on the section of freight line to Bootle. (Bird, 2000)

"Hotting"

> Teenage joyriders have turned the wrecking of expensive cars into a meticulously orchestrated late-night entertainment involving performances at 100 mph and spectacular handbrake turns.
> Residents of an Oxford council estate complain that they are being kept awake night after night by a new youth cult, which draws spectators from as far away as Bournemouth. A gang of 150 youths regularly gathers to watch an Audi 80 or Volkswagen Golf being driven into the ground.
> Police estimate that between 30 and 50 cars – mainly GTi models – have been stolen in recent months. They say that the cars are made to "perform." A local youth revs it up, drives it at up to 100 mph and executes handbrake turns for the cheering spectators, to the sound of screeching tyres and crashing gears. The entrepreneurial joy riders charge local members of the audience £1 and outsiders £2. (Cohen, 1991b)

The French do it too (Sage, 2000).

Fire-raising

Finally, young children are prone to experiment with matches; so how about this?

> (*It is dark. A car draws up, a young man jumps out and pours petrol from a bottle over the seats. He then strikes a match and throws it into the car. The car bursts into flames and burns furiously.*)
>
> **Adam:** There's always the same feeling, a good feeling, when it burns, whatever car it is, when you burn it out. Sometimes I'll burn three, four cars out a day. It's still the same feeling. It's still as good as the first one. It's the sense of power – that you've destroyed something. It's a sad thing to say, but I enjoy it, destroying other people's stuff. That I've done it, I've destroyed it, and no one else can touch it back. 'Cos it's me there, and it's like in your own world; it's just me and whatever's on fire. I'm just stood beside it, whatever. Just watching it burn and knowing no one else can stop it; and it's just me there, no one else can do, just me, in my world. It's like a step from reality, you're in your own world, where everything's good. And it's not like normal day life, where things go wrong. When I set a car on fire, it's like heaven. (Cosgrove, 1994)

Relationship to instinctive fear

All these leisure activities, which evidently provide some sort of "buzz," involve stimuli or situations that might be expected to interact with the "prepared" fears hypothesized in chapter 2. Evidence was cited in that chapter to support the idea of an instinctive fear reaction to heights (skydiving and bungee jumping; cf. the visual cliff; Gibson & Walk, 1960), to rapid motion in a forward direction (biking; cf. "looming"; Ball & Tronick, 1971), and, less securely, to snakes (Prechtl, 1950). Only fire-raising seems lacking in direct support, though wild animals do show an instinctive fear of fire.

That relationship suggests that these particular activities are exciting because they interact with an instinctive fear mechanism and it is the mild to moderate anxiety experienced in consequence that is described as "the buzz." If that conjecture be correct, then we should look for other activities which might similarly engage instinctive fear mechanisms and yet others (e.g., boxing; see chapter 13) which excite by engaging other instinctive motivations.

QUESTIONS FOR DISCUSSION

1 If people find doing nothing, doing literally nothing, so excessively un-pleasant, might there not be some instinctive pattern of behavior that is being frustrated?

2 In the sensory deprivation chamber, participants are motivated not by some critical stimulus but by the complete absence of stimulation. How does our concept of motivation need to be revised?

3 Fear seems to be the internal sensation we get from an instinctive system, similar to pain, that protects us against remote threats. Why then do people go biking, and skydiving, and bungee jumping, and why do they handle snakes?

6

SOCIAL CONVENTIONS

To this point I have been concerned with domains of motivation that are essentially individual – fear, sex, boredom – and with responses to extraneous stimuli of the kind that one might observe in any animal species. But humankind is different. The way in which *we* respond to motivational triggers is modified by the requirements and expectations of people around us. How do those social constraints work?

This interview with a burglar puts the question more acutely.

> To me my job is burgling. Jail becomes an occupational hazard. If you get caught you go to jail, but I've got one of the best-paid jobs in the country, guaranteed, best-paid jobs in the country, because every time I go out I come back with £600 in my pocket, £700 for being out of my house for two hours; £300 per hour is a lot of money when you put it that way. (Kirby, 1993)

So why do we not all turn to burglary, if it pays so well? There are a small number of criminals who enjoy rich pickings by flouting the mores of society. What hold does society have over the rest of us that prevents everyone turning to burglary? This introduces another profound group of questions which will ultimately be answered by a third fundamental idea in chapter 9.

Traditionally, the authorities of all religions have taken it upon themselves to tell us what things are "right" and what are "wrong" and many people suppose that that kind of pronouncement is what matters. For example, the UK government, in the person of Dr Nick Tate, chief curriculum adviser, has laid such a duty on schools – "Schools 'need lesson in teaching morals'" (Judd, 1996).

This chapter is the first of four concerned with the psychological reality of moral constraints. It is possible to study this question *ab initio* chiefly because of a famous series of experiments by Stanley Milgram which open up the debate to scientific examination. But I must emphasize that I am not concerned with *content*, not with moral values themselves – it is not my place to usurp religious authority and tell anyone what they should, or should not, do. I am concerned with the *nature* of moral imperatives, that is, with the *psychological meaning* of the words "right" and "wrong."

MILGRAM'S EXPERIMENTS

Ordinary townspeople from the New Haven community were recruited by advertisement. On arrival at the laboratory there were two participants, one who had responded to the advertisement and another who was a confederate of the experimenter – an actor engaged for the purpose, the same actor throughout. It is explained to both that the experiment is to do with the effect of punishment on learning and the two subjects draw lots to decide who shall be teacher and who pupil. The drawing is rigged and the real participant always draws the role of teacher. He or she then helps to strap the pupil (that is, the confederate) into a chair in a cubicle and attach an electrode to his wrist through which the punishment (electric shock) will be delivered.

The pupil's task is to learn a list of word pairs such as "Boy–Girl." The list is read through once and then the first word of each pair only with a choice of four words for the response. The teacher is instructed to administer an electric shock for each response that is wrong, beginning at 15 volts and increasing the level by 15 volts each time up to a maximum of 450 volts. The teacher samples a real electric shock (at 45 volts) before beginning the experiment to persuade him or her that the shocks are real.

As one might expect, some of the participants were uncertain about administering the electric shocks. The experimenter had a series of "prods" prepared to induce the teacher to continue:

1 "Please continue" or "Please go on."
2 "The experiment requires that you continue."
3 "It is absolutely essential that you continue."
4 "You have no other choice, you must go on."

These "prods" were delivered in increasing order of urgency as required. If the teacher asked about physical injury to the pupil, the experimenter replied: "Although the shocks may be painful, there is no permanent tissue damage, so please go on." If the teacher said that the pupil did not want to go on, the experimenter replied: "Whether the learner likes it or not, you must go on until he has learned all the word pairs correctly. So please go on" (Milgram, 1974, p. 21). The pupil, of course, received no shocks at all, and the experiment had nothing to do with the effect of punishment on learning. It was concerned with the obedience of the naive teacher. At what point will he or she rebel and refuse to continue?

Proximity of Teacher and Pupil

Table 6.1 sets out the brief details from 12 of Milgram's experiments, and figure 6.1 displays the results from the first four, together with aggregate predictions from a group of 39 psychiatrists. The psychiatrists were informed of the experimental

Table 6.1 Summary of the experiments by Milgram (1974) discussed in the text

Experiment[a]	Procedure	Percentage continuing to 450 volts
Predictions by psychiatrists	At what levels of shock would 100 Americans of diverse ages and occupations break off and refuse to continue?	0.125
1	Pupil pounds on the cubicle wall at 300 volts; gives no further answer after 315 volts.	65.0
2	Vocal protests added to the protocol of Experiment 1.	62.5
3	Same protocol of protests as in Experiment 2, but the pupil was now placed in the same room as the teacher.	40.0
4	As Experiment 3, except that the pupil received a shock only when his hand was in contact with a "shock-plate." At 150 volts the pupil refused to keep his hand on the shock-plate and the teacher was ordered to force his hand onto the plate.	30.0
5	A replication of Experiment 1 with a standard schedule of pupil protests now recorded on audiotape.	65.0
7	The experimenter gave his initial instructions in person and then left the room; further orders, prods, etc. were given by telephone.	27.5
11	Participants were allowed to choose their own level of shock for 30 critical (shock) trials.	Average 45 to 60 volts
13	The experimenter was called away before his instructions were quite complete. An additional confederate then proposed: "Let's advance one step [15 volts] each time."	20.0
13a	Confederate takes over the shock generator when the real participant refuses to continue.	nom. 68.75
16	Two experimenters and only one participant, so one of the experimenters serves as pupil.	65.0
17	Two additional confederates in the role of participants assigned subsidiary tasks. The confederates refused to continue beyond 150 and 210 volts respectively.	10.0
18	The operation of the shock generator was assigned to a second confederate; the real participant merely assisted with some subsidiary task.	92.5

[a] The numbers given to the experiments here are Milgram's (1974) enumeration.

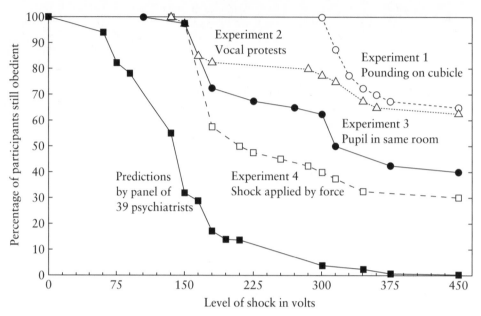

Figure 6.1 Proximity of teacher and pupil. Milgram's Experiments 1–4 and predictions from a group of psychiatrists.

procedure, though not of the outcome, and asked to say at what levels of shock they thought 100 Americans of diverse ages and occupations would break off and refuse to continue. Collectively, the psychiatrists predicted that only 1 person in 800 would remain obedient throughout. But the results were quite different.

In the first experiment the pupil pounded on the cubicle walls when the shock level was raised to 300 volts and above 315 volts made no further answers; 26 participants out of 40 continued to 450 volts. The second experiment added some vocal protests, but still 25 participants out of 40 continued to 450 volts. In Experiment 3 the pupil was brought into the same room as the teacher and this degree of proximity reduced the level of compliance to 16 out of 40. In Experiment 4 the pupil was required to place his hand on a shock-plate to receive his punishment. When the shock level was raised to 150 volts the pupil refused to do so and the teacher was ordered to force the pupil's hand on to the shock-plate; 12 out of 40 participants still proceeded all the way to 450 volts.

What is Going On?

Under instruction from a suitable authority most people – most *ordinary* people – will undertake tasks – administering potentially lethal electric shocks – which, so far as they can tell, cause intense suffering to someone else. Did Milgram collect a specially sadistic group of participants? Milgram (1974) repeated the experiment with both students and townspeople and obtained the same level of compliance. Smith and Bond (1993, p. 20) have tabulated replications of Milgram's work elsewhere. Most of these replications gave a higher level of compliance than even Milgram obtained.

But are people generally as sadistic as this? A comparison with the personalities of people who have been trained to administer torture suggests that sadism has nothing to do with it. The torturers who served the Greek military regime from 1967 to 1974 have been studied by Dr Haritos-Fatouras, Professor of Clinical Psychology at the University of Thessalonika.

> . . . the first rule for those selecting potential torturers is: do not hire a sadist. A delight in inflicting pain is a disadvantage; a sadist might make it personal. . . . torturers must be able to control themselves; must go as far as is necessary and no farther; and must have goals that are both important and impersonal.
>
> Men with potential were sent to torture school and underwent a process of desensitisation. They took food to prisoners, mopped up the blood and performed minor or group torture sessions, under supervision.
>
> The strange thing is that outside the camp, many of the torturers led normal lives. . . . One of the cruellest had a girlfriend who had many friends involved in the struggle against the regime and he would go with her to cafés, where they would sing songs against the dictatorship. And then he would go back to work. (Daly, 1992)

Alternatively, were Milgram's participants seeing through the hoax whereby the pupil received no shock? After the experiment was over the real participants were asked, among other things, whether they "believed learner was (probably) getting shocked"; 80 percent reported that they did so believe. A similar proportion reported being tense and nervous. But in a situation such as this with apparently lethal levels of shock, participants would actually need to *know* that the pupil was not getting shocked before being happy to continue to a pretended level of 450 volts. Mere belief or suspicion would not be sufficient to make a participant continue all the way with no concern at all. Only 2.4 percent reported that they were certain the pupil was not getting the shocks.

In addition, the participant is under an obligation to the experimenter. In the first place, he or she has volunteered to do the experiment and accepted payment of expenses ($4.50) before beginning. For most of these volunteers a "psychological experiment" is an entirely new milieu. They do not know what conduct is appropriate in that milieu and are inclined to accept the experimenter's suggestion. There is also an element of pressure that leads to conflict with the social mores of the larger society to which each participant ultimately returns.

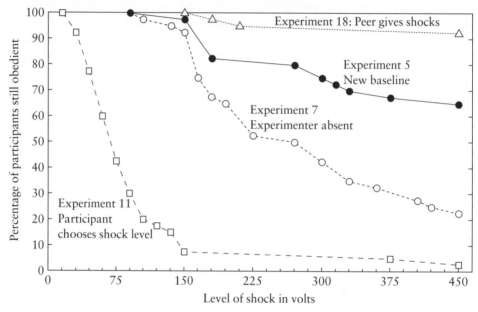

Figure 6.2   Relaxation of the conflict. Milgram's Experiments 5, 7, 11, and 18.

Relaxation of the Conflict

Milgram's experimental procedure evolved during the first four experiments in figure 6.1. The confederate developed a standard set of cries and protests that were then recorded onto audiotape and incorporated into the experimental procedure. The protests changed from a mere "Ugh!" (at 75 volts) to references to a "heart condition" (150 volts) to agonized screams and "Let me out of here" (270 volts) to an "Intense and prolonged agonized scream" at 330 volts, following which there was complete silence. Experiment 5 established a new baseline with respect to this standard set of protests for comparisons with subsequent experimental manipulations. The results of Experiments 1 and 2 were replicated; 26 out of 40 participants continued obediently to 450 volts. The results of this experiment and three others are displayed in figure 6.2.

Experiment 7 shows that the physical presence of the experimenter is needed to ensure compliance. The experimenter gave his initial instructions in person and then left the room; further orders, prods, etc. were given by telephone. The degree of compliance was now less – 11 instead of 26 out of 40. In addition, the level of shock actually administered for each error was covertly recorded and several participants were found to be giving shocks at a lower level than they had been instructed to give. Some participants assured the experimenter that they were raising the shock level while, in fact, they were repeatedly administering only 15 volts. Refusal to continue typically occurred at a lower level of shock; but if the experimenter returned to the laboratory, he could often reimpose his authority. In comparison with Experiment 5, this experiment makes it clear that the physical presence of authority is important to secure compliance.

What level of shock do the participants think appropriate in circumstances such as this? In Experiment 11 participants were allowed to choose their own level of shock for 30 critical (shock) trials. The pupil's protests were linked (according to the schedule established for Experiment 5) to the actual level of shock administered. The average level remained at 45 to 60 volts throughout. But when, in Experiment 18, the operation of the shock generator was assigned to a second confederate, while the naive participant merely assisted with some subsidiary task, only 3 out of the 40 participants refused to complete the experiment.

It is plain that the participants' view of what level of shock is appropriate is quite different from that imposed by the experimenter. For that reason the task generates internal conflict and continued pressure from authority is needed to ensure compliance. If the experimenter is out of sight, his authority is undermined and the level of compliance reduced. But if, on the other hand, the naive participant is removed from the actual administration of the shocks, resistance to the experimenter's demands is less.

The Importance of Social Structure

Figure 6.3 summarizes three further experiments. Experiment 13 shows that the experimenter has a special authority in his laboratory. There was an additional confederate who was assigned a subsidiary task (recording the duration of the shock) at the experimenter's desk. The experimenter gave his instructions as usual, but was called away by a prearranged telephone call before those instructions were quite complete. The additional confederate then proposed a rule for selecting the level of shock: "Let's advance one step [15 volts] each time." That same instruction from someone who appeared to be a fellow participant was much less effective than when it came from the experimenter himself. Only 4 out of 20 participants continued all the way to 450 volts.

When the real participant in Experiment 13 refused to continue, the additional confederate took over the operation of the shock generator and asked the real participant to take over the recording of the duration of the shock at the experimenter's desk. In charge of the shock generator the confederate, of course, continued to "advance one step [15 volts] each time." This manipulation constituted Experiment 13a. What is of particular interest is the reaction of the naive participants.

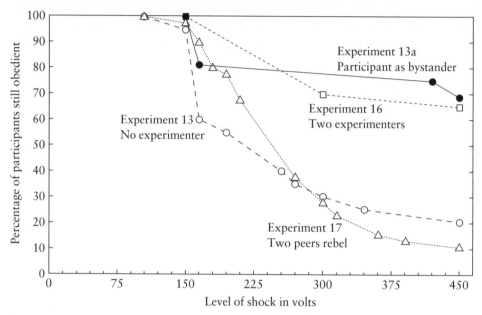

Figure 6.3   The importance of social structure. Milgram's Experiments 13, 16, and 17.

> Of the sixteen subjects exposed to this situation, virtually all protested the ac-
> tions of the coparticipant; five took physical action against him, or the shock
> generator, to terminate the administration of shocks. (Several attempted to dis-
> connect the generator from its electrical source; four physically restrained the
> coparticipant.) One, a large man, lifted the zealous shocker from his chair, threw
> him to a corner of the laboratory, and did not allow him to move until he had
> promised not to administer further shocks. (Milgram, 1974, p. 97)

Eleven out of 16 participants equates to 68.75 percent nominally acquiescing in
continuation to 450 volts. This should be compared with Experiment 18 where
92.5 percent were obedient to the end.

The special status accorded to an experimenter is not preserved when he serves as
a participant. In Experiment 16 there were two experimenters, and only one participant; the second participant has failed to turn up – that is, the usual confederate
is introduced as an experimenter rather than as a participant. In this emergency, one
of the experimenters (the confederate) agrees to serve as a participant. Of the 20
participants in this experiment, 65 percent remained compliant to 450 volts. This is
exactly the proportion obtained in the baseline condition (Experiment 5).

If, however, the naive participant has some support (from other participants), he
will rebel at lower levels of shock. In Experiment 17 there were two additional
confederates seated one on either side of the naive participant at the shock generator.

One of these confederates reads the word pairs and the second tells the pupil whether he is correct. The task of administering the shock is left to the naive participant. However, one of the confederates refused to continue beyond 150 volts and the second gave up at 210 volts. At those particular points many of the real participants rebelled too.

So, the experimenter has a particular authority in his laboratory. But that authority is not preserved when an experimenter serves as participant; nor is it shared by another participant (a confederate) taking over the experimenter's role in his absence. Indeed, in this latter case authority is conspicuously lacking. The experimenter's authority is not absolute, however; it is in competition with the lesser authority of fellow participants (the two additional confederates). When these confederates refuse to continue they provide support for the real participant, if he or she is also minded to give up, in a manner that we shall examine in greater detail in chapter 10.

SOCIAL CONVENTIONS

Three elements are needed to understand Milgram's experimental results of which the first is the basic idea of a social convention. By this I mean a pattern of behavior that is implicitly expected by the society in which one is placed. Many agreements between people are no more than verbal, but it is still expected that they will be kept. The London Stock Exchange's motto is "My word is my bond." In 1987 the British Petroleum privatization share issue was announced at 120p (part paid) just before the stock market crashed on October 19 that year. The part-paid trading price sunk to 70p, which was a floor set by the government's buy-back price. About 270,000 applicants had already submitted bids (at 120p) before the stock market crashed. Only 2 percent or so of those 270,000 reneged on their offer to purchase (Tomkins, 1987). In the same way, having volunteered their services and presented themselves at the laboratory, Milgram's participants acknowledged an obligation to cooperate with the experimenter.

In 1990 Dr Penelope Leach reported a convention emerging spontaneously amongst teenagers. It appears that

> Teenagers have invented their own secret institution to legitimize sex before marriage. Young people show their commitment to each other by exchanging pledges – often ribbons plaited on to the wrist in such a way that they can only be removed by cutting.
>
> Being in love is not considered by young people to be sufficient to have a full sexual relationship, but it is all right if you are "engaged" – this is the term that they used for their exchange of pledges.
>
> By "engaged" they did not mean engaged to be married because on average they did not expect to be married until they were 23, and expected to be engaged for no more than two years beforehand. (Gillie, 1990b)

Laws are often a codification of existing conventions; but when a law is in conflict with convention (e.g., speed limits on motorways), it is widely flouted and impossible to enforce. For example, private cars on British motorways travel at 75 to 85 mph, notwithstanding that the speed limit is 70.

> More than half of all the 70 million cars monitored on Britain's motorways by the Department of Transport last year . . . were found to be travelling at more than 70 mph.
>   Nearly one-fifth of the drivers were travelling at more than 80 mph. Nearly three-quarters of the cars monitored in urban areas were breaking the 30 mph speed limit. (Lean, 1996)

The content of a social convention may be any aspect of behavior: (unsocial) working hours; time of arrival at parties (in the UK you turn up late, though not too late); fashions in dress. "The dress code for entry to the stewards' enclosure [at Henley Regatta] . . . says: 'Ladies will not be admitted if their skirts do not have a hemline below the knee or if wearing divided skirts or trousers of any kind'" (Young, 2000). When the behavior of one person impinges on the freedom, well-being, or status of another, ethical considerations enter into the reckoning. So moral standards are (roughly speaking) a subset of social conventions.

Cannibalism

Perhaps the most widespread and most stringently enforced convention of all is the prohibition on the eating of human flesh. Since humankind lives in such close-knit societies, it is easy to see why this prohibition is needed. Without it, no one would be safe. But it is social convention, not instinct. This is the conclusion from a recent survey of the evidence (Korn, Radice, & Hawes, 2001).

In the first place, archeological excavations have failed to produce the number of skeletons from prehistoric societies that might have been expected. Instead, there have been finds of human bones alongside animal bones, both showing the same kinds of score marks where the flesh had been stripped off for consumption. It is not possible to know whether this was a consumption driven purely by shortage of food (as has happened in diverse places in recent times) or whether it had a ritual significance (as used to be the practice in South Pacific societies). But it is probable that cannibalism was widespread in prehistoric societies and has been progressively prohibited (for the obvious reason) as human societies became more closely knit. The cannibalism discovered by missionaries to the South Pacific appears to have been the last survivor of a practice that was once widespread.

To people living within those South Pacific societies, cannibalism seemed entirely natural and proper. It is reported that when Captain Cook went to Tonga, the inhabitants could not believe that he did not eat human flesh – that he was profoundly revolted by the whole idea. South Pacific cannibalism was a ritual eating of enemies from neighboring tribes, especially enemies killed in battle, in the belief that eating one's enemy gave the eater a supernatural advantage over the enemy. It was accompanied by a religious ceremony that protected against the possibility that humankind would eat its own kith and kin. Cannibalism of one's own tribe was strictly prohibited, again for the obvious reason.

Instances of cannibalism in recent times have mostly been driven by extreme starvation. A well-known incident occurred when an airplane crashed in the Andes in 1972. Some of the passengers were killed in the crash, others survived relatively uninjured. The living survived for 72 days, until rescued, by eating the dead. While it took a while for the survivors to bring themselves to eat the cadavers of their dead colleagues, it was commented that thirst and cold were much more difficult to contend with than was the prospect of eating human flesh (Read, 1974). There are also stories of shipwrecked sailors in even greater extremes of hunger drawing lots to determine who should be the first to be killed and eaten (e.g., the shipwreck of the whaler *Essex*; Philbrick, 2000).

Social Conventions are Different in Different Societies

The extent to which our lives conform to social convention is revealed only by comparing our society with another. Social conventions differ between one society and another – this is the second element needed in understanding Milgram's results.

In Britain it is bad manners to rest your hands or elbows on the dinner table; in France it is bad manners to keep them out of sight on your lap; and in Hungary it is exceptionally bad manners to stick your elbows out while eating and to eat with the fork upside down (as is polite in the UK), jabbing at the food.

The caste system in India

In India a man's and a woman's places in society, and the opportunities open to them, depend on their caste.

> The Hindu religion contains four main castes: the priests (Brahmins), warriors, artisans/merchants and labourers. Within the Sudra, or labourers caste, there are as many as 3,700 subcastes. . . . Untouchables, categorised by the Indian government as scheduled castes, are deemed so low that they are placed outside the caste system, along with animals and insects.
>
> When the former Indian prime minister, Vishwanath Pratap Singh, announced his intention to increase the number of reserved places for backward castes last year, he unleashed a fury of resentment and a new phenomenon – high-caste teenagers turned themselves into human torches in protest against proposed restrictions on jobs that are already in short supply. The riots eventually led to Mr Singh's resignation. (Aziz, 1991)

The social pressure exerted by one's caste can lead to lynching.

> The parents of a young Indian woman watched as their daughter and her boy-friend were hanged in a village lynching because they were having an inter-caste relationship.
>
> Hundreds of their neighbours looked on as the pair were taken to the roof of a house in India's largest state of Uttar Pradesh . . . and killed.
>
> Vishal, 19, and his 18-year-old lover, Sonu, died after they failed to heed warnings from their families to stop seeing each other. . . . She was an upper-caste Brahmin and he was a member of the Jat community, which is lower in the rigid Hindu hierarchy. (*The Times*, 2001a)

Indian immigrants have brought their caste system with them to Britain.

> "Why would a Jat Sikh boy marry a Chuhra girl? He's making trouble for himself and he won't be proud of himself. There are plenty of Jat girls to marry," says Pritam Sidhu, a journalist and Jat. His words are reminiscent of an anti-apartheid white who cannot understand why his daughter wants to marry a black. The newspaper he works for, *Des Perdes*, carries advertisements for marriage partners clearly stipulating caste. "Handsome British Punjabi Khatik, age 28, graduate engineer, 5ft 7in, seeks educated Khatik girl aged 21–26."
>
> Jasvir Kaur, a Jat, fell in love with a fellow student, Ram Kumar, a Christian Untouchable. When her family realised she was spending time on her own with him, they booked a flight for her to India and an arranged marriage.
>
> "At the airport I pretended I was going to the toilet and phoned Ram to come and get me. He left the house in his pyjamas and just raced into the airport hall and picked me up and rushed me to the car." Despite opposition from her family, she and Ram were married. Her family refused to attend the wedding and have not seen her since. (Aziz, 1991)

The social status of women

The freedom enjoyed by women *vis-à-vis* men in western societies is not tolerated in Muslim countries . . .

> "She was frightened and wanted to escape," Ali Musrati later told police about the night he gagged and murdered his 16-year-old sister Amal to cleanse the stain on his family's honour.
>
> Ali and a second sister, Yasmin, of the Arab village of Ramle in Israel, had decided to kill Amal after she twice ran away from the family. When she returned home the second time they tied her up and left her in the middle of the road, where Ali ran over her with his car several times until she was dead. The use of the car was a clumsy attempt to pretend that Amal's death was an accident, but police rapidly decided that her death was an honour killing. Amal, suspected of having sex with a man after she ran away, was judged by her family to have so shamed them that their reputation could only be restored by her death. (Cockburn & Nolen, 1995)

... nor in Hindu countries:

> More than 11,000 young Indian wives have committed suicide or been murdered in the past three years because of illegal dowry demands, according to figures released last month. The government statistics, given in Parliament, confirm the fears of women's organisations that more and more Indian families are flouting the law to demand increasing quantities of money and consumer goods from the families of young brides.
>
> "We're so poor, we could not give the dowry to save my child," one mother told reporters earlier this month after her recently and unhappily married 21-year-old daughter was found dead.
>
> At the top end of the social scale, dowry money is believed to account for a significant proportion of India's black economy, estimated at up to $30 billion. Demands among the middle and upper classes include houses, imported video recorders and stereos. At the bottom of the pile, social workers say, even beggars have to find pots, pans and a bit of gold jewellery to marry off their daughters.
>
> The new statistics, given in response to a question from a woman deputy, show that, of the 11,259 dowry-related deaths registered in 1988, 1989 and 1990, 4,038 were suicides. ... Newspaper commentators note that it is always young women whose saris catch fire as they bend over kerosene stoves, while such reported accidents rarely happen to elderly, infirm women who might be thought more vulnerable. (Pitchford, 1991)

That custom has a natural consequence.

> World-wide, for every 100 men, there are 105 women; in India, the average has fallen to 93 women for every 100 men, but in some regions there are fewer than 85 women per 100 men.
>
> Traditionally, villagers think that having daughters is a waste of money and food, since they grow up, marry, move away, and are unable to provide for their own parents. "Having a daughter is like watering your neighbour's garden," is one proverb. But even among many middle-class families, sons are preferred to daughters and are generally better treated. A study by a Ludhiana teaching hospital showed that out of every 100 children admitted, 84 were boys. When girls were finally brought for treatment, parents had waited until their daughters were near death. (McGirk, 1996)

Arranged marriages

On the Indian subcontinent it is customary for parents to arrange marriages for their children. People (of all ethnic groups) who have migrated thence to the UK have brought that custom with them. The story of Jasvir Kaur and Ram Kumar has been told above. Gurmeet is another young woman, a Sikh, who was tricked into visiting India with the covert intention that, once there, a marriage would be arranged for her. She was rescued only on the day of her official engagement by the intervention of a First Secretary from the British High Commission in collaboration with the local police in Chandigarh (Frean, 2000). In Britain a forced marriage is invalid and consideration is being given to classifying it as "abduction." "It is estimated that at least 1,000 young British women are forced into marriage each year, although there are no reliable statistics. Women's groups believe that the true figure is far higher. The Southall Black Sisters, a women's group in West London, deals with at least 150 cases a year" (Ford, 2000).

Administration of capital punishment

Britain does not have capital punishment, but, when it did, it was carried out by hanging. In America, in different states of the Union, it is accomplished by electric chair or by lethal injection. Iran uses other methods.

> A court in Iran has sentenced a woman to be stoned to death for adultery and helping her lover to murder her husband in Tehran.
> The lover, who is the woman's cousin, is to be hanged. Both will receive 100 lashes first.
> If the woman manages to survive being stoned, she will have to serve 15 years in jail. Survival is unlikely because she will be buried up to her neck.
> Men sentenced to be stoned to death are buried waist-deep in the ground. If they have confessed to their crimes and manage to escape, they can go free. (*The Times*, 2001b)

Social Conventions also Differ between Subgroups within the One Society . . .

. . . though less so than between distinct societies. There is one standard of behavior at church on Sunday and a different standard at work on Monday. This is the third element that I bring to bear on Milgram's results.

C. vs. S.

C. vs. S. was a *cause célèbre* in February 1987. Two students met at a party; they went home together and to bed. For the man, that was the end of the affair – a one-night stand. But the woman realized that she had been imprudent and went to her doctor for "morning-after" contraception. Four months later a medical investigation of a chest infection, which included a body scan, revealed that she was also pregnant. Two doctors were found to sign a certificate that continuation of her pregnancy posed a greater risk to her life and health than its termination. Then C. and S. chanced to meet again. The woman tells the man that she is four months pregnant and about to have an abortion. One can understand that a young woman in such a predicament would feel a need to talk to someone, but . . .

To confide in him was a strange decision. As a member of the Society for the Protection of the Unborn Child, his views were well known. In the same month as their brief affair, he had written a searing article describing abortion as "an unseen holocaust."

According to friends, the pair now thrown into the national spotlight were from the beginning an unlikely match. He is a poet and an atheist, studying "the moral universe in classical literature." Colleagues say they are mystified at his strength of feeling. "He is a nice, quiet liberal," said one, "but when I heard him speak about abortion, I was shocked at the vehemence."

She is a churchgoer who has an apparently chaste relationship with another long-standing Christian boy-friend. (Thynne, 1987)

Now to the point of the story: The man's behavior as escort for an evening was one thing and his behavior as a member of the Society for the Protection of the Unborn Child (SPUC) quite another. As a prospective father, he sought an injunction in the High Court, then the Court of Appeal, and was finally refused leave to appeal to the House of Lords – an injunction to prevent an alleged breach of criminal law, namely, the aborting of a fetus which would be "born alive" within the meaning of the Infant Life [Preservation] Act, 1929. There was never any suggestion that an infant, born that early, could actually survive.

The fetus was variously said to be 18 to 21 weeks, and legal abortion must take place before 28 weeks. The legal action imposed a stress on the woman who was already under treatment for depression. Oxford Area Health Authority was not willing to carry out an abortion until all legal procedures had been completed. Counsel for the plaintiff refused a concession to allow the abortion to go ahead while the legal case was argued. It all looks like spite and vindictiveness – like the Society for the Persecution of Damsels in Distress – though presumably not. In the first place, SPUC would have welcomed the publicity. Second, the man becomes temporarily a prominent member of that society. Finally, there were legal costs estimated at £50,000 (no doubt borne by SPUC).

After entering hospital twice in March 1987 for a late abortion, the woman changed her mind and gave birth to a baby girl in July 1987. Thereafter the father brought the child up by himself (Langley, 1988).

UNDERSTANDING MILGRAM'S RESULTS

Human societies – families, workgroups, sports clubs, religious societies – function because each member knows what is expected of him or her, what he or she may do and may not do, and also knows what to expect from other members of the society. These mutual understandings promote harmony between different members of the society; they are maintained by continued social intercourse. Without mutual understanding of that kind there would be conflict.

But such mutual understandings do not necessarily exist between *different* societies, between Anglo-Saxon British and Asian societies, because the social intercourse needed to maintain them is lacking. So, British law and Asian custom are in conflict. While the Asian parents who coerce their daughters into marriage are aware of the legal constraints in Britain, they nevertheless see it as entirely proper to choose their daughter's future husband for her. It is British law that is "wrong."

The same disparity in convention develops, but to a lesser extent, between different social groups in the one country, because people of a common society and nationality nevertheless belong, transiently, to different social groups, maybe several different groups, which develop different moral standards. This provides the possibility of conflict that emerged in Milgram's experiments.

Stanley Milgram invited naive participants into a psychological laboratory as volunteers in an experiment whose purpose was kept hidden. For Milgram's participants this was an unfamiliar milieu. They did not know what social conventions applied and for that reason were generally compliant. But Milgram's laboratory was set within a larger society to which participants would, in due course, return. They are therefore subject to a conflict between different moral imperatives; they have obligations to the experimenter, from whom they have already accepted payment of expenses, and also to society at large. Milgram's results depend upon his participants being uncertain which moral imperative is (temporarily) the more important. In a continuing society (Nazi Germany, the military regime in Greece from 1967 to 1974, the Soviet Union in the 1930s under Stalin, Cambodia under Pol Pot) the moral imperatives evolve. In Milgram's Experiment 18 an even greater proportion of participants (37 out of 40) acquiesced when someone else was operating the shock generator. The acquiescence of the German people under the Nazi regime would seem to need no further explanation.

Nevertheless, the question is still asked: "How did Hitler make millions follow him?" (LeBor & Boyes, 2000a, b). Imagine that Milgram's participants are *employed* to teach "stupid" pupils to learn pairs of words. They work at this "teaching" day after day and are paid for doing it. In the world outside their workplace, they are encouraged as patriotic workers carrying out a vital task. The two important differences I have introduced are, first, that there is no return to a society where this particular administration of potentially lethal electric shocks is considered "wrong" and, second, that they are publicly praised for their work. If Milgram can achieve complete obedience from 65 percent of his volunteer participants in the course of an hour's experiment, the evolution of the Nazi regime, however evil it now seems to our sensibilities, is not to be wondered at. Indeed, prior to 1939 Hitler enjoyed noticeable sympathy amongst the British ruling classes, including King Edward VIII and his future consort, Wallis Simpson, as a potential ally in the battle against communism.

Military Obedience

Stanley Milgram's experimental research was motivated by two particular issues: (1) the acquiescence of the German people under the Nazi regime and (2) the obedience of soldiers under arms. It has happened from time to time that soldiers, on command, have slaughtered gatherings of unarmed civilians, sometimes of their own people, and such episodes provide a direct parallel to Milgram's findings. The historic list of such massacres includes St Peter's Fields, Manchester, 1819; "Bloody Sunday," Belfast, 1972; St Petersburg, 1905; Lidice, Czechoslovakia, 1942; My Lai, Vietnam, 1968; and Tiananmen Square, Beijing, 1989. Here are brief accounts of the last two.

My Lai, Vietnam, 1968

My Lai is a village in central Vietnam. On March 16, 1968, C Company of the 1/20th US infantry were sent there on a "search and destroy" mission. The 1st Platoon under 2nd Lieutenant Calley killed about 500 villagers – old men, women, and children.

> Denis Conti was a member of the 1st Platoon led by 2nd Lt. William Calley, who held another briefing for his platoon after Medina's [Captain Medina, commander of C Company]. "Calley told us that 90 per cent of the population were VC [Viet Cong] or VC sympathisers. 'If you see a man, he is carrying a weapon; if you see a woman, she is carrying a pack.' He said something about children, also, something like they could be future VC. He said cattle and crops were VC food. Calley struck me as all psyched up. He said not to hesitate to kill anything that moves. That stands out in my mind. He reminded us that we had lost a lot of men in that area, and we were going to make up for it." (Bilton & Sim, 1989)

Calley's platoon not only killed – they also scalped, raped, mutilated, and burned.

Ronald Haeberle was a US Army photographer, sent to cover the My Lai operation for *Stars and Stripes*, the army's official newspaper. The official photographs he took are generally innocuous. But Haeberle also carried his own camera, and his own photographs tell a quite different story. They show bodies strewn along a path; an old man thrown down a well; a group of seven peasants, mere seconds from slaughter; and every home set on fire (Bilton & Sim, 1989, pp. 30–1). These photographs were published when news of the massacre leaked out some 18 months afterwards; and this was the work of ordinary American youngsters with an average age of about 20, most of whom had been in Vietnam for just seven weeks. My Lai, more than any other event, turned American public opinion against the Vietnam War.

Tiananmen Square, Beijing, 1989

The story begins with Hu Yaobang, a popular, though deposed, Communist Party chieftain, dying from a heart attack on April 15, 1989. The mourning at his funeral spontaneously erupted into a rally in Tiananmen Square in support of democracy and free speech. The Communist Party leadership was divided what to do. For reasons connected with political face, they could not do anything during the seventieth anniversary of the May 4th Movement, nor during the visit of Mikhail Gorbachev, Chairman of the USSR Supreme Soviet, on May 16 that year. For these reasons the rally in Tiananmen Square was allowed to continue for a month.

But once the summit meeting with Gorbachev was over, martial law was declared, on May 20, and the army, deploying 50,000 troops, was summoned to restore control. The army hesitated for two weeks, probably because of internal divisions within the leadership. Then unarmed assaults on the protesters failed to displace them. So on the night of June 3/4, 1989, the Chinese People's Liberation Army cleared Tiananmen Square by firing live rounds at the Chinese people. That attack was filmed by news reporters and broadcast around the world (e.g., Independent Television News, June 4, 1989). Photographic documentation is also extensive (e.g., Dejevsky, 1989; Fathers & Higgins, 1989).

The most recent such incident in the UK, to my knowledge, was at Rotherham in 1893 when there was a bitter coal strike.

> "Three men killed and ten injured" is in brief the result of Wednesday's rioting in the home county.
>
> It remained for the authorities in the south-western division to teach the miners a lesson which they will not soon forget. Mob law has reigned for the past fortnight, but the stringent measures which have now been adopted bid fair to nip in the bud any further outbreaks.
>
> Capt. Barker ordered the front rank to kneel, and four files to fire in the midst of the mob. The report of firearms was followed by cries and groans, and ten or a dozen were seen to drop. (*Sheffield and Rotherham Independent*, 1893; cited by Vanson, 1985)

THE STANFORD COUNTY PRISON EXPERIMENT

One can imagine that soldiers, accustomed to obeying orders without question, will, on command, fire even on their own people. But what about a civilian population, what about the evolving society in Nazi Germany from 1933 to 1945? Surely people there could see that the persecution of the Jews was wrong? Sadly, that is how ordinary people do react – American university students, for example. This was shown to be so in a dramatic experiment by Haney, Banks, and Zimbardo (1973).

A prison was simulated in a basement at Stanford University. A total of 24 male participants were selected from a pool of 75 volunteers. These 24 were selected as being the most mature and stable, as assessed by tests of personality and by interview. They were previously unknown to each other and were assigned at random, half to be prisoners and half to be guards. The prisoners were initially picked up by the Palo Alto police, taken through the induction procedures that usually follow arrest, and then transferred to the simulated prison. The guards were divided into three shifts, each shift on duty for 8 hours at a time. The subjects were provided with uniforms; the guards wore khaki shirts and trousers, the prisoners loose-fitting smocks with an identification number front and back and a chain and lock around one ankle. Everybody was paid $15 per day and it was intended that the experiment should continue for 14 days. But ...

> At the end of only six days we had to close down our mock prison because what we saw was frightening. It was no longer apparent to most of the subjects (or to us) where reality ended and their roles began.
>
> We had to release three prisoners in the first four days because they had such acute situational traumatic reactions as hysterical crying, confusion in thinking and severe depression. Others begged to be paroled, and all but three were willing to forfeit all the money they had earned if they could be paroled. By then (the fifth day) they had been so programmed to think of themselves as prisoners that when their request for parole was denied, they returned docilely to their cells. (Zimbardo, 1972, p. 4)

And these were university students selected as being especially mature and stable in personality!

The differences in behavior between guards and prisoners were not due to differences in personality. In any ordinary prison, prisoners and guards are drawn from different populations and the very great differences in their attitudes and behavior might arise because they are different kinds of people. But the methods of selection and assignment in the Stanford County Prison experiment mean that such differences were induced *entirely* by the different roles to which prisoners and guards had been randomly assigned. The guards were specifically prohibited from using physical punishment or physical aggression, but were otherwise allowed to decide for themselves how to manage the prison. That management regime evolved, with intensified harassment and aggression, so rapidly that the experiment had to be terminated after only six days. Zimbardo had a consultant, "an ex-convict with 16 years of imprisonment in California's jails, [who] would get so depressed and furious each time he visited our prison, because of its psychological similarity to his experiences, that he would have to leave. A Catholic priest who was a former prison chaplain in Washington, D.C. talked to our prisoners after four days and said they were just like the other first-timers he had seen" (Zimbardo, 1972, p. 6).

Interviews with both guards and prisoners were characterized by negative attitudes and outlook.

> "They [the prisoners] didn't see it as an experiment. It was real and they were fighting to keep their identity. But we were always there to show them just who was boss."

> "... I began to feel I was losing my identity, that the person I call ——, the person who volunteered to get me into this prison (because it was a prison to me, it *still* is a prison to me, I don't regard it as an experiment or a simulation . . .) was distant from me, was remote until finally I wasn't *that* person, I was 416. I was really my number and 416 was really going to have to decide what to do." (Haney et al., 1973, p. 88)

All this consequent purely on the roles to which these young men had been assigned by chance!

Philip Zimbardo was able to terminate his experiment once he perceived that conditions in his simulated prison were evolving out of his control as superintendent. But what happens in a real prison?

> The head of the Prison Service yesterday described six jails in England and Wales as "hell holes" which too many staff accepted as terrible places unable to be reformed.
>
> He said that he was unwilling to go on being an apologist for failing prisons and attitudes that treated prisoners as a sub-species.
>
> Mr Narey described the appalling conditions he found at Birmingham jail. Rooms in the health care centre were dirty despite a nurse on duty saying they had been cleaned that morning. "The stench from one cell in which a patient was held pervaded the corridor," he said. "As I visited at 3.45 p.m., the evening meal was being served. The Board of Visitors were adamant that there was no physical abuse at Birmingham. I do not share that confidence."
>
> The Director-General pre-empted the Chief Inspector of Prisons' forthcoming report on Birmingham by disclosing some of its contents. Mr Narey said that Sir David found filthy conditions and appalling hygiene. "He will speak of a mentally ill prisoner denied a change of clothes for several weeks." (Ford, 2001)

The lesson to be learned from the Stanford County Prison study is that the structure of the society in which individuals are placed greatly shapes what they do and what they say. This has two immediate implications. First, conditions in Birmingham and in other prisons do not result from sadistic warders but from the structure of a prison society *per se*. To reform the internal conditions that the director-general finds appalling, it will be necessary to rethink the whole notion of criminal punishment. Second, the evolution of German civilian society under the Nazi regime should present no psychological problem at all. What needs to be studied is how a very few people – Dietrich Bonhoeffer was one – could bring themselves to resist.

This chapter has been concerned to describe Milgram's experiments and their results and to map out some of the implications for our understanding of human society. But there is still a deep question that these experiments do not directly answer: How can the requests and actions of such an authority have so profound an effect on what people will do? That question is for chapter 9. Meanwhile the next chapter provides many more examples of social conventions, to emphasize the extent to which they govern and constrain our social lives.

QUESTIONS FOR DISCUSSION

1   Why did Milgram's participants, ordinary American citizens, administer (as they thought) 450-volt shocks to an innocent pupil?

2   Why do some societies (Muslim, Hindu) allow women so much less freedom than western societies?

3   How far are our lives governed by the structure of the society in which we are placed?

7

THE RATE FOR THE JOB

Milgram's experiments in the preceding chapter and the Stanford County Prison study can be understood on the basis that much of our social life is governed by convention. Social conventions specify who has authority in our society, who may do what. They specify what we should do in this situation and that, though, in practice, the actual outcome in terms of behavior is modified by the particular people we are with. It happens that conventions differ somewhat as between one social group and another.

This chapter elaborates the idea of a social convention with further examples. It has this particular message: Different subgroups in our society develop their own social standards and conventions. Examples include animal welfare groups protesting about the transport of veal calves to the continent; anti-hunt saboteurs; anti-road protesters; directors of large public companies; and MPs, so far as their private business interests are concerned – these subgroups have all made it to the national news headlines during the last few years. Where social conventions concern a subgroup's particular purpose in being, they tend to develop independently of the larger society within which the subgroup exists and may even come into conflict with the conventions of that larger society to which members of the subgroup also belong.

The most frequent examples arise in business, so this chapter could have been entitled "Business ethics." But this would not be the ethics taught in business school, how business dealings ought to be conducted, but the psychological reality, how business *is* conducted in the real world. But the most frequent conflict of standards in business concerns how much someone should be paid for what they do; hence "The rate for the job."

HOW MUCH DO DIFFERENT PEOPLE EARN?

In business money is the great incentive. But its distribution is ultimately arbitrary and you might expect squabbles over how much someone should be paid for their work. Society has evolved some informal principles (social conventions) to preempt those squabbles. There are three rules of thumb.

1 People Doing the Same Job Get Paid the Same (Irrespective of How Well They Do It), Unless, Sometimes, They Happen to be Women

On January 31, 1996, the House of Commons was debating the highly sensitive issue of members' pay.

> Mr Hoyle, MP for Warrington North, said: . . . "I believe that MPs' pay has fallen behind the pay of other European parliaments and other professions outside the House." (MacIntyre, 1996)

The government is at present trying to displace this principle with the introduction of "merit pay" and meeting with continued resistance.

But that principle is applied only with reluctance to comparisons between the earnings of men and women.

> A report by the Equal Opportunities Commission (EOC) reveals that women lag behind men in the pay stakes by as much as 20%. Worse, it could take almost half a century for women to catch up.
> The EOC report reveals that salary sexism knows no bounds. It does not matter where you work, what kind of job you do, or the hours you put in – as far as income is concerned, it is still a man's world. (Caine & Davidson, 1997; see also New Earnings Survey, 1997, tables A.13, A.14)

But people in different jobs are paid different amounts, sometimes very different. The differences of pay between different occupations (one occupation from each decile of the distribution of incomes) as at April 2000 are set out in figure 7.1. Why the variation? While there is a certain element of supply of, and demand for, particular kinds of labor, that is not the full story, not with 1 million people out of work. In fact, the supply of work is limited, so the pay you receive depends on how readily you can get your hands on the money. That leads to the second rule of thumb.

2 Those People Closest to the Money are Paid the Most

The best-paid jobs for university graduates are in banking, accountancy, and financial management. School teaching is poorly paid because, except for the small private sector, education is not marketable. Here are some examples.

Waitress £9,335   Cleaner £10,766   Builder's mate £14,320   Warehouseman £14,895   Stewardess £16,473   Paramedic £19,193   Photographer £21,400   Estate agent £24,692   Company secretary £33,691   Doctor £54,353

Figure 7.1 Approximate annual earnings in different occupations – one occupation from each decile of the distribution of incomes – as at April 2000 (data from Francis, 2000, table A12).

Liliane Preisler

Liliane Preisler was a "currency swaps" broker.

> She puts in contact with each other banks, companies and pension funds which want to maximise their investments and minimise risks by swapping the interest owing on debts they hold in one currency for interest in another.
>
> It is an arcane but hugely profitable part of the City's business. According to the International Swaps Dealers Association, the global volume of swaps in sterling alone amounted to £28bn last year [1990]. Most of that business was done in London. (Rocco, 1991)

At that time Liliane Preisler was 31 years old, spoke four languages fluently, and was earning about £150,000 a year including bonuses from Euro Brokers Capital Markets. She took leave to have a baby. Before returning to work Liliane Preisler asked for a pay rise, which was refused; she claimed the she was worth at least £200,000 a year. When she returned to work after seven months, six of her best clients had been given to other brokers. Now, an important part of her remuneration was her bonus, and that bonus depended on the amount of business she conducted (to motivate individual employees). That explains the importance of "best clients" – business can, to some extent, be allocated. Liliane Preisler claimed "constructive dismissal." She won her case before the industrial tribunal, but was awarded only one month's pay and benefits.

Bill Brown

Bill Brown is a reinsurance broker, chairman of Walsham Brothers who exchange risks between different syndicates at Lloyds. Roughly speaking, his company lays off bets as between one syndicate and another. In 1989, Walsham Brothers reported post-tax profits of £20.4 million on a turnover of £36.6 million. In that year Bill Brown paid himself £8.2 million salary and over £9 million in dividends. But in 1991 recession began to bite . . .

> The highest paid company director in Britain has taken a pay cut of £792,000 and is now having to struggle along on a mere £7.3m a year.
>
> However, Mr Brown's employees have set a far more impressive example. Their average pay has been cut by 61 per cent, according to records for 1990 filed at Companies House. (Moore, 1991)

Jan Leschly

More recently, Jan Leschly, chief executive of SmithKline Beecham, the pharmaceuticals firm, benefited from pay, bonus, and gains on share options amounting to £27 million in 1997 (Lynn & Hamilton, 1998). It is possible, however, for a company director to take too much.

> SmithKline Beecham is to meet leading institutional investors in an attempt to head off a shareholder revolt over the level of pay and options packages enjoyed by the board of the drugs group.
>
> The five leading directors picked up total pay, options and other incentives worth as much as £25 million during 1997. The pay and incentive schemes were worth more than £10 million alone to Jan Leschly, the chief executive, during the year. His accumulated options and bonuses are now worth up to £66 million. (Nissé, 1998)

So, how much should people in different occupations be paid? That question is usually resolved by convention, but with one exception, which provides the third rule of thumb.

3 If Someone Can Earn More by Negotiating a Private Deal, Well, Good Luck to Her or Him

Supermodels

Supermodels provide the example above all others of young women who can negotiate exceedingly lucrative private deals. Linda Evangelista, Cindy Crawford, Naomi Campbell, Claudia Schiffer, Christy Turlington, Kate Moss – their faces are very well known from fashion magazines. Their fees are typically £6,000–£10,000 a day (Jobey, 1991). Iman once earned $50,000 for 20 minutes' work at a Paris fashion show (Tredre, 1992a). But why such high fees?

In the first place, fashion shows in Paris, Milan, or London are not actually about selling *haute couture*.

> Success is not calculated on the basis of how many women actually buy – there is no expectation of making money on a collection even when Ivana Trump pays $36,000 (£21,800) for a beaded jacket at Lacroix. Bernard Arnaud, the financier behind Christian Dior and Lacroix, considers couture to be the advertising facade for a series of businesses including perfume and licensing spin-offs.
>
> No more than 1,500 orders are placed in total each season by a relatively fixed customer base, which is variously estimated to total between 300 and 1,000 women worldwide. Couture's role now is simply to add glamour value to the ready-to-wear accessories and, most importantly, scent, upon which the houses' profits are really based. (Tredre, 1990)

This is where the money is really made. Not in flogging the outrageous and sometimes wonderful flights of fancy you see billowing down the runway. That's all for publicity. It's the accessories, stupid. In the Eighties you couldn't open a bathroom cupboard door without finding a bottle of Paco Rabanne's aftershave or Chanel Pour Homme. In the Nineties everyone was wearing Calvin Klein's Eternity before they moved on to Obsession. This is what designers are really fighting for, a space in your shower cabinet. (Coles, 2000)

So, the money to pay the supermodels' fees comes from cross-subsidy.

But why such exorbitant fees when there are so many "wannabes" who would do it for nothing (Tredre, 1992b, c)? The fashion market is not unlimited. There are only a limited number of glossy magazines – *Vogue, Harper's & Queen, Marie Claire, Elle, The Face*, and their foreign counterparts – in which pictures of fashion models are routinely published for public appreciation. It follows that only a limited number of fashion models can become truly well known.

The real purpose of a fashion show is publicity for the fashion house.

> The best seats in the house are right at the end of the catwalk where the wives of leading politicians are sometimes joined by film stars such as Catherine Deneuve and Mireille Matthieu. As these little groups assemble the photographers set frantically to work adding to the general air of excitement. Also in the best seats are the leading fashion journalists. The fashion editors wield real power in this world. They receive a personal escort to their seats and during the year they are showered with gifts. The little Christmas box from Chanel is awaited with particular interest it seems. One personal client of Emanuel Ungaro's told me that she found the fashion writers' comments totally unhelpful, but that is not a dispute which a lone male would be well-advised to join. (Marnham, 1990)

> As head of the world's most powerful fashion magazine, [Anna] Wintour [Editor-in-Chief of American *Vogue*] . . . can make the career of a designer, model, or photographer with a nod of her elegantly coiffed head – and she regularly does. (Rickey, 2001)

A fashion house must use the best-known models, whatever they cost, to get that publicity. That circumstance breeds the supermodels.

The common view is that people (in general) earn what they do because their labor is worth that much (so that conventional salaries are seldom contested) and that view is extrapolated to the earnings of supermodels. ". . . only a handful of girls . . . have what it takes to be a supermodel, sought after for both catwalk and photographic work, their faces familiar from glossy magazines and raw tabloids" (Armstrong, 1991). "It's all about marketing a product. The very best models stand out a mile; they can make indifferent clothes look rather special" (Chris Moore, cited by Tredre, 1991) – but that is because their faces are well known. The supermodel's appeal is not intrinsic – many other women could wear those clothes with equal grace. The supermodel's appeal depends upon her face being well known from glossy fashion magazines like *Vogue*. The quality of the clothes she models is evaluated from the model who is wearing them. The number of supermodels is limited by the number of fashion magazines and that number, in turn, by the total readership. Supermodels' earnings are ultimately set by the ratio of the number of fashion magazines to the number of fashion houses putting on fashion shows.

The Allegra Coleman nobody knows

If you dispute that line about publicity . . .

> Just ask **Woody Allen.** Or **David Schwimmer.** Or **Tarantino.** . . . **Allegra Coleman** is Hollywood's Next Big Thing. She's the It Girl of '96, a ripe, fresh young actress just bubbling with essence and making her very first national magazine appearance in the cover of *Esquire*'s November issue. . . . **Martha Sherrill** – who recognises star quality when she sees it . . . gushes: "She's the most compelling celebrity I've ever written about . . . Allegra defines what Hollywood is all about in the nineties."
> The only thing is, **Allegra Coleman** does not exist. She's a fictional creation, and Sherrill's interview is a parody of the celebrity journalism that's run wild in the '90s. (Vertes, 1996)

Then who was that on the front cover of *Esquire* for November 1996?

> The real face on the cover belongs to Ali Larder, a model.
> Inevitably, the story has also turned Larder into a celebrity. Hollywood deal-makers are reportedly rushing to sign her. A star is about to be born. (Allen-Mills, 1996)

Boardroom Pay

Cedric Brown was appointed chief executive of British Gas in 1992. Then, on November 21, 1994, it emerged in the national press that he was to receive a pay rise that would take his remuneration from £270,000 a year to £475,000. There were storms of protest, not least in the House of Commons. "It is way, way over the top" (Sir Andrew Bowden, MP, on *The World at One*, BBC Radio 4, November 21, 1994; cited in Brown & MacIntyre, 1994). Well, actually, it wasn't. At that time British Gas was the seventh largest company in the country. Cedric Brown was merely catching up with the pay levels of chief executives in other companies of similar size (Rule 1 above).

This issue has arisen before. In July 1989 Lord King, chairman of British Airways, received a rise of 116 percent to bring him to £386,000. At that time the top 30 company directors averaged £534,000; the largest income was earned by Lord Hanson with £1,239,000 per year (Beresford, 1989). More recently, in 1995, the chief executives of the 100 largest companies shared £125 million between them (Rhoads & Patterson, 1996); this amounts to a 100 percent increase over the space of six years – much greater than the rate of inflation. And in October 1998, "The pay of top FTSE 100 executives has soared by 45% since last year. The average boss now earns £1m" (Lynn, Hamilton, & Coffer, 1998). Company directors are at the top end of the range of pay; they receive such excessive remuneration because they are close to the money (Rule 2 above).

Who sits on the boards of companies? How are they appointed?

In the darker recesses of the Athenaeum's reading room, newspapers rustle. Sir Peter Holmes, the lean and fit chairman of Shell, comes here to relax. So do Lord Armstrong of Ilminster and Sir David Orr, his non-executive colleagues.

Orr is chairman of Inchcape. Among the non-executives who sit on his board are Armstrong and Sir Peter Baxendale, himself the chairman of Shell until 1985. Orr has sat on the Shell board since 1982 – the same year he left his post as chairman of Unilever and first became chairman of Inchcape, a job which he has now held twice. In 1986, he stepped down from office to become deputy chairman but was also looking around for another non-executive director. The newly retired Baxendale, already a friend, was an obvious choice. (Kay, 1992)

Directors are appointed by other directors who propose people they know. "Up to 80% of outside appointments to the boards of large British companies are still made on the old boy network" (a casual comment from Sir Adrian Cadbury, chairman of the Committee on the Financial Aspects of Corporate Governance, cited by Kay, 1992).

Just four days after he stepped down as chief executive of British Airways, Sir Colin Marshall has already landed on a new corporate runway. He was yesterday named as the new chairman of Inchcape, the struggling motor distributor and marketing group. He joins the board with immediate effect. . . .

He will be paid £200,000 a year for a 1.5 to two-day week. He will continue to spend two days a week at BA as chairman, although his modified BA salary has not yet been decided. Inchcape says it will share Sir Colin's car and chauffeur expenses with BA.

Sir Colin's appointment renews several long-standing acquaintances. Charles Mackay has sat on the same board as Sir Colin at both HSBC and BA. At Inchcape Sir Colin will sit at the same board table as Liam Strong, who is a non-executive director and was formerly marketing director of BA. (Cope, 1995)

A natural consequence is that few company directors are women. Amongst the full-time executive directors of the companies listed in the FTSE 100 index, only 10 out of 555 (1.8 percent) are women. Of 695 non-executive directors, just 55 (8 percent) are women (Ashworth, 2000, citing the FTSE Female Index).

How is directors' pay fixed?

A director's pay is usually determined by a remuneration committee which is itself composed of directors, most of them non-executive directors – that is, they are not also employees of the company. But they are very likely to be executive directors of other companies. As of November 1991 Sir Colin Marshall was an executive director of British Airways, and also a non-executive director of Midland Bank (HSBC) and of Grand Metropolitan Hotels and on the remuneration committees of both those companies (Rodgers, 1991). Multiple appointments of that pattern assist the remuneration committee in making comparison with the pay of directors in other companies (Rule 1 above) – but they also foster an unhealthy degree of inbreeding.

There have been repeated public protests about the excessive level of remuneration of the directors of the top public companies. The Conservative government passed that buck to the shareholders.

> Ask any chairman of a major public company – annual salary somewhere in the region of £500,000 – and he will tell you that the commonest question on pay at his meetings with institutional shareholders is not whether the board is paying itself too much, but the exact opposite. Are executives being given a big enough financial incentive to perform? (*Independent*, 1994c)

Higher pay at the very top enables higher pay slightly lower down for those executives with whom institutional managers identify.

Are directors worth their pay?

We don't know. A company's financial success (or failure) depends in large part on factors outside the directors' control – the rate of inflation, interest rates, and other parameters of the economy. It would be wrong for directors to be personally penalized for lack of success due to outside causes such as these – and usually they are not. On that basis the board of Guardian Royal Exchange paid itself one-third more in 1990, while the company moved from a profit of £148 million to a loss of £157 million (Macrae, 1991). But much business success is due to the very same factors working in the opposite direction. It would be wrong for directors to be rewarded with bonuses on that account – but they are.

Mountleigh was a company that invested in property in the late 1980s.

> In its heyday, and even in its low days, Mountleigh was a company that illustrated some of the worst excesses of the Eighties. Directors came and went, earning huge fees before going off to pastures new.
>   In 1991, a year in which Mountleigh made pre-tax losses of £96.1m, Nelson Peltz, the American entrepreneur chairman . . . was awarded a salary of £457,000,

a 50 per cent increase on the previous year. His fellow directors enjoyed similar increases – and all this before the planes and the big black Bentley that went with the job. (Hellier & Nissé, 1992)

Mountleigh crashed in May 1992.

Do directors know how to do their jobs?

Gerald Ratner used to be a jeweler with a nationwide chain of high street shops, 1,000 strong. When he took over the family business in 1984 at the age of 34, he went to view a rival jeweler in Newcastle who was said to be "taking £1m a month and had a queue half way to Sunderland" (Randall, 1991) and copied his rival's sales pitch. By 1991 his shops were taking more money per square foot than any other retailer in Europe (*The Times*, 1991) and, with that success behind him, Gerald Ratner was invited to address the Institute of Directors at their annual convention at the Albert Hall. He told them

> We sell things like a teapot for two quid or an imitation open book to lay on your coffee table. The pages don't turn – but they have beautifully curled up corners and genuine antique dust. I know it is in the worst possible taste, but we sold a quarter of a million last year.
>   We also do cut-glass sherry decanters complete with six glasses on a silver tray – that your butler can serve you drinks on – all for £4.95. People say how can you sell this for such a low price. I say because it is total crap.
>   Some people say they cannot even see the jewellery for all the posters and banners smothering the shop windows. It is interesting, isn't it, that these shops, that everyone has a good laugh about, take more money per square foot than any other retailer in Europe.
>   We even sell a pair of earrings for under £1, which is cheaper than a prawn sandwich from Marks & Spencers. But I have to say the earrings probably won't last as long. (*The Times*, 1991)

"Stockmarket operators . . . seemed to like what they heard in Mr Ratner's speech. The share price jumped 6p to 184p on Tuesday and added another 2p when trading opened yesterday" (Cash, 1991). But Ratner's sold its jewelry with a "money back" guarantee if the purchaser was dissatisfied and returned the goods within one month of purchase. Bob Derbyshire was a shop manager for Ratner's at the time.

> I saw the words "crap" all over the newspapers and that was the first I'd heard. And I was gobsmacked.
>   The day after the speech was made customers would be coming back into the store, bringing their jewellery back that they'd recently purchased, and wanting their money back.
>   They came back the following day, and the day after, and the day after that. (Mirsky, 1996)

When asked, Gerald Ratner said: "How much did the speech cost me? Well I think it could have cost the company a few hundred million pounds, maybe – a hundred million, two hundred million. But it cost me personally, obviously, it cost me – everything" (Mirsky, 1996). Gerald Ratner was ousted from the company that he had built up. His business expertise was of a "trial-and-error" kind. He did not understand what not to do.

In practice, the most important thing about business is knowing other business-men with whom to do business. Profits are made by increasing the volume of business done (even if only slightly), and the volume of business depends on whom one knows to do business with. It therefore makes some sense to appoint people to directorships whom one knows and who are known to have useful contacts. That is still true whether the individual is good at directing business or only mediocre. But it leads to a subsociety of directors of top public companies who, collectively, milk their companies for their own benefit. It is not only businessmen who take away excessive salaries; hospital consultants, judges, and lawyers do it as well when they get the chance. So also do MPs.

MPs' Financial Interests

The market is governed by profit, not enlightenment. It is the responsibility of government to so regulate the market (by imposing minimum conditions of work, etc.) as to force it (the market) to a more socially enlightened equilibrium. There is a long history of Factory Acts and much present-day Health and Safety at Work legislation designed to protect the workforce from exploitation. The philosophy of high rewards as an incentive to work harder and create more wealth is simply an excuse to shift the market in the opposite direction. Members of Parliament them-selves are not averse to that kind of shift!

Parliament's responsibility is compromised by the financial interests of its members. Since those personal interests might influence an MP's contribution to debate, there is a Register of Members' Interests in which MPs are required to list all earnings and benefits received outside of their parliamentary salary and allowances. The Register is designed to prevent corruption and was introduced in the wake of the Poulson corruption scandal in 1974.[1] MPs are also required to declare all relevant interests when speaking in a debate or lobbying ministers. This is how it is done.

---

[1] John Poulson, an architect involved in public sector development, conspired with a local council leader to use bribery and illicit influence to win building contracts in the north of England and elsewhere. John Poulson paid civil servants, local councillors, council officials, nationalized industry and NHS employees, and MPs various amounts in cash and in gifts in his bid to secure contracts. A number of people were jailed as a result, and a Royal Commission into Standards in Public Life was set up to provide new rules for the conduct of local government.

Parliament, May 8, 1990

> *Sir Peter Blaker:* Mr Speaker, I have declared an interest in the subject as chairman of a company [Maclean Hunter Cablevision Ltd.] which has six cable franchises but does not aspire to obtain any more.
>
> (You have to state that you have such an interest if you have it; you have to register it, you have to declare it in debate, and that enables your colleagues to say: "Is Peter Blaker putting this proposal forward solely for his own interest, or is he putting it forward because it's a good proposal?" And they have to judge.) (Hayes, 1992)

The conflict of interest is obvious. How does an MP make sure that he or she is always voting in the public interest, and putting forward the views that the public has, and not in his or her own financial interest?

If an MP is merely asking a question in the House, he or she is not actually required to declare his or her interest explicitly.

Parliament, November 30, 1989

> *Mr Jerry Wiggin:* Is my right honourable friend aware that the proposed plant of British Sugar will consume some 750,000 tons of straw a year, some 10 per cent of annual production? . . . that because of the innovative nature of the technology and the high risk involved, will need a substantial contribution from government? Will he make representations to the Department of Trade and Industry in due course, strongly in favour of this excellent British enterprise? (Hayes, 1992)

As an example of the operation of the Register, in February 1990 the Select Committee on Members' Interests found that John Browne, MP for Winchester, had left significant interests undeclared (Pienaar, 1990; Waterhouse, 1990b). John Browne was suspended for 20 days and he stood down at the subsequent (1992) general election. That episode focused the attention of the national press on members' interests. Research uncovered 37 out of 373 Conservative MPs who had commercial interests in political lobbying firms or in public relations companies.

MPs are being employed as "parliamentary consultants" to lobbyists. Some MPs are even setting up their own companies, selling their expertise and advice.

Consultancy can be a lucrative sideline for MPs, supplementing their £26,701 [1990] basic annual salary. Fees normally average between £6,000 and £10,000 a year for each client. Some MPs list several regular consultancies.

In 1986 Sir Alex [Fletcher], a former junior minister in the Scottish Office and Department of Trade, offered to help Dutton-Forshaw Motor Group, which was in the queue to buy British Leyland's truck and Land-Rover divisions.

His services did not come cheap. After a meeting with Dutton-Forshaw executives he proposed a briefing fee of £5,000 and a monthly retainer of £5,000 plus expenses. He suggested a minimum guarantee fee of £15,000 if no deal was concluded and a bonus of £25,000 if it was – in addition to the retainer. His offer was declined.

Peter Fry (Wellingborough) is a director of and shareholder in Countrywide and Political Communications.

Mr Fry appeared before the select committee on parliamentary lobbying in April last year [1989]. A Labour member, Dale Campbell-Savours, said he had cross-referenced every parliamentary intervention Mr Fry had made since 1983. He pointed out that each parliamentary question cost the taxpayer about £2,000 to answer.

"I have to tell you that in one year, 1985, half your parliamentary interventions can be related directly to clients of public relations companies with which you had a direct involvement.

"There is a very clear linkage between these questions and the client list. I have done this every year since 1983 and in every year there is a clear correlation and linkage." (Waterhouse, 1990a)

What is the going rate for a former Tory cabinet minister? Until last week it was, according to City headhunters, between £200,000 and £250,000 – the rate commanded by recent recruits such as Nigel Lawson and Norman Tebbit.

But last week Lord Young, the former trade secretary, raised that substantially when he confirmed that he would become executive chairman of Cable & Wireless next October. His undisclosed salary is expected to be about £400,000. (Rafferty & Roy, 1990)

In July 1994 there were rumors abounding that some MPs were willing to ask a question in Parliament in return for payment. A *Sunday Times* reporter approached 20 MPs, chosen at random, offering a £1,000 payment for asking a (bogus) parliamentary question. Graham Riddick (Colne Valley) and David Tredinnick (Bosworth) took the bait and were dismissed from their posts as parliamentary private secretaries (Chittenden, Skipworth, Calvert, & Ramesh, 1994). Then in October 1994 Mohammed al Fayed, the owner of Harrods, revealed that Tim Smith, Minister for Northern Ireland, and Neil Hamilton, Minister at the Department of Trade and Industry, had accepted payment from him for asking questions in the House between 1987 and 1989 whilst they were still backbenchers. They had been paid £2,000 per question. Tim Smith resigned immediately; Neil Hamilton five days later. A standing committee was set up under the chairmanship of Lord Nolan to oversee standards of probity in public life (MacIntyre, 1994; MacIntyre & Brown, 1994).

There still remains the question of MPs who, openly and legitimately, take on extra employment. As of January 1995, David Mellor, MP for Putney and former Heritage Secretary, held 12 consultancies and had further earnings from journalism and television and radio appearances. Other MPs listed 11 or 10 directorships and consultancies. "200 out of 243 (83 per cent) Tory MPs, excluding ministers [who are precluded from such employment] hold a total of 276 paid directorships and 356 consultancies" (Clement, 1995).

Why do they do it? For the money, obviously. But surely MPs are elected to serve their constituents? It is alleged that MPs are so poorly paid and resourced that outside emoluments are necessary to make ends meet. But they could take jobs elsewhere . . . But what salary would these particular MPs command outside the House, without the cachet MP? For some (but certainly not all), election to Parliament is the stepping stone to publicity and commercial contacts and directorships; that is to say, some members appear to enter Parliament for the sake of the money on the side.

What Has This Chapter Really Been About?

The stories presented in this chapter support these generalizations.

1 A subgroup, occupied in some particular purpose, develops its own social conventions, somewhat independently of the larger society in which it exists. Examples are money brokers in the City, supermodels and Hollywood actresses, directors of large public companies, and MPs – but there are many more.
2 Those social conventions include the hours someone is expected to work (money brokers and politicians work excessively long hours; supermodels and directors rather short hours), how well they are expected to perform, and so on. But the most obvious subject of convention is how much someone is paid for their work.
3 The distribution of remuneration in our society is ultimately arbitrary (and therefore preeminently the subject of a social convention), but there are three rules of thumb which seem to be generally accepted:
    (a) People doing the same job should be paid the same.
    (b) Those working closest to the money get paid the most.
    (c) If anyone can get themselves paid more through a private deal, good luck to them!
4 A neat categorization of the different conventions evolving within each subgroup is not possible. The content of each subgroup's particular conventions depends too much on its reason for being. For example,

(a) Fashion houses are concerned above all else with attracting publicity. They therefore hire the best-known models, whatever their fees, and kowtow to fashion editors.

(b) Money brokers and other financial intermediaries jealously preserve their business contacts, whence come their bonuses. They expect to take those contacts with them when they move from one job to another.

(c) Directors are more concerned with who is fit to be appointed to a director-ship (that is, who already belongs to the informal subgroup of company directors). Actual ability to direct business efficiently seems not to figure. For example,

> Cedric Brown is to leave British Gas in April [1996] with a pension of £247,000 a year, after a coup the City believes was orchestrated by Richard Giordano, the company's chairman. (Rodgers, 1996)

Cedric Brown is a man who did not fit the usual mold of company director. He had no Oxbridge degree or MBA. He had left school at 16, joined British Gas as a laboratory assistant, and worked his way up (Cope, 1994). To put the matter succinctly, he was not really a member of the company directors' subsociety at all – just a jumped-up gas engineer! That would explain the protests at the time of his pay rise and at the subsequent annual general meeting:

> when nearly 5,000 shareholders descended on the London Arena in Docklands, east London, he [Cedric Brown] arrived to find an inflatable pig hoisted above the stadium. "Cedric the Pig" became a symbol of boardroom greed. (Cope & Rodgers, 1996)

During all this time Richard Giordano, the British Gas chairman, was receiving £450,000 a year for working a three- to four-day week. No one protested about that, no one at all! Richard Giordano is a real professional director, a genuine member of the directors' subsociety.

(d) On the other hand, membership of Parliament is independently determined by election and there can be no doubt over who is, and who is not, a member. Consequently, MPs' concerns are different; they are concerned with what additional remuneration it is permissible to accept on the side.

This chapter has fleshed out a picture of a society much constrained by social convention – who may do what and get away with it. But the ultimate question, how those conventions are enforced, has yet to be answered. We are not yet ready to address that question. There is another preliminary which will show that the moral sanction, when we get to it, does have the force and compulsion that are obviously needed to modify the expression of other, more primitive, motivations. So the next chapter looks at the intolerable effects of social isolation.

QUESTIONS FOR DISCUSSION

1 What would our society be like if subgroups – money brokers in the City, supermodels and Hollywood actresses, directors of large public companies, and MPs – had not evolved their own social conventions?

2 Some people – members of animal welfare groups, anti-hunt saboteurs, and anti-road protesters provide clear examples – argue that what certain other people are doing is "wrong." What does that word "wrong" mean?

8

LONELINESS

This chapter examines the effects of being alone, entirely on one's own, for a long period of time. Solitary confinement in prison would be one example; but the scope of "Loneliness" includes anyone who for any reason at all has spent a long time entirely by themselves. So I shall also be looking at the experiences of single-handed sailors and some polar explorers, as well as prisoners in solitary confinement. These are all people who, after a normal upbringing in human society, happen to spend a long period of time alone, effectively isolated from all others. But that is not the end of the matter. There are also historic reports of feral children who (very exceptionally) have somehow survived in the wild from a young age and have never known human society. They also are of interest. In fact, the effects of these two kinds of isolation, people who have for any reason become isolated from human society and children who have never known human society, are quite different and the comparison is instructive.

By "loneliness" I mean an unrestricted use of the senses, but no, or at the most only very limited, communication with any other person. There is no kind of sensory deprivation involved, but, nevertheless, some bizarre experiences emerge that invite comparison with the phenomena described in chapter 5. The chief difference is that the phenomena in this chapter take much longer to show. Social isolation is important to the question of how society exercises control over its members because, continued long enough, isolation proves as intolerable to the individual as does sensory deprivation over the shorter time. In short, the threat of extrusion provides society with an exceedingly powerful sanction against single individuals.

THE EXPERIENCE OF BEING ALONE

I look first at some anecdotal reports of what it is like to be alone from individuals who happen, for one reason or another, to have spent a long period of time virtually without human companionship. I am concerned with how they felt, how they described their experience, with the intention (vide chapter 4) of interpreting their descriptions in terms of what social isolation, as an environmental factor, does to the individual.

Joshua Slocum

Joshua Slocum was the first man to sail around the world alone. He accomplished this in a sloop, *The Spray*, 37 ft o.a., from 1895 to 1898, before the days of radio communication. He was a very experienced sailor, aged 51 at the time. Here are some of his reflections on the very first leg of his voyage across the Atlantic Ocean from Halifax, Nova Scotia, to the Azores (islands in the mid-Atlantic at the latitude of southern Spain).

> During these days a feeling of awe crept over me. My memory worked with startling power. The ominous, the insignificant, the great, the small, the wonderful, the commonplace – all appeared before my mental vision in magical succession. Pages of my history were recalled which had been so long forgotten that they seemed to belong to a previous existence. I heard all the voices of the past laughing, crying, telling what I had heard them tell in many corners of the earth.
>
> The loneliness of my state wore off when the gale was high and I found much work to do. When fine weather returned, then came the sense of solitude, which I could not shake off. (Slocum, 1900, pp. 26–7)

After leaving the Azores, Slocum suffered stomach cramps and, in this condition, ran into a storm with his sails only reefed, rather than stowed altogether.

> I am a careful man at sea, but this night, in the coming storm, I swayed up my sails, which, reefed though they were, were still too much in such heavy weather; and I saw to it that the sheets were securely belayed. In a word, I should have laid to, but did not. I gave her the double-reefed mainsail and whole jib instead, and set her on her course. Then I went below, and threw myself upon the cabin floor in great pain. How long I lay there I could not tell, for I became delirious. When I came to, as I thought, from my swoon, I realized that the sloop was plunging into a heavy sea, and looking out of the companionway, to my amazement I saw a tall man at the helm. His rigid hand, grasping the spokes of the wheel, held them as in a vise. One may imagine my astonishment. His rig was that of a foreign sailor, and the large red cap he wore was cockbilled over his left ear, and all was set off with shaggy black whiskers. He would have been taken for a pirate in any part of the world. While I gazed upon his threatening aspect I forgot the storm, and wondered if he had come to cut my throat. This he seemed to divine. "Señor," said he, doffing his cap. "I have come to do you no harm." And a smile, the faintest in the world, but still a smile, played on his face, which seemed not unkind when he spoke. "I have come to do you no harm. I have sailed free," he said, "but was never worse than a *contrabandista*. I am one of Columbus's crew," he continued. "I am the pilot of the *Pinta* come to

aid you. Lie quiet, señor captain," he added, "and I will guide your ship to-night. You have a *calentura*, but you will be all right to-morrow." (Slocum, 1900, pp. 39–40)

That vision reappeared several times during gales in the course of Slocum's three-year voyage.

Admiral Byrd

Admiral Byrd was a very experienced aviator and explorer, having visited both the North and South Poles. He was the leader of an expedition in 1934 to Little America, a survey station at 78° 20′ S on the Ross ice shelf in Antarctica. He attempted to man an inland weather station at 80° 08′ S (near the southern end of Roosevelt Is.) alone throughout the Antarctic night. The plan had been for three men (not two) to man this weather station, but it proved impossible to transport enough supplies for three men to that remote spot. Byrd lived in a shack buried in the snow, alone, for 136 days (March 28–August 11, 1934), with the temperature outside sometimes down to −80°F. He kept a diary which he was persuaded some four years later to prepare for publication (Byrd, 1938).

During his solitary sojourn he suffered extreme cold and also a low level of carbon monoxide poisoning due to faulty ventilation. He reported a near-death experience.

> I won't even attempt to recall all the melancholy thoughts that drifted through my mind that long afternoon. But I can say truthfully that at no time did I have any feeling of resignation. My whole being rebelled against my low estate. As the afternoon wore on, I felt myself sinking. Now I became alarmed. This was not the first time I had ever faced death. It had confronted me many times in the air. But then it had seemed altogether different. In flying things happen fast: you make a decision; the verdict crowds you instantly; and, when the invisible and neglected passenger comes lunging into the cockpit, he is but one of countless distractions. But now death was a stranger sitting in a darkened room, secure in the knowledge that he would be there when I was gone.
>
> Great waves of fear, a fear I had never known before, swept through me and settled deep within. But it wasn't the fear of suffering or even of death itself. It was a terrible anxiety over the consequences to those at home if I failed to return. I had done a damnable thing in going to Advance Base, I told myself. Also, during those hours of bitterness, I saw my whole life pass in review. (Byrd, 1938, pp. 179–80)

He had only very primitive radio communication with base, dependent on an electric generator which ultimately failed.

> In the afternoon I eavesdropped on Little America's weekly broadcast to the United States. One reason was that prudence suggested testing my handiness

with the battery-powered emergency set. But the moving reason was a hunger for familiar voices. (Byrd, 1938, p. 195)

His colleagues at main base became anxious about his fate and ultimately made the journey through the Antarctic night – they used tractors and took about 93 hours (August 7–11) to cover 123 miles – to rescue him. It was still perpetual night and there was no possibility of return until daylight came on October 11. So four men lived in the shack, 9 ft × 12 ft, for 64 days. Byrd ultimately wrote 300 pages on his experiences whilst alone, but only three pages on those last 64 days.

Alexander Selkirk

In 1708 an English privateer discovered a Scots sailor, alone, on the otherwise uninhabited Juan Fernandez Islands off the coast of Chile. This was Alexander Selkirk, who was long thought to be the model for Robinson Crusoe (Defoe, 1719). He had been marooned there for four years. The captain of the privateer reported:

> At his first coming on board us, he had so much forgot his language, for want of use, that we could scarce understand him, for he seemed to speak his words by halves. We offered him a dram, but he would not touch it, having drunk nothing but water since his being here. (Cited in Shattuck, 1980, p. 193)

Christopher Burney

These three examples are all people who accepted isolation voluntarily. Christopher Burney (*Solitary Confinement*, 1952), on the other hand, was imprisoned. He was a British Army officer, captured in 1942 whilst on a clandestine operation in occupied France. He spent 526 days in solitary confinement in prison at Fresnes, a suburb of Paris. His chief problem in captivity was how to pass the time. After the war he wrote 150 pages on his experiences in solitary, but two pages only on his removal to Buchenwald, one of the most notorious of the German concentration camps, and nothing at all on his life there. It was the solitary confinement that was traumatic.

The effects of social isolation on people's behavior, especially on their reduced ability to interact with others, are analogous to those of sensory deprivation, but less dramatic, and require a longer timescale in which to develop.

Applications of Research into Social Isolation

Social isolation, and especially the isolation of small groups of people, has been studied with reference to the manning of space craft, nuclear submarines, isolated radar and missile stations, and remote scientific outposts. Experimental studies cannot achieve the length of isolation that sometimes occurs in real life and anecdotal reports will always be important for that reason. The severe effects occur, of course, in solitary isolation, and the results from surveys of small groups are very variable. Here is one survey of behavior in small groups.

Mullin (1960) interviewed 85 members of small groups (12 to 40 members) overwintering in Antarctic scientific stations. The interviews were conducted toward the end of the winter. Mullin's conclusions are set out below and are modified here by comments (in italic) from a personal friend who has overwintered twice in the Antarctic.

1   Danger, hardship, and cold were not important stresses on the individual. (*This is true within 500 m of base where there are guide ropes, because the dangers are well known. But accidents, such as getting lost in a blizzard, do happen through disregard of safety rules.*)
2   The main problems were (a) adjustment to the group, (b) the perpetual "sameness" of the milieu, and (c) the absence of emotional gratification. (*There is boredom and having too much to do is better than having too little, so that scientists cope with this problem better than do mechanics. There are "cubby holes" where small groups will gather to pass the time. But, in truth, one's only private space is one's bunk.*)
3   Overt hostility between people is rare, because no one can afford to alienate the group. (*This again is true, but there are verbal rows which do not come to blows.*)
4   Headaches were extraordinarily common, possibly as a reaction to the suppressed aggression.
5   Insomnia was also common, but only in the winter. (*People sleep better in summer when part of the day is spent outside working, and the insomnia is probably related to the absence of a diurnal cycle.*)
6   Interviewees reported an intellectual inertia (as in sensory deprivation). Many began the winter with plans how they would use their leisure time – plans that were rarely realized.
7   Interviewees also reported impaired memory, alertness, and concentration.
8   People overate; weight gains of 20 to 30 pounds over the winter were not uncommon. (*But people lose weight again in the spring.*)

"Brainwashing"

Notwithstanding that "brainwashing" in its original sense of wiping the mind clean and reprogramming it with a different ideology is science fiction, there have been repeated attempts to coerce belief or, at least, compliance. In chapter 5 I mentioned the cases of Cardinal Mindszenty and of the UN prisoners in Korea. What was done to these people in captivity to secure their apparent compliance?

Cardinal Mindszenty

Cardinal Mindszenty was sentenced to life imprisonment in February 1949; but in October 1956 there was an uprising in Hungary. Mindszenty was momentarily released from prison and took refuge in the US embassy. He was allowed to leave Hungary some years later and ultimately published his memoirs in 1974 (Mindszenty, 1974). In that book he tells how he was broken down.

He was interrogated at night. He was beaten with a rubber truncheon when he refused to sign a confession and was not allowed to sleep. He ate little food in case it had been drugged. Under this regime his resistance was broken in about 14 days. Then came the "Mr Nice and Mr Nasty" technique. Certain of his interrogators who had previously been hostile suddenly began expressing deep sympathy with the cardinal and suggesting ways of ameliorating his likely sentence. At this point Cardinal Mindszenty was socially disoriented and unable to distinguish genuine offers of advice from bogus ones. Accordingly he wrote two letters in his own hand, one to the US ambassador to Hungary asking for an aircraft to be laid on to help him escape and a second to the Minister of Justice, confessing to every charge against him, agreeing to collaborate in the future, and suggesting that his trial was no longer necessary. Both these letters were produced at his trial (Közi-Horváth, 1979, pp. 39–49)

UN prisoners of war in Korea

In the first place UN prisoners of war in Korea were segregated by rank so that private soldiers were deprived of military leadership. In addition, spontaneous leadership, wherever it emerged amongst the prisoners, was broken up by moving the key figure elsewhere. The intention was that communist authority should be allowed to assert itself unopposed.

Access to news from outside the prison camp was permitted only through communist-approved newspapers. Private mail was censored and sometimes withheld altogether as support for the argument that the prisoners' relatives at home did not care about them. Promises were made of better conditions and earlier repatriation for those who agreed to serve on "peace committees" and to collaborate with the communists in other ways. There were compulsory indoctrination lectures, each followed by a group discussion at which the prisoners had to reach the "right" conclusion. A "wrong" conclusion – for example, that North Korea had begun the war by invading the South – was followed by a repetition of the lecture and the discussion. Finally, there was a systematic use of Chinese spies, and also of informers from within the prisoners' own ranks.

When the war was over, 21 US servicemen ultimately refused repatriation. One might read that as a modest success; but "Most men returned from prison camp expressing strong anti-communist feelings" (Schein, 1958, p. 333). It would be more appropriate to consider the mean effect on the prisoners as a whole (assuming that a "mean" can be estimated) and, on that basis, there was arguably no significant effect, except that in the absence of the constraints of American society, individual prisoners varied rather more in their reactions to Chinese propaganda than would otherwise have been the case.

The breaking up of the preexisting social structure had a substantial effect on the behavior of the prisoners. There was a breakdown of discipline amongst the US prisoners when separated from their officers and NCOs. Discipline is important to a man's very survival under such harsh prison conditions; but out of 7,190 US Army prisoners, 2,730 (38 percent) died in captivity in Korea. This is a greater proportion than in any previous war in which American soldiers have been engaged, including the War of Independence. On the other hand, out of 229 Turkish prisoners (who were Muslim), not one died. At most two (of those 229) could even be said to have collaborated. The difference was a matter of group discipline.

> I asked Colonel Perry how the Turks had reacted toward indoctrination, and he replied that they had withstood it almost one hundred per cent. Because their chain of command remained unbroken, they were able to present a completely united front to pressure, despite the fact that their officers and men were segregated like the rest of the prisoners. To illustrate this, the colonel read to me from the account of a Turkish officer's prison experience, given to one of our interrogators. "I told the Chinese commander of the camp that while we were a unit, I was in charge of my group," the Turkish officer said. "If he wanted anything done, he was to come to me, and I would see that it was done. When he removed me, the responsibility would fall not on him, but on the man next below me, and after that on the man below him. And so on, down through the ranks, until there were only two privates left. Then the senior private would be in charge. They could kill us, I told him, but they couldn't make us do what we didn't want to do. Discipline was our salvation, and we all knew it. If a Turk had responded to an order from his superiors to share his food or lift a litter the way I understand some of your men did, he would literally have had his teeth knocked in. Not by his superior, either, but by the Turk nearest to him." (Kinkead, 1960, pp. 165–6)

The breakdown of discipline amongst American prisoners of war should be compared with Milgram's Experiment 7 (p. 108) in which the experimenter gave his initial instructions and then left the room – further orders, "prods," etc. being given by telephone. In that experiment compliance was much less than in the baseline condition – 27.5 percent instead of 65. What these examples demonstrate is an acute need for human company – not just any human company, but the company of others with whom the individual has common sympathies and understandings – and the role that company plays.

FERAL CHILDREN

It has sometimes happened in the past that a child has been abandoned in the wild and has survived long enough to return to human society. Most reports of such children are little more than hearsay (Malson & Itard, 1972), but the discovery of Victor, the Wild Boy of Aveyron (in southern France), in 1800, and the subsequent attempts at his rehabilitation are exceedingly well documented. This historical case teaches us that when a child has never known human society, his reactions to social isolation are entirely different. The "need" is not a need for *any* human society but for the society (family, work group, institution – even a prison society) to which the individual has become accustomed, and that applies equally when the society is a *society of one*. That contrast with the examples set out above needs to be borne in mind throughout the rest of this chapter.

Victor

In 1797 a naked child was seen playing entirely alone in the woods of Lacaune in the département of Tarn. He was captured for the first time in a place called La Bassine but escaped for a further fifteen months. In July 1798 he was spotted in a tree by some hunters, captured once again and taken to the house of a widow in the village nearby. There he stayed for a week but managed to get away once more and according to Guiraud, a local government official, spent the long winter months in the woods. On 9 January 1800 at seven in the morning he strayed on to the road and was recaptured eight hundred metres from the village in the garden of a man named Vidal, a dyer from the district of Saint-Sernin-sur-Rance [where there is now a statue to commemorate his capture] in the département of Aveyron. On 10 January Victor was placed in the hospital at Saint-Affrique and on 4 February he was taken to Rodez where he was given his first examination by the naturalist Bonaterre who also wrote the first report about him.

The boy was about four and a half feet tall and his knee ligaments were normal. He murmured while he ate, was subject to sudden fits of anger, liked fires, slept according to the sun, tried constantly to escape and could not understand his reflection in the mirror – he always looked for the person he was sure was hiding behind the glass. The newspapers carried various stories about him and a government minister became interested in his case. Victor was taken to Paris for further studies and examined by Pinel, the most celebrated psychologist of the day. He reported that far from being a normal child deprived of all faculties by his extraordinary experiences, Victor was rather a congenital idiot exactly like the many others in the Bicêtre asylum. Itard, recently appointed consultant to the Institution des Sourds-Muets [Deaf Mutes] in the Rue Saint-Jacques, took the opposite view. He had read Locke and Condillac and was convinced that man is not "born" but "constructed." He agreed the child was an idiot but denied that this was necessarily due to a defect of birth, arguing that it might equally well be explained by his cultural loss. He hoped to disprove his opponents by awakening the boy's mind. Victor was accordingly entrusted to his care so that he might have the opportunity of demonstrating his theory.

When he first arrived at the Institute, the boy's face twitched nervously, he kept rubbing his eyes, gnashing his teeth and jumping up and down. He suffered convulsions and made constant attempts to run away. His mood swung erratically from nervous excitement to complete passivity. He loved playing in the snow and enjoyed gazing Narcissus-like into the still waters of the pond. At night he would stare long and admiringly at the moon. He was incapable of imitation and showed not the slightest interest in the other children's games, although he enjoyed setting fire to some ninepins that someone gave him. The only work he could do, and this he must have learnt at Rodez or in the wilds, was shelling beans.

The doctor was struck that, at the age of puberty, his attempts at sexual satisfaction were absolutely futile, and that he did not seem to notice sexual differences. Itard was equally struck by some of the boy's other traits. His skin, though delicate, seemed insensitive to pain: he would readily pick burning logs out of the fire. He could not smell snuff even when it was put up his nose, and paid no attention to the noise of a gun fired right behind him, although he would turn at the sound of a nut being cracked. He disliked sleeping in a bed and was able to tolerate intense cold and damp. Foul smells did not trouble him at all. He ate berries, roots and raw chestnuts and disliked sweet things, spices, spirits and wines. He loved the rain and the storm clouds which announced its coming. In short, Victor scorned the products of civilization and preferred his nature plain and simple.

His powers of concentration were very poor and the slightest movement was sufficient to distract him. He was incapable of distinguishing a picture from the object it depicted and seemed not to hear music or the sound of the human voice, though he recognized at once the sound of a chestnut being shelled. He used to sniff at everything he came across, whether it was branches and leaves, stones, soil, or flesh. He was more helpless than a chimpanzee and could neither open a door by himself nor climb on to a chair to reach what he wanted. He was as incapable of speech as an animal and uttered only a single, formless sound. Victor's backwardness was revealed unmistakably in his face. His expression would change rapidly from a sullen scowl to a curious sneer, a muscular contortion meant to be a smile. (Malson, 1972, pp. 71–3)

Victor was aged somewhere between 10 and 12 years when captured. He had been in the wild for at least three years, and probably much longer; where he came from we do not know.

Jean Itard, a young doctor in Paris, undertook to try to rehabilitate him, an attempt funded by the government. He achieved a certain amount of socialization – Victor became genuinely fond of Mme. Guérin who looked after him day to day. Victor learned to utter and to recognize some linguistic sounds, but never used language in a representative mode, as we do – he was never able to recount his previous experience, so that his origins were lost forever.

Victor's attempted rehabilitation ended in 1806, at about the age of 17. The reason for terminating that attempt casts additional light on the nature of sexual motivation (chapter 3):

But there is something in the emotional system of this young man which is even more astonishing and which defies all explanation: it is his indifference to women, in spite of all the signs and symptoms of a well-developed puberty. I have awaited this moment with great keenness, envisaging it as a source of new sensations for my pupil and of fascinating observations for myself, watching out carefully for all the preliminary phenomena of this moral crisis; every day, I waited for a breath of that universal emotion which stirs and stimulates all creatures, expecting it to move Victor in his turn and enlarge his moral existence. I have seen the arrival – or rather, the explosion – of this long-desired puberty, seen our Savage consumed by desires of an extreme violence and a fearful continuity without once realizing their purpose or feeling any form of preference for any woman. Instead of that burst of enthusiasm which urges one sex towards the other, he has shown only a sort of blind instinct, a rather indistinct preference which makes the society of women more agreeable to him than the company of men, but without actually experiencing any true emotion in this connection. I have seen him sometimes in the company of women, trying to find some solace for his feelings by sitting next to some young lady and gently squeezing her arms, hands and knees, carrying on thus until his restless desires were increased rather than calmed by these strange caresses; and then, unable to see an end to these painful emotions, suddenly change and angrily thrust aside she whom he had eagerly sought, only to turn to yet another in his search for fulfilment. One day, however, he took his endeavours a little further. After a few preliminary caresses, he took the lady by the hand and pulled her – though without violence – into a small alcove.

There, he seemed at a loss to know what to do next, his face and behaviour revealed a curious mixture of gaiety and sadness, boldness and uncertainty, and finally he tried to persuade the lady to caress him by offering her his cheeks; he walked round and round her thoughtfully and then threw his arms round her shoulders and hugged her tightly. This was all he did and the demonstrations of love came to an end, like all the others, with a burst of vexation which made him push away the object of his transitory desires. (Itard, 1972, pp. 175–6)

Itard had it wrong. He thought Victor did not know what to do with a girl. But courtship requires continued interplay between male and female. Which girl wants a husband who is half savage and cannot speak? The women in question simply did not respond to Victor in that way – and that is not at all surprising.

I was wrong to compare my pupil to an ordinary adolescent whose love for women often precedes or at least accompanies the excitement of the sex organs. This concordance of needs and desires could not possibly be found in a creature who had not been taught to distinguish between men and women and who had to rely on instinct alone to grasp the difference between them, without ever being able to usefully apply whatever knowledge he might have gained. I did not doubt but that if I had dared to reveal the secret of his anxieties and the reason for his desires to this young man I would have reaped an incalculable benefit. But on the other hand, supposing that I could have tried such an experiment, would I not have revealed to our Savage a need he would doubtless have sought to satisfy as publicly as his other needs and which would have led him into acts of great indecency? (Itard, 1972, pp. 177–8)

So, Victor's attempted rehabilitation came to an end and he spent the rest of his days quietly, as it were, in retirement. He died at the age of about 28.

Genie

One might suppose that in our present state of civilization it would be impossible for a child to grow up in isolation from all human society. Nevertheless, in 1970 a 13.5-year-old girl was discovered in Los Angeles who had been confined since the age of about 20 months in a bare upstairs room with the door shut and the curtains drawn. One member of the family entered her room just long enough to feed her baby food. She had never been toilet-trained and spent her time strapped naked to a potty-chair. Since the age of 1 year Genie had had almost no human contact and only a few magazines with pictures in them to look at. She was discovered when her mother, blind and hitherto under the father's domination, managed to escape from the family home with Genie and make contact with social services (Curtiss, 1977).

At the age of 13.5 Genie could not stand erect, walk, talk, chew solid food, or control her bodily functions. She had no language – in fact, throughout her childhood she had been systematically punished for making any noise at all – and provided certain American research workers with a seemingly ideal opportunity for testing Noam Chomsky's (Chomsky, 1965) thesis that humans have an innate biological capacity for language (a natural language) and, at the same time, Eric Lenneberg's (Lenneberg, 1967) thesis that there is a critical period ending at puberty for learning one's native language. Susan Curtiss (Curtiss, 1977) undertook the greater part of that linguistic training as a young graduate student. Under Curtiss's tuition Genie acquired a wide vocabulary of individual words, but never learned to speak ordinary grammatical English. Genie also made dramatic social progress in the first few years, but, even so, never made up for her lack of interaction with others during childhood. Then the research funding ran out, and today Genie lives in a home, under supervision.

John

Malson (1972, pp. 80–2) catalogs 53 reports of feral children, many of whom had been allegedly cared for by some wild (subhuman) species – wolves, bears, leopards, and apes. In case this sounds implausible, very many humans are attracted, in an affectionate manner, by the young of many mammalian species, this being a projection of the instinctive care which adult humans generally show for babies and very young children, especially, of course, their own. If humankind feels this way toward the young of other species, it ought not to surprise us if some of those other mammalian species sometimes display similar sentiments toward young humans. John is a recent case from a remote village about 100 miles from Kampala, Uganda.

As John tells his story (Cutler, 1999), when he was about 5 years old he ran into the jungle to escape his father who had just killed his mother. John feared that he also would have been killed. In the jungle he was taken care of by a group of monkeys who brought him food to eat, bananas especially. But there was no water – John, surprisingly, says he did not drink any water during this time. After some period of time he was discovered and restored to human society. It is near impossible to estimate how long a period of time that was, but when discovered his body, all except for his buttocks, was clothed with hair – a feature noted with other "wolf" children.

Of course, the question to be asked is: How much of this is true? The verdict of Professor Douglas Candland (Cutler, 1999) is that it is all plausible. Shown a book of pictures of different species of monkeys, John picked out a local species, green vervet monkeys. Faced with a troop of green vervet monkeys, John's reaction was quite unlike that of other Ugandan children. It is arguable that he knew, from actual experience, possibly even socialization, how to interact with them. But John has now made a happy readjustment to human society and so has little to teach us here. The critical difference with respect to Victor and Genie is that he spent his first 5 years in normal human society and acquired his native language before becoming lost in the jungle.

What May We Conclude from the Attempted Rehabilitation of These Three Children?

There is a long history of anecdotal reports of the recovery of feral children. Such children were of much interest to eighteenth-century philosophers: How much of human nature is innate and how much acquired? What is that innate nature like, and to what extent is man a "noble savage" corrupted by society? What distinguishes humans from other animals? . . . and other questions besides. Victor and Genie are the two well-recorded cases on which we might attempt to address those questions. John is another case of which the true details are still somewhat uncertain.

It is tempting to see Genie as another Victor, but that would be too simple. Both children grew up in near-isolation from human society, but there the resemblance ends. They grew up under different kinds of deprivation. After her discovery, Genie enjoyed being with other people, but Victor repeatedly tried to escape. Victor was never able to say anything about his previous feral existence, but Genie acquired enough language to tell her carers many details that they would never otherwise have known. John, by contrast, has made a near-complete readjustment to human society. This may be because his sojourn in the wild was relatively short, maybe only a few months, or it may be consequent on his initial human socialization. He had already acquired his native language. The complete absence of language – more precisely, the complete inability to acquire language after capture – does suggest that Victor was abandoned or lost at a very early age.

The most significant comparison, however, is between Victor and Genie separately and those others, brought up in ordinary human society who subsequently happened to spend long periods in near-complete isolation. Whereas Joshua Slocum, Admiral Byrd, and Christopher Burney longed for human companionship, Victor repeatedly tried to run away. So the longing is not for human society *per se*, but for the particular society to which one belongs. Each individual is a product of the society in which he or she grows up, including, in Victor's case, a society of one, and we cannot talk about human nature independent of that social background.

Communication between its members is essential to human society, and it is arguable that deafness is a greater handicap than blindness. Victor never learned to communicate (except at the crude level of a pet animal). Lenneberg's hypothesis proposing a critical period for acquisition of a first language, a period which terminates at puberty (see Newport, 1991, pp. 116–21), would explain Victor's linguistic difficulty. Genie probably heard a minimal level of speech throughout her incarceration, though she never had the opportunity to speak herself. That might account for her greater linguistic achievements relative to Victor.

Jean Itard, on the other hand, saw Victor's difficulty as the prior acquisition of a feral culture – a culture of one. For example, Victor never (so far as we know) had any opportunity to play with other children. Play is natural, not only to children but to the young of all mammalian species. The question as Itard would have formulated it is: Can an individual change his culture once he has grown up? It is difficult to adapt to a different human culture, to say the least, and perhaps impossible without language. It might be that Victor did not even see himself as human, as a member of the same biological species!

As an example, here is Victor's attitude to clothes (and I emphasize that Victor could see how other people around him dressed without the need for any verbal explanation).

> One morning, after a heavy fall of snow, as soon as he awaked, he uttered a cry of joy, leaped from his bed, ran to the window, afterwards to the door, going backwards and forwards, from one to the other, with the greatest impatience, and, at length, escaped half-dressed into the garden. There he exhibited the utmost emotions of pleasure; he ran, rolled himself in the snow, and taking it up by handfuls, devoured it with an incredible avidity. (Itard, 1972, pp. 103–4)

Victor's behavior should remind us of Kinsey's observation (p. 52) that the wearing of clothes is chiefly to do with taboos on nudity, not with keeping warm.

However, an evaluation of Victor's difficulties in socialization are hindered by not knowing anything about his origin. He may, for example, have been abandoned because he was mentally retarded or autistic. Nevertheless, the survival of a child, once abandoned, in the wild over a period of years is uncommon, and many more children who are abandoned or get lost fail to survive. So Victor's survival attests to a certain innate ability. We do not know.

We do, however, know that Genie was hidden away because her father believed her to be mentally defective. That idea of mental retardation was supported by Jay Shurley on the basis of Genie's abnormal brainwaves (Garman & Poole, 1994). If that be so, then the many tests monitoring Genie's partial rehabilitation cannot be reliably interpreted, nor extrapolated to other hypothetical cases.

But the lesson from these two children remains, that we are all of us products of our early environment to a much, much greater extent than we realize. We can identify some patterns of behavior that are manifestly acquired, and not innate, by comparing one culture with another, in the same way as (pp. 113–16) we can identify social conventions that are specific to the society. Cultural differences cannot be innate. But there may be, and probably are, more profound developmental changes during childhood which, though common to all cultures, are still dependent on social interaction. Such changes would not be identifiable from cross-cultural comparison. Only comparison with a history such as Victor's can give us even a clue as to what such developmental changes might be.

CONCLUSIONS ON SOCIAL ISOLATION

Setting aside the special cases of feral children, continued interaction with other people is needed to maintain social skills, to maintain one's language as a means of communication. I have already mentioned Alexander Selkirk; here is another.

Jacob Bronowski – mathematician, poet, inventor, playwright, latterly life-scientist – was born in Poland in 1908. He emigrated to England at the age of 13 and thereafter spoke English. At the end of his life, age 65, he wrote:

> I speak English, which I only learned at the age of thirteen; but I could not speak English if I had not before learned language. You see, if you leave a child speaking no language until the age of thirteen, then it is almost impossible for it to learn at all. I speak English because I learned Polish at the age of two. *I have forgotten every word of Polish.* (Bronowski, 1973, p. 421; italics supplied)

Social interaction is also needed for social acclimatization, to prevent boredom and social disorientation. Learning is progressive; what a child learns today depends on his or her previous state of development. A childhood spent in isolation means that the background of previous experiences which society takes for granted is lacking, and further learning may fail simply for that reason. This was Itard's argument with respect to Victor's difficulties. One might usefully look at the experiences of feral children as socialization with respect to a different society, and their difficulties as analogous to, but very much greater than, a child transported from one culture to another today.

Social isolation is unpleasant – long continued, it is exceedingly unpleasant and is used as a formal sanction by society (i.e., imprisonment) as punishment for criminal behavior. Whilst in America in 1842, Charles Dickens visited the Eastern Penitentiary in Philadelphia.

> The system here is rigid, strict, and hopeless solitary confinement. I believe it, in its effects, to be cruel and wrong.
>
> Standing at the central point, and looking down these dreary passages, the dull repose and quiet that prevails, is awful. Occasionally, there is a drowsy sound from some lone weaver's shuttle, or shoemaker's last, but it is stifled by the thick walls and heavy dungeon-door, and only serves to make the general stillness more profound. Over the head and face of every prisoner who comes into this melancholy house, a black hood is drawn; and in this dark shroud, an emblem of the curtain dropped between him and the living world, he is led to the cell from which he never again comes forth, until his whole term of imprisonment has expired. He is a man buried alive; to be dug out in the slow round of years; and in the meantime dead to everything but torturing anxieties and horrible despair.
>
> The first man I saw, was seated at his loom, at work. He had been there six years. He stopped his work when we went in, took off his spectacles, and answered freely to everything that was said to him, but always with a strange kind of pause first, and in a low, thoughtful voice. "And time goes pretty quickly?" "Time is very long, gentlemen, within these four walls!" He gazed about him . . . and in the act of doing so, fell into a strange stare as if he had forgotten something.
>
> In another cell, was a German, sentenced to five years imprisonment for larceny, two of which had just expired. He had painted every inch of the walls and ceiling quite beautifully. The taste and ingenuity he had displayed in everything were most extraordinary; and yet a more dejected, heart-broken, wretched creature, it would be difficult to imagine. I never saw such a picture of forlorn affliction and distress of mind.
>
> There was a sailor who had been there upwards of eleven years. "I am very glad to hear your time is nearly out." What does he say? Nothing. Why does he stare at his hands, and pick the flesh open upon his fingers, and raise his eyes for an instant, every now and then, to those bare walls which have seen his head turn grey? (Dickens, 1957, pp. 99–104; cited by Brownfield, 1972, pp. 22–3)

There are two quite distinct categories of isolation. There are

1 people who, after a normal upbringing in human society, happen to spend a long period of time alone, effectively isolated from all others. The effects of their isolation are reminiscent of sensory deprivation, though requiring a longer period of time to show.

> The solitary sailors . . . relate that the first days out of port are the dangerous ones; awe, humility, and fear in the face of the sea are most acute at this time. Bombard [Bombard, 1954] states that if the terror of the first week can be overcome, one can survive. Apparently, many do not survive this first period.

Many single-handed boats have not arrived at their transoceanic destination. We have clues as to the causes from what sometimes happens with two persons on such crossings. There are several pairs of ocean-crossing sailors in which one of the couple became so terror-stricken, paranoid, and bent on murder and/or suicide, that he had to be tied to his bunk. (Lilly, 1956, p. 3)

There are also

2   feral children who (very exceptionally) have somehow survived from near birth in the wild and have never known human society. Depending on the length of their isolation and the extent of their prior social development, they seem unable to make up for their lost childhood. Some socialization is achieved, but it is rarely complete.

The effects of these two categories of isolation are quite different and the comparison instructive.

The fact that people cannot tolerate social isolation for any substantial period of time – that, long continued, it becomes traumatic – suggests, as in chapter 5, the frustration of some instinctive behavior. Whether the maintenance of interaction with other people is really instinctive and whether that instinct, if such it be, is distinct from mere relief of boredom I am not at all sure. But the real importance of social isolation to the study of human motivation is its use as a sanction, not just in formal committal to prison, but spontaneously by society at large. Here, I believe, is the lever which society uses to compel a practical level of conformity from its members. That argument is the subject of the next chapter.

QUESTIONS FOR DISCUSSION

1   Why does "brainwashing" (in its practical application) work, and why are its effects not permanent?

2   Why is loneliness intolerable, and why are feral children not distressed at being alone?

9

THE MORAL SANCTION

Philip Lawrence was headmaster of St George's School, Maida Vale, London. On December 8, 1995 he intervened to protect one of his pupils who was being attacked by two youths outside the school gates. In the continuation of that attack Philip Lawrence was stabbed through the heart. Nearly a year later, October 17, 1996, Learco Chindamo was found guilty of Mr Lawrence's murder. On the following day, Philip's widow, Frances Lawrence, found herself momentarily the focus of press attention and took advantage of that moment to appeal nationally for a moral revival. Her personal manifesto appeared in national newspapers on October 21. She called specifically for a ban on combat knives of the kind which had been used to kill her husband and for "good citizenship" lessons in schools.

John Major, the then Prime Minister, and Tony Blair, then Leader of the Opposition, quickly added their public support. As the leading politicians of the day, they could not afford *not* to be seen supporting such an initiative. There was immense support from the general public as well, with the outcome that the government agreed to introduce a bill to ban combat knives, notwithstanding the difficulty of defining what is, and what is not, a "combat knife."

Now I have no wish to decry Frances Lawrence's initiative – it had a noticeable effect on the nation's conscience and she made good and effective use of her moment of attention. But the question does need to be asked: Will it work? The manifesto Frances Lawrence published was of a kind to which most other people would also subscribe – moral prescriptions proclaimed by political and religious authorities of unimpeachable integrity. But it still needs to be asked: Will it work? because, while government can find a way to make "combat knives" illegal, they cannot eliminate sharpened screwdrivers or even machetes or meat cleavers. It is not sufficient for a moral crusade to get to the 99 percent of people who abide by the law; it must get to the violent in our society – the Learco Chindamos – as well. That is the problem I address here.

THE MORAL SANCTION

How do social constraints work? What is the sanction that induces most people to conform? The burglar interviewed at the beginning of chapter 6 "earned" £300 an hour. Why do we not all turn to burglary if it pays so well? What hold does society have over the rest of us? It is now time to propose a direct answer to this question.

Legal penalties are not that answer. There are several reasons that might be cited.

1   Many crimes go undetected;
2   severe penalties do not systematically reduce crime;
3   a law which contravenes social custom – the speed limit on motorways, or the prohibition on smoking cannabis – is impossible to enforce;
4   but, chiefly, the same mechanism of social control extends to many activities which are not illegal.

The thesis of this chapter is that the ultimate penalty is extrusion from society. This is not to say that a threat of extrusion is patent on each and every occasion on which society as a whole disciplines one of its members, but, rather, that if defiance of society's requirements is pursued too far, extrusion of the deviant member results. It means that milder indications of disapproval are effective, because the threat of ultimate extrusion is latent. That latent threat is the real reason why social isolation (in the preceding chapter) is important. It is the intolerable nature of isolation that maintains social conformity.

But the operative threat is *extrusion*, the process of being excluded, not the exclusion itself. The *underclass* (Murray, 1984, 1990) is excluded from mainstream society. Its members develop their own society with their own mores and continued exclusion has little or no effect on them. So *exclusion* is not itself the operative threat. Extrusion works because society threatens to sever the individual's *existing* social ties, and that severance proves intolerable. Members of the underclass, on the other hand, have their own intragroup ties already established and find exclusion from the mainstream more than merely tolerable. It is, however, difficult to be sure when most of the evidence is anecdotal.

An Experimental Study of Extrusion

The thesis that social conformity is maintained by the threat of extrusion is not new. Schachter (1951) cites Thrasher (1927) and Sherif and Cantril (1947), who have expressed the same idea. Moreover, the thesis has been tested by experiment.

Schachter (1951; replicated by Emerson, 1964) set up some clubs for students. There were four different kinds of club, but the differences need not concern us

Table 9.1 Assignment of confederates to committees in the experiment by Schachter (1951)

Confederate	Opinion		Percentage assigned to . . .		
		Consensus	Executive	Steering	Correspondence
"Mode"		●	30.7	42.8	26.5
"Deviate"	●		23.9	28.1	47.8
"Slider"	○ ⟶	●	35.1	30.2	34.7

here. Each club consisted of five to seven students together with three paid participants, confederates of the experimenter, who pretended to be ordinary students like
the other members of the club. The clubs were set to review the case of "Johnny
Rocco," a juvenile delinquent awaiting sentence for a minor crime. In the discussion
of what should be done with him, one of the paid participants, the "mode," took
a position corresponding to the consensus of the real participants. Another paid
participant, the "deviate," took an extreme disciplinarian position, as deviant from
the rest of the participants as possible, while the third, the "slider," started out as
the "deviant" did, but allowed himself to be persuaded to the consensus position.
At the end of the meeting, each member of the club was asked to nominate colleagues
for membership of three committees to carry forward the work of the club, the
Executive Committee, to select topics for future discussion, the Steering Committee,
to prepare discussion materials, and the Correspondence Committee, the least prestigious of the three. The total number of committee members required was such
that each member had to nominate every other member to exactly one committee.
Then the meeting was brought to an end by explaining that this was not a meeting
of a club at all, but an experiment.

The purpose of the experiment was to see to which committees the three paid
participants would be assigned, and the results are set out in table 9.1. The "deviate"
was mostly nominated for the Correspondence Committee, the least prestigious of
the three. The "deviate" was also the least preferred of the three in a sociometric
ranking. These findings match the anecdotal examples which follow. But it cannot
be emphasized too strongly that what was achieved in this experiment is but a
very pale reflection of what happens in the world outside the laboratory. It would
not be valid to extrapolate to the situations we shall meet below; and I press
this point, not as a criticism of Schachter's (and Emerson's) skill as experimenters,
but as a comment on the intrinsic limitations of laboratory research into social
structures.

It is often not feasible to set up an experiment that matches what is observed to happen in the real world. Even if some way were found to keep an experimental society in being for long enough without the behavior of its members being compromised by the fact of the society being experimental (cf. Orne, 1962), the experimental manipulations required would certainly be deemed unethical by today's criteria. The argument in this chapter therefore rests chiefly on anecdote, and I present a variety of stories to support different facets of my thesis.

Whistleblowers

Extrusion of the deviant from society is shown most simply by the treatment of "whistleblowers." A whistleblower is someone who deliberately brings malpractice to public notice, usually by telling the press or a regulatory authority where to look and what to look for. Here are some examples.

Graham Pink

Graham Pink was a charge nurse on a geriatric ward at Stepping Hill Hospital, Greater Manchester.

> [He] was sacked because he breached the confidentiality of a dying elderly patient during a campaign to increase hospital staffing, an industrial tribunal was told.
>
> Charge nurse Graham Pink, 63, had written a "torrent of words" in letters up to and including the Prime Minister in his campaign over night nursing levels on geriatric wards in Stepping Hill Hospital, Stockport, Greater Manchester, John Hand QC, for Stockport Health Authority, said.
>
> Mr Pink had appeared in newspaper articles and on television. But Mr Hand told the hearing in Manchester, where Mr Pink is claiming unfair dismissal, that he had told a newspaper of an incident concerning a dying patient in such a way that it had identified him to his friends and relatives and caused "great distress."
>
> Mr Hand said that Mr Pink, a night charge nurse on three geriatric wards, had presented a "lurid and negative picture" of working life on the wards. "He has complained that he was dismissed because of this campaign."
>
> But Mr Hand told the tribunal: "The respondent's case is that Mr Pink was dismissed because, in the course of his campaign, he breached the fundamental principle of patient confidentiality." (*Independent*, 1993)

The merits of Graham Pink's case are unclear. After 10 days of the hearing (and £90,000 costs), Stockport Health Authority abandoned its defense and conceded £11,000 damages, which was the maximum that the industrial tribunal could award for unfair dismissal.

There is an implicit conflict in the National Health Service (NHS) between management, who are concerned, above all, with containing costs (which means limiting the numbers of staff), and the staff, who see themselves burdened, at times, with more work than they can cope with, so that standards of patient care suffer. There are many NHS employees who are concerned about standards of health care and any complaint they make about those standards implicitly challenges manage-ment, who are responsible for providing the resources. But staff cannot be dismissed merely for complaining; so management look for some other pretext for dismissal that, in another employee, one who has not complained, would be overlooked.

Stephen Bolsin

Stephen Bolsin used to be a consultant anesthetist at the Bristol Royal Infirmary. His experience shows that Graham Pink's dismissal had nothing to do with his being relatively lowly in the health service.

Two senior cardiac surgeons at the Bristol Royal Infirmary, James Wisheart and Janardan Dhasmana, had a quite unacceptable record of failures in operations intended to correct birth defects in babies' hearts. Their unit's mortality rate was much in excess of the national average. The problem was that James Wisheart was "so painstakingly slow that babies were often left for up to five hours on heart bypass machines, often causing complications that would kill them; while Janardan Dhasmana was too new at the switch operations [an operation to interchange the arteries of the heart in a baby born with them back to front] to be fully competent" (Barrowclough, 2000). The poor performance of these doctors was widely known in medical circles. But there is a longstanding culture in medicine that you do not criticize other doctors' performance. Nevertheless, Stephen Bolsin went to the General Medical Council and, after the longest hearing in its history, James Wisheart was struck off the medical register and Janardan Dhasmana was dismissed from his post. As for Stephen Bolsin, the only post that he could obtain was at Geelong Hospital in Australia.

> I think you should know that you are employing one of the most hated anaes-thetists in Europe. (Barrowclough, 2000, p. 3)

PC Adrian Dart

Adrian Dart was a young probationary police constable based at Longbridge in Birmingham. On his second day on duty he arrested Junior Patrick Williams, a West Indian worker at the British Leyland car plant, on suspicion of stealing material from the plant. It was Adrian Dart's first arrest. He took Mr Williams back to Longbridge police station and handed him over to Detective Sergeant Brian Morton and two other detectives. They took Williams into an interview room from where, a few moments later, PC Dart heard sounds of disturbance. He could hear Williams crying and someone shouting, "Admit you did it." This was followed by sounds of banging and slapping and more sobbing. When the door opened, DS Morton emerged half carrying Williams whose face was covered in blood. Inside the room the other detectives, DCs Martin Lambert and Graham Stephen, were wiping blood off the floor. One of them shouted to Dart to get out of the station. When he came back on duty, PC Dart reported the incident to his sergeant. He was immediately transferred to another station, Belgrave Road three miles away. A few weeks later he was transferred again, this time to Smethwick. PC Dart persisted with his complaint, however, and the matter was eventually taken up by the Police Complaints Department at Lloyd House. According to PC Dart, there were three other policemen on duty at Longbridge who witnessed the incident but each of them returned what are known as negative statements. They had heard nothing and seen nothing. PC Dart was on his own.

As a result of PC Dart's action, DS Morton and the other detectives were suspended from duty and charged with assault. From that moment on, PC Dart was an outcast. Only two of the twenty or so officers on his shift at Smethwick would speak to him. When he went into the canteen, other officers would get up and walk away. On one occasion, in the toilet, one young officer apologised for not speaking to him. He was a Panda car driver and he did not want to be put back on the beat, he said.

As the trial got nearer, the harassment intensified. PC Dart's car, parked outside the station, was damaged. Inside the station his locker was broken open with a crowbar and his clothes stolen. He started receiving hate mail. Someone stuck his picture on a wall and drew a noose around his neck. Underneath was the caption, "If all else fails . . ." (Mullin, 1986, pp. 220–1)

That harassment extended to PC Dart's work and even included senior officers.

In November, 1983, DS Morton and DCs Lambert and Stephen were found guilty of assaulting Junior Patrick Williams. PC Dart gave evidence against them. Morton was sentenced to one year's imprisonment, half of it suspended. The others received six months each, half suspended.

Three months after Morton was sentenced, PC Dart resigned from the police force. "I couldn't stand the harassment any longer," he says. (Mullin, 1986, p. 222)

The police, in particular, form a closed subsociety. It is only too easy for them to get away with a wide variety of irregularities provided none of them bears witness against his or her fellows. Any police officer who cannot be trusted not to testify in that way is forced out.

Jim Smith

Jim Smith was part-time financial director of Aish & Co. of Poole, Dorset, who are specialist naval and marine electrical and electronic engineers. He was dismissed in June 1981. "I was made to leave the company premises in the middle of a board meeting at the very point in time when I would not ratify the company's accounts because they sought to conceal excess profits on government contracts" (Committee of Public Accounts, 1986, p. 44). Aish & Co. subsequently repaid £400,000 excess profits to the Ministry of Defence (MoD). Jim Smith sued for unfair dismissal, but lost the case. As of 1987, Jim Smith was still out of work (Elliott & Kiley, 1987).

When there is only one company with the technical expertise needed to carry out the work, MoD contracts are offered on a "cost plus" basis, which means that the company is entitled to recover its costs plus an overhead which varies from 6.4 to 12.5 percent. That kind of contract provides a company with an opportunity to charge work done for other customers to the MoD as well, thereby receiving payment twice over. The MoD is meant to check the costing of such contracts, but where do you look for fraud? The whistleblower tells the MoD where to look and what to look for.

The House of Commons Public Accounts Committee, especially Dale Campbell-Savours MP, is concerned about fraudulent applications of public money. But the MoD seems not to want to know. After all, such knowledge would sour the relationship with the client company, and if there is no other company with the technical expertise to carry out the work (as often there is not in this kind of case), the MoD is left with a problem.

Other people outside of the Public Accounts Committee also do not want to get involved. Mr Smith contacted the MoD through private contacts immediately on his dismissal in June 1981. But Aish & Co. say that it was the company itself which first revealed to the MoD the details of the excess profits in May 1982. Officials from the MoD, speaking individually, do not support Mr Smith's story. They do not dispute their meetings with Mr Smith on specified dates in 1981, but typically say that the matter of excess profits was not raised at those meetings (Committee of Public Accounts, 1986, p. 34).

Social conventions in business and conventions in the world outside, especially in the Public Accounts Committee, are different to the point of being in conflict. The whistleblower resolves that conflict in favor of the outside world. Thereafter, no business will employ him – he is an "industrial grass."

Examples from the Wider Society

Whistleblowing occurs within industrial or commercial or administrative organizations with a formal hierarchical structure of management. Although such cases fit well into the thesis of extrusion as the ultimate social sanction, they could also be seen as some senior manager exacting a purely personal revenge. So I turn now to cases from wider society where there is no formal hierarchical structure and the "revenge" interpretation of that society's counteraction is hardly tenable.

Megan's Law

Pedophiles at large in the community present a continuing threat to young children. The case of Colin Hatch (p. 49) has already been recounted. In July 1994 Megan Kanka, aged 7, was raped and killed by a twice-convicted pedophile who had settled just across the road in her street in Hamilton Township, New Jersey. The people of Hamilton Township were outraged. A petition was begun within 24 hours of Megan's death; 7,500 attended a vigil five days later; the petition attracted 400,000 signatures within the space of three months; and "Megan's Law" passed through the New Jersey legislature just 89 days after she died. Megan's Law provides that communities should be told of any convicted pedophile living in their vicinity and that convicted pedophiles should be recorded in a public register. "If a paedophile is living on my street, I want to know," says Mrs Kanka. "If I had known they were there, I could have warned my daughter, and she would be alive today" (Catliff, 1997a, b). Some people ask that pedophiles should also be identified in Britain. Let us see what would happen.

> A convicted paedophile was moved to a secret address under police guard yesterday after demonstrators besieged the hostel where he was staying.
> Alan Christie, 50, with an anorak covering his head, was escorted by two CID officers from his DSS [Department of Social Security] bed-and-breakfast accommodation on a rundown Stirling estate. A cordon of six police officers protected him from the crowd. As he was driven away, lying under a blanket on the back seat of the car, about 50 women chanted: "Beast out, beast out." (English, 1997)

On July 1, 2000, Sarah Payne, aged 8, was abducted from a field behind her grandparents' home at Kingston Gorse, Sussex. The search for her rapidly achieved national attention, with nightly broadcasts on television news and her photograph (showing a very appealing 8-year-old) in the national press. But, sadly, her body was found two weeks later in a shallow grave 12 miles away. While Britain does have a register of pedophiles, it is not open to public inspection. The *News of the World*, a national Sundays-only newspaper, sought to remedy this defect by publishing details of known sex offenders. Its campaign of "naming and shaming" convicted pedophiles was subsequently withdrawn after continued and very public pressure. But the event that finally led to the ending of that campaign is of particular interest.

The Paulsgrove estate houses about 16,000 people on the northern fringes of Portsmouth. Night after night in August 2000, about five weeks after Sarah Payne's death, there was a march of about 150 people, mothers, families, young children, some in baby carriages and strollers, shouting "What do we want?" "Paedophiles out!" Two registered sex offenders on the estate simply disappeared. In addition, four innocent families had to flee and another family came back from holiday to find that their car had been firebombed. The marchers are not accurately informed. But they are generally unrepentant and, so long as they continue marching, the authorities have to do something (Reid, 2000). To put the matter succinctly, pedophiles are not going to be allowed to live on the Paulsgrove estate.

Kelly Turner

Kelly Turner from Barking, in Essex, had once had a boyfriend, Nicky Fuller, whom she had dumped after three days. Two weeks later . . .

> Nicky (who hadn't given up hanging around) boasted to Kelly that he "had beaten up a Paki." Kelly thought he was only trying to impress her. But then she saw television pictures of the bloodied, swollen face of Muktar Ahmed, who had been attacked by a gang of white youths in the East End, one Tuesday night . . . and was critically ill in the London Hospital (and whose face, two years on, is still a mess). (Bedell, 1996)

Kelly went to the police.

> Even now, when Nicky Fuller has been convicted and has served his sentence, . . . opinions are divided on the pavement outside Kelly's old school as to whether she did the right thing. A girl called Elizabeth, who was a year below Kelly and is now doing GCSEs, said: "It was completely out of order what she done. I wouldn't shop my boyfriend." An overgrown boy of the same age, spotty in his West Ham scarf, was keen to find reasons to exonerate Fuller. "It depends why he did it. If his sister had been the victim of a race attack . . ."
>   "She hadn't."
>   "No, but if she had, it would have been wrong to go to the police."
>
> One of Kelly's middle-aged neighbours has refused to speak to her since she went to the police. She has been beaten up, threatened, abused. The family's dog was fed meat spiked with glass.

The attack on Muktar Ahmed was racially motivated. One might therefore expect that social reaction would divide on racial lines. But Kelly Turner had transgressed another convention that transcends even the racial divide. In the kind of society in which she lived no one goes to the police. The police are "them" and we, all of us, are "us."

> In the eight months between the attack and Nicky's trial, Kelly was subjected to a venomous campaign of abuse. Asian people as well as white apparently thought her guilty of some appalling act of near miscegenation: there was a series of silent and heavy-breathing telephone calls which were traced to an Asian man; at school, Kelly says she was called "slag, bitch, wolf's meat, Paki-lover, whore. People would say: 'Are you going up Barking to see some monkeys?' I got beaten up in the toilets twice. A girl threatened to get petrol and set light to me."

There were death threats over the telephone, sometimes from a man, sometimes a woman. . . . Kelly was followed in Romford by one of the boys who hung around with Nicky, who told her he knew where she went and who she was with. A boy at school – a black boy, oddly enough – beat her up in the classroom after telling her that she shouldn't have grassed on her boyfriend. Other pupils had to drag him off. His girlfriend later pulled out a knife, stabbed it into the paintwork, and said that if Kelly had been there she would have stuck it in her. (Bedell, 1996)

Anne and Daniel Wiseman

Orthodox Jews take a similar stance toward the police. Anne and Daniel Wiseman (these are not their real names) used to employ Eli Cohen, aged 17, as babysitter for Debbie (aged 5) and Thomas (10). The children revealed that Cohen had been abusing them, sexually, while the parents were out in the evenings. Now orthodox Jews do not involve the secular authorities in their affairs. So Mrs Wiseman went to the rabbis, demanding that Cohen be sent out of the community. The rabbis, one rabbi in particular, refused to take any action, and eventually the Wisemans went to the police. Here is how the orthodox community reacted.

It started with hate mail to Anne and Daniel and continued with death threats to members of her family. The community began to take sides – but precious few sided with the people they regarded as *moisers*. "Many people we considered friends ostracised us," Anne said. "Some shops refused to serve me. It was astonishing. I'd walk down the street with Debbie, and other mothers would run out of their houses and drag their children in. Women would pinch their noses and hold their heads in the air as I walked past. Several walked up to Debbie and said she was an evil liar."

Two weeks ago [re August 11, 1991], when Eli Cohen was sentenced to six months' youth custody (later reduced to 12 months' probation by the Court of Appeal), the family were subjected to a riot outside their home. More than 250 people emerged at *motzei shabbos*, the ending of the Sabbath, and gathered outside chanting "Get out of town!" and, predictably, "*Moisers!*"

A brick came through the window. Large numbers of police arrived as eggs were thrown and CS gas canisters let off. Wearily, Daniel says: "It was very frightening."

Hinda Style, the independent counsellor, went to offer her support when Daniel called her. They were concerned because Anne had gone to a friend's house to take some night-clothes for Debbie, who, they thought, would be safer out of the way.

"On the way back," Mrs Style says, "Anne called us on the car phone. She had broken down and a mob of about 35 people had spotted her and surrounded the car. It was awful. Daniel has an open phone that we could all hear, and we heard people hitting the car, trying to smash the windows to get to Anne.

"It was horrible. We could hear Anne screaming as it was happening. The police got there in time and rescued her, but she believes – and I can't really disagree – that they would have killed her if they'd got into the car." That was when they were put into a police safe house. (Boggan, 1991)

It is understandable that the more tightly knit a community is, the more distinctly its members see themselves as different from the wider society around them, the more stringent are that community's demands on its members. That greater stringency is needed to maintain the distinctiveness of the community. It is also understandable that when those demands are transgressed, the counterreaction is correspondingly fiercer. Coalmining communities in South Wales provide another example.

John and Joy Watson

Members of trades unions do not cross picket lines, not their own, nor any other union's. Miners in South Wales who flouted this convention during the 1984–5 strike faced extrusion from their community, not just from their union, but from the entire community within which they lived. John Watson was one such. His wife, Joy, was interviewed on television, just after the strike had ended, in a program on recriminations within the mining community (Lewis, 1985).

(*View of graffiti on a house wall*: "DEATH TO WATSON SCAB."
Crowd shouting: "Scabby bastard!" and "Dirty rotten..."
outside Aberdare colliery, March 1985. Mrs Watson leaving colliery. Her car is pelted with bricks and stones which break the car near-side window and shatter the windscreen.)

Reporter: This is Mrs Watson. Her husband worked during the strike. She had just dropped him off at the plant in the first week after the strike ended.

Mrs Watson: I wouldn't like to think that we'd always have to live as we are today. We're not happy, and we wish that we could make amends to these people in some way. But they don't seem to accept that we also have a right to our opinion.

Reporter: Do you regret what your husband did?

Mrs Watson: No, not at all. I don't regret it one little bit. I'm rather proud of what he's done; we would do it again. (Lewis, 1985)

John and Joy Watson eventually moved house, away from South Wales.

Angelina Mavrides

Finally, an example which shows that the moral sanction transcends even families' loyalties. An Austrian tourist went for a night-time stroll in London in the autumn of 1996. She was attacked by a gang of youths beside the Regent's canal.

> At least two of the gang were high on drugs: their victim was forcibly stripped, kicked and punched in the head and repeatedly raped by each of them while they chanted "f*** the white bitch." After an hour she was asked if she could swim and, sensing a chance to escape, she said no. The boys threw her into the canal. . . . She swam to the far bank and cried for help, naked, shivering and bleeding. (Driscoll, 1999)

The gang's swift arrest was due to Angelina Mavrides whose own son, just 16, was one of them. She sent a message to the police.

> Angelina has lost her home, her friends and any hope of civilised relations with her former husband. She has been spat on, sent hate mail and threatened with a knife.
> She was grabbed in a telephone box outside her home shortly after the arrests; a knife was held to her throat and she was told that if she testified, she would die. (Driscoll, 1999)

SOME INTERIM CONCLUSIONS ON EXTRUSION

Extrusion from society – from work in both the formal sense of being dismissed and the social sense of being sent to Coventry, from religious community and from the neighborhood, even from the family – is sometimes applied as a sanction against those who flout social conventions. The "sometimes" needs emphasis since the anecdotes recounted here represent the extremes of human social reaction. Much more often, milder expressions of pressure achieve the conformity that is demanded. But these stories do suggest that the effective moral sanction which binds individual members into the social fabric is ultimately the threat of extrusion.

1 Extrusion is Spontaneous

In some instances at least – the marches on the Paulsgrove estate in Portsmouth – the social reaction appears to be spontaneous. Here is another.

On February 12, 1993, whilst his mother was momentarily distracted, James Bulger, aged 2, was led away from the Strand shopping precinct, Bootle, by two 10-year-old boys and murdered. The circumstances of the murder evoked great revulsion in the local community. A security video revealed that James's abductors had been young boys, leading to a search for possible juvenile perpetrators.

> A boy aged 12 [not one of the two abductors] whose arrest in connection with the abduction and murder of James Bulger sparked off a minor riot was in hiding last night after being released by Merseyside police.
>
> Detectives said that the boy, who was arrested at his home in Kirkdale, Liverpool, on Tuesday night, had been eliminated from the inquiry.
>
> Local anger over the killing is so intense that the boy will not be returning to the house where he was arrested. To ensure their safety he and his family have been moved to a secret address.
>
> A crowd of eighty people gathered outside the house on Tuesday and there were shouts of "murderer" as he was taken away with a blanket over his head into one of a convoy of eight police vans. (Bennet & MacKinnon, 1993)

Another example comes from prison society. The prisoners are unrelated and initially unacquainted with each other; there is no preexisting social structure. But prison society soon sorts itself out. Here is part of an interview with a serial rapist, but a man who attacks adult women, not children.

> *Interviewer:* Rapists who volunteer for treatment can feel physically at risk. Inside prison, there is a perverse hierarchy, where bank robbers and burglars are at the top, and sex offenders at the bottom. And the lowest of the low are the child sex offenders, subject to attack from all.
>
> *Rapist:* On the course that I did [voluntary therapy sex offenders] – I did two courses – on the first one, the breakdown was that there were eight offenders, of whom seven were offenders against children, and me.
>
> *Interviewer:* Did that worry you before you joined the course?
>
> *Rapist:* Somewhat. It worried some other people so much that they would not in fact join the course. While on the wing I was actually serving on this was comparatively mild, in the prison system as a whole, the prejudice against offenders against children is so strong that one is liable to be attacked for associating with them or even working with them. In some prisons it would simply be physically impossible or just very, very dangerous to do it. (Burge, 1996)

Sex offenders, especially child sex offenders, are extruded even from prison society. That not only suggests that extrusion from society is the effective moral sanction, but that it is possibly instinctive. Certainly the effects of long-term social isolation (see chapter 8) are sufficiently unpleasant for it to work as a sanction.

2 Moral Constraints are Subconscious

One might suppose the ethics of this course of action or that to be a matter of conscious deliberation, but that appears not to be so. Brigadier Marshall was an intrepid military historian of World War II, observing the conduct of infantrymen in battle first hand, in both the European and Central Pacific theaters of war.

> ... we found that on an average not more than 15 per cent of the men had actually fired at the enemy positions or personnel with rifle, carbines, grenades, bazookas, BARs, or machine guns during the course of an entire engagement. Even allowing for the dead and wounded, ... the figure did not rise above 20 to 25 per cent of the total for any action. (Marshall, 1947, p. 54)

Here is one particular example from Marshall's research.

> In the attack along the Carentan Causeway [in Normandy] during the night of June 10th, 1944 [four days after D-Day], one battalion of the 502nd Parachute Infantry was strung out along a narrow defile which was totally devoid of cover and where throughout the night the men were fully exposed to enemy bullet-fire from positions along a low ridge directly in front of them. The ridge was wholly within their view and running off at a slight angle from the line of advance of the column, so that the Americans were strung out anywhere from 300 to 700 yards from the enemy fire positions.
>
> In this situation the commander, Lieutenant Colonel Robert G. Cole ... was able to keep moving up and down along the column despite a harassing fire, and observe the attitude of all riflemen and weapons men. This was his testimony, given in the presence of the assembled battalion: "I found no way to make them continue fire. Not one man in twenty-five voluntarily used his weapon. There was no cover; they could not dig in. Therefore their only protection was to continue a fire which would make the enemy keep his head down. They had been taught this principle in training. They all knew it very well. But they could not force themselves to act upon it. When I ordered the men who were right around me to fire, they did so. But the moment I passed on, they quit. I walked up and down the line yelling, 'God damn it! Start shooting!' But it did little good. They fired only while I watched them or while some other officer stood over them." (Marshall, 1947, p. 72)

The first of those reports was cited by Hebb (1955, p. 251), in his historic paper on motivation, as an example of the "paralysis of terror." But, in truth, the second episode is much more reminiscent of Milgram's Experiment 7 in which the experimenter gave his initial instructions in person and then left the room. Compliance was now less, and several participants were found to be giving shocks at a lower level than they had been instructed to do. But if the experimenter returned to the laboratory, he could often reimpose his authority. That comparison with Milgram's work makes the problem on the Carentan Causeway sound as though the order to fire is opposed by some moral imperative. The same idea is suggested by the following incident that Marshall observed in the Pacific theater of operations.

> In the 184th Infantry Regiment's sector during the Kwajalein battle, we saw two objects floating by, 200 yards out in the lagoon. They looked like the heads of swimming men. From forwards of us, there was a spattering of fire which kicked up the water around the objects. The riflemen close around me – there were about ten of them – held their fire. I then turned my field glasses over to them, saying: "Take a look and you will see that those men are wasting their ammunition on blocks of wood." They did so, and within a few seconds they were all firing like mad at the objects. (Marshall, 1947, p. 77)

This also suggests that infantrymen do not use their weapons in case they kill someone! And that suggestion is confirmed by the following remark.

> Line commanders pay little attention to the true nature of this mental block. They take it more or less for granted that if the man is put on such easy terms with his weapon in training that he "loves to fire," this is the main step toward surmounting the general difficulty. But it isn't as easy as that. A revealing light is thrown on this subject through the studies by Medical Corps psychiatrists of the combat fatigue cases in the European Theater. They found that fear of killing, rather than fear of being killed, was the most common cause of battle failure in the individual. (Marshall, 1947, p. 79)

The most plausible reading of Marshall's observations is that moral imperatives ("Thou shalt not kill") are not set aside in war. In fact, they hinder the fighting. It is easy to see that a conscious consideration of the moral issue would deliver a quite different result and this operation of the moral imperative has to be subconscious. Of course, the force of that moral constraint is different for different individuals and Marshall's observations relate to conscripted men. Certain infantrymen do fire their rifles in battle (the same ones each time), while certain others do not. By selecting those men who use their weapons without that moral restraint, one can assemble a much more effective fighting force. The Special Air Service (SAS) and Special Boat Service (SBS) are effective because all their men fight.

A similar lesson may be drawn from the experience of mixing men and women in combat. "The British army still keeps women out of combat – with the frequently quoted rationale of the experience of the Israelis who, apparently, found that men would stop fighting in order to look after women wounded in battle. Good chivalry, bad warfare" (Cotton, 1997).

All this suggests that moral imperatives act subconsciously; they are precognitive and for that reason cannot be taught in school like other subjects. They are "motivation," not "knowledge."

3 The Sanction of Extrusion is Powerful

The ultimate threat of extrusion from society supports social conventions in all domains of social life; in particular, it modifies behavior driven by more obvious kinds of motivation like sex. In chapter 3 I argued that sexual behavior is quasi-mechanical. Most men do not habitually force their female partners, though the men of Pitcairn Island (population 44) are reported to be an exception (d'Antal, 2001). That restraint is a matter of social convention, because it applies differently in different societies. In Bangladesh a man whose proposal of marriage is not accepted revenges the slight to his masculine honor in a truly horrific manner. He goes to a garage and buys a can of sulfuric acid – and not for his car battery either. There is an Acid Survivors Foundation rehabilitation center in Dhaka, caring for the women who, after an acid attack, are cast out by society. More than 200 acid attacks were recorded in 1998 (Farrell, 2000). Such behavior is possible only because the society tolerates it. Ordinarily the threat of extrusion constrains courtship behavior within acceptable social limits. That threat must therefore have a power comparable to more obvious motivations like sex and is, arguably, itself instinctive, quasi-mechanical in operation like other motivations.

4 The Underclass

If extrusion from society is the ultimate moral sanction, then, for those already extruded, extrusion is no longer a sanction and social control is lost. Those people already extruded from mainstream society form the "underclass," a concept introduced by Charles Murray.

> By underclass I do not mean people who are merely poor, but people at the margins of society, unsocialised and often violent. The chronic criminal is part of the underclass, especially the violent chronic criminal. So are parents who mean well but who cannot provide for themselves, who give nothing back to the neighbourhood and whose children are the despair of the teachers who have to deal with them. (Murray, 2000)

A good example is this 11-year-old joyrider in Hartlepool.

Reporter:	At half past ten this morning, Norman Watson was opening the gate of his corner house, on Hartlepool's West View Estate. Suddenly, there was a screech of brakes and a stolen car ploughed through the fence a few feet from where he was standing. At the wheel was the eleven-year-old boy; in hot pursuit, the police.
Mr Watson:	He was at the wheel. I saw him – the first thing I saw him – trying to get the wheel round, you know, to get round the corner, but obviously he couldn't get it round far enough – too small.
Reporter:	Minutes later, there was a cheer from the gang of youths and swaggering along the road came the eleven-year-old joyrider. Word had spread fast. He was now something of a hero. After an hour and a half at the local police station, he'd been summoned for aggravated "taking without the owner's consent" to the Juvenile Panel and then released. Now he was free, back at the scene of the crime, and apparently blaming the police.
As the youngster was patted on the back, the older youths openly admitted that many of them were TWOCers and arrogantly refused to accept that there was anything wrong with it.
Boy:	Them joyriders. And the only reason we're joyriders is because there's nowt else better for the kids to do, so they're pinching cars. There's no work for the kids round here.
Another boy:	You get a real buzz out of it, man, a good buzz! (Network North, 1993)

Another example is Lee Ridley.

> Last summer [1992], the chairman of the Newport Juvenile Bench collared one young delinquent – Lee Ridley, a local boy with dozens of convictions – on the courtroom steps.
> "What do you do it for? It's pointless. We see you in court week after week. Why can't you stop?"
> "Because it's boring here," the 15-year-old replied. "What the fuck else is there to do?" (Cohen & Durham, 1993)

Finally, there was a 13-year-old in Sunderland who had stolen more than 200 cars in two years (Qualtrough, 1993). This boy, still so thin and small that he needed a cushion to see over the steering wheel of the cars he hijacked, was blamed for half of the then recent car thefts in Sunderland, including 40 in one weekend.

Police attempts to arrest him are complicated by a network of tiny spies, some as young as 7, who advise him when and where to flee. When the police do catch him, they can only bring him before the magistrates who can then only send him to a remand home from which he immediately absconds. His other offenses include assault, theft, robbery, and burglary.

The underclass have their own social conventions, just like other subgroups in our society, and judicial sanctions against juvenile delinquency do not work, because a law in conflict with social convention cannot be enforced. Learco Chindamo comes from the underclass. Frances Lawrence's moral crusade is not going to reach people such as Learco Chindamo. It is essential, first, to reintegrate the underclass back into society at large.

This chapter completes a sequence of four that have explained what social conventions are, with many examples of what they achieve. Purely "animal" instincts like eating, drinking, sex, and fear would elicit near-mechanical responses except for their modification by social constraint. Extrusion from society is the ultimate sanction that forces conformity with convention and is what makes human society civilized. But, while the ultimate sanction from which social conventions derive their power and authority has been identified, we have yet to examine the process by which that power is realized – to put it simply, how conventions operate in human society. Such an insight is provided by a series of inspired experiments by Solomon Asch.

QUESTIONS FOR DISCUSSION

1 How are social conventions maintained in human societies?

2 Why do so many infantrymen not use their weapons in battle?

3 Can moral rules be ascertained by reasoned argument?

10

PEER PRESSURE

Our social lives are lived within a web of social conventions that constrain nearly everything we do. The ultimate sanction which gives society this power over us is extrusion – those who deviate too much from the requirements and expectations of people around them are simply ejected from the web. But how do social conventions actually exercise their power? How do they function on the small scale, at the level of personal interaction? These are questions that can be addressed, in part, in light of a remarkable series of experiments by Solomon Asch (1952, chap. 16; 1956, 1958). Asch's experiments establish some of the ground rules according to which people influence one another. They show that the influence exerted by a concerted group of people on another person can be very powerful indeed. The experiments are cruel; they would probably not pass ethical scrutiny today. But the social applications that these experiments illumine are, some of them, even more cruel, and the lessons from Asch's research have yet to be absorbed.

SOCIAL CONFORMITY

Asch's experiment is best introduced by means of his instructions.

> This is a task involving the discrimination of lengths of lines. Before you is a pair of cards [figure 10.1 shows a sample pair]. On the left is a card with one line; the card at the right has three lines differing in length; they are numbered 1, 2, and 3, in order. One of the three lines at the right is equal to the standard line at the left – you will decide in each case which is the equal line. You will state your judgment in terms of the number of the line. There will be 18 such comparisons in all.
>   As the number of comparisons is few and the group small [about eight], I will call upon each of you in turn to announce your judgments, which I shall record here on a prepared form. Please be as accurate as possible. Suppose you give me

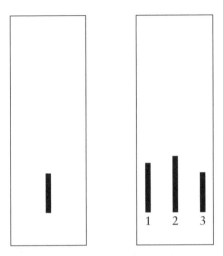

Figure 10.1 A pair of stimulus cards in Asch's experiment.

your estimates in order, starting at the right in the first row, proceeding to the left, and then going to the second row. (Asch, 1956, p. 4)

The first two rounds of judgments are uneventful. The decisions to be announced are obvious; surely, no one would ever get it wrong! Figure 10.1 displays the stimulus cards for the third round. Looking at these cards, the first participant to announce his judgment says "1." The second participant also says "1"; the third likewise, and then the fourth, fifth, and sixth participants – they all say "1." Imagine that you are the next participant to announce your judgment: What would you say?

What you do not know is that all the other participants in the experiment, the first six and the eighth, are confederates of the experimenter who have been instructed to give the same wrong answer on certain critical rounds, though not on every round. The point of the experiment is the behavior of the one critical participant (in seventh position). Will he go with the unanimous, but wrong, majority, or will he hold out and give the correct answer (which is, of course, "3")?

Out of the 18 rounds of judgments in the experiment, 12 were critical; these were the rounds on which the experimenter's confederates all gave the same wrong answer. There were 123 uninstructed participants, tested one at a time in company with an instructed majority. Their average number of errors (out of 12) was 4.4; that is, the uninstructed (critical) participants followed the wrong majority response 37 percent of the time. That percentage of errors was in no way due to the difficulty of the judgments because a control group of 37 uninstructed participants tested alone (without the confederate majority) made only three errors between them out of a total of 444 (0.7 percent). The 4.4 average errors were due to the pressure of majority opinion. (These results and others to come are summarized in table 10.5 at the end of the chapter.)

The miners' strike, 1984–5

It might be tempting to suppose that the opposition of an isolated individual by a concerted majority, as in Asch's experiments, is something that happens only in a contrived laboratory experiment; but that would be wrong. Here is a miner going in to work alone during the miners' strike in 1985.

Reporter:	One man goes to work during the miners' strike – alone, but for the taunts.
Women and children:	(*lining the approach to Cynheidre Colliery, South Wales*) Scab, scab, scab …
Reporter:	"Scab," the cruel catchword of the dispute …
Women and children:	Scab, scab, scab, …
Reporter:	"Scab," the word for those who cross the picket lines, whether in their thousands as in Nottinghamshire or in small groups as in Yorkshire and Wales. Today, the divisions born of the strike between working miner and striker live on. One working miner, too frightened to be filmed, explains what is happening to his family.
Working miner:	As soon as I go out to work the wife's getting phone calls. She's been very strong, you know, she's been able to take it right up to this last few weeks. But now they seem to have a campaign, "Get the wife." And the kids – they haven't been outside since August, you know, since we went back to work, because they've threatened to get the kids as soon as they go out on their own. (Lewis, 1985)

To explain the background to that scene: In 1981 Arthur Scargill had been elected President of the National Union of Mineworkers (NUM). Under his more militant leadership there had been three national ballots over strike action, in January and October 1982 concerning pay offers and in March 1983 over the proposed closure of Tymawr Lewis Merthyr Colliery in South Wales. Each of these ballots went against a strike, the second and third by 61 to 39 percent (Crick, 1985, pp. 93–6).

On March 1, 1984, the National Coal Board (NCB) announced that Cortonwood colliery in South Yorkshire was to close. At that time the NUM's Rule 43 stipulated a 55 percent majority in favor of action before a national strike could be called. In light of the three previous national ballots, the National Executive Committee (of the NUM) did not believe that a 55 percent majority could be obtained. They therefore decided to call a strike under Rule 41. This rule was intended to give the National Executive Committee control over strike action in individual areas of the NUM's regional organization, but was now used, as it were, in reverse, to initiate technically separate strikes in each of the NUM's constituent areas without running the risk of failing to achieve the required majority in a national ballot. As a result of these maneuvers, a strike was begun with the union leadership and its officials almost entirely in favor, but with the miners themselves deeply divided.

Many of the miners resented being called out without a ballot. There were, in fact, ballots in ten of the NUM's constituent areas of which none achieved a 55 percent majority.

> At Bilston Glen, Scotland's biggest pit, 1,900 attended a stormy three-hour meeting, and several came to blows as local officials refused to call a vote, and a large part of the labour force expressed its intention to work on regardless. In South Wales, men at sixteen pits and several transport and washery plants initially voted to ignore the strike call, causing Emlyn Williams [Area President], who had set the whole dispute in motion, to reflect: 'I've been leading the South Wales miners for twenty-five years and never before encountered a rejection like this.' But the six Welsh collieries which did down tools provided enough pickets to bring out the entire coalfield by the end of the second week. (Wilsher, MacIntyre, & Jones, 1985, p. 57)

The organized leadership in South Wales provided the "unanimous majority" against which the unorganized workforce was helpless.

INFORMATIONAL AND NORMATIVE INFLUENCES

A pinpoint of light in an otherwise completely dark room appears unstable. Sherif (1935, 1937) showed that when people are asked to judge the distance through which the light moves (the light is stationary throughout), they find that judgment exceedingly difficult (because there is no way in which they can relate the position of the light to themselves) and are greatly influenced by any judgments they happen to hear from other people. It is likely that those extraneous judgments merely provide the participant with "information" about the distance moved by the light (notwithstanding that the "information" is false) and the influence exerted might be described as "informational." But in Asch's experiment the judgments are easy, and it is difficult to suppose that participants are merely uncertain about which answer is correct. There appears to be a substantial element of pressure to agree with the majority (notwithstanding that the majority is wrong) and that kind of influence is called "normative." These terms were introduced by Deutsch and Gerard (1955).

Informational Influence

Informational influence acts in a vacuum; it has its effect to the extent that participants do not know, or cannot tell, what the correct answer is.

Standard line paired with a single comparison

Asch (1956, Expt 6, pp. 60–2) manipulated the difficulty of the judgment by pairing a standard with a single comparison line. In this experiment each card carried only one line. The card on the left presented a standard length (3, 5, 7, or 9 in) and the card on the right a comparison length longer or shorter by 0.25, 0.5, or 0.75 in. The participants were asked whether the line on the right-hand card was longer than, equal to, or less than this standard. The confederate majority, again unanimous and of substantial size, judged in the wrong direction on the critical rounds. The percentages of errors are set out in table 10.1.

It is easy to see that, for a fixed discrepancy, the percentage of errors increases with the length of the standard, and, for a fixed standard, decreases inversely as the discrepancy; that is to say, the more difficult judgments produce more errors, notwithstanding that they are still fairly easy. We therefore need to think of the pair of stimuli as providing information – easier pairs providing more information – in opposition to the wrong majority. A part of the majority influence is informational.

Table 10.1 Percentages of errors in relation to length of standard and magnitude of discrepancy

Magnitude of discrepancy	Length of standard (in)			
	3	*5*	*7*	*9*
±0.25	41.7	58.3	61.1	66.7
±0.50	25.0	25.0	33.3	50.0
±0.75	25.0	25.0	25.0	27.8

Source: Asch (1956, p. 61, table 21). © 1956 American Psychological Association. Reproduced with permission.

Normative Influence

Normative influence consists in pressure to agree with the majority, irrespective of the stimulus comparison, possibly under the ultimate threat of extrusion from the group of experimental participants. Normative influence is also present.

The critical participant writes his answers

Asch (1956, Expt 4, pp. 56–8) arranged that the critical participant should arrive "late," after the experiment had "started." Turning up at the appointed time, this participant found the experiment already in progress. The uninstructed participant is ushered to the one empty chair, last but one in the order of recall; then, because the experimenter has already started filling out his prepared form for the other seven participants by themselves, the new arrival is asked to write his judgments instead of announcing them to the experimenter.

> The experimenter offered an acceptable reason for not being able to include the subject in the procedure of public announcements, but invited him to take a seat . . . and to put his estimates in writing. In the course of this explanation the experimenter managed to include the full instructions. In addition, the experimenter explained that he was interested in the time relations of the judgments, that he would signal to each member with the help of a metronome, when to announce his response, and that the critical subject was to wait with writing his estimate until his turn came. (Asch, 1956, p. 56)

So, the uninstructed participant heard all the judgments uttered by the others, unanimously wrong on certain critical rounds, before writing his own judgment down, but did not have to expose his own judgments to the majority. As a result the proportion of pro-majority errors decreased to 12.5 percent from the original 37 percent. It is clear that the expected reaction of the majority to the critical participant's public response is important in producing the large proportion of errors, and that is a normative effect. It would be wrong, however, to attribute all the 12.5 percent, when answers are written down, to purely informational influence, because the critical participants said they assumed the experimenter would compare their written answers with the majority judgments later.

Awareness of majority

The critical participants were almost always aware of the influence of the majority, conscious of a conflict, and uneasy. Asch (1955, pp. 31, 33) has published photographs of an experimental session in progress. Those photographs show the agony experienced by one participant when making a critical decision, notwithstanding that that particular participant fell in the category (below) of "confident resistance" and made no errors at all. The conflict is actually reduced when the judgment is less clear – then the majority effect is even more pronounced: "the majority achieves its most pronounced effect when it acts most painlessly" (Asch, 1958, p. 182).

Group Cohesiveness

The element of conflict is also reduced when the participants are not face to face. Deutsch and Gerard (1955) replicated Asch's experiment exactly, except that their participants were separated by partitions that prevented them from either seeing or talking to one another. They indicated their judgments, not by voice, but by pressing buttons. This enabled the experimenter to run every participant as a "critical participant," with no confederate majority. Each participant was told that he was No. 3 (out of a group of four) and the judgments attributed to the other three participants were rigged. Deutsch and Gerard recorded an average of 2.77 errors per participant (23 percent). However, this should be compared with an average of 3.00 errors (25 percent) when Deutsch and Gerard ran similar groups of four participants (three of them confederates) face to face, and 4.0 errors (33.3 percent) from Asch (1958) for groups of the same size.

But Deutsch and Gerard (1955) were able to increase the proportion of errors in a further replication which introduced a group reward designed to increase cohesiveness between the participants. The participants, again separated by partitions, were told:

> This group is one of twenty similar groups who are participating in this experiment. We want to see how accurately you can make judgments. We are going to give a reward to the five best groups – the five groups who make the fewest errors on the series of judgments that you are given. The reward will be a pair of tickets to a Broadway play of your own choosing for each member of the winning group. An error will be counted any time one of you makes an incorrect judgment. That is, on any given card the group can make as many as four errors if you each judge incorrectly or you can make no errors if you each judge correctly. The five groups that make the best scores will be rewarded. (Deutsch & Gerard, 1955, p. 631)

In that variant of the experiment the average number of errors was 5.60 (47 percent). Cohesiveness – a common purpose in being – enhances the effect of the majority. The experimental participants form a social subgroup; the critical participant risks extrusion from that subgroup on account of his deviant judgments. The critical participant's situation is analogous to the extrusion of whistleblowers, or a lone miner going in to work during the miners' strike, or to schoolchildren taking recreational drugs.

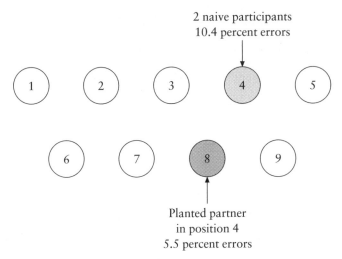

2 naive participants
10.4 percent errors

Planted partner
in position 4
5.5 percent errors

Figure 10.2 Effect of a non-unanimous majority.

WHAT HAPPENS IF THE MAJORITY IS NOT UNANIMOUS?

Asch (1958, pp. 179–80) reported an experiment in which there were two uninstructed participants seated in the fourth and eighth positions in a group of (presumably) nine. The experimental situation is depicted in figure 10.2. The presence of an uninstructed partner reduced the number of pro-majority errors to 15 out of 144 (10.4 percent). This should be compared with the 36.8 percent for a single isolated participant.

The miners' strike again

In Nottinghamshire the NUM officials were similarly in favor of the strike. They controlled the lines of communication so that individual members of the workforce, most of them against the strike, were isolated from each other, forming separate minorities of one. At this point, enter Chris Butcher, a blacksmith at Bevercotes colliery, who initially became known to the media under the sobriquet "Silver Birch."

> At the end of March [1984], Butcher decided to organise something. He started making telephone calls to people he knew in other collieries and listing names. Forty or so met at a pub in Stanton Hill, and were frightened enough to tell the police what they were doing and ask for protection. Most were from North Notts, as there was virtually no contact with the South Notts pits, even a few miles away. "Area were little islands, we weren't united." But then, at Mansfield on 1 May [a May Day rally], there were thousands of working miners, all

milling, leaderless, in a large field. Butcher had brought little slips of paper with his name and telephone number, and started circulating, introducing himself as a rank-and-file member who didn't like what was being done. He found himself often talking to forty or fifty at a time, and when he got home that night, the phone started ringing. Eighty men attended the second Stanton Hill meeting, and the Nottinghamshire Working Miners' Committee was born. (Wilsher et al., 1985, pp. 111–12)

Forming minorities of more than one, even though they were still minorities, made it easier to resist the pressure. This was especially so once the minority was organized and could undertake concerted action.

Butcher's contribution was to create an atmosphere where working miners could believe it possible to organise and resist the enormous pressures, moral, social and intimidatory, to support the majority line. He was not, at least initially, interested in promoting a back-to-work movement. His address book, a blue-covered NCB notepad, was lettered on the cover "The link-up of friendship," and the threefold objectives of his committee were to set up an information network among the twenty-five Notts pits "to stop rumours spreading" through-out the coalfield; to assist miners who were still working, especially those being threatened or attacked; and to "reaffirm democracy within the NUM . . . not to break or replace it." Numbers swelled, the meetings were changed to the Green Dragon at Oxton, . . . and funds started to build up. (Wilsher et al., 1985, pp. 114)

Minorities greater than one means that the "majority" is no longer unanimous. Resistance becomes easier, especially when the minority itself is also organized. The increased power of an organized minority provides the reason for the treatment of prisoners of war in Korea (who were stripped of all leadership) and for the structure of Chinese communist society as a whole.

Deliberations in the jury room

The jury room is another setting in which majority pressure is exercised. Very little is known in the UK about how juries go about their business. While members of a jury may talk about their experiences in general, it is a criminal offense to reveal how and why the jury adjudicated a particular case in the manner that it did. But in the United States the attitude is more liberal. Investigators may not listen into, nor record, jury proceedings, but they are allowed to question jurors afterwards. On that basis Kalven and Zeisel (1966) analyzed reports on 3,576 criminal jury trials in the United States (from 1954/5 and 1958) submitted by 555 different judges together with supplementary material from post-trial interviews with jurors. Nearly all these juries had to reach unanimous verdicts and individual jurors were therefore under pressure to agree with the majority.

Table 10.2 Initial voting in 225 jury trials analyzed by Kalven & Zeisel

Number of guilty votes on first ballot	Number of trials	Final verdict		
		Not guilty	Hung	Guilty
0	26	26	0	0
1–5	41	37	3	1
6	10	5	0	5
7–11	105	5	10	90
12	43	0	0	43

Source: Adapted from Kalven & Zeisel (1966, pp. 487, 488).

The discussion which follows is based upon the results of a pilot study in which Kalven and Zeisel were able to reconstruct the voting in 225 actual jury trials in Chicago and Brooklyn. Juries seem invariably to begin with an initial ballot, and in these 225 trials the initial voting went as in table 10.2 (Kalven and Zeisel, 1966, pp. 487, 488).

The first ballot was unanimous in only 31 percent of these trials; nevertheless, the final verdict usually went the way of the majority. In only six of the remaining 146 trials did the minority win the majority over to their point of view.

> But this is only to say that *with very few exceptions the first ballot decides the outcome of the verdict*. And if this is true, then *the real decision is often made before the deliberation begins*.
>
> The upshot is a radical hunch about the function of the deliberation process. Perhaps it does not so much decide the case as bring about the consensus, the outcome of which has been made highly likely by the distribution of first ballot votes. The deliberation process might well be likened to what the developer does for an exposed film: it brings out the picture, but the outcome is pre-determined. (Kalven & Zeisel, 1966, pp. 488–9; italics original)

A further insight may be gained by looking at those trials in which the jury was not initially unanimous. The details are set out in table 10.3 where it can be seen that in only 13 out of 155 trials did the jury fail to reach a unanimous verdict.

> The table shows that juries which begin with an overwhelming majority in either direction are not likely to hang. It requires a massive minority of 4 or 5 jurors at the first vote to develop the likelihood of a hung jury.
>
> But the substantial minority need exist only at the beginning of the deliberations. During the process it may be whittled away [to just one] . . .
>
> Nevertheless, for one or two jurors to hold out to the end, it would appear necessary that they had companionship at the beginning of the deliberations. The juror psychology recalls a famous series of experiments by the psychologist

Table 10.3   Outcome of 155 trials in which the jury was not initially unanimous

First ballot		Number of trials	Jury	
for conviction	for acquittal or undecided		reached a verdict	unable to agree
11 } 10 } 9 }	1 } 2 } 3 }	78	78	0
8 } 7 } 6 } 5 } 4 }	4 } 5 } 6 } 7 } 8 }	52	42	10
3 } 2 }	9 } 10 }	22	19	3
1	11	3	3	0

Source: Adapted from Kalven & Zeisel (1966, p. 462).

Asch and others which showed that in an ambiguous situation a member of a group will doubt and finally disbelieve his own correct observation if all other members of the group claim that he must have been mistaken. To maintain his original position, not only before others but even before himself, it is necessary for him to have at least one ally. (Kalven & Zeisel, 1966, pp. 462–3)

Inversion of Majority and Minority

In another experiment Asch (1952, pp. 479–80) reversed the sizes of the uninstructed and confederate groups. There was, in this experiment, one confederate only seated in the seventh position amongst a total of 16 otherwise uninstructed participants. The confederate, primed as before to give wrong answers on the same 12 rounds of judgments, could exert no effect on the judgments of the other 15. Instead, they just laughed at the confederate's "errors."

That was David Icke's experience too. David Icke has had a varied career, as goalkeeper, as broadcaster, and as a member of the Green Party. He gave a press conference on March 27, 1991.

Hereford United's former goalie smoothed his turquoise clothes, carefully chosen to "resonate with the universe," checked his watch and prepared to announce the end of the world.

In the same bouncy voice David Icke used in his old incarnation as a BBC sports presenter, he called the press conference to order. "I am a channel for the Christ spirit. The title was given to me very recently by the Godhead."

Mr Icke, who resigned as a national spokesman of the Green party after having the truth revealed to him by Socrates, Jesus and others in the spirit world, expected to be laughed at – he was. (Cohen, 1991a)

But many other men (and not a few women) say similar things in public in equally unusual garb every Sunday and they are not laughed at. The reason is revealed in a further experiment. When the two groups were of nearly equal sizes (a group of 9 confederates with 11 uninstructed participants), the uninstructed participants showed much greater respect for the "judgments" of the confederates (Asch, 1952, pp. 480–1). It is simply a matter of the size of one's claque; empirical veracity, or truth, does not enter into it at all.

HOW LARGE DOES THE MAJORITY HAVE TO BE?

Asch (1958) explored the power of a (wrong) majority to influence the judgment of an uninstructed participant by comparing majorities of 1, 2, 3, 4, 8, and 10–15. The percentages of errors are shown in figure 10.3. If a single uninstructed participant is

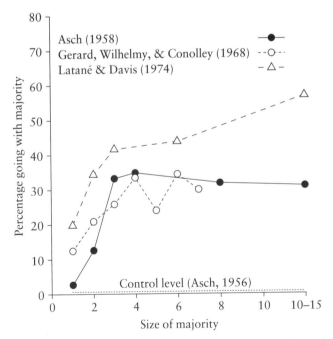

Figure 10.3 Percentages of errors in the judgment of Asch's lines in relation to the size of the wrong majority.

faced with one confederate only, the influence is negligible (2.75 percent). But, faced with a majority of two, uninstructed participants made 12.75 percent errors, compared with 36.8 percent in the original experiment; and a majority of three is sufficient to reveal the full effect. This means that a team of three police officers, two to ask the questions and one to record the answers, is enough to coerce a suspect held incommunicado in a police station. The control data (0.7 percent errors) in figure 10.3 are from Asch's (1956, p. 10) original control condition in which 37 participants wrote their answers down.

Replications of Asch's experiment have generally shown an impact which increases steadily with the size of the majority. Gerard, Wilhelmy, and Conolley (1968) had their participants in cubicles, with the instructions given over headphones and the answers indicated by lights on a panel, the setup employed by Deutsch and Gerard (1955; see above). Their data are also shown in figure 10.3.

Latané and Davis (1974; cited in Latané & Wolf, 1981, p. 443) asked students at Ohio State University for their opinion of the adequacy of local newspapers. Students were asked to add their name to a questionnaire with "Yes" and "No" columns and 1, 2, 3, 6, or 12 signatures already in place in one column and none in the other. After a correction for chance, they obtained the data in figure 10.3 from a total of 1,008 respondents.

Why the difference?

Asch had his participants face to face, which (presumably) produces the greater peer pressure. More to the point, different participants respond differently to Asch's manipulation of peer pressure (a matter I examine below) with very wide variation in their degree of compliance. This means that the mean numbers of errors are determined chiefly by the varied personalities of the participant cohort, a factor which is independent of the actual size of the majority. One possibility, then, is that Asch's face-to-face encounter forced compliance up against a limit determined by the personalities of the participant cohort and that limit was reached with a majority of three. The less confrontational situations used by Gerard et al. (1968) and by Latané and Davis possibly require a larger majority to press against the same limit.

Individual Differences between Participants

The number of errors (out of 12) made by individual participants varied very widely. The numbers of participants in Asch's original sample of 123 who made each different number of errors are set out in table 10.4. Twenty-nine of the 123 participants made no errors at all, while, at the other extreme, six participants went with the wrong majority every time. This looks to be a difference in personality.

Table 10.4 Distribution of numbers of errors in Asch's original sample

Number of errors	Control group (37 participants)	Experimental group (123 participants)
0	35	29
1	1	8
2	1	10
3		17
4		6
5		7
6		7
7		4
8		13
9		6
10		6
11		4
12		6

Source: Adapted with permission from Asch (1956, p. 10). © 1956 American Psychological Association.

Five categories of reaction

After each experimental session the experimenter interviewed the one uninstructed participant, asking about his reactions to the experiment and ultimately explaining that all the other participants had been instructed to utter certain wrong answers according to a specific schedule. Based on this interview, Asch (1952, pp. 465–73) distinguished five different categories of reaction:

1 *Yielding without awareness*. A very few participants went with the majority without realizing that the majority was wrong. These few participants perceived the stimuli as the majority judged them; they yielded to majority opinion without being aware that they were, in fact, doing so.
2 *Belief that own judgment was wrong*. Other participants said that they believed that their own covert (correct) judgments were wrong. These participants said they went with the majority in order not to spoil the experiment.
3 *Compliant*. Some participants simply lacked the confidence to declare their own judgment in the face of a unanimous and contrary majority.
4 *Resistant, but assailed by doubt*. A fourth group of participants generally resisted the influence of majority opinion, but were constantly assailed by doubt. Generally, these participants were convinced that the majority were right and that their own judgments were inaccurate.

5   *Confident resistance.* A fifth category of participant resisted confidently. Some
    of these participants rationalized the situation by supposing that the majority
    were subject to some illusion from which they were free. Nevertheless, despite
    the confident nature of their resistance to majority opinion, these participants
    still showed signs of deep disturbance (see Asch, 1955).

Interrogation by the Police

The very varied degrees of conformity shown by Asch's participants illuminate one
frequent source of miscarriages of justice. Suppose a crime has been committed; you
are asked to go to the police station for interview. There, you are interrogated by
two police officers, while a third writes down your answers. A majority of three to
one, face to face, seemingly exerts the full pressure of majority opinion. What this
means is that while some suspects in such a situation (29 out of 123 in table 10.4)
will resist police suggestion throughout, others (6 out of 123) will cave in completely, and yet others may compromise themselves sufficiently seriously to be sent
for trial.

Planted partner

Asch (1958, pp. 179–80; see figure 10.2 above) found that the presence of an
uninstructed partner reduced the number of pro-majority errors to 10.4 percent.
Accordingly, when the police have two or more suspects arrested under suspicion of
involvement in the same crime, they interrogate them separately, keeping them
always apart. In a repetition of this experiment, Asch put a confederate in the
fourth position, a confederate who always responded correctly, in opposition to
the wrong majority. The uninstructed participant therefore heard the confederate's
correct answer before giving his own judgment. This manipulation reduced the percentage of errors from the real participant in eighth position to 5.5 (see figure
10.2 again).

   When you are interrogated at a police station, you are entitled to have a solicitor
with you. But the police prefer to interview suspects before they have had access to
a solicitor. A solicitor plays the role of the "true" confederate in Asch's experiment.
The influence of the majority in Asch's experiment depends on its physical presence
and is at an end as soon as the experiment is over. So it is with suspects under
interrogation. Innocent suspects who have "confessed" to the police interrogation
repudiate their confessions when they get to court. But by then it is usually too late.
Experienced criminals, of course, already know the ropes; it is the innocent who are
most at risk.

The Guildford Four

Paul Hill, Gerrard Conlon, Patrick Armstrong, and Carole Richardson can speak to that risk. On October 17, 1989, these four were released from prison after serving nearly 15 years for a crime in which, it is now widely agreed, they had no part whatsoever. They had been charged with murder, specifically with planting bombs on behalf of the Irish Republican Army (IRA) in two public houses at Guildford on October 5, 1974. They were convicted solely on the basis of confessions they had made whilst in police custody. Why did they sign confessions to a very serious crime about which they knew nothing beyond what they had read in the newspapers?

Gerry Conlon:	I was absolutely petrified in the police station. I was being beaten. I was being degraded. I was being humiliated. I wasn't given any food. I wasn't – wasn't given any sleep. And then they come round and they said to me, "We know where your mother works. She works in the Royal Victoria Hospital; she works shift work. Your sister works in the Dublin Road which you know is a very dodgy area. A lot of sectarian murders have been committed round there." They told me they could arrange an accident. And then things were taken out of my hands – How would you have felt, if they'd – put it to you and you'd have said – you didn't sign the statement and they murdered your mother? That's what was going through my head, that they were – were capable of murdering my mother. And I honestly believe that they would have murdered my mother and that's why I signed the statements.
Paul Hill:	I mean, you can't imagine – I mean, I was absolutely terrified – terrified, you know. They had firearms pointing at me. I was told I would be left in a lane like a person by the name of Lennon – just up the road in Surrey – you know – at the side of the road. I mean, where I came from Northern Ireland lots of people get left at the side of the road. You know, I was – it was put to me in no uncertain terms, that it could happen to me, it could happen to certain members of my family.

Carole Richardson: You know, you are in that sort of situation. It's – well, a case of getting away from it than – anything. Just – give them what they want and they'll sort of leave you alone. And stick you back in your cell for another however many hours it is until they decide they've got something else they want to tell you.

Gerry Conlon: At one point it come and I thought: "Jesus Christ, I've done this and I can't remember." It actually went through my mind, "Gerry, you've done this and you can't remember." I thought, I may have been smoking drugs or taking a trip or what, and I had actually done it.

Patrick Armstrong: Policemen rolling in now and threatening through your windows and threatening to 'phone up Belfast about getting your mother sorted out and your family sorted out. I mean, I've never seen anything like that before in my life. So it was a very frightening experience. So to me, signing a confession, if that was going to get the pressure off my family and then, I mean, gladly – I signed it.

Carole Richardson: It was like the world being turned upside down. – They'd come out with lines like "If he wasn't there I'd splatter you all the way round the room" and – "If you don't ans – you know, say something, well, yeh – you're going to have to give in in the end; we can hold you for days." 'Cos I – all I kept asking for was my diary and my solicitor. "You can't have your solicitor. We can hold you for seven days." – You know, "We don't have to tell anybody where you are." – And you feel so powerless, so helpless, so out of control. – They move you around from police station to police station. – I don't know, everything was – designed to – make you feel insecure and threatened and alone and – just out of control. There was nothing there – nothing, there wasn't anything you could turn to that was familiar. – (*shaking head*) I just couldn't handle it, couldn't cope. (Franey & McKee, 1989)

There are some parallels between what the Guildford Four said in their television interviews and remarks by some of Asch's participants in the course of debriefing. Compare Gerry Conlon's

> At one point it come and I thought: "Jesus Christ, I've done this and I can't remember." It actually went through my mind, "Gerry, you've done this and you can't remember." I thought, I may have been smoking drugs or taking a trip or what, and I had actually done it.

with

> My whole mental processes were working abnormally [from a participant who made six errors]. (Asch, 1956, p. 28)

and

> May be something's the matter with me, either mentally or physically [this from a participant who went with the wrong majority every time]. (Asch, 1956, p. 28)

Carole Richardson's final comment may be compared with:

> There were so many against me that I thought I must be wrong. Toward the end I got mixed up. I thought I heard the directions wrong. I was beginning to become confused and was more prone to their influence [from a participant who made 10 errors]. (Asch, 1956, p. 44)

Asch's participants were students who volunteered to serve in an experimental session lasting about 20 minutes. In the course of that session about one-third of their judgments, simple judgments about what they were looking at, were subverted by the contrary majority. The Guildford Four, on the other hand, were held for up to seven days under the then recently enacted Prevention of Terrorism Act, without access to a solicitor or anyone else. The police were able to continue their interrogations as long as they pleased – Carole Richardson was interviewed for a total of over 20 hours (Kee, 1986, p. 137) – and to bring the suspects back for further interrogation again, as and when they pleased. For the Guildford Four the "experimental session" went on virtually forever. Given that the police arrested more than 40 people on suspicion of complicity in the Guildford bombs, it would have been surprising indeed if none of them had broken down under interrogation.

The Bridgewater Three

The facts of this case are simple. On September 19, 1978, Carl Bridgewater (aged 13) was shot at point blank range when he disturbed a burglary whilst delivering a newspaper to Yew Tree Farm, Prestwood, Staffordshire. On October 8, 1979, Patrick

Molloy, James Robinson, Vincent Hickey, and Michael Hickey were sentenced to life imprisonment on the basis of Patrick Molloy's confession whilst in police custody. Patrick Molloy died in 1981, and could not thereafter retract his evidence. But on February 21, 1997, the other three were released on bail pending an appeal which the prosecution declared they would not contest. The convictions on the three were quashed on July 30, 1997.

After he was released on bail, James Robinson was interviewed on television.

> At one stage – or a couple of stages – they had me there lying in bits – absolutely – absolutely in bits, thinking "Have I had a mental blackout? Have I killed the baby? Have I blotted it out of my mind? No way!" (Dowd, Sutcliffe, Lord, & Renn, 1997)

Compare Asch's participant (resistant, but assailed by doubt):

> At first I felt there was something wrong with me, that there was something about my make-up that caused me to be different, then I gained more confidence and thought I might be as right as they [that participant made no errors]. (Asch, 1956, p. 28)

SUMMARY

Social conventions develop and are maintained through interactions between individual members of society. Asch's experiments set out some of the ground rules governing the effectiveness of those interactions. The principal results are listed in table 10.5 and may be summarized as follows.

1   When a single uninstructed individual was confronted by a unanimous, but wrong, majority, that individual went with the majority 37 percent of the time.
2   This was dependent
    (a)   on hearing the majority's judgments (a control group who all wrote their answers without hearing any majority judgments made only 0.7 percent errors) and
    (b)   on having to announce the judgments publicly in the hearing of the unanimous majority (participants who wrote their answers, while still hearing the majority calling theirs out, made only 12.5 percent errors).
3   The full effect (about one error per three critical trials) was achieved with a majority of three or more . . .
4   . . . but it is important that the majority be unanimous.
    (a)   Two uninstructed participants together made only 10.4 percent errors.

Table 10.5 Principal results from Asch (1956, 1958) and from Deutsch & Gerard (1955)

Experimental condition	No. critical participants	Average no. errors	Percent errors
Asch (1956)			
Baseline condition	123	4.41	36.8
Control condition	37	0.08	0.7
Written answers	14	1.50	12.5
Deutsch & Gerard (1955)			
Separated by partitions	13	2.77	23.1
Face to face	13	3.00	25.0
Group reward	15	5.60	46.7
Asch (1958)			
2 critical participants	12	1.25	10.4
Planted partner	–	0.66	5.5
Size of majority:			
1	10	0.33	2.8
2	15	1.53	12.8
3 or more	82	3.75–4.20	31.3–35.0

    (b)   A single uninstructed participant with a planted partner (who always responded correctly) made only 5.5 percent errors.

5 (a)   A single confederate had no effect on an uninstructed majority (of 15); the confederate's "errors" were simply greeted with laughter.

    (b)   But when the groups were equal (11 uninstructed participants, 9 confederates giving unanimous wrong answers), much more respect was paid to the "judgments" of the confederates.

6 The magnitude of the effect depends on:

    (a)   The difficulty of the discrimination. The percentage of errors increased as the difference in length decreased and also as the lengths to be compared increased.

    (b)   The participants and confederates seeing each other face to face. Replications with the participants in booths, not visible to each other, have given a somewhat smaller proportion of errors (e.g., 23 percent). On the other hand, when the groups achieving the greatest number of "correct" judgments were promised a group reward (a pair of tickets to the Broadway play of their choice), errors increased to 47 percent (the participants still being separated from each other in booths).

There appear to be two distinct kinds of social influence operative in these experiments.

1 *Informational* – one person's opinion simply provides a suggestion to help resolve the uncertainty in another person's mind.
2 *Normative* – the judgments of other people generate pressure to conform, possibly under threat of extrusion from the group.

Asch's experiments on varying the difficulty of the discrimination §6(a) and on the effect of being allowed to write one's judgment down §2, rather than call it out aloud, show that both kinds of influence were operative, but the distinction is, nevertheless, a real one.

Different participants made very different numbers of errors, ranging from none at all up to 100 percent. Debriefing after the experimental session revealed something of the differences in personality underlying these different numbers.

Asch's results have application to a wide variety of social situations, detailing in particular the circumstances in which a majority can coerce a minority. But in informal society the sizes of majorities and minorities change spontaneously so that the majority influences charted by Asch act in a partially random manner. That becomes especially important in a crowd temporarily isolated from the mainstream of society and to that situation we turn next.

QUESTIONS FOR DISCUSSION

1 Why do some people, sometimes, say what they hear other people say in opposition to what they can clearly see with their own eyes?

2 It matters that the wrong majority be truly unanimous. Why?

3 What do Asch's results tell us about the reliability of confessions made whilst under interrogation by the police . . .

4 . . . and about verdicts reached in the jury room?

11

THE CROWD

THE PROBLEM

In the first place, people in a crowd sometimes exhibit a marked similarity of action as though the crowd was itself an organism. The FA Cup quarter-final match between Luton and Millwall on March 13, 1985, was a watershed in the development of violence on the part of football spectators in the UK. After Millwall's defeat by a single goal, one of their disgruntled supporters ripped up a seat and threw it onto the pitch. What a good idea! There followed a rain of seats descending on the police trying to restore order, sufficient to force the police momentarily to retreat (Jones, 1985). In some cases the demonstration is preplanned (the riot instigated by COMBAT18 at the England vs. Ireland football match on February 15, 1995, at Lansdowne Road, Dublin, is a case in point), but such allegations are not sustainable every time.

Second, the actions of people in a crowd are liable to run out of control to the point that they sometimes do things that they would never, ever consider attempting on their own. On February 1, 1995, Jill Phipps was one of a group of demonstrators protesting against the export of veal calves from Coventry airport. She somehow got herself crushed under the wheels of a lorry.

> An hour after she arrived on the day she died, the lorry appeared. Most of the protesters were further down the road but a small group, including Ms Phipps who had arrived earlier, were at the entrance of the airport when the articulated lorry came up the road. As it bypassed the main group of campaigners, she ran, arms outstretched, headlong towards it. She clambered up the front wing. Her sister watched in horror as she slipped and fell beneath the wheels.
>
> Another protester, Gill Gates, was just yards away. "She was just behind me," she said. "I turned around for a second and my friend was on the ground. I don't know if she slipped, fell or was knocked over by the truck. Police yelled for the lorry driver to stop and it did, but with the wheels right on her body." Paramedics tried emergency treatment but she was dead on arrival at hospital. (Vallely, 1995)

In a crowd the ordinary motivation of individual behavior seems to be suspended. People somehow act in concert and are liable to do things they ordinarily would not. This chapter looks at the behavior of people caught up in a crowd. The argument will be that what people do is simply the result of a random series of interpersonal interactions of the kind examined in the previous chapter; but, because those interactions are substantially random, in a crowd temporarily isolated from the rest of society, the evolution of that crowd's behavior can prove quite unexpected.

These problems have been considered before, many times, and these different ways of looking at crowd behavior have been proposed.

The Flashpoint

Writing about the riots in Brixton, April 10–12, 1981, Lord Scarman said:

> The incident which sparked off the disorder on Saturday was nothing unusual on the streets of Brixton – two plain-clothes police officers questioning a suspect, a hostile crowd gathering and complaining of police harassment, an arrest, and a final violent protest as the police sought to remove the arrested man. Usually, however, such an incident would end there: the protesting crowd would, after a little while, disperse and normality would return. Why, on this occasion, did the incident escalate into a major disorder culminating in arson and a full-scale battle against the police?
>
> The tinder for a major conflagration was there: the arrest outside the S&M Car Hire Office was the spark which set it ablaze.
>
> There is no need to probe deeper for the immediate cause of the Saturday riot. I have heard no evidence to suggest that there was any prior organization or conspiracy . . . the immediate cause of Saturday's events was a spontaneous combustion set off by the spark of one single incident. (Scarman, 1981, pp. 65–6)

Lord Scarman draws an analogy with lighting a fire or detonating an explosion. But compare the St Paul's riot in Bristol on April 2, 1980.

> As the first group of police reached the grass area there was a pause. Then an old man walked up to a parked panda car and kicked in its lights. There was a loud cheer and missiles were flung at the police. These were exposed on all sides and after a while were so fiercely pressed that they were forced to fall back towards City Road. (Reicher, 1984, p. 9)

The trouble with a "flashpoint" is that, on looking back, one can always find some event which just preceded the outbreak of riot, but that event can be identified only in retrospect. Would the same old man kicking in the lights of a panda car have sparked a riot elsewhere? And how do we account for those crowds which do not riot?

"Group Mind"

This idea asserts that individuals are subordinate to the crowd which itself follows different rules and standards of behavior to the rest of society. The "group mind" effectively denies any role to the social context of the crowd, but otherwise explains nothing.

The Random Evolution of Crowd Behavior

It is easily demonstrated that social conventions evolve in course of time; my thesis here is that behavior in a crowd is simply the same process speeded up. This is possible in a subgroup temporarily isolated from the rest of society. One Millwall supporter tears out a seat and throws it onto the pitch; the others think, "What a good idea!" and copy. That copying gives the crowd an appearance of organic unity. But if members of a crowd all copy each other like that, their behavior will be indeterminate in its evolution – and will appear random.

I expand this idea in a series of propositions below. The chief problem to be addressed subsists in the assertion that the evolution of social conventions, which is ordinarily a very slow, gradual process, can happen sufficiently quickly in a small, isolated subsociety to account for the sometimes very rapid development of crowd behavior.

1 SOCIAL ATTITUDES, STANDARDS, CONVENTIONS EVOLVE

The history of sexual license in broadcasting provides a clear example. In the 1940s and 1950s the BBC code governing sexual license in radio broadcasting was widely seen by the public as the prohibition of any mention of any items of ladies' underwear. At that time radio comedy was recorded in front of a live audience (because the comedians could not perform successfully without the immediate response of an audience). The late Jimmy Edwards, the principal star of *Take It From Here!*, brought the house down on one occasion by specifically *not* mentioning a certain item of ladies' underwear. One minute later he brought the house down again – with the same joke repeated. Today his joke would be seen as childish – playground humor at best. But in the early 1950s it was a sidesplitter.

As of 1996 (at a time when program titles were straightforward) Channel 4 broadcast "Red Light Evenings." On a more regular basis one could watch *Eurotrash* (Channel 4, Saturdays at 10.35 p.m.), *The Girlie Show* (Channel 4, Fridays at 11.05 p.m., repeated on Sundays at 12.10 a.m.), *The Good Sex Guide . . . Late* (ITV, Saturdays at 1.00 a.m., repeated on Thursdays at 2.40 a.m.), *Hotel Babylon* (ITV,

Saturdays at 12.20 a.m., repeated on Wednesdays at 2.25 a.m.), and *Pyjama Party* (ITV, Sundays at 1.30 a.m.) (Leapman, 1996). In March 1997 Channel 5 was launched with a penchant for soft-porn films. "The inclusion, for its own sake, of erotic material in a free-to-air television service is a step change in the use of sex on British television" (statement by the Broadcasting Standards Council; cited by Hellen, 1999). Then, in 1998, "Channel 4 breaks the last sex taboo with bestiality film" (Hellen & Barot, 1998).

2 SOCIAL CONVENTIONS CAN EVOLVE RAPIDLY

It is clear that social conventions evolve, but those changes in sexual license in broadcasting have taken place very slowly over a period of 50 years. Could such a process run its course quickly, in a matter of minutes?

Broadcasting, especially by the BBC, is a service to the nation. Broadcasting standards are a matter of public debate, and in the UK there is a Broadcasting Standards Council to consider complaints about violence, sexual conduct, taste, and decency on television, on radio, and in advertisements. The Broadcasting Standards Council provided the initial outlet for the late Mary Whitehouse and her National Viewers' and Listeners' Association. It receives complaints, inquires into the facts of the matter, and adjudicates as a committee. This means that the consideration of any one complaint takes a substantial time. Moreover, the entire nation is its constituency, so evolution in matters of broadcasting standards is slow. There is great inertia, and that accounts for the BBC's overcautious approach.

But envisage a much smaller group, with direct communication between individuals – a crowd. A look at the simplest crowd of all – car drivers on the M25 motorway around London – shows that the evolution of ideas and action – at what speed to drive – can be very rapid.

Motorway driving

On a crowded motorway each driver chooses his or her speed according to the speed of the surrounding vehicles; this is essential, to avoid collision. There is, therefore, an interaction between individual drivers. Each driver can react rapidly to the speed of adjacent cars – rapidly enough to match the occasional explosion of crowd behavior. That is demonstrated by the phenomenon of traffic density waves.

Envisage a knot of vehicles joining the motorway at a junction. That knot of vehicles creates a local increase in traffic density and following vehicles have to slow to avoid collision. In heavy traffic, when the density of vehicles on the motorway is so great that they impede each other, that local increase in density propagates

Figure 11.1   A traffic density wave on the M25 motorway. Traffic in the right-hand lane is traveling toward the camera. In the distance there is an increased density of traffic (a density wave) that has been progressively moving away from the camera, contrary to the flow of traffic. Photograph © Stewart Goldstein.

backwards against the direction of traffic flow as a wave of increased traffic density. Backward propagation happens when the reactions of successive drivers are so quick that the change in speed propagates from one vehicle to the one following behind faster than the vehicles themselves are moving forwards. Figure 11.1 shows such a traffic density wave on the M25. Traffic in the right-hand lane is traveling toward the camera. In the distance there is an increased density of traffic that has been progressively moving away from the camera, contrary to the flow of traffic. Mathematically speaking, the increased concentration of traffic is a shock wave, analogous to waves breaking on a shelving beach and falling back toward the sea (Haberman, 1977, p. 312).

Such a backwards-traveling density wave presents a hazard. It is a common experience whilst driving at 70 mph on the M25 to suddenly find oneself catching up very quickly indeed on the car ahead. It sometimes proves necessary to brake suddenly to perhaps 30 mph or even less to avoid a collision; sometimes even to come to a halt. Thereafter cars slowly thin out as the density wave passes further back against the traffic flow. That phenomenon is entirely mediated by the transmission of changes in speed from one driver to another. Occasionally there is a rear-end collision. But the very low frequency of such accidents (in relation to the number of cars using the motorway) testifies to the rapidity with which car drivers can respond to each other.

The funeral of Diana, Princess of Wales

If you are still reluctant to agree that car drivers on a motorway constitute a real crowd or that people can respond to each other as quickly as that . . .

> A sound like a distant shower of rain penetrated the walls of Westminster Abbey shortly before noon yesterday. It rolled towards us. Then it was inside the church. It rolled up the nave, like a great wave.
>
> It was people clapping, first the crowds outside and then the 2,000 inside. People don't clap at funerals; and they don't clap because people outside are clapping. But yesterday they did. It was dense, serious applause and it marked the moment at which the meaning of what was happening on this incredible day was made plain.
>
> It was the end of Earl Spencer's tribute to his sister, Diana, Princess of Wales, that had raised the emotional tension to this breaking point. (Appleyard, 1997)

The crowd in Westminster Abbey and on Palace Green was of a conventional kind. The applause began and rose to its climax within a minute. In a crowd, behavior can, indeed, sometimes does, evolve that quickly. Here are two further examples.

Bob and Dot Dunderdale

Bob and Dot Dunderdale used to run a corner shop on a council estate in Lincoln. In June 1993 their shop was destroyed by mob violence over four days of rioting.

> The corner shop is quiet now. Every door and window has been boarded up and is covered with graffiti.

A month ago this little corner of Macauley Drive and Swift Gardens in Lincoln wasn't quite so tranquil. It was a scene of violent clashes between police and youths as petrol bombs were thrown. Over four days it erupted from a minor confrontation to rioting.

Lincolnshire Police, local councillors and residents on the city's St Giles estate were astounded. No one was more surprised than Bob and Dot Dunderdale, who had run the shop for five years, building it up from an empty shell to a thriving business.

Their shop took the brunt of the mob's anger. The police took the rest. The shop was ransacked and looted, and the Dunderdales were forced to move to a secret address.

Mr Dunderdale speculates it might have started from a random incident. "A person was injured during a disturbance at a wedding reception being held nearby. Someone came in and asked to use the shop telephone to call an ambulance. The person who made the call only telephoned for an ambulance. I know because I was holding the telephone." The police arrived with the ambulance and he thinks people believe he called them. That night somebody broke one of his shop windows. In the following weeks the shop had several windows broken and had two break-ins.

Several weeks later came the riot.

The Dunderdales are still seeking an explanation for what happened next. "I got a phone call from the local police. They asked me to go up because windows had been smashed," Mr Dunderdale said. When he arrived he was confronted with a frightening scene. "There were lots of people milling around, kids and adults. The atmosphere was very tense."

When he heard the next morning there had been a riot, he broke down. (Connett, 1993)

The Heysel Stadium, Brussels, May 29, 1985

On May 29, 1985, Liverpool Football Club were scheduled to play Juventus of Turin in the final of the European Cup at the Heysel Stadium, Brussels. Spectators began entering the stadium about 3 hours before the kick-off. Juventus fans were assigned to one end of the stadium, and Liverpool to the other – except that some Italians got into Block Z, which comprised one-quarter of the "British" end. The Juventus and Liverpool fans there were separated by only a narrow accessway and some lightweight fencing. With 40 minutes still to go before the kick-off, the Liverpool fans, tightly packed, broke the fencing down and thronged into Block Z. The Italian fans panicked, the perimeter wall collapsed, and 38 people were crushed to death and about 400 injured (Popplewell, 1986). Consequent on that riot, English football clubs were excluded from European competition for five years, until the 1990/91 season.

3 THE EVOLUTION OF SOCIAL CONVENTIONS IS ESSENTIALLY RANDOM

I have just described the change in broadcasting standards over a period of 50 years; but how did it come about?

The Broadcasting Standards Council is concerned with what is acceptable to the public as a whole. What is deemed acceptable today is judged by reference to what was acceptable yesterday, and the vagaries of human judgment mean that standards drift (though not in any specific direction). That drift results, in part, from particular public events, of which the trial over the possible obscenity of D. H. Lawrence's novel *Lady Chatterley's Lover* in 1960 was particularly influential. But broadcasting standards could have evolved in a different direction – the loose, profligate society of the early nineteenth-century Regency period gave way to the sober, straitlaced attitudes of Victorian days.

Rumor

Rumor consists of the spread of unsubstantiated assertions and provides an opportunity here to exhibit the random character of such transmission.

There was an earthquake in the Indian province of Bihar on January 15, 1934. The earthquake lasted for about 3 minutes and destroyed all communications in Northern Bihar. There happened to be a psychologist on hand to record the rumors that spread about the damage done by the earthquake and to check those rumors by personal observation.

> (1) *Four thousand buildings in Patna city have collapsed, causing innumerable deaths, and immense loss of property.* (January 15th, 1934).

Parts of several houses had collapsed, and many were damaged. This was not an entirely false report, but highly exaggerated, as found by personal verification.

> (2) *The Patna College Building has collapsed, and the Chemistry block of Science College has sunk four feet down into the ground.* (January 15th, 1934).

Only the top portions of the Patna College Building (old block) had fallen down, and the Chemistry block was merely suspected to have sunk by inches, which was hardly noticeable. It was a highly exaggerated report. Personally verified. [. . .]

> (4) *The arch of the General Post Office crumbled down as a result of the second shock on the morning of January 16th, 1934.* (January 16th, 1934).

False. Personally verified.

(5) *The water of the river Ganges disappeared at the time of the earthquake, and people bathing were embedded in sand.* (January 17th, 1934).

This is a fabrication, as I subsequently ascertained. (Prasad, 1935)

Prasad (1935) lists a total of 30 rumors together with his verifications. Some rumors were complete fabrications, others were wild exaggerations of actual events. In the absence of normal communications, news is obtainable only by word of mouth; and in the absence of any factual corroboration, rumors evolve as they circulate. The individuals who pass them on have no basis (except plausibility) on which to dispute them.

In a subsequent paper Prasad (1950) collected data from historical earthquakes in India and surrounding countries and noted certain consistent themes in the resulting rumors. Often there is some factual basis, but it is exaggerated; other rumors introduce supernatural elements. Ordinarily, credibility is constrained by what normally happens in the world; following an earthquake, that constraint is largely suspended. In addition, information is scarce so fabrications are introduced to fill the void. Those fabrications are sometimes of a cultural or religious origin – hence the supernatural elements.

Bob and Dot Dunderdale again

Such propagation of rumor is by no means specific to Indian society. The events outside the Dunderdales' corner shop in Lincoln have already been described. But why did it happen? "Last week residents on the estate said the shop was attacked because the Dunderdales were 'grasses'" (Connett, 1993, p. 6). More precisely, one of the things one must not do in certain areas of the UK (and evidently the St Giles estate is one of them) is to go to the police.

But why was the Dunderdales' shop attacked? "When pressed, residents on St Giles estate have no evidence for the informer allegation but are not concerned it might be untrue. They quickly cite other reasons why the shop was singled out" (Connett, 1993, p. 6). It is quite clear that there was intense local resentment at the Dunderdales which found expression in apparently baseless allegations as reasons for the riot. How does public resentment originate? How does it escalate into riot? It looks to be driven by no more than rumor – the result of random interactions between individuals.

Public Protest

Protest groups protesting against the export of veal calves, against new roads, against hunting are self-organizing – they form crowds – and their collective behavior is liable to evolve randomly for that reason. The reaction against the proposed move of the Gracewell Clinic to Upton-upon-Severn is typical of spontaneous public protest.

The Gracewell Clinic

The Gracewell Clinic in Birmingham was founded by Ray Wyre for the treatment of men convicted or accused of sexual offenses against children. It is highly respected within the profession. But in October 1993 it was ordered to close on account of contravening planning regulations, coupled with a protest signed by 1,600 local residents (Waterhouse, 1993).

The Faithfull Foundation is a child protection charity founded by 83-year-old Baroness Faithfull to take over Gracewell's work. It sought to open a residential clinic for male child sex abusers at The Boynes, a large Victorian house 1 mile outside Upton-upon-Severn. The local people formed a protest movement. They exhibited posters and placards – "NO to sex offenders," "NO PERVERTS IN UPTON." They picketed The Boynes. They took direct action, including arson, to prevent the establishment of the clinic (Hodgkinson, 1993). But why?

There is a powerful reaction, almost certainly instinctive at heart, on the part of mothers against any perceived threat to their children. Pedophiles are one such threat. I have already described (pp. 163–4) the reaction of the people living on the Paulsgrove estate in Portsmouth. They marched, night after night: "What do we want?" "Paedophiles out!" (Reid, 2000). They objected to registered sex offenders living, effectively unsupervised, on their estate. But the people of Upton-upon-Severn were faced with a different kind of threat. While they may have had visions of child molesters lurking behind hedgerows, waiting to pounce, the kind of child abusers treated by Gracewell operate by first winning the trust of a child; they are definitely not violent. Moreover, the Gracewell Clinic has a high reputation amongst professionals in childcare and provides them with training courses. So Upton children would actually have been safe because the possible threat would have been known and monitored – especially safe except, possibly, from an undetected pedophile living in their midst. The protest by the people of Upton-upon-Severn was driven chiefly by rumor; it did not matter that the perceived threat was largely imaginary.

Campaigners against abortion

Many people are opposed to abortion; the Society for the Protection of the Unborn Child (SPUC) and Life are two pressure groups lobbying Parliament in the UK. In the United States there is Operation Rescue.

Operation Rescue, in the United States, runs "boot camps" that aim to train the "shock troops of the anti-abortion movement." They give instruction in the tracing of car licence numbers of clinic employees and patients, in electronic surveillance, jamming of phone lines and similar skills. "These," their director told the *New York Times* last week, "are the field exercises for what is to come." (Fenton, 1993)

So what *is* to come?

Dr David Gunn, 47, was shot dead outside a clinic in Florida during an anti-abortion demonstration sponsored by Rescue America [not the same group as Operation Rescue], a group known for its extreme views. Michael Griffin, an outspoken "pro-lifer," was heard to shout "Don't kill any more babies" as he fired three shots into Gunn's back. He later gave himself up to police. Witnesses said other demonstrators appeared pleased by the killing. (Reeves, 1993)

On the Sunday before the murder he [Michael Griffin] reportedly led a prayer at a fundamentalist church that Dr Gunn should "give his life to Christ." (Fenton, 1993, p. 23)

That is the extreme to which the "pro-life" movement has evolved in America. Of course, "Rescue America . . . said it did not condone the killing of Dr Gunn. But Don Treshman, the national director of the group, said, 'While Gunn's death is unfortunate, it's also true that quite a number of babies' lives will be saved'" (Rohter, 1993). Dr Gunn's murderer is another example of someone in a crowd doing things he would surely not have considered doing on his own. On the other hand, Dr Gunn has not been the only doctor to be shot at: "four or five shots were fired at Dr Tiller after he left his clinic in Wichita, Kansas, . . . and climbed into his van. He was slightly wounded in each arm" (Reeves, 1993, p. 10).

The anti-abortion movement is a semi-isolated subgroup that has evolved its own extreme standards of behavior in violent conflict with the conventions of the larger society within which its members also exist. "Pro-life" means anti-abortion, but it does not always mean anti-murder! Those deviant conventions which have evolved within the subgroup are rationalized by appeals to a perverted religious morality.

4 THE LIKELIHOOD OF DISORDER, OF RIOT, DEPENDS ON THE CROWD'S REASON FOR BEING

If the evolution of the behavior in a crowd is random, that would explain why some crowds riot, while others do not; why some communities protest and others do not – at least, do not protest effectively. But there is more to it than that.

The possibility of a riot requires the people forming the crowd to be brought together. But most aggregations of people come together for some common purpose, such as commuters traveling to work, and that common purpose determines what they do. Briefly, commuters do not riot. We therefore need to distinguish between an "army" and a "crowd."

By an *army* I mean a diverse aggregation of humankind under a single overall command. The Falklands task force in 1982, which consisted of 39 warships and 60 support ships, 171 naval aircraft and a similar number from the Royal Air Force (RAF), 5,000 combat troops and their supports, provides a prime example. Different units act in concert according to a single strategic plan of campaign dictated from above. They have to, to secure victory. Some things go wrong in the heat of battle. It was alleged that some Argentine prisoners of war were executed on Mount Longdon (Hilton, 1993). The Falklands task force was a less than perfect army.

By a *crowd*, on the other hand, I mean a contiguous group of people entirely devoid of leadership or common purpose. The Liverpool fans waiting for the match against Juventus to begin – how were they going to pass the time? Killing time is an essentially random activity and liable to evolve – possibly rapidly. As a further example I compare two rallies of miners in Sheffield in April 1984 (Waddington, Jones, & Critcher, 1989, chap. 2).

Two rallies of miners in Sheffield, April 1984

As I have already explained (pp. 176–7), the miners' strike in 1984–5 was called on an area-by-area basis. But some coalfields refused to strike without a national ballot. So the National Union of Miners (NUM) held two delegate conferences in Sheffield in April 1984 to try to persuade those reluctant coalfields to come out. The rallies of miners which interest us here were assembled to lobby the delegates to these two NUM conferences.

The first rally on April 12 consisted of about 7,000 miners outside the NUM's national headquarters in St James's Square, Sheffield. They were protesting against the motion to hold a national ballot. There was much pushing and shoving against the police. The motion was actually ruled out of order and was referred to a Special Delegates Conference called for the following week. After the rally, there was some further disorder as the miners returned to their coaches to go home.

The second rally on April 19 required a larger venue and was held at Sheffield City Hall. Both the NUM and the police were anxious to avoid a repetition of the disorder of the previous week. So a platform was erected outside the City Hall, and the demonstrators listened to speeches and were entertained while the conference was in progress. There was about the same number of miners at the rally as on the previous Saturday, but now under the control of the NUM's own marshals. The rally was peaceful. However, after the rally, with the entertainment over and the miners returning to their coaches, a near-riot broke out with 68 arrests and about 100 injured. Outside the City Hall the rally was well controlled, like an army. But once that control ceased, the crowd's behavior began to evolve rapidly, leading to disorder and violence.

5 THE LIKELIHOOD OF DISORDER, OF RIOT, ALSO DEPENDS ON THE SOCIAL SETTING

The people of Brixton, south London, rioted in 1981, in 1985, and again in December 1995. In 1981 there were also riots in Birmingham, Bristol, Liverpool, Manchester, and Wolverhampton – inner-city areas with relatively large proportions of black people. Does this mean that black people have an intrinsic propensity to riot?

From 1981 on unemployment nationally was between 2.5 and 3 million. But that unemployment was not evenly distributed; ethnic minorities living in poor inner-city areas fared much the worst. Early in 1981 unemployment in Brixton was 13 percent; but among black youths under the age of 19 it was estimated to be 55 percent. What are those black youths going to do if they have no work to go to? The unemployed (of any and every ethnic origin) have much time to loiter, but little money to spend on anything. They tend to congregate on the street and form a crowd – exactly a crowd – with nothing to do.

Brixton, December 1995

Brixton erupted again in December 1995. On December 5, Wayne Douglas was arrested by the police for a minor theft after a chase at the end of which, some witnesses said, he had been overpowered by the use of the police's long batons. One hour later he was dead. Scotland Yard released preliminary details of a postmortem which suggested that he had died as a result of a heart condition, but black people in Brixton were in no mood to accept that. Eight days later there was a protest rally outside Brixton police station with some inflammatory speeches. Then the crowd embarked on a march, not authorized by the police, which brought further conflict. That conflict escalated into rioting, looting, and violence, with running battles fought against the police.

If the riot had broken out on the day Wayne Douglas died, it would have fitted Lord Scarman's "flashpoint" mold well. As it was, it took eight days to reach that climax, but what is clear is that there had to be a background of animosity against the police for the conflict to spiral out of control. Why such a background when, following the riots in 1981, so much money and official concern had been poured into the regeneration of Brixton (Boggan, 1995)?

> Hubert James, director of Brixton community law centre, said the area had always suffered from an atmosphere of tension arising out of police treatment of young men.

"The council has closed many of the resources for youth around here. The youth clubs are disappearing and often those facilities that are left aren't available to the black youths because they can't afford them. All they've got left to do is stand around on street corners." He said as a result they came into conflict frequently with local police. "I don't believe people should burn down businesses, but there is a lot of anger around here." (Bennetto & Victor, 1995)

The Marsh Farm estate, Luton

Rioting is in no way the preserve of black people, nor of those who live in inner-city areas. In July 1995 there were three days of rioting on the Marsh Farm estate, Luton. This is not an inner-city area.

Connoisseurs of miserable housing estates would stroll through Marsh Farm with surprise. Not riots here, surely, among these green fields, scattered with nice houses, gardens front and back? Here is a recreation centre with pool, shops, a library, a community centre, a health centre, church and schools – in short, the ideal London overspill, circa 1967. But they petrol-bombed or bricked the windows of every public building.

The Vicar of Holy Cross, the modern Anglican church beside the shopping centre, expressed brisk and not particularly Christian sentiments about the rioters. "I go up to them and ask them why. 'Nothing to do,' they say. What do you mean, nothing to do? There is everything here for you. What do you want? 'Dunno,' they say. 'Not bothered.'"

Some of the young men he is talking about were mooching in a corner of the car park. Nothing, nothing, nothing, they said. Recreation centre? It costs a lot. The free sessions for those on benefits are at a few peculiar random hours. Community centre? They turn up their nose, nothing really in it for them. Jobs? "I don't try any more. I was dead keen when I first left school. Not now. No point." Unemployment on the estate is officially 10 percent, but among the young it is far higher. (Toynbee, 1995)

This rioting on the Marsh Farm estate at Luton illustrates my thesis well. Unemployed youths with much time on their hands tend to loiter in each others' company. What to do? They borrow ideas from each other, in a circular fashion. That is to say, they form a crowd, by contiguity, entirely without purpose or leadership. Their behavior evolves, possibly rapidly, independently of the wider society within which they live. That is a scenario with the potential for riot. In Brixton in similar circumstances, evolving behavior brings young unemployed men into conflict with the police who have a duty to preserve order in public places. That conflict, oft repeated, creates a simmering undercurrent of distrust – the "tinder" of which Lord Scarman spoke. "Flashpoint" is an apt metaphor for describing what sometimes happens, but the underlying cause is the economic degradation which the young unemployed suffer.

SUMMARY

By a "crowd" I mean a circumscribed subset of people, temporarily cut off from the external influence of wider society purely by reason of geography. They are not distinguished by any particular purpose in coming together; they have no leadership. Individual members of this subsociety interact with each other by virtue of contiguity, and their collective behavior evolves independently of wider society.

The evolution of a crowd's behavior is no more than the ordinary evolution of an independent social group, but greatly speeded up. Given a crowd of sufficiently small size, with sufficiently rapid communication between its members (with sufficient coherence), behavior *en masse* can evolve very quickly – once one football fan has thrown a seat, many others copy – to give the crowd an appearance of organic unity.

That process of evolution of behavior can be studied (at slower speed) in subsocieties generally. That explains the relevance to this chapter of the spread of rumor and the behavior of protest groups.

The evolution of a crowd's behavior may, however, depend on how the crowd came into being, how the people making up the crowd came to be together in one place. An army is under one command and its behavior is centrally directed. If a crowd has met together for some purpose (a trade union rally), that purpose constrains its behavior. But if young unemployed youths simply congregate on the street (to pass the time), they have no purpose in being and the behavior of that crowd is likely to evolve at random. That means that riot cannot be predicted in advance; it explains why many "flashpoints" do not lead to riot.

But the evolution is spontaneous, not generally orchestrated. That in turn suggests that the interactions between individuals that drive that evolution, the copying of actions by one person from another, are, possibly, instinctive. We have, then, a conflict between instinctive reaction and social convention. But perhaps the greatest interplay between "animal" instinct and social convention is seen in aggressive behavior, and to that I turn next.

QUESTIONS FOR DISCUSSION

1 Why do crowds sometimes run out of control?

2 What can be done to control football supporters . . .

3 . . . and to revitalize rundown inner-city neighborhoods?

12

RAGE . . .

Tracie Andrews

A young father has died after a passenger in a car he overtook stabbed him at least 15 times and slashed his throat at the end of a three-mile chase along unlit country lanes.

Lee Harvey . . . was left bleeding from multiple wounds in the middle of the road as his attacker's car drove off. He died in the arms of his fiancée, who was slightly injured.

Detectives were last night looking for the shabby F-registration Ford Sierra that chased the couple between Burcot and Alvechurch . . . late on Sunday night.

Mr Harvey, 25, and his fiancée, Tracie Andrews, had been on their way home from an evening out . . . when they overtook the Sierra along the A38 near the Forest public house. The other driver gave chase, flashing his lights, driving bumper to bumper and exchanging obscene hand gestures with Mr Harvey.

The pursuit continued . . . until the Sierra overtook Mr Harvey, who . . . was forced to stop in Coopers Hill, a few hundred yards from his home. As Miss Andrews looked on from the car, the two drivers argued, pointing their fingers and shouting.

The confrontation appeared to end and the Sierra driver returned to his car. But as he did so, his passenger climbed out and attacked Mr Harvey, stabbing his head, neck and upper body. He continued to slash his victim after he fell to the ground and when Miss Andrews tried to intervene, she suffered a cut eyebrow. The Sierra then drove off, leaving Mr Harvey to die in the road. (Farrell, 1996)

That was Tracie Andrews's story about the events on the evening of December 1, 1996. But the police did not believe her – her story did not tally with any of the forensic evidence – and neither did the court. Tracie Andrews was sentenced to life imprisonment for murder. Subsequently she confessed to the killing in a letter sent from prison to the *News of the World*. In that letter she wrote that she had "lost all control" (Sherwin, 1999). But I do not think that Ms Andrews was telling all of the truth in that letter and still have to ask: What really happened?

It is known that the couple had a meal at the Marlbrook pub in Bromsgrove where they were seen to be arguing over dinner. I conjecture that the argument continued in the car on the way home and Tracie eventually took a knife to her fiancé whilst the car was still in motion. Lee Harvey naturally stops the car and gets out, but the attack continues until he is dead.

This couple had a history of violent rows.

> Neighbours reported screaming matches lasting for hours, punctuated by the sounds of breaking furniture. Mr Harvey occasionally pushed his fiancée around, but never hit her. He expressed his anger by smashing objects, once throwing a television set out of a window. She, on the other hand, would not hesitate to lash out and was often overheard shouting that she "hated" him.
>
> Police were called to their flat on several occasions but the couple would often continue fighting even in their presence and would have to be restrained. They split up many times, but would always be reunited. (Bale, 1997)

But why?

The couple were planning to marry in June 1997. That intention makes the attack quite irrational. But Tracie Andrews is excessively given to violence and loss of temper, even from childhood. The fatal episode on December 1 was a straight loss of self-control, a takeover by an instinctive aggression. This is actually the most typical pattern of murder in our society, a loss of self-control leading to a violent attack on someone one knows. The patterns presented in detective stories and television dramas are atypical (see Berkowitz, 1993, chap. 9). Tracie Andrews's violence was far from being preplanned. On Wednesday December 4, she was admitted to hospital following an overdose of paracetamol, aspirin, and tranquilizers. Well, what else did life have for her after her fiancé's death?

WHY ARE PEOPLE AGGRESSIVE?

The episode just described suggests that rage is a takeover by instinctive behavior patterns in defiance of both social convention and rational considerations and that it constitutes another category of compulsive behavior. Violence is often triggered by actions undertaken by the victim – in this case by Lee Harvey continuing the argument – which lead to a simple loss of control on the part of the aggressor. Anger is the emotional counterpart.

The nature of such behavior is brought out by a comparison with tigers. Cats are territorial. Lions will share territory; but other species of cat do not. If a dominant male tiger dies, other males will fight for possession of his territory (Birkhead, 1997). The struggle is instinctive. This comparison suggests that similar instinctive behavior is natural to humans, but is normally held in check, overlaid by social constraints.

But there are other ways of looking at aggression.

Frustration

One idea is that aggression results from the frustration of some other goal-directed activity – for example, the cuckolded husband discovering his wife with her lover (Dollard, Doob, Miller, Mowrer, & Sears, 1939). Sexual behavior is instinctive, quasi-mechanical. Its forcible interruption creates a conflict between the person and the source of the interruption, a conflict we experience subjectively as frustration. It is very plausible that such a conflict should eventuate in some other kind of motivated activity and rage seems a natural outcome.

One woman who had suffered violence at the hands of her partner said, "I have been raped, punched, bruised, mainly because I didn't consent to sex" (cited by Mooney, 1994, p. 37). Here is another contemporary example.

> A drunken passenger who went berserk on a jumbo jet after being ticked off for watching porn on a laptop computer was jailed for three years for what was described as the "worst ever case of air rage."
> Ian Bottomley, 36 . . . injured three stewards, caused £30,000 of damage and invited a former soldier to "step outside" seven miles above the African jungle. Finally, after a "violent struggle," he was overpowered, handcuffed, gagged, strapped down and repeatedly sedated in an attempt to restore order. But minutes later it became necessary to crowbar the seats in front of him from their fittings to stop him trying to head-butt them. (Howe, 1999)

> Trouble flared when he was told by Mr Stevenson [cabin crew] to stop ogling the "hardcore" pornography. "Bottomley just jumped up and lunged at me with both fists," Mr Stevenson said. (Poole, 1999)

Envisage that at the time of the interruption Mr Bottomley was sexually excited by the pornography he was looking at. Envisage that Mr Stevenson's intervention interrupts his sexual sequence – sudden frustration, turning immediately into rage. Some aggression certainly results from the frustration of other motivated behavior, but not all aggression arises in this way. Tracie Andrews would seem to be a counterexample.

Negative Affect

As a modification of the idea of frustration as its source, Berkowitz (1983, 1989) has proposed that aggression is what happens when one is feeling "out of sorts," a reaction to aversive environmental circumstances, to stress. Some aggression probably does result from external stress, but again not all of it.

> A boy of 12 killed his baby brother with a kitchen knife after a row with his mother, a court heard yesterday.

The boy stabbed the six-month-old baby 17 times in his cot, cutting off his left hand. He then walked to his local police station where he handed over the knife and told officers what he had done.

Police arrived at the family home to find his mother dozing on the sofa with another child, unaware of what had happened in the baby's room.

. . . the boy had had an argument with his mother over school dinners. Later she told the boy to take a bottle to his baby half-brother. Instead he took a knife from a kitchen drawer and went upstairs. Five minutes later he came down and let himself out of the house. He walked into a police station near his home . . . and said: "I've stabbed my brother. I think he might be dead."

Later the boy told the police: "I went to the kitchen drawer and got a knife. When I got it I was thinking to hurt the baby. I went to the bedroom, walked to the cot and stabbed him. I didn't look down. I just looked at the cupboard.

"I was in the room for a couple of minutes. I felt the knife go into the baby. I was aiming to hurt him. I don't know why." (de Bruxelles, 2001)

Retaliation

Schachter and Singer (1962 – this experiment was described in chapter 2, p. 26) proposed a two-factor theory of emotion, which says that arousal is one thing and how that state of arousal is interpreted is another. Aggression results when someone else's behavior is interpreted as hostile, as an attack. But why someone else's behavior should be interpreted as hostile is left unexplained.

AGGRESSION AS INSTINCT

Each of the preceding ideas accords with *some* patterns of aggression, but not with all. In fact, like fear, aggression might be a rather disparate group of behaviors. I argue that it is instinctive, in which case it should be observable in infants, like the visual cliff, looming, and the reaction to snakes in chapter 2.

The "Terrible Twos"

It is well known that young children are prone to temper tantrums. Here is Penelope Leach describing the pattern of behavior commonly observed in 2-year-olds . . .

Temper tantrums are the result of too much frustration just as phobias result from too much anxiety. More than half of all two year olds will have tantrums at least once or twice a week while very few children will reach their third birthday without ever having experienced one.

A tantrum is like an emotional blown fuse; it is not something which the toddler can prevent. The load of frustration builds up inside her until she is so full of tension that only an explosion can release it. While the tantrum lasts, the toddler is lost to the world, overwhelmed by her own internal rage and terrified by the violent feelings which she cannot control.

Children's behaviour during a tantrum varies, but your particular child will probably behave similarly each time:

She may rush around the room, wild and screaming. Remember that she is right out of control so anything movable that happens to be in her path will be knocked flying. If you do not protect her she may bang into solid walls and heavy furniture. She may fling herself on the floor, writhing, kicking and screaming as if she were fighting with demons. She may scream and scream until she makes herself sick. She may scream and turn blue in the face because she has breathed out so far that, for the moment, she cannot breathe in again. (Leach, 1977, pp. 324–5)

. . . and here is an eyewitness account:

Last week I was sitting on the train opposite a little girl of about two, who was happily absorbed in a book. She tried to turn the page but couldn't manage it, quickly became frustrated and was furious when her mother tried to help. The book went flying across the carriage and she threw herself on the floor, kicking and screaming at the top of her voice. In seconds she was transformed from a calm, cheerful toddler to a small writhing heap of utter rage. (Collins, 2000)

I am suggesting that temper tantrums are simply an instinctive pattern of aggression. In a 2-year-old they are manageable, because the adult is so much larger and stronger than the child. But in an older child – the boy of 12, described above, who killed his baby half-brother – they are intolerable. Adult aggression (e.g., Tracie Andrews) is the same instinctive pattern as the infantile form, but modified by socialization.

INSTRUMENTAL AND EMOTIONAL AGGRESSION

Social psychologists (e.g., Berkowitz, 1993) distinguish two categories of aggression:

1 *Emotional aggression* – "blind rage," the pattern exhibited by Tracie Andrews.
2 *Instrumental aggression*, aggression in "cold blood" – a contract killing at the behest of a Mafia godfather. There are no hard feelings on the part of the killer toward the victim, just a job to be done – but that job happens to be a bullet in the head.

Tracie Andrews's killing of her fiancé defies all social rules and conventions; and, although a contract killing at the behest of a Mafia godfather might appear equally to flout convention, it does not flout convention within the Mafia family whence the killing was ordered – quite the contrary. I therefore prefer a different emphasis on the distinction between emotional and instrumental aggression. As before, there are two categories of factors, but I think it more meaningful to distinguish, first, the level of motivation – the intensity of the rage – and, second, the restraining power of social sanctions. In human society aggressive behavior is restrained by social conventions and legal constraints. With this different emphasis, emotional aggression or rage results from an excessively high level of motivation such that social restraints are simply overwhelmed (Tracie Andrews again); but instrumental aggression results when social restraints are ineffective. In this case the level of motivation is not excessive, but criminals do not regard ordinary social conventions – they have their own different codes of conduct. These two categories are the two ends of a continuum and actual instances of aggression lie, of course, somewhere in between.

EXPERIMENTAL METHODS

There is a long history of laboratory experiments on aggression. The experiments use a rather standard procedure which I will illustrate with an experiment by Lang et al. (1975).

There were two participants, one was a confederate of the experimenters, one naive. They did a mirror-tracing task together. This task consisted of tracing around a six-pointed star with one's hand visible only in a mirror. In the mirror the front/back direction (but not the left/right) is reversed. This task is known to be difficult at first, but to admit much improvement in the course of training (Snoddy, 1920). While the experimenter was out of the room, the two participants compared their respective performances.

> While the experimenter was absent, there was time for a brief conversation between the confederate and the subject. The entire verbal interaction was tape recorded for subsequent analysis. In the provocation conditions, the star diagram which the confederate produced was a standard excellent one which he had prepared beforehand. The subject's relatively poorer tracing served as the basis for the confederate's insulting and belittling remarks, which constituted the provocation manipulation. In a sarcastic and condescending manner, the confederate asked if the subject's attempt had been serious, if he had ever before looked in a mirror or drawn anything, if he had to cheat to stay in school, and generally questioned the subject's intelligence. In the no-provocation conditions the confederate's star diagram was also a standard one, but one which he had actually produced on his first attempt with the apparatus. In this case, his comments to the subjects were friendly and suggested that, although neither of them had done very well on the task, it was probably nothing to worry about. (Lang et al., 1975, pp. 511–12)

There followed a learning task of the kind employed by Milgram (chapter 6 above) with the real participant as teacher. The confederate, as pupil, was set to learn 40 three-consonant "code items," each with a two-alternative forced-choice response. If the response was wrong, the teacher administered an electric shock using the Buss aggression apparatus.

The Buss Aggression Apparatus

There is a stimulus panel on the accomplice's side that contains four lights, any number of which will be lit on any given trial. The accomplice responds by pressing the "A" button or the "B" button, with the "A" button being correct whenever the upper left light on the panel is lit; the "B" button is correct whenever the upper left light is not lit. This is the concept that the accomplice is ostensibly to learn.

The subject is given a sequence that randomly presents patterns of lights to the accomplice. The stimulus panel is lit by depressing the stimulus buttons marked 1, 2, 3, and 4 on the subject's side, and the accomplice's response is indicated by the lights just above the stimulus buttons. Upon noting the accomplice's response, the subject decides whether it is correct or not and presses the "correct" button on the left or one of the shock buttons. The shock is delivered by means of electrodes fastened to the third finger.

Since the subject should discover how much shock is represented by the 10 buttons, the electrodes are attached to him, and he is shocked. He is administered shock from buttons 1, 2, 3, and 5 and is told that the intensity of the shock continues to increase to button 10. The shock level is set so that 1 is slightly above touch threshold and is essentially only a signal that the response was incorrect. As the intensity of the shock increases through 2 and 3, it becomes painful; at 5 it is an extremely noxious stimulus. (Buss, 1960, pp. 48–9)

The Buss aggression apparatus was developed about the same time as Milgram's procedure and the similarity is obvious. The chief difference in Buss's procedure is that the teacher chooses his own level of shock without any instructions. The teacher's level of aggression is assessed by his choice of level of shock, and the essential comparison in the experiment by Lang et al. (1975) is between the levels of shock delivered by provoked, versus those by control, participants. That comparison is shown in figure 12.1 (to be discussed later).

The general circumstances of this procedure raise serious questions about its validity. Two strangers meet in an experimental laboratory. One abuses the other. Subsequently the one who suffered the abuse gets an opportunity to administer painful electric shocks (as he thinks) to the other who delivered that abuse – all this within the formal framework of an experiment. Do the results of such an experiment really extrapolate to real aggression, unobserved, in the world outside? Apart from the unreality of the experimental situation, there is the difficulty that the naive participants might perceive themselves as expected by the

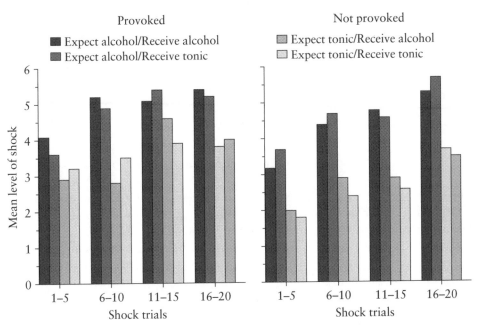

Figure 12.1   Mean shock levels in the experiment by Lang et al. (1975). Reproduced with permission from Lang et al. (1975, p. 515). © 1975 American Psychological Association.

experimenter to react in certain ways, and participants are usually ready to oblige (Orne, 1962). The question cannot be answered without comparing experimental result with anecdote.

The whole question of the validity of laboratory experiments on aggression is discussed by Berkowitz (1993, chap. 13). Berkowitz first points out that the level of shock that participants choose to administer, the number of shocks, and the length of time for which the shock button is depressed are typically correlated with each other, as one would expect, and are greater in those participants who have been provoked in the experiment. On the other hand, the participants are well aware that they are being observed and are concerned with their image. They therefore tend to hold back on the punishment. "Most laboratory experiments therefore attempt to lower the subjects' restraints against aggression by giving them a socially legitimate excuse for punishing the victim. Otherwise very little if any aggression would be seen" (Berkowitz, 1993, p. 422). Laboratory experiments therefore provide a guide to understanding aggressive behavior in the real world, but their results must be extrapolated with caution because of the social constraints on aggression which obtain outside.

Table 12.1 Mean reaction times in the experiment by Lang et al. (1975)

Experimental condition		Mean RT (ms)
Tonic water only		1,065
Vodka + tonic	Not provoked	1,174
	Provoked	1,294

The Effects of Alcohol

The experiment by Lang et al. (1975) is of interest as one of many experiments investigating the effects of alcohol. Alcohol has long been known to affect human behavior, but precisely what effect does it have? What does it do?

Lang et al. (1975) selected eight groups of 12 (real) participants from among "heavy drinkers" defined as people within the top 10 percent of alcohol consumption within the general population. These eight groups were arranged in a $2 \times 2 \times 2$ design according to these factors:

(a) Vodka + tonic vs. tonic only;
(b) "Expect alcohol" vs. "expect tonic only";
(c) Provoked by confederate vs. no provocation (control).

The results are set out in figure 12.1.

1 There is a systematic increase in the level of shock administered over successive trials. Lang et al. (1975) say that such an increase is common with the Buss apparatus and might reflect an increasing frustration on the part of the participant.
2 The shock levels administered during the learning task depended only on expectation (b) and scarcely at all on the administration of alcohol (a). The principal difference in figure 12.1 lies between the two sets of dark gray bars ("Expect alcohol") and the light gray ("Expect tonic"). This independence of aggression from alcohol suggests that it might be thought socially excusable to be aggressive when one is (thought to be) under the influence of drink.
3 In the learning task (40 three-consonant "code items" with a two-alternative forced-choice response) the teacher was instructed to acknowledge the pupil's response as quickly as possible by pressing a separate button. This constituted a simple reaction time to be measured. Reaction time was independent of expectation and depended only on the ingestion of alcohol. The mean reaction times are set out in table 12.1. Alcohol slows reaction time, as is well known; but anger slows it even more.

Notwithstanding the result (2 above) that the level of shock administered depended only on what the participant had been led to believe, whether he had received alcohol or not in the experiment, it is the actual ingestion of alcohol that is associated with crime and violence.

> As a source of antisocial behavior, alcohol is implicated in nearly 70% of fatal automobile accidents, 65% of murders, 88% of knifings, 65% of spouse battering, 55% of violent child abuse, 60% of burglaries, and so on, causing the National Commission on the Causes and Prevention of Violence (1970) to conclude that "no other psychoactive substance is associated with violent crimes, suicide, and automobile accidents more than alcohol" (p. 641). For some individuals, of course, drinking alcohol becomes something they cannot control – the other head of the beast. In 1985, nearly 10.5 million people in the United States were addicted to alcohol (Williams, Stinson, Parker, Harford, & Noble, 1987). (Steele & Josephs, 1990, p. 921)

Alcohol myopia

The problem with alcohol is that its effects are so varied. They vary from one drinker to another. Many husbands, more than one-half at some time or other in their lives, use violence on their wives, most often after drinking; but drink does not drive every husband to violence, nor does it drive the potentially violent husband every time. So the effects of alcohol also vary for the same drinker from one time to another.

A plausible synthesis runs as follows:

1 Alcohol restricts the range of cues, social as well as sensory, that we perceive in a given situation.
2 Alcohol reduces our ability to understand those cues that we do perceive. Hence . . .
3 . . . under the influence of alcohol our behavior is directed by the more salient cues only. This makes behavior more extreme in every respect.

On October 13, 1996, it was widely reported that Paul Gascoigne, footballer for Glasgow Rangers and England, had battered his wife of 14 weeks, and not for the first time. Gascoigne has a reputation as a carouser, but at the same time was teased by teammates for being unable to hold his liquor. "It was alleged that he became abusive over dinner on Sunday. His wife reportedly fled to her room, pursued by her husband, and they fought while the children slept in the next room. Pictures of Mrs Gascoigne with facial bruises, a bandaged hand and her hand in a sling appeared in the *Daily Mirror* yesterday" (English & McCarra, 1996). Paul Gascoigne was very contrite afterwards ("Gascoigne asks forgiveness for 'the rage inside me'"; Hughes, 1996). This is a common pattern in wife-battering; the battery results from an acute loss of self-control which is contritely acknowledged as such after the event. But that does not prevent the loss of self-control from recurring, and there were public calls for Gascoigne's omission from England's football team.

Alcohol not only makes some people more violent, it makes others more benevolent. Lynn (1988) took a job as a waiter in a restaurant in Columbus, Ohio, and kept a record of how much alcohol each party drank and how large a tip they left after the meal. Those parties who drank alcohol gave bigger tips, and the size of the tip increased with the number of drinks.

The increased violence under the influence of alcohol is well established. The increased divergence of behavior in other directions as well seems to be a fact, but its basis is less certain, chiefly because violence attracts public attention to an extent that other kinds of behavior do not. The idea that this results from a decreased sensitivity to social stimuli is plausible. Steele and Josephs (1990) call it "alcohol myopia." But what especially fails under the influence of alcohol seems to be the restraint of social convention, rather than immediate social pressure. Taylor and Gammon (1976) arranged for participants to deliver electric shocks to an aggressive opponent. They introduced an "observer" (a confederate of course) into the experimental room who then made suggestions to the (naive) participant what level of shock to administer. Mild social pressure restrained the behavior of both sober and intoxicated participants. But Sears (1977) found that intoxicated participants were more responsive than sober ones when pressed to *increase* the level of shock (see Taylor & Leonard, 1983).

AGGRESSION IN EVERYDAY LIFE

Domestic Violence

Domestic violence is common (Gelles & Straus, 1988). A survey of 1,000 men and women in Islington, north London, in 1994 revealed that 37 percent of the female respondents had suffered "mental cruelty" at some time in their lives, 27 percent had faced threats of violence or physical force, 6 to 32 percent had suffered various kinds of actual physical violence, 27 percent had been injured, and 23 percent had been raped (Mills, 1994, citing data from Mooney, 1994).

Here are two examples.

The victim

Anne Vickers does not doubt that had her new husband not come to her rescue, her previous partner would have killed her.

He had called round unexpectedly claiming he wanted to discuss access arrangements for their child. Instead, he pinned her to the stairs and rained blow after blow on her prone body. "I saw something flash and I thought it was a knife," she said. It turned out to be a screwdriver.

The attacks, verbal and physical, started shortly after the couple moved in together when Anne [not her real name] was 18. At first they were relatively minor – a poke in the face, a slap around the head. He was always contrite, often tearful and said he would change.

With the birth of their child a year later, the frequency and intensity of his violent outbursts increased – he had twice tried to strangle Anne, once causing her to black out. Anne left. (Mills, 1994)

The abuser

"The tea wasn't on the table when I'd got home. I'd had a very bad day at work and I just saw red," Brian [not his real name] said. . . .

"I remember dragging my wife upstairs by the hair and tying her on the bed. I then paraded around the house shouting and screaming. I worked myself up into a real frenzy."

He fetched petrol, poured it on the bed and for an hour tormented her by playing with matches. "She was petrified. I have to admit I used to enjoy seeing her like that. I need to feel in total control." (Mills, 1994)

Both these examples tell of a loss of control and a giving way to instinctive fury (and the second story also provides a good example of "negative affect"; Berkowitz, 1983, 1989).

Women do also attack men, mostly in self-defense. But sometimes the woman is the initial aggressor, though much less frequently so than the man. What is striking about such cases is that the men *do not fight back* (Ferguson, 1999). Why? Because there is a social convention that men do not assault women.

Domestic violence contravenes a widely and strongly held social convention. It occurs in private; husbands and wives seldom quarrel in public. This has two consequences. First, the public in general do not know how widespread domestic violence is, and wives who suffer do not know where to turn.

Sheryl Gascoigne . . . who was divorced . . . after three years of marriage, described how she suffered in silence because she did not know that help was available. "You always think it will get better and you become optimistic and think if you don't do this or that, then he won't behave in that way. He always said: 'Just don't you tell anyone.'" (Coates, 2001a)

Second, in the previous chapter I identified a crowd as a group of people temporarily isolated from the larger society within which they live. In private, the family is a "crowd." Under those circumstances family conflicts can escalate out of control, cut off from all outside social constraint. Escalation is facilitated by alcohol – Steele and Josephs (1990) reported a 65 percent involvement in family violence – and also by economic hardship that also provokes domestic violence.

As many as 14,000 Russian women a year are killed as a result of domestic violence . . .

Interior Ministry figures given to the United Nations show that four fifths of violent crime in the country can be attributed to domestic violence and statistics suggest that a third of all murders are committed by husbands killing their wives.

Only 3 per cent of violent crimes committed in the home are reported to the police and domestic disputes are still regarded by the authorities as a private matter between husband and wife. An article in *Komsomolskaya Pravda* recently reported that helplines for battered women were dealing with five to six times more calls than usual since the beginning of the Russian economic crisis in August, indicating that financial difficulties can aggravate already difficult domestic situations. (Blundy, 1998)

Road Rage

Here is an example. On October 6, 1997, in the evening, Toby Exley and Karen Martin were driving west along the A316 (the Great Chertsey Road).

[A] saloon car is said to have come up behind the couple's Ford Fiesta in the fast lane heading westwards at Hanworth at about 8.50 p.m. The driver became impatient with their speed and rammed into the back of their car three times.

Mr Exley could not move into the slow lane because of traffic but moved to the right to let the saloon pass. The saloon then hit him again, catching the left hand rear of his car and forcing him to veer right into the wooden central reservation. (*The Times*, 1997)

Both Toby and Karen were killed in the crash that followed. The driver of the saloon car was ultimately apprehended and sentenced to 12 years for manslaughter (Jones & Lee, 1998).

Road rage is common. There are, as yet, no statistics for the UK, but Louis Mizell Inc. maintains a database of crime reports in the United States. Compiling reports from 30 major newspapers, 16 police departments, and claims on insurance companies, it has counted totals, specifically for "aggressive driving," mostly involving death or serious injury, which have increased from 1,129 in 1990 to 1,800 (estimated) for 1996; that is a more than 50 percent increase in six years (Mizell, 1997). Most offenders are young, male, poorly educated, with a criminal record; but Louis Mizell's database does include all kinds of people.

In January 1995 the Automobile Association (AA) surveyed 526 drivers in the UK, asking them about their experiences of "road rage." Eighty-eight percent of the sample said they had suffered some form of road rage over the past 12 months, though only 60 percent confessed to being responsible. The percentages of different forms of aggressive behavior are shown in table 12.2. It is systematically the case that more drivers complain of having been the victim of a particular kind of

Table 12.2 Percentage incidence of road rage in Britain in 1994

Behavior complained of	As victim	As perpetrator
Aggressive tailgating	62	6
Flashed lights to demonstrate annoyance	59	45
Aggressive or rude gestures	48	22
Deliberate obstruction or preventing a maneuver	21	5
Verbal abuse	16	12
Physical assault	1	[a]
None of these	12	40

[a] One case in the sample of 526.
Source: Adapted with permission from Joint (1995, pp. 21–2). © 1995, The AA Foundation for Road Safety Unit. Contact by email: motorist@theaa.com

aggressive behavior than will confess to being the perpetrator, and one might easily suppose that this happens because some drivers were simply unwilling to confess to what they had done. But there is a simpler explanation.

Social Cognition

Social cognition is concerned, among other things, with ability to recognize motivational and emotional states in other people. A high level of agreement has been demonstrated amongst different viewers for the kind of emotion (afraid, angry, disgusted, happy, sad, and surprised) expressed in different faces. Moreover, the identification of emotion is accurate when compared with the emotional state of the individual at the time his or her face was photographed (Ekman & Friesen, 1975). But on the road one can seldom see another driver's face and the driver's intention has to be inferred from the motion of his or her car. How might that be accomplished?

There is a fundamental question whether conscious judgment of the state of emotion expressed in someone else's face – judgment, at least, of the kind recorded in a laboratory experiment – is causal with respect to our reaction to that person. The reason is that we also react to other people's body language, to the nonverbal cues people unwittingly display, and that reaction is itself nonverbal (Bull & Frederikson, 1994). One of the best known of such cues is the size of the pupils. The pupil dilates in low light levels under control of the parasympathetic nervous system; but it also responds under sympathetic control to the individual's emotional state and such a dilation would have to be subconscious. Hess (1965) has shown that a photograph of a woman's face with pupils enlarged is more attractive to male participants than the same photograph with pupils constricted. Some participants said that the first photograph was "more feminine" or "softer," but none noticed the difference in pupil size.

Enlarged pupils generally signal interest and Hess suggests that the photograph with enlarged pupils is more appealing because it is interpreted, by the (male) viewer, as indicating increased interest in the viewer as a person. But, it is only a photograph and cannot possibly signal such an interest, so the reaction of the viewer would have to be quasi-automatic. Hess (1975) argues on the basis of a variety of semi-informal experiments that the attractiveness of large pupils is innate in the sense in which ethologists use that term. For example, pupil dilation on the part of the viewer (indicating increased attractiveness of the image) can be elicited by a highly schematic pair of eyes (no face), though not by a single schematic eye, nor by three in a row. There was also a difference in reaction to a female visitor by infants of 3 to 3.5 months of age depending on whether the visitor's eyes had been artificially dilated, or constricted, by application of an appropriate drug. The mothers of the infants visited by this experimenter also described her in different terms according to the dilation or constriction of her eyes.

Research into nonverbal communication has, generally, proved rather difficult for the elementary reason that even the research psychologist is largely unaware of the subtle cues that people display and use at a subconscious level. While the recognition of emotional expression in a face might appear to be a conscious, learned, discrimination, there might, at the same time, be an underlying, subconscious, reaction in which the face functions simply as "body language." Ekman (1980) reports studies in the identification of emotion with the South Fore people who live in the highlands of New Guinea. The question put is whether the identification of emotional expression is universal – would the South Fore people who at that time had had virtually no contact with the outside world make the same emotional identifications as participants from the United States and elsewhere? Except for confusion between expressions of fear and surprise, the South Fore people recognized the same emotions. Coupled with other studies reviewed by Ekman, this suggests that emotion is generally recognized across cultures and that recognition is therefore innate, not culturally acquired. Cultures do vary in the occasions on which it is permissible to display emotion, but not, it seems, in the facial expression once that expression is permitted.

How, then, might the underlying intention of another driver be inferred from the motion of his or her car? One possibility is by treating another motorist's car as if it were a person, extrapolating the subconscious interpretation of body language. But the motivation of the driver is not necessarily expressed in the motion of the car, and thereby hangs a quite different interpretation of the discrepancies in table 12.2. Quite simply, the difference between the columns may be the results of misperception, with an instinctive bias toward seeing another motorist's actions as threatening.

The specific incidences of "aggressive tailgating" (62 and 6 percent), that is, of driving dangerously close to the vehicle in front, may, however, admit a simpler explanation still. It happens that it is much easier to judge distance in front of one's vehicle, looking through the windscreen and over the hood, than through the rear window, where there is a much larger blind area. So, the same distance that looks safe to the driver of the car behind, looking ahead, might appear dangerous to the driver of the car in front when viewed in the rear-view mirror.

Crowding

There appears to have been a progressive increase in incidents of "road rage" in recent years. Although the evidence collected by Mizell (1997) does not have the reliability of experimental data, it is nevertheless persuasive. At the same time the density of vehicles on our roads has been increasing and this has suggested a parallel with crowding in animal populations. The idea stems from an article by Calhoun (1962).

Calhoun confined naturally increasing populations of Norway rats in a relatively small space. When the population increased above the density that would be tolerated in the wild, the behavior of the rats fell apart, as it were. Under the stress of overpopulation, there were disorders of eating, drinking, and social organization, including increased aggression and cannibalism. Following the publication of Calhoun's article, it became popular to suggest that human aggression was the consequence of overcrowded living conditions in cities. But the most salient effect of overcrowding in Calhoun's population was infant mortality, which reached 96 percent in one regime and 80 percent in another.

This popular view has recently been challenged by de Waal, Aureli, and Judge (2000). Looking at populations of monkeys and chimpanzees and extrapolating from *those* populations to human society (on the face of it, a much more reasonable extrapolation), the thesis appears to break down. Monkeys and chimpanzees are stressed by overcrowding – that much is clear – but their reaction to that stress is not an increase in aggressive behavior.

I shall return to this question below. For the present I note that an unnatural increase in aggression has been reported amongst ducks farmed indoors in overcrowded accommodation (Prentice, 2000). The *Times*'s report relied largely on evidence provided by Viva!, an animal rights group. Viva!

> secretly filmed dead and injured birds in and around apparently crowded sheds . . . [The farm] imports day-old Barbary ducklings from France whose beaks and claws have already been trimmed, according to Viva! This farm . . . claims that the Barbary must be treated in this way or they will mutilate one another in the factory farm sheds. Viva! says this is because aggressive behaviour is caused when the ducks become so crowded together that they have to fight for space.

Viva!, of course, is an animal rights group and has an axe to grind. On the other hand, the *Times*'s journalists were refused permission to visit – and the mutilation was illustrated with photographs.

Less controversial, because the video recording was broadcast on the *BBC News*, is an instance of aggression amongst pigs. Consequent on the outbreak of foot and mouth disease (February 29, 2001) in Britain, in many areas of the country movement of pigs, sheep, and cows was prohibited for any reason whatsoever. One consequence was that pigs had to stay in their pens, notwithstanding the progressive overcrowding. The *BBC 10 O'Clock News* report of April 11, 2001, showed pigs fighting with one another in very crowded conditions, with wounds on one animal's back.

Three Principal Factors

Returning to "road rage" by human drivers, there seem to be three principal factors contributing.

1   A car is, for most people, the second most valuable purchase (after a house) that they will ever make. It is expensive to repair and the occupants are at risk of possibly serious personal injury in a crash. So car drivers insist on maintaining a personal space around their vehicle. Infringement of that territory is seen as aggressive (like the tigers at the beginning of this chapter). "He cut me off"; "They kept tailgating me." When that requirement is combined with the increasing congestion of traffic on the roads, there is inevitably an increase in "road rage."

2   There are laws and conventions to prevent collisions on the road. They specify who gives way to whom. (The "Rules for Avoiding Collisions at Sea" are very explicit.) But the traffic on a section of road can change quickly. So, imagine two drivers in two cars who both perceive the fast-moving events around them less than completely, and therefore differently. They thereby come to have different perceptions of their respective rights and wrongs in a quickly changing pattern of traffic. Add to that an instinctive tendency to respond to perceived aggression with aggression. The recipe is complete for an escalation of any incipient or merely accidental conflict, leading to an outburst of "road rage."

3   Unintended conflict is a potential feature of ordinary daily life and we have procedures for preventing its escalation. In a crowded room or on a street, accidental collisions between individuals are unavoidable. We say "Sorry" or "Please excuse me." This is not just a human characteristic; it can be seen in animal societies as well.

In our dogs, in the wolf, and in other members of the same family, submissive or appeasing movements have evolved from juvenile expression movements persisting into adulthood. This is not surprising to anyone who knows how strong the inhibition against attacking pups is in any normal dog. R. Schenkel has shown that a great many gestures of active submission, i.e. of being submissive and, at the same time, *friendly* to a "respected" but not feared, higher ranking animal, arise directly from the relation of the young animal to its mother: nuzzling, pawing, licking the corners of the mouth, movements which we all know well in friendly dogs, are derived, according to Schenkel, from movement patterns of sucking and begging for food.

Expression movements of social submissiveness, evolved from the female invitation to mate, are found in monkeys, particularly baboons. The ritual presentation of the hindquarters, which for purposes of visual emphasis are often incredibly colourful, has in its present form almost nothing to do with sexual motivation. It means that the individual performing the ritual acknowledges the higher rank of the one to whom it is directed. Even quite young baboons perform this ceremony without having been taught. When Katherina Heinroth's female baboon, which had lived with human beings since shortly after birth, was let into an unfamiliar room, she performed the ceremony of "presenting her behind" to every chair that apparently evoked her fear. (Lorenz, 1966, pp. 115–17)

Rhesus monkeys forced into crowded accommodation groom each other more. While there is increased aggression amongst unrelated females, the general reaction to crowding is an increase in grooming which communicates a specifically nonviolent intent. Chimpanzees adapt even more successfully. In the wild they are very territorial and will attack and even kill neighboring colonies. But in crowded accommodations they actually show a lessened frequency of aggression. This is not because they are not stressed by the crowding; but that they react to overcrowding with behavior that specifically does not evoke reaction, like human beings do when squeezed into a lift (de Waal et al., 2000). Such behavior is the primate equivalent of "Sorry" or "Please excuse me." But you cannot say "Sorry" to a driver in another car, and an attempt to do so may even be interpreted as hostile! So car drivers on the road react more like rats and ducks and pigs because, on the road, they cannot send appeasement signals in the manner that dogs, monkeys, and chimpanzees do.

There is only one way to avoid involvement in "road rage" incidents: Do not respond directly to any other driver on the road (except for formal vehicle signals), whatever your perception of the rights and wrongs of the situation.

Football violence

The world has become inured to violence from football fans, but this episode is different. In 1997 Paolo di Canio joined Sheffield Wednesday and finished that season as the club's top scorer. In the game against Arsenal on September 26, 1998, his temper flared.

It all began when Vieira [the Arsenal midfield player] brutally pulled down Jonk [Di Canio's teammate]. I ran up to Vieira to ask him why the hell he had done it. Keown [the Arsenal defender] was near by and stopped me by painfully elbowing me in the nose. We came to blows but instead of calling both Arsenal players to him, the ref showed me the red card. It was an obvious injustice. I'd never seen anything like it. (Kempson, 1998)

Neither had the spectators seen anything like what followed because Di Canio retaliated by pushing the referee to the ground!

I pushed the referee in the stomach and he took three or four backward steps like someone diving to win a penalty. (Kempson, 1998)

That is to say, he then accused the referee of deliberately falling over, as professional footballers sometimes do, to make the assault look more serious than it really was.

Football is watched by millions of people. Television exposure and the worldwide audience that the broadcasts reach mean enormous rewards for the top teams, the teams whose games are watched around the world, and immense pressure on the players in those teams to succeed. There are professional tricks that include covert violence on opposing players (Di Canio's view on Keown's elbow) and falling over in the opponents' penalty area to make a challenge look illegal (Di Canio's view on the referee's stumble). It is instinctive to react to aggression with aggression, even when such a reaction is manifestly unwise, and on the professional football field loss of control is only just below the surface.

SUMMARY

Rage is another category of compulsive behavior; the individual is taken over by seemingly instinctive patterns of aggression in defiance both of social restraints and rational considerations. There is at least a superficial parallel with fighting between animals of the same species; cats will fight instinctively for the control of territory. In humans, we see a straight loss of self-control; anger is the emotional accompaniment.

There is a long history of research into the origins of aggression and the ideas have been explored that (1) rage results from the frustration of some other motivated activity, or that (2) aggression is a reaction to aversive environmental circumstances, or that (3) aggression results when someone else's behavior is interpreted as hostile. While each of these ideas accords with some patterns of aggressive behavior, none of them accommodates all aggression.

There are two distinct factors underlying aggressive behavior; there is (1) the level of motivation and (2) the restraining power of social sanctions. Emotional aggression results from an excessively high level of motivation, so high that social restraints are simply overwhelmed, while instrumental aggression is what happens when social restraints are simply ineffective.

There is a long history of laboratory research into aggressive behavior using procedures similar to those used by Milgram. While these procedures might look excessively contrived and unreliable, comparison with anecdotal report suggests that the experimental results nevertheless extrapolate to ordinary human behavior in the world outside.

While it has long been known that alcohol has an obvious and serious effect on people's behavior, there is a problem in that its effects are so variable, both from one drinker to another and also on the same drinker from one time to another. The most plausible idea, at present, is that alcohol has the effects that it does by restricting people's responsiveness to the most salient social cues only. As a consequence, behavior under the influence of alcohol is more extreme in every respect – more altruistic as well as more violent.

Rage is common in the home and on the football field. Instances of road rage (and also "air rage") seem to be on the increase. We have procedures for avoiding conflict in a crowded room or on a street. But those procedures cannot be used when the potential conflict is with a driver in another vehicle and, so far, no alternative procedure has evolved to supply that need.

But some acts of violence, e.g., murder of children by children, take even hardened commentators by surprise and everyone asks: Why did they do it? Was it from watching video nasties? That question is so common, on so many people's lips, that it deserves a chapter to itself.

QUESTIONS FOR DISCUSSION

1 Why do toddlers throw tantrums? What does this tell us about adult rage?

2 Why does alcohol make people behave aggressively?

3 Can we trust the findings of laboratory experiments on aggression?

13

...AND ARE WE PROVOKED TO VIOLENCE BY THE MEDIA?

On February 12, 1993, James Bulger, aged 2, was led away by two 10-year-olds from the Strand shopping precinct, Bootle, Merseyside.

> James was dragged, often in tears, through the streets, on to a covered reservoir, and finally to the railway line at Walton, Liverpool, two and a half miles from the precinct. There Thompson and Venables inflicted 42 injuries. Among the 22 wounds on his face and head were those that caused his death. The killers struck more than 30 blows with bricks and an iron bar. They sexually abused James's body, removing his trousers and underpants. (Foster, 1993)

And everyone asked: "Why did they do it? From watching video nasties?"

VIDEO NASTIES

To tell the truth, video nasties are not important to the study of human motivation, and some justification is needed for a chapter devoted to them. But video nasties are what every layperson thinks of when some horrific story is made public and what newspaper columnists debate. Consequently, their role has been well researched and there is now a fairly clear answer to the question. Setting out the answer to that question will accomplish two things. It will, first, identify a wider set of (human) environmental events which interact with aggressive instincts and, second, it will reveal how difficult it is to answer even a seemingly simple question like the effect of video nasties.

Murder of children by children is very rare, which means that there is ordinarily no basis on which anyone could attempt to explain why those two 10-year-olds should have killed James Bulger; except that there is an uncannily close parallel to that tragic story – so close a parallel as to invoke some simple underlying pattern of behavior. On April 11, 1861, at Stockport (only 30 miles from where James was murdered) two boys, 8 years old at the time, led George Burgess, aged 2, away to a brook, undressed him, beat him savagely, and then held his face under a few inches of water (Sereny, 1995). There were no video nasties for those boys to watch. But their behavior would have been shaped by the brutality of the society in which they were growing up. They did to George Burgess ("beat him savagely") what grown-ups had done to them. People, children, copy what they see others do around them. So, this chapter is not just about video nasties; it is about a whole range of events in the human society around us that might provoke some of us to violence.

"COPYCAT" MURDERS

On 30th March 1981 President Reagan was just leaving the Washington Hilton Hotel at about 2.30 p.m. when John Hinckley fired six shots, wounding President Reagan and three others. On investigation the police found a letter (unposted) to Jodie Foster in Hinckley's apartment in which he detailed his plans to assassinate the President. Now Jodie Foster had recently played the role of a prostitute in the film *Taxi Driver*. "The film concerns a mentally disturbed cab driver who plots to kill a U.S. Senator and who at one point tells his teen-aged prostitute paramour, 'If you don't love me, I'm going to kill the President.'" (Bishop, 1981)

John Hinckley seems to have been acting out a fantasy. That fantasy explains why his attempted assassination took that particular form, but does not necessarily explain why he attempted an assassination in the first place. We must distinguish carefully between two questions: (1) Why was the assassination attempted at all? and (2) Why did it take the form that it did? The episode in *Taxi Driver* provides an answer to the second question; it evidently suggested a *modus operandi* to Hinckley. But it is more than possible that if he had not seen that film, he would still have made his attempt, but in some other fashion. That is to say, the episode in the film does not necessarily provide the motivation to kill, merely a scenario for doing it.

The Columbine High School shooting

"Copycat" actions are far from uncommon. On Tuesday April 20, 1999, at about 11.20 in the morning, Eric Harris and Dylan Klebold walked into Columbine High School in Denver, Colorado – their high school – dressed in trenchcoats and started shooting. They were armed with a 9-mm semi-automatic pistol, a 9-mm semi-automatic carbine, and two sawn-off shotguns, to say nothing of numerous bombs. They killed 12 fellow pupils and one teacher, besides injuring more than 20 others, before finally killing themselves (Rhodes, 1999).

The motivation for Harris's and Klebold's actions presents, of course, a profound and difficult problem; but that is not the point here. I am interested in the "copycats."

> In Colorado Springs, four teenagers were charged with trespassing after arriving at a school in trenchcoats and masks. In Ohio, a 13-year-old boy was taken into custody after threatening to shoot all the people he did not like at school.
>
> In Texas five 14-year-olds were taken into custody for allegedly making plans to assassinate teachers and students at Danforth junior high school in Wimberley, 35 miles southwest of Austin. (Rhodes, 1999, pp. 26–7)

From Washington, DC, a week later,

> In the eight school days since the deadly rampage at Columbine High School, panic has swept schools in nearly every state as administrators and teachers scramble to deal with hundreds of copycat incidents – most often bomb threats or scares, but in a few cases acts of violence.
>
> The incidents have ranged from a boy tossing chemical bombs outside a Michigan high school and four Texas boys plotting a bomb attack on their middle school to an Alaska boy who brought a stolen .44-caliber Magnum pistol to his middle school.
>
> Washington area schools have been plagued by bomb threats and rumors of student "hit lists" since the Colorado shooting. The trend continued yesterday, with bomb searches at schools in Arlington and Fairfax counties and the arrests of two Prince George's County students on charges of making threats. (Cooper, 1999)

Copycat crime can begin at a very young age. Kayla Rolland, aged 6, was shot and killed at Buell Elementary School, north of Flint, Michigan, on February 28, 2000. The 6-year-old boy accused of the killing "took the gun from under a bed at home and afterwards said that what he had done 'kind of happens on TV'" (Whitworth & Macintyre, 2000).

We are thereby brought to face this question: Do video nasties also prompt violence, as well as shape it? That proves to be a difficult question to answer for these reasons:

1　Of necessity homicides cannot be subject to experimental manipulation. So any investigation of the effects of video nasties on propensity to kill must depend on surveying the frequencies of naturally occurring homicides. But homicides are rare events and such a survey would need a prohibitively large sample.
2　In addition, the use of survey data means that the presentation of the video nasty, or whatever else, is not subject to experimental control either.
3　One could, of course, select particular homicide stories from the news television broadcasts; but, notwithstanding that homicides are rare events, the number of homicide stories, fictional as well as real, presented in news and television broadcasts is much too great for the analysis of the effects of individual stories to be feasible.

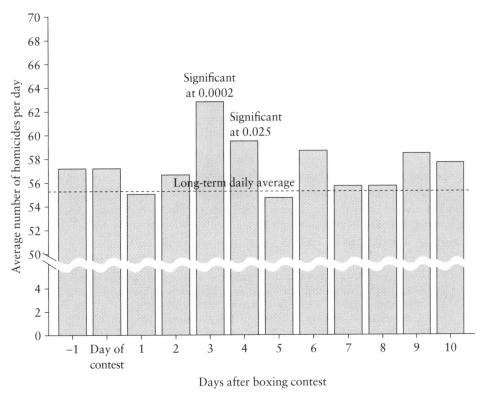

Figure 13.1 Average number of daily homicides in the United States following a heavyweight boxing contest, 1973–8.

Phillips (1983) devised a most elegant solution to this otherwise difficult problem. Heavyweight championship boxing contests are

1 relatively infrequent, so that the influence of individual contests on people's behavior can be distinguished, one contest from another;
2 heavily publicized, so that the potential size of the survey sample is huge; and
3 the violence is presented as real; as exciting; as (morally) uncriticized; as justi-fied; as rewarded; and it is known that each boxer actually intends to hurt his opponent. These are all factors which are alleged to facilitate imitation of the violence (Comstock, 1977).

Phillips calculated a linear regression of the number of daily homicides in the United States on the successive days following a heavyweight boxing contest, with controls for the day of the week, the season, the year, and for public holidays. His results are shown in figure 13.1. The increase of 7.47 above the daily average of

55.4, three days after the fight, is small but nevertheless significant at 0.0002; the increase of 4.15 on the following day is also significant. There is no countervailing drop in frequency on the days following so that the heavyweight contest does not just bring forward homicides that were going to take place anyway. It appears to effect an absolute increase in frequency. But why?

BOXING

Many sports make their top exponents multimillionaires. The money to reward the top sportsmen and women comes from sponsors in return for advertising the sponsor's name. Formula 1 motor racing is perhaps the most extreme example. But one sport has always been able to make its champions millionaires without sponsorship. That sport is heavyweight boxing. People will pay large sums for a seat at the ringside to watch two very powerful men batter each other. Here's why.

> Billy Schwer ducks and bobs, dances and punches as a thousand followers from his home town, Luton, call out his name, their voices rising and swelling in a chilling chorus, like the sound of storm winds blowing through the great dome of the Albert Hall: "Bee-lay, Bee-lay . . ." His opponent, Carl Crook, sways and buckles. His face is bleeding; the blood runs down Schwer's back. It's nasty but it's compelling. The crowd explodes with excitement.
>
> Piercing their incantations is a high-pitched woman's voice. "Jab him, Billy," she yells. She's jumping up and down on her ringside chair, her blonde hair making light waves around her head. She's small and curvy, wearing a white plunge-neck T-shirt, hot pants, a spangled velvet waistcoat and chunky high-heeled shoes. When Crook's head goes back in response to a punch, she goes wild. Beside her a more sedate but equally enraptured young woman calls out a milder message: "Come on Billy!" She bites her lip. She is wearing black leather trousers and a body-hugging black shirt. Both young women wear gold bracelets and necklaces. Beside them an older woman watches, her expression fearful. She transmits nervous messages: "Keep your hands up, Billy!" Her voice is quieter.
>
> The women are Billy's two sisters Mandy and Lisa, both in their twenties, and his mother, Wendy. It is Mandy, the elder sister, whose voice is the loudest. As the fight reaches its bloody climax, amazing reserves of fury find their way out of Mandy's delicately drawn mouth: "Hurt him Billy! Break his ribs! Box his lights out! Finish him off Billy!" Crook goes down, his nose broken, and Billy's fist is raised in victory. The crowd is beside itself. The women gather up their handbags, chattering happily among themselves. (McFadyean, 1994)

And here is Koula Solomon, sister to Rocky "The Cyprus Cyclone" Milton.

> She would hate it if Rocky really hurt anyone, she says: yet, she adds, with great feeling and no embarrassment: "Blood gets me going. When I see blood on Rocky's opponent it makes me want to shout louder. It makes me want to jump in the ring with him."

"When he's in the ring it brings the animal out in me," she says. "I feel wild, I rage, I go crazy when I see the blood. When my brother causes pain enough for blood to come oozing out of his opponent's face, it's almost as if I can taste it, as if it's the sweet success pouring out. Blood means winning."

She feels that she changes when she gets to a fight. "It's that powerful aura surrounding the ring: the people, the faces, the expectations. It's live, it's raw, it's powerful. Those half-naked bodies are an instant turn-on. They send out body messages, body heat, the sweat trickling down their backs – I feel an excitement deep within myself. It's like an orgasm only more so – the violence, the ecstasy, the terror." (McFadyean, 1994)

There is an instinctive response to seeing others fight, to vicarious aggression. People get worked up simply from watching. Berkowitz (1965) has published a series of laboratory experiments to underline this point. Here is the third experiment in that series.

The Effect of Watching a Boxing Match

Berkowitz employed a conventional design with each real participant paired with a confederate who was introduced as a graduate student in physical education and a "former college boxer." The experimental procedure was divided into three phases.

Phase 1. The two participants were both given a 5-minute intelligence test during which the confederate disparaged the real participant's performance or was neutral. This phase set up the usual comparison between provoked and control conditions.

Phase 2. Both participants next watched a 6-minute clip from the film *Champion* in which the hero (played by Kirk Douglas) gets badly beaten up in the ring. There is a prior summary to set the scene which portrays Kirk Douglas's character as either (a) a basically nice person (to elicit sympathy for the character so that the punishment he receives will be perceived as morally wrong – people do not get worked up over prohibited violence) or (b) unpleasant and exploitative (so that the punishment is now seen as deserved).

Phase 3. The real participant is now asked to evaluate the confederate's work on an unrelated task, devising "an original and imaginative floor plan for a house." The real participant administers one shock for "very good," up to 10 shocks for "very bad." From figure 13.2 it can be seen that provoked participants deliver more shocks – that is, they exhibit a higher level of aggression. The mean number of shocks interacts with the scene set for the film clip. The "justified beating" (which means "it's all right to get worked up about it") amplifies the effect of provocation, so that the "provoked × justified beating" condition generates the highest level of aggression. The experimental effect is small, but is readily repeatable (Berkowitz, 1993, pp. 214–17).

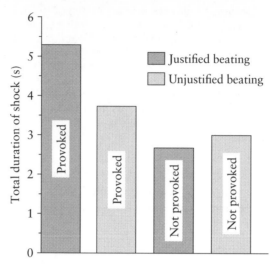

Figure 13.2   Mean numbers of shocks delivered in the experiment by Berkowitz (1965, Expt 3). Reproduced with permission from Berkowitz (1993, p. 216). © 1993 McGraw-Hill Education.

The appeal of boxing lies in the emotional arousal it generates amongst the spectators. It has an appeal like skydiving, bungee jumping, biking, and handling poisonous snakes (cf. chapter 5). In our society there are social constraints against all sorts of violence. At a boxing match those constraints are vicariously set aside; that is especially so if one has been brought up in a boxing family . . . or is otherwise given to violence!

NEIGHBOR DISPUTES

Although enjoyment of a boxing match is restricted to aficionados – though there are many of them – the propensity to get worked up when watching someone else's conflict is widespread, and probably universal. That explains the great popularity in the UK of a new TV genre featuring the presentation of neighbor disputes – *Neighbours from Hell* (ITV), *Neighbours at War* (BBC1). The neighbors are in conflict over a variety of different causes – unsocial behavior; noise, especially during the night; boundary or driveway disputes; Lawson's cypresses, and worse. The different neighbors develop different perceptions of the rights and wrongs of the dispute – they view it from different points of view – and there follows an instinctive continuation and escalation of the conflict.

These disputes are mostly pursued just within the law, seemingly with a maximum of spite and bitterness. The BBC report that 1 in 14 households have reported a neighbor to the police; 1 in 25 households have threatened to take a neighbor to court (Woodford, 1998). Conflict between neighbors is widespread. Usually neither party benefits; often both are faced with crippling legal costs.

> A long-running neighbour dispute over a few square feet of land finally ended at the Court of Appeal yesterday after 28 court hearings that generated an estimated £100,000 in legal bills.
> Rejecting a claim by Clive Pearson, a property manager, to a ten-yard strip measuring between one inch and three inches, . . . (Gibb, 1999)

There are two questions to ask here.

1 Why do so many neighbors get into these kinds of dispute, often pursued with great acrimony? I suggest there is an instinctive tendency in each of us to respond to aggression, real or merely imagined, with aggression. Ordinarily, such a response is limited by social constraints; but let one party disregard the constraints of civilized behavior and the scene is set for an escalation, with the conflict getting progressively out of hand.
2 Why does such an escalation of conflict provide so popular an entertainment? It clearly does; it appeals in the same way as boxing, but is free of the obloquy attaching to the "noble art." People seem to get aroused by watching other people in conflict – by boxing, by neighbor disputes – and by what else?

Sympathetic Motivation

Richard Gelles and Murray Straus are world experts on the incidence of domestic violence and its impact on other people. So imagine you are a pediatrician examining a little girl who has come into Accident and Emergency with bruises, broken bones, and cigarette burns on her back.

> Most clinicians know they should not take out their anger and frustration on either victims or offenders. Yet, dealing with family violence does produce anger and frustration. Often, the anger is directed at other professionals: physicians get angry with social workers, social workers get angry with physicians, and they both direct fury at the criminal justice system. (Gelles & Straus, 1988, p. 184)

Live sex shows are another example (cf. chapter 3). Kinsey et al. (1953, p. 661) noted that "commercialized exhibitions of sexual activity" have been provided since the days of ancient Rome (but only for men – women are generally unaroused by them). "The males of practically all infra-human species may become aroused when they observe other animals in sexual activity. Of this fact farmers, animal breeders, scientists experimenting with laboratory animals, and many persons who have kept household pets are abundantly aware" (Kinsey et al., 1953, p. 661).

The propensity to become excited oneself when observing highly motivated behavior in others may be a quite general phenomenon. If so, it would provide a basis for the present-day demand for pornography of all kinds and also for romantic literature (Mills & Boon novels etc.) and horror films – "TV puts on festive orgy of sex, horror and violence" (Midgley, 1998a).

SUICIDES

Attempts at suicide provide another example and are an increasing problem.

> A rise in young men attempting suicide has pushed Britain to a record level of self-destruction, with one in every 250 people in England a year admitted to casualty for self-harm. . . .
> Deliberate overdoses or other self-injuries are now in the top five of all emergency admissions . . . Paracetamol overdose is the most common.
> Suicide-attempt rates have mirrored recent recessions. The most likely to die by suicide are now male, unemployed, in poor physical health and living alone. "The rates have gone up spectacularly for men under 30." (Rumbelow, 1998)

The potential suicide is, of course, depressed. But what tips him over the edge?

Phillips (1974) listed the suicides appearing on the front page of the *New York Times* from 1947 to 1968. He then examined the numbers of suicides each month in relation to the month of publication of each story, adjusting those monthly statistics for trends and seasons. For example, on November 1, 1965, Daniel Burros, a leader of the Ku Klux Klan, committed suicide when newspapers revealed that he was Jewish. Comparing November 1965 with the average of November 1964 and 1966 gives an increase of 58 (3.5 percent) in the month of Daniel Burros's suicide. This calculation is set out in table 13.1.

Table 13.1 Numbers of suicides in the United States for November 1964, 1965, 1966

Month	No. suicides	No. suicides
November 1964	1,639	
November 1965		1,710
November 1966	1,665	
Average (November 1964 and 1966)		1,652
Difference		58

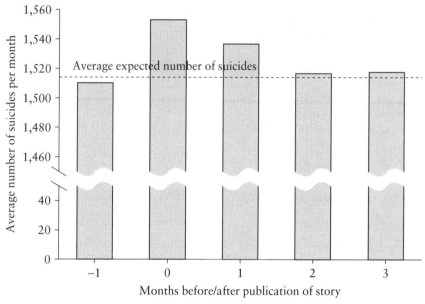

Figure 13.3 The number of suicides in the months before, during, and after the publication of another suicide story (from Phillips, 1974).

Figure 13.3 shows the fluctuation in the numbers of suicides before, during, and after a well-publicized suicide. The average excess in the month of the story is 39. Especially famous people produce a greater effect. Marilyn Monroe killed herself in August 1962. Her death led to a 12 percent (198) increase in the number of suicides in the United States and a nearly 10 percent increase in Britain (Berkowitz, 1993, p. 205). The frequency of suicides is influenced by the media.

THE LONG-TERM EFFECT OF TELEVISION VIOLENCE

Video nasties (and heavyweight boxing contests, assassinations, murders, suicides, executions, etc.) demonstrably modulate the temporary frequency of violent crime. But maybe the effect is only transitory; maybe these were crimes that were going to happen anyway. Do video nasties also increase the long-term frequency of violence? The complication here is that the intrinsically violent may well have a preference for watching violence on television. But does the watching, of itself, make the adult more violent than he would otherwise have been?

One frequent view (e.g., Damasio, 1994, p. 247; Berkowitz, 1993, pp. 223–4) is that the presentation of so much vicarious violence on television and elsewhere

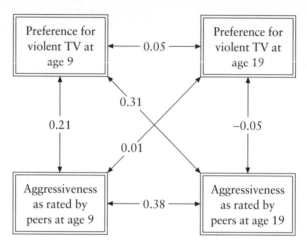

Figure 13.4 Cross-lagged correlations between preference for violent television programs and peer-rated aggression for 211 boys at ages 9 and 19. Reproduced with permission from Eron et al. (1972, p. 257). © 1972 American Psychological Association.

simply dulls the emotional response. Transposing that idea from personal view into camera view, it amounts to this: That the prevalence of violence on television, apparently divorced from social constraints, restructures the individual's view of society and makes violent behavior seem (to the individual) less unacceptable. That may well be so, and the examples of copycat crimes that I have already cited support that view. But the question I address now is whether watching violence on television makes any *noticeable* difference to the individual's behavior, bearing in mind that that behavior may be governed by other social constraints, much more powerful in their influence than television. This is the ultimate question and it proves very difficult to answer. But it has been addressed.

Eron, Huesman, Lefkowitz, and Walder (1972) conducted a longitudinal study of 427 children in Columbia County, New York. They measured each child's preference for violent television programs and also the child's aggression as rated by peers at both ages 9 and 19. The correlations between each pair of these variables are set out in figure 13.4.

The calculations look conclusive. The forward cross-lagged correlation,

TV preference (at age 9) → Aggressiveness (at age 19),

0.31, is significant at 0.01. It is much stronger than the backward correlation,

TV preference (at age 19) → Aggressiveness (at age 9),

0.01; the difference between the two is also significant at 0.01. So it seems that aggression at age 19 must, to some extent, be consequent on television preference at age 9. If there were no such consequential relationship, one would expect these two correlation coefficients to be about the same, reflecting simply a static relationship between individual preference for violence on television and innate aggressiveness.

The survey by Eron et al. (1972) has been repeated in Finland, in Israel (with city children), in Poland, and in Chicago with similar results, but in Australia and Israel (with kibbutz children) no relationship between preference for violence on television and subsequent aggressiveness was found. In 1994 the island of St Helena began television broadcasting.

> St Helena, in the south Atlantic, got television for the first time only three years ago. Children there, whose behaviour has been monitored since they began watching, have shown no signs of copying violence or altering their conduct.
>
> The children have been watching the same amounts of violence, and in many cases the same programmes, as British children. But they have not gone out and copied what they have seen on TV.
>
> The study involves 59 pre-school children who will be monitored until they are 13 and all 800 children of first and middle school. Researchers monitored hours of television programmes viewed by the St Helena children to establish that they were watching the same levels of violence as British children. This was backed up by secret videoing of the children as they played at school to see if the television violence was transferred into play.
>
> Bad behaviour is virtually unheard of in the playground, and our footage shows that what is viewed is not repeated. (Midgley, 1998b)

However, the cross-lagged correlation of 0.31 between television preference at age 9 and aggressiveness at age 19 means that television preference at age 9 accounts for only 10 percent ($(0.31)^2$) of the variance in aggressiveness at age 19. So the effect of violence in television programs on children's behavior or on adult aggressiveness is, at most, weak. Its appearance probably depends on the structure of the society in which the child grows up (so that different results are obtained from surveys in different countries), and social structure and family constraints are thought to be especially stable on St Helena. But if that stable, disciplined social framework be taken away . . .

The Ridings School, Halifax

The Ridings School at Halifax was created in January 1995 by the merger of two unsuccessful secondary modern schools. The pupils from these two constituents never gelled and the teachers gradually lost control. There developed a breakdown in discipline, regular vandalism, and contempt for the teachers. The headmistress eventually resigned, and the school was closed on October 31, 1996 – and then reopened under a hand-picked troubleshooter as headmaster.

> As an experienced "trouble shooting" headteacher called in to rescue a school
> branded the worst in Britain, Peter Clark was braced for a battle. What he found
> shocked even him.
>
> Pupils aged 11 to 18 were so undisciplined that when they were angry they
> smashed furniture. Staff were regularly assaulted. Demoralised teachers no longer
> knew how to defuse emerging crises and parents sided with their violent off-
> spring, refusing to recognise the school's authority.
>
> "One of the most noticeable behaviour patterns among the pupils was their
> tendency to fly off the handle at some minor perceived slight," says Clark. "In a
> normal school this would result in fights and swearing – at the Ridings during
> these first few weeks, it involved throwing a piece of furniture."
>
> Many children found it "almost impossible" to control their tempers and threw
> "spectacular tantrums." Instead of just one or two troublemakers in a class,
> most were intent on disruption, making it virtually unteachable. (O'Reilly, 1997)

In most schools the pupils concentrate on their work. Those pupils who would
prefer to play around, disrupting the class, are restrained by discipline. Experience
at the Ridings School shows what happens when a disciplined social framework is
lacking. Once the teachers lost control, the pupils' behavior evolved beyond all
civilized bounds; the educational function of the school collapsed.

One might suppose that this chaos resulted simply from a lack of skill or experience or "losing it" on the part of the teachers. But that would be too simple.
Torsten Friedag was brought in as a "superhead" to rescue the Islington Arts and
Media School from ignominious failure. As part of that rescue Islington Education Authority undertook a radical refurbishment of the school premises; but local
bureaucracy was so cumbersome that the building work was hopelessly delayed and
the new school year had to begin on a virtual building site. Those circumstances
of themselves placed additional burdens on a school already encumbered with the
legacy of recent failure, and discipline failed again.

> There were between 40 and 60 boys and girls who would not or could not behave.
>
> The most notorious incident was a stand-off between screaming and swearing
> gangs of 40 to 50 girls, backed up by reinforcements from outside called in on
> their mobile phones. It took 10 police officers to help staff to bring the riot under
> control.
>
> There were rumours of weapons and one boy brought a metal pole for this
> purpose, but that was all that was found. (Torsten Friedag in interview;
> Waterhouse, 2000)

Torsten Friedag resigned after fewer than two complete terms (Thirkell, 2000). He
is one of four superheads, out of 16, who have taken on problem schools in Britain
and given up, having failed to turn their school around. French teachers have a
similar problem of discipline (Sopel, 2000). It is not just the skill and devotion of
the teachers that matters; it is the entire milieu, much of which (the school buildings
and the support from governors and the local education authority) is outside the

teachers' control. It is not surprising that the development of aggressive behavior from watching violence on television depends, among other things, on the social milieu within which the children grow up.

The Medway Training Centre

Another problem arises, of course, from the pupils themselves. The Medway Training Centre opened in April 1998 to take 40 young offenders between the ages of 12 and 14. There were 100 staff to look after them. Seven months later,

> Britain's first child jail is undergoing a sweeping overhaul after months of turmoil during which young offenders wrecked classrooms, their rooms and kitchens.
> More than £100,000 has been spent replacing and repairing facilities at the purpose-built Medway Secure Training Centre at Rochester in Kent.
> There have been 97 assaults on staff, 27 of whom needed medical treatment.
> The specially toughened bedroom windows have been replaced after the children smashed them with their fists and feet. Wooden doors reinforced with steel are being replaced after the wood was hacked away. CCTV cameras have been destroyed and all bedroom door locks replaced. (Ford & Kennedy, 1998)

The Medway Training Centre takes in the most disadvantaged of children. These are children who mostly have been denied the parental care and the start in life that everybody else takes for granted. They are the "unadoptable" ones. The center opened under a management philosophy of "Education, Care, Discipline." But the staff, carefully chosen for having cool tempers, rapidly lost control. A riot in June 1998 had to be brought under control by police wearing riot gear, accompanied by dogs (Kennedy & Ford, 1998).

SUMMARY

When some particularly sickening act of violence catches the media's attention, people ask: Why did he do it? Was it from watching video nasties?

It is clear that some people do copy crimes that they see on the screen or hear about in the media. But that does not necessarily make the video nasty the cause of the crime; it might merely shape it. A crime that was going to be committed anyway is committed in this way, rather than in some other fashion. The question of causation requires more careful investigation.

Analysis of the numbers of homicides in the days following heavyweight boxing contests has shown that the media do have some effect. Well-publicized suicides temporarily increase the rate of suicide. Watching a boxing match gets the spectators worked up and they become more aggressive in consequence. That increased aggression has been confirmed by experiment. It provides an explanation for the audience appeal of boxing – people like to be worked up – an appeal which extends to the broadcasting of neighbor disputes on television.

But this still does not address the ultimate question whether watching violence on television produces a long-term increase in aggressive behavior. The longitudinal study by Eron et al. (1972) has produced different answers in different cultures and the best answer that can be given today is that the effect of video nasties is, at most, weak, and probably dependent on the social structure of the society under examination. Some societies show no effect at all. On the other hand, if social discipline be entirely undermined, as happened at the Ridings School in Halifax and at the Medway Training Centre, then violent behavior becomes unrestrained.

This chapter completes my consideration of those sources of motivation which might be considered instinctive in humans. I have not covered all the basic instincts that can be identified, just those which have important social implications in our society today. But this is not the end of human motivation. The motivational force of money is manifestly acquired; different countries use different systems of coinage and the coins that are motivationally significant in one country may have little impact in another. But, as a source of motivation, money is just as powerful as any instinct, as we shall see next.

QUESTIONS FOR DISCUSSION

1 Would our society be less violent than it is without television, films, and videos?

2 Why do some spectators get so excited over a boxing bout?

3 Why do disputes between neighbors sometimes escalate beyond all reason . . .

4 . . . and why is the incidence of "road rage" increasing?

14

MONEY

In the language of animal behavior theory, money is an incentive; that is, its motivational significance is acquired rather than innate – it does not engage any instinctive behavior directly. Nevertheless, money functions like any other motivator. There are people who are unmoved by money, of whom St Francis of Assisi is the best known. He was born Francesco di Pietro di Bernadone in 1181 or 1182, the son of a cloth merchant. As a young man he renounced all material goods and family ties in order to embrace a life of poverty; his disciples evolved into the Franciscan order of monks and friars. Such people do exist – but they are very rare. For nearly everybody else money seems to have the same strength of motivational force as basic instincts like fear and rage and sex, as the examples in this chapter will show.

To illustrate the power of money as a motivator, Schwab (1953) asked participants to hang by the arms from a bar above the ground. Supporting one's weight in that way is very fatiguing. The arm muscles are more than strong enough, but they ache and this experiment looked at the participants' toleration of that discomfort. The (normal) control instruction was "For as long as you can" and that produced an average endurance of 48 s. Under strong suggestion to the same participants that they could do better (hypnotic suggestion in some cases), the average increased to 72 s. But when each participant was offered $5 if he improved on his previous performance, the average endurance increased yet again to 112 s.

In this chapter I am concerned, in the first place, to illustrate the kinds of things people will do for money – many of them in varying degrees illegal. Chapter 7 showed that the distribution of monetary rewards in our society is arbitrary and very unequal, and that social conventions and laws are needed to maintain that inequality. As a result there are some members of society who think they haven't got enough money and I shall look at what such people do to get themselves more. But it is not everybody who is actuated in this way; it is certain kinds of people and we shall see what kinds of people they are – the Machiavellians and the psychopaths.

Two Ways to Become Rich

To put the matter simply, there are two ways to become rich. In the first place, you can sit and wait for money to drop into your lap. If you have wealthy parents or grandparents, patience will ultimately pay off. But there are other expectations that might also be fulfilled.

Compensation for post-traumatic stress

Suppose you suffer an accident or are involved in a disaster, or a close relative is killed and you are there when it happens, or you see it happen on television, or you are a police officer on duty at the time. If the accident or disaster achieves a sufficiently high public profile, you can sue for the psychological distress you have suffered. On April 15, 1989, the FA Cup semi-final between Liverpool and Nottingham Forest was scheduled to be played at Hillsborough in Sheffield. The football match started on time, but was stopped after 6 minutes because the crowd in the Leppings Lane stand had imploded. Spectators pressing in to already overfilled stands, eager not to miss any of the play, compressed those other spectators already inside to the point that 95 of them were crushed to death. Without examining here how and why and who was responsible, it is relevant that 150 police officers sued South Yorkshire Police authority for compensation for post-traumatic stress disorder. As of July 15, 1996, 113 of those cases had been withdrawn, 14 litigants had been awarded £1.2 million, and 23 cases were pending of which six were awaiting appeal (Davies, 1996). There is no mention of therapy in that report, and one must presume that the litigants' post-traumatic stress disorder had been left untreated for seven years, because a successful treatment would have reduced the amount of damages.

The parents and siblings of the 95 spectators who died also sued. Barry Devonside lost his 18-year-old son Christopher at Hillsborough.

> People are very upset and bitter about the compensation they expect. We do not want the money for ourselves, but it is important that someone is made to pay for the terrible events of that day.
>
> I lost Christopher and all I'm entitled to is compensation for the trauma and pain he suffered before dying, which I am told will be around £2,000. (*Independent*, 1990)

> For a while after the tragedy, the families were wholly united in grief and formed a family support group, initially as a place where they could grieve together. Later it became a pressure group to lobby for their interests.
>
> Six years on . . . Hillsborough remains unfinished business for the families of the dead. There have been suicide attempts, long-term relationships have broken up and families have fallen out with one another as they continue their struggle for justice. (Crace, 1995)

Eye Need

If you do not have wealthy parents or other expectations, you could still put an advertisement in the satirical magazine *Private Eye*'s personal column, *Eye Need*. Margaret Evans (an *Independent* journalist) wrote to 20 box numbers asking the advertiser to contact her. Their reason for advertising? "Loads of people advertise in the *Eye* so it must work" – it doesn't!

> Jonathan Sale, a journalist, who advertised "Father, householder, cyclist seeks funds to keep family career and wheels on the straight and narrow," was sent a chain letter. His post also contained 50p from someone salving a "guilty conscience," a new puncture-repair kit from "a fellow father and cyclist" and £1.72 in used and unused stamps. He beat Brian Jenner's attempt to raise funds for *The Hypocrite*, the satirical paper of Brasenose College, Oxford. The only contact he made was mine.
>
> The ads cost £1.40 a word plus £7.50 for the use of the box, so evidently there is some money lining the advertiser's purses. The "young continental male artist-painter . . . seeking generous sponsors" had forked out £49.50. Compare that with unemployment benefit at £37.35 a week." (Evans, 1991)

There are two ways to become rich and the second way is to take money from somebody else – and you had better not be too scrupulous about it. The rest of this chapter is about various schemes for taking money from other people, not necessarily legally, and why they work and what they tell us about human motivation. I shall be asking what kind of people operate these schemes and it will help, as a point of reference, to look straightaway at the psychopathic personality.

THE PSYCHOPATHIC PERSONALITY

The concept of a psychopathic personality was developed especially by Hervey Cleckley (1976) who saw it as a mental disorder with the characteristics set out in table 14.1. Cleckley's indicators relate mostly to the long-term integration of social behavior. That suggests that the psychopath is variously unresponsive to social constraints, like normal people under the influence of alcohol (cf. chapter 12, pp. 219–20). That lack of responsiveness leads to a diverse variety of antisocial behavior, including crime and delinquency (see Mealey, 1995).

Legally, psychopaths are not insane, and they are sent to prison for the crimes they commit. Characteristics 2 and 3 in table 14.1 mean that psychopathy is unrelated to the conventional psychiatric categories of insanity and neuroticism. Characteristic 1 signifies that the psychopath knows how to get on in society, while the insane do not, and it is arguable that psychopaths are not even abnormal, but simply one extreme of a natural variation in personality (e.g., Smith, 1978). That

Table 14.1 Characteristics of the psychopathic personality

1	Superficial charm and good "intelligence"
2	Absence of delusions and other signs of irrational thinking
3	Absence of "nervousness" or psychoneurotic manifestations
4	Unreliability
5	Untruthfulness and insincerity
6	Lack of remorse or shame
7	Inadequately motivated antisocial behavior
8	Poor judgment and failure to learn by experience
9	Pathological egocentricity and incapacity for love
10	General poverty in major affective reactions
11	Specific loss of insight
12	Unresponsiveness in general interpersonal relations
13	Fantastic and uninviting behavior with drink and sometimes without
14	Suicide rarely carried out
15	Sex life impersonal, trivial, and poorly integrated
16	Failure to follow any life plan

Source: Cleckley (1976, pp. 337–8).

idea is supported by the examples of many lesser degrees of psychopathic behavior that we shall meet below.

Psychopathic personality seems to have evolved into a psychiatric category solely because the psychiatrist is the natural "port of call" for people with any kind of personality or social problem. Psychopathic personality, roughly speaking, is the residue of cases left after all other categories – psychoses, neuroses, congenital deficiencies – have been separated out. There is no effective treatment.

MACHIAVELLIANISM

It will also help to look at the concept of Machiavellianism as a component of the personality of certain people. Niccolò Machiavelli was a sixteenth-century Florentine diplomat and political philosopher. Richard Christie and Florence Geis (Christie & Geis, 1970) constructed a scale of Machiavellianism which may be loosely characterized as an ability or willingness to manipulate other people. They selected 20 statements from Machiavelli's two books, *The Prince* and *The Discourses*. These statements, which are set out in table 14.2, were given to the respondent with instructions to indicate agreement or disagreement on a five-point scale, ranging from "strong disagreement" to "strong agreement." Half of the statements (e.g., No. 1) are phrased as Machiavelli would have put them, half (e.g., No. 2) were

Table 14.2 Scale items in the test of Machiavellianism

1   The best way to handle people is to tell them what they want to hear.
2   When you ask someone to do something for you, it is best to give the real reasons for wanting it rather than giving reasons which might carry more weight.
3   Anyone who completely trusts anyone else is asking for trouble.
4   It is hard to get ahead without cutting corners here and there.
5   Honesty is the best policy in all cases.
6   It is safest to assume that all people have a vicious streak and it will come out when they are given a chance.
7   Never tell anyone the real reason you did something unless it is useful to do so.
8   One should take action only when sure it is morally right.
9   It is wise to flatter important people.
10 All in all, it is better to be humble and honest than important and dishonest.
11 Barnum was very wrong when he said there's a sucker born every minute.
12 People suffering from incurable diseases should have the choice of being put painlessly to death.
13 It is possible to be good in all respects.
14 Most people are basically good and kind.
15 There is no excuse for lying to someone else.
16 Most men forget more easily the death of their father than the loss of their property.
17 Most people who get ahead in the world lead clean, moral lives.
18 Generally speaking, men won't work hard unless they're forced to do so.
19 The biggest difference between most criminals and other people is that criminals are stupid enough to get caught.
20 Most men are brave.

Source: Adapted with permission from Christie & Geis (1970, pp. 17–18). © 1970 Academic Press.

inverted, to correct for any intrinsic bias to agree or to disagree *per se*. The sum of the ratings, with the ratings for the inverted statements reversed, gave a simple measure of the extent to which the respondent agreed with Machiavelli's dicta. Does that measure of agreement correlate with any observable characteristics of people's behavior?

The $10 Game

There are three participants seated round a table. These are their instructions.

> This is a bargaining game in which you will have a chance to make some money if you are good at bargaining. Ten $1 bills will be placed on the table in front of the three of you. The money will belong to any *two* of you who can agree with each other as to how you will divide the $10 between you. (You will not be

Table 14.3 Number of participants in the final coalition in relation to score of Machiavellianism

Machiavellianism score	Included in final coalition	Excluded from final coalition	Average winnings
High	7	0	$5.57
Medium	5	2	$3.14
Low	2	5	$1.29

Source: Adapted with permission from Christie & Geis (1970, pp. 164, 165). © 1970 Academic Press.

> allowed to divide the money among all three of you.) The two prospective part-
> ners can divide the $10 any way they choose. For example, they might split it 5
> and 5, 8 and 2, or any other split. Of course, the third man, who at the time is
> being left out of the agreement, can also make offers to either of the two bar-
> gainers, and try to win one of them over to making the agreement with him. The
> game is over when any two players have made an agreement which the third
> player cannot get them to break. The money belongs to the two who have made
> the agreement and is divided accordingly between them. (Christie & Geis, 1970,
> pp. 161–2)

Christie and Geis ran seven triads of participants. The 21 participants were first scored on Machiavellianism, and each triad was composed of a high, a medium, and a low scorer. To receive a share of the $10, a participant has to be in the final coalition. Table 14.3 shows how membership of that coalition related to each participant's score on the test of Machiavellianism. The high Machiavel is always included, the low Machiavel usually excluded. The relationship is significant at 0.016; so also is the relationship to average winnings (Christie & Geis, 1970, pp. 164–5). Machiavellianism is a real personality factor with demonstrable beha-vioral outcomes.

Further study showed that Machiavellianism was uncorrelated with IQ and with most other personality and demographic variables. So what is it about Machiavels that enables them to win? That proves to be surprisingly difficult to answer, but some indications are provided by the "con game."

The Con Game

The con game (Geis, 1970) is another three-person bargaining game with the participants again assigned to triads according to their Machiavellianism score. But the con game is more complicated than the $10 game and its additional complica-tions enable one to see how the bargaining develops. It turns out that the low and

Table 14.4 Bargaining in the con game: (a) offers made and (b) offers accepted

(a) *To*	High Machiavel	Medium Machiavel	Low Machiavel
By High Machiavel	–	3.76	3.74
Medium Machiavel	3.87	–	3.12
Low Machiavel	3.58	2.92	–

(b) *From*	High Machiavel	Medium Machiavel	Low Machiavel
By High Machiavel	–	1.81	1.33
Medium Machiavel	1.78	–	1.08
Low Machiavel	1.40	1.28	–

medium Machiavels direct more of their bargaining to the high Machiavel and do not bargain so much with each other. Table 14.4(a) shows that the low and medium Machiavels make more offers of a coalition to the high Machiavel than they do to each other, and table 14.4(b) shows that they accept more offers from the high Machiavel. But why?

In the $10 game the participants were previously unacquainted, and one can only infer that the high Machiavel was intrinsically more attractive as a person. (It is certain kinds of people who make money in our society.) This inference calls to mind the "Superficial charm and good 'intelligence'" of the psychopath. The relationship between Machiavellianism and psychopathy has been studied more recently by McHoskey, Worzel, and Szyarto (1998) who administered Mach-IV (the test set out in table 14.2) and similar tests for psychopathy to groups of university students and examined the intercorrelations. They concluded "that the Mach-IV is a global measure of psychopathy in noninstitutionalized populations ... and that the primary differences between MACH and psychopathy are not traceable to substantive theoretical issues but to the different professional affiliations they are associated with: personality and social psychology and clinical psychology, respectively" (McHoskey et al., 1998, p. 192). So, how does Machiavellianism work out in practice?

Pawnbroking

A pawnbroker lends money for a short period against a pledge as security. If the loan is not repaid on time (a likely outcome), the pledge is forfeit. How does the amount lent relate to the value of the pledge?

> Islington council purchased new jewellery for £175 and then visited five local pawnbrokers to compare the loans on offer. The largest loan was £30, and the smallest just £15.
>
> The London Pledge Company had the highest APR [annual percentage rate] of the brokers surveyed, quoting a figure of 100 per cent but calculated by Islington at 156 per cent. (Gosling, 1993)

Some loan companies make a handsome profit out of the poor.

> Denise Burrow works 30 hours a week at home. Her last job was packing Christmas tags into fiddly cellophane packs. For her pains she earned £7. Why bother?
>
> "Well it pays my loan company £2 a week and then the £5 I use on a weekend for food . . . normal food. Basically we wouldn't have meat at the weekends so it supplies meat and even a loaf of bread, a pint of milk." This is a desperate woman.
>
> Denise lives in Bramley, Leeds, on a run-down council estate. For the past 14 years she's been in hock to the tallyman.
>
> When the charges they make can push up the annual borrowing rate, in effect, to 500 per cent or more, one has to ask why they're still in business. (Pennington, 1995)

There are other people, not quite so poor as Denise, who nevertheless get into debt, and there are companies who make a profit out of them. "Debt problems? Mr Stephenson was paying . . . £980 per month we restructured his payments to . . . £149 per month. One single affordable payment." But if you think Mr Stephenson has cut his debt by 85 percent, he hasn't; he has increased it with fees to Baines & Ernst. Also – "Need a car but can't get credit?" If you do not have a credit rating, you will surely pay through the nose for finance. Then you will have to ask Baines & Ernst to reschedule your debts.

By law, moneylenders have to be licensed. But in Glasgow there are unlicensed moneylenders who will lend money without a pledge, and to people without the resources to pay it back. Paul McCabe is one such. How does he make it pay?

> Until McCabe's conviction earlier this year [1992] for "operating a moneylending business without a licence," he and his collector . . . would hang out in the foyer of the Bell Street hostel, openly lending and collecting.
>
> By all accounts – mostly from borrowers anxious to remain anonymous – McCabe didn't have any trouble with bad debts. He has 10 convictions for assault.

McCabe charged a simple but punitive rate of interest. Usually it was 25 per cent per week [APR 10,947,544 percent], so on a £50 loan, £62.50 would be repayable the next week. On occasions the rate was doubled. (Rohrer, 1992)

If a borrower fails to repay, he is visited by the "heavies." If he resists, his face is slashed. If he goes to the police, his jaw, or arms or legs are broken.

Eye Contact

Such methods are brutal. Much more sophisticated is some kind of financial deception which depends on an ability to lie convincingly or, at the least, to be "economical with the truth." Convincing one's intended victim is assisted by maintaining eye contact with him or her. How do Machiavels score on eye contact?

Exline, Thibaut, Hickey, and Gumpert (1970) conducted an experiment in which two participants were interviewed under conditions in which the direction of gaze of one of them (the naive participant) could be recorded. They were then given 10 decision problems of increasing difficulty to solve together. The problems consisted of estimating the number of dots and the shape of a figure on a card exposed for 5 s. The two participants were required to agree on their answer. After the sixth of these 10 problems the experimenter was called away to take an "important long-distance telephone call." In the experimenter's absence, one of the participants (a confederate of the experimenter) persuades the other (the naive participant) to look at the answers to the remaining problems which happen to be available face down on the desk. After all 10 problems have been completed, there is a further interview in which the experimenter asks about the methods used to solve them, culminating in an accusation of cheating. The critical measure in this experiment is the amount of eye contact from the naive participant during this interview as a function of the naive participant's Machiavellianism score.

That critical measure is displayed in figure 14.1. Compared with a baseline measure, based on a 2-minute interview before the experiment started, all participants made less eye contact after they had been cheating, as measured by the average number of seconds per minute during which the participant looked at the experimenter during interview; but the high-scoring Machiavels showed a lesser reduction than did low scorers. That is, Machiavels are better able to "brazen it out." Being able to brazen it out is an important accomplishment if you are to take money from other people.

Credibility When Lying

As one might also expect, Machiavels are more credible when lying. This was demonstrated in an experiment by Geis and Moon (1981). Participants were

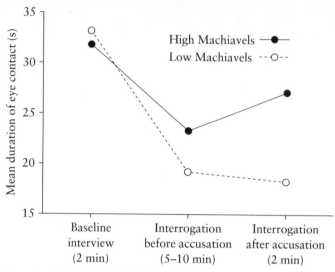

Figure 14.1 Mean duration for which critical participants looked at the experimenter during the experiment by Exline et al. (1970). Redrawn with permission from Christie & Geis (1970, p. 67). © 1970 Academic Press.

engaged to play the "prisoner's dilemma" game for real money (with payoffs of $2 to $7). Although this game ordinarily requires two players only, in this version of the game there were two pairs of players, each pair playing in consultation. Of the four players involved, one was naive and the other three confederates of the experimenter. In the course of the game half of the naive participants were induced by their confederate partner to steal a small sum of money, while the other half served as "no theft" controls. In due course the other pair of players, both confederates, accused the first pair of stealing some of their winnings. The same accusation was made in both experimental and control conditions, with the accusers not knowing which condition applied. It thus happened that all of the naive participants were accused of the same theft, when half of them had indeed stolen the money, while the other half had not. Their denials were surreptitiously videotaped and subsequently viewed by another set of participants (the judges) who were asked simply whether the original naive participant accused of theft was lying or not. The judges recorded their beliefs on a six-point scale (mid-point 3.5) and the mean credibility scores are shown in figure 14.2.

The naive participants were, of course, evenly divided into high and low scorers on the Mach scale. When there had been no theft (the control condition), there was no difference between the high and low Machiavels in credibility. But while in the theft condition both groups suffered in credibility, the judges were significantly less inclined to believe the low Machiavels. The high Machiavels are better able

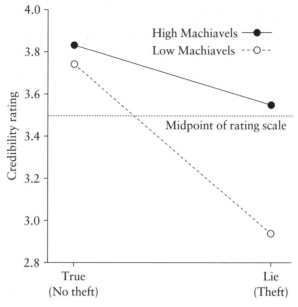

Figure 14.2 Credibility of high- and low-scoring Machiavels when lying and when telling the truth (data from Geis & Moon, 1981). Redrawn with permission from Geis & Moon (1981, p. 772). © 1981 American Psychological Association.

to convince when they are lying. However, that is not quite the end of the story. The experimental design required 64 naive participants, but 81 participants were actually run. Of the 17 participants who were lost to the final analysis, 10 (9 high Machiavels and 1 low) refused to go along with the theft; 6 (2 high Machiavels and 4 low) confessed to stealing the money, and 1 (a low Machiavel) refused to allow her videotape to be passed to the judges.

Research on personality differences based on Christie's Mach scale has recently been summarized, with particular reference to its relationship to the psychopathic personality, by Mealey (1995, pp. 534–5).

The Edward L. Green letter

The most common reply to advertisements in *Eye Need* was a chain letter. There is a technical problem of legality here in that a straightforward chain letter would be begging and begging is illegal. This problem is circumvented by the "Edward L. Green" letter. Recipients are invited to order copies of four financial reports ("How to make £250,000 by multilevel mail order sales," "The major corporations and multilevel sales," "Sources of the best mailing lists," and "Evaluating multilevel sales plans") for £5 each, ordering each report from a different one of four people whose addresses are listed one below the other. You then retype the order form, omitting the bottom address, dropping the top three addresses down one place, and inserting your own name and address at the top. You then mail hundreds of these letters to whomever you can think of. Edward L. Green claims "I've made over four million pounds and retired after having sent out 16,000 letter packets." My own copy arrived (entirely out of the blue) with four testimonials from people who had allegedly made a pile and a personal message from the sender.

> But the reports are only one or two pages long and contain no useful information. Money is made not from reading the reports but from reselling them.
> For most of those who participate, the cost of advertising, responding to enquiries and copying the reports far outweighs any income generated. (Thompson, 1991)

A simple calculation shows that Edward L. Green's "four million pounds" is someone else's loss and the only people who can expect to make a profit are photocopying shops and the postal service.

Pyramid Selling

Another way to make money is by selling water filters. Here is Clarissa's story (as of December 1992). Clarissa was an architect; but the recession that developed in 1990–1 meant that her work disappeared.

> In her late forties, she looked in vain for another job. There were none around.
> "When I was made redundant, a friend who had lost his job at the same time tried to interest me in the idea of selling water filters," she remembers. "I said, 'Oh my God, how disgusting, get away from me.'"
> A year went by, Clarissa (not her real name) fell £10,000 into debt.

And money can overcome even revulsion.

> A month later, after going to meetings about water filters and reading about water filters and ruminating about water filters, Clarissa entered the great pyramid of National Safety Associates of America (UK) Ltd, or NSA, at the only place where it is possible to enter it – the ground floor.
> To get started, Clarissa bought four water filters at £100 each and four air filters at £121 each, wholesale. Because she was already in debt she bought them on NSA's own credit scheme, borrowing the £300 deposit from her own sponsor and paying off the rest at £60 per month over ten months. Including the interest on the loan, the bare minimum Clarissa will have paid to get started in NSA will be more than £1,000.

The investment provides a powerful incentive for the fledgling dealer to begin working the telephone. In her first month Clarissa went at it furiously. "They tell you NSA stands for 'Never Sleep Again,' and in the first weeks you eat, sleep and dream water filters," she says. Overcoming powerful misgivings, she began going down the list of 100 friends which her sponsor had had her draw up. In the first month she gave 18 demonstrations and made five sales. Her £1,000 investment yielded an income of about £30 per sale, a total of £150.

But in the same period she also started to build her own pyramid: she "got three people across," as they say in the trade.

Every time Sophie and the others in Clarissa's downline make a sale, Clarissa gets a percentage of the wholesale price, paid to her by NSA as her commission – and she will continue being paid a small percentage on her downline, as long as it is industrious, for up to five "generations." (Popham, 1992, pp. 23, 26)

Selling water filters is a job for the Machiavellian who has no qualms about manipulating her friends. But some people are simply not like that.

Many others give up in disgust. Ann Strenger, an American living in Oxford who has a master's degree in poetry, became involved in selling water filters but hated what it did to her friendships. "It's OK with one's immediate family, but once beyond that I felt most uncomfortable. They're asking you to trade on what is always a personal part of your life . . . I'm pretty much deciding that I don't want to use my friendships like that. They say one is helping friends to be successful, but that's not how it feels." (Popham, 1992)

According to NSA only 2 percent of British households have a water filter, so the potential market is immense. (Personally I had no idea that British water was so unpotable.) But what is being sold? Water filters, obviously; but for use in purifying water or merely for demonstration purposes? And to whom? To the general public or to would-be water-filter salespersons? It is estimated that 80 percent of entrants to NSA drop out (having bought their demonstration stock) and it could be that most of the market is sales to failed franchisees!

Commissions for Financial Services

Another way to take money from other people is in the form of commission on handling their deals on the stock market. The futures market is a forum in which it is particularly difficult for the amateur investor to deal without a professional intermediary. A futures contract is an agreement to buy or sell – it could be coffee – at a given price and at some specified date in the future. If you are a manufacturer of instant coffee, you need to be assured of a continuing supply of raw material at a predictable price and therefore buy in advance at a time when the price is acceptable.

This is the reason why: "The price of coffee yesterday soared by 25 per cent after a second frost damaged Brazilian coffee plants and led to fears that as much as half of the crop could be destroyed" (Torday, 1994). You can also buy coffee futures, even though you are *not* a manufacturer of instant coffee, in the hope of a severe frost in Brazil pushing the price up. A futures contract requires a deposit of only 10 percent of the contract price until the coffee is delivered, so you can "invest" ten times as much as you have capital. The profits, as a percentage of the 10 percent stake, can be spectacular. So also can the losses.

> KC writes: Last January I opened an account with DPR Futures Ltd – after much persuasive telephoning by a representative. I said I would invest only the proceeds of the sale of my BAA, BA, TSB and Rolls-Royce shares, and I sent the certificates to DPR. On January 13, DPR invested my money in deutsch-mark futures, and on January 15 the whole investment was wiped out.... I am now being pressed by DPR's liquidators for $680. So much for DPR's selling technique of promising that not all my money was at risk. (Hetherington, 1988)

Here is DPR's *modus operandi*.

> Two company directors in their twenties who awarded themselves £1 million each, drove four company cars – a Ferrari, Porsche, BMW and Mercedes – and channelled large sums of money into Swiss bank accounts, heard their firm described as "a menace to the investing public" in the High Court yesterday. Three years ago Mr Andrew Page and Mr David Rycott were a second-hand car sales-man and a student respectively.
>
> The court closed down their firm, DPR Futures, which had made millions of pounds by badgering private investors over the telephone to put their money into highly speculative investments and charging them exorbitant rates of commis-sion. DPR Futures salesmen would telephone investors at home and at work, sometimes as often as 40 times a day, to persuade them to invest in futures and options contracts which were speculative and invariably unsuitable.
>
> DPR's hard-sell tactics and high commissions – often five times the normal rate – made the firm exceedingly profitable. In the last three months of 1987 it made profits of more than £3 million. DPR's commission charges were some-times as much as two-thirds of the investors' stake money and overall averaged 50 per cent of the stake. This meant investors had to make 100 per cent profits just to stand still.
>
> *The Times* has a large file of complaints from unhappy investors who lost thousands of pounds through DPR. (Lever, 1988)

DPR Futures was wound up by the Securities and Investments Board following the Financial Services Act, which came into force in the UK on April 29, 1988. However, although the four directors were tried, they were found not guilty of fraudulent trading (Warner, 1990).

Table 14.5   A brief history of Barlow Clowes and Partners

1973	Barlow Clowes and Partners sets up in business, offering a financial management service.
1978	Elizabeth Barlow resigns. Business continues under Peter Clowes's management.
1983/1984	Department of Trade and Industry (DTI) concern about Barlow Clowes dealing in securities without a license.
May 1984	Warnings from Stock Exchange "that it [Barlow Clowes] would have difficulty in paying the high minimum rate of return offered without eating into capital, and feared it might be pooling client's funds [which have to be kept strictly separate from the company's funds]."
October 1985	Barlow Clowes eventually secures a license from a reluctant DTI. If the license had been refused, there would have been problems in unscrambling unauthorized deposits and, in addition, the DTI might have been sued by Barlow Clowes for loss of business.
June 1986	Barlow Clowes sets up in Gibraltar, beyond surveillance by the DTI.
May 1988	Barlow Clowes declared insolvent.

Source: *The Times* (1988).

Barlow Clowes

After buying a house, most people think next about saving for retirement. A secure investment is highly desirable and that can be provided by investing in British government bonds (known as "gilts"). But so also is a "maximum return," and Barlow Clowes and Partners exploited people's mild cupidity with a very traditional kind of fraud. So far in this chapter all the financial schemes I have described (except for the loan sharks in Glasgow) have been within the law (even if "only just"); the two that follow were most certainly illegal.

A very brief history of Barlow Clowes and Partners is set out in table 14.5. It needs perhaps to be emphasized that, because of the opportunities for dishonesty when handling other people's money (of the kind detailed below), a license is required before any company may take deposits from the public. Continuation of that license depends, among other things, on the proper keeping of accounts. Of course, so long as a company can meet its commitments (chiefly repaying investors promptly), irregularities in internal accounting can often be kept hidden, but if ever the company becomes insolvent, they are necessarily exposed.

> The basic dishonest scheme was simple and as old as the hills.
> You persuade people to entrust their savings to you by telling them that they will be kept safe in a particular rock-solid investment. You don't put the money in a rock-solid investment but use it to live the life of Riley. You make good the

deficiencies that come up with fresh money from new investors, and you lie and cheat to cover your tracks.

Over the years until its collapse in May 1988, Barlow Clowes' off-shore business attracted £225m from 11,000 mainly elderly investors, promising them the security of an investment in British government stock, or gilts. Until the collapse, investors had little cause for complaint. Monthly income cheques arrived on time and withdrawals were paid promptly.

Yet when liquidators came to pick over Barlow Clowes' carcass, they found only £1.9m in gilts when there should have been £115m. The rest seemed to have gone on yachts, an executive Lear jet, large houses, antique furniture, a French vineyard, expensive cars and on buying stakes in public and private companies. (Durman, 1992b)

New investments were obtained by promising a higher return from gilts than any other fund manager was offering. Naturally, people living in retirement on limited savings were attracted by this slightly bigger return. But, ultimately, the stock market collapsed to the point that the firm could not meet its obligations and its financial state was exposed. Peter Clowes was sentenced to 10 years' imprisonment (Durman, 1992a).

But "10 years" does not actually mean 10 years inside. Peter Clowes was released from prison in February 1996 after serving only four years. On release, he "still refuses to accept that he is a thief. 'I have never stolen anybody's money. . . . I have never lined my nest with anybody's money'" (Popham, 1996). Twenty-one months later, "Peter Clowes, former head of the Barlow Clowes investment empire, appeared before magistrates in Macclesfield, Cheshire, yesterday, charged with benefits fraud. Mr Clowes, 55, of Stockport, Greater Manchester, denies two charges of false accounting relating to the submission of jobseeker's allowances forms in November last year" (Ashworth, 1997). Peter Clowes was ultimately jailed for four months (*The Times*, 1999a).

The psychiatrists tell us that there is no cure for the psychopath.

Dunsdale Securities

But if one were seriously looking for a reincarnation of Niccolò Machiavelli, Robert Miller, sole director of Dunsdale Securities, would be the candidate. He operated essentially the same fraud as Peter Clowes, promising some clients a 20 percent return from investments in gilts. (That is not possible – gilts never pay that much.) What is especially chilling about Robert Miller is that he took deposits from his immediate family and friends. They found him charming, while he was taking them for every penny they had (Hawthorne, 1991).

Over 10 years Miller took money from more than 200 clients, purportedly to be invested in low-risk gilt-edged securities, according to Brian Barker QC, for the prosecution. None of the money went into gilts.

More than £1.9m was spent on private residences, £272,000 on credit card purchases and £23,000 on sponsoring an opera evening. Mr Barker said that Miller bought his sister a Peugeot and his first wife, Deborah, a £16,400 BMW and put £53,000 into her bank account. His mistress, Rosalind Alexander, received a £40,000 Mercedes. His second wife, Naomi, had £15,000 placed in her bank account and was given a Range Rover.

At his Park Lane offices, Miller convinced his staff he was buying gilts by making calls on a telephone marked with the name and number of a City stock-broker, Alexanders, Laing & Cruickshank.

His membership of Fimbra, the watchdog for financial advisers, added credibility. Miller forged the company secretary's name on accounts for 10 years. He also forged a stock note from ALC.

He was able to pay out to people wanting to withdraw money by recruiting new clients. . . . As his wife said at one stage, "People couldn't wait to give him money." (Hosking, 1991)

Ordinary people's mild cupidity makes them easy prey for men like Robert Miller (who, of course, are utterly devoid of conscience). A sufficiently clever accountant can always fool the regulatory authorities for so long as he can meet his financial obligations. "Fimbra [Financial Intermediaries, Managers and Brokers Regulatory Association], which took responsibility for regulating Dunsdale in the middle of 1988, gave it a C3 rating, one of the highest obtainable. . . . A representative from Fimbra visited Dunsdale in August last year [1989]. . . . a few minor points were raised but otherwise Dunsdale was given a clean bill of health" (Nissé & Cole, 1990). Dunsdale's accounts were described as "neat but meaningless." This particular fraud was exposed when investors experienced difficulty in obtaining repayment. Liquidators were appointed following legal action.

There is one other arena where money, very large sums of money, provide an incentive that actuates nearly everyone. That arena is the casino, or other forms of gambling, which we examine next.

QUESTIONS FOR DISCUSSION

1 Some people make money out of their friends and family. How can they bring themselves to do it? Is it just cupidity or is there something else in their makeup?

2 Why are some people much more successful at bargaining than others? What do the successful have that other people do not?

3 How does money come to have such force as an incentive?

15

GAMBLING

The National Lottery used to use as its advertising slogan "IT COULD BE YOU."
It *is* Beverley Miles:

> A woman is so addicted to lottery scratchcards that she even bought them with
> money intended for a hypnosis course to cure her of the habit . . .
>   Beverley Miles, 37, often goes without food to buy the cards out of her dole
> money. In court at Harrogate, North Yorkshire, she admitted stealing a fridge, a
> chest of drawers and a coffee table from her rented flat to finance her spending
> of up to £60 a week.
>   Miles told police that she planned to replace the furniture with money she is
> convinced is just around the corner. In fact, she has won only £50 twice.
>   . . . shops near her home had banned her to help her to beat the craving.
> Afterwards Miles said: "I wish it had never been invented. The addiction has
> taken over. The lure of the big win keeps me hooked. Now I am hundreds of
> pounds in debt and have to rely on my mother for a good meal." (Wilkinson,
> 1997)

The question for this chapter is: Why does Beverley Miles gamble and keep on
gambling despite repeated losses?

THE PREVALENCE OF GAMBLING

Table 15.1 shows the prevalence of gambling in the UK in 1995/96. If you went to
a casino or bet on the horses you could expect to have about 80 percent of your
stake money returned to you as winnings. Much more popular, though, was the
National Lottery, which returned only 50 percent as prize money. But 9 million
people staked a total of £556 million on football pools of which only £128 million
was returned as winnings – only 23p for every pound staked. So, why do people
gamble and keep gambling despite heavy losses (Rachlin, 1990)?

Table 15.1 Prevalence of gambling in Britain, 1995/96[a]

Gamble	Number of participants	Amount staked (£m)	Exchequer (£m)	Profits and expenses (£m)	Returned to punters (£m)	% return
Casinos	–	2,548	80	370	2,098	82
Gaming machines	4,201,000	9,000	130	1,670	7,200	80
On-course betting	708,000	761 ⎫	448	881	5,315	80
Off-course betting	3,174,000	5,883 ⎬				
Bingo	2,787,000	1,161	94	255	812	70
National Lottery	31,684,000 ⎫	5,260	583	732 (and 1,473 to good causes)	2,472	47
Instants	12,505,000 ⎬					
Football pools	8,990,000	556	131	297	128	23

[a] The most recent year for which I have been able to assemble all these statistics.

Rationality

I must begin by explaining what "rational" means in this context. Suppose I am offered a gamble to win £x with probability p and £y with probability (1 – p). My

Expected winnings = £$\{px + (1 - p)y\}$,

and this is the most that a rational man should be willing to pay to participate in this particular gamble. If I pay more than this, then, in the long run, I shall be out of pocket. But gamblers repeatedly flout this principle – they buy bets for more than their expected values – and it is necessary that they should do so to provide a margin for the casino and the lottery promoter. All this means that gamblers keep on gambling despite losing. Here is one at the Casino Club, Lytham St Anne's.

Maggie Harding:	I've lost for about the last three months, I would say. And I've just won tonight, so that's good.
Interviewer:	You've lost pretty solidly, as well?
Maggie Harding:	Yes, yes.
Interviewer:	So totting that up, what's it come to?
Maggie Harding:	What's sixty times twelve? About six hundred, seven hundred pounds. (Nelson, 1998)

Commonsense intuitions about how and why people learn suggest that, if you lose your money often enough, you will eventually give up. In this respect common sense coincides with psychological insight; a simple application of learning theory – any learning theory – says that repeated losses should extinguish the habit. What makes gambling so profound a puzzle is that in this particular case psychological insight is wrong. Gamblers seldom give up!

Some people, including some psychologists, have suggested that the money does not matter.

> For gambling addicts – nearly always men – money is rarely the object. Winning means the game is over.
> . . . researchers now think that, unlike social gamblers, men who gamble compulsively are indifferent to the money involved, disappointed when they win – and may even prefer to lose. (Rowlands, 1996)

To this I can only retort, "Try pulling the other one – it comes off!" On January 6, 1996, the National Lottery had its first double-rollover jackpot.

£60m spent in one day as Britain goes lottery mad.

After struggling to cope with sales which broke records from 7am onwards, the machines crashed just before 1pm as the lottery's two main data processing sites in Watford and Liverpool proved unable to cope.

Tens of thousands of punters stayed in long queues as technicians rectified the fault.

Sales for the biggest gamble in British history later peaked at up to eight million tickets an hour, and at one point 5,000 per second, helping to build a record total of £128m for the week. (Varley, 1996)

Gamblers are motivated by money, especially by the prospect of a very big win – never mind the odds. But why? Let us suppose, as a working hypothesis, that gamblers are unable to estimate the probability (not the "odds," but the absolute probability) of winning.

The Estimation of Probabilities

I have explained in *Human Judgment: The Eye of the Beholder* (Laming, 2004) why this is so. The basic principle is that all judgments, of whatever kind, are relative.

There is no absolute judgment – all judgments are relative, comparisons of one thing with another.

Even more,

The comparisons (of one thing with another) are little better than ordinal.

If one makes a chain of judgments – "How likely am I to win this next time?" – an error in one judgment is passed along the chain, because each judgment uses its predecessor as a point of comparison. In consequence, when people are asked to judge auditory frequency or intensity or some other sensory attribute, they are unable to achieve an accuracy exceeding the use of five categories without error (Garner, 1962, chap. 3). In gambling decisions are based on the informal estimation of probabilities. A probability is not a stimulus – it is a mathematical abstraction – and cannot be "presented" to participants for direct comparison, to be compared with another probability, in the conventional manner. So, in estimating probabilities, the greatest accuracy one might expect is that shown in figure 15.1.

Contraceptive pills

The applicability of this idea to the judgment of probability is illustrated by this episode. On October 18, 1995, the Committee on Safety of Medicines issued a

Horses	Contraceptive pill
Certain	
"Sure Thing"	Dangerous
"Maybe"	Risky
"No way"	Safe
Impossible	

Figure 15.1   Five different levels of estimated probability.

warning, in a letter to doctors, that third-generation contraceptive pills had been found to carry an increased risk of thromboembolism, compared to second-generation pills. Women using third-generation pills (about 1.5 million of them) were advised to consult their doctor to review their prescription and switch to another brand on completion of their present monthly course (Laurence, 1995).

> The telephone lines were jammed and the queue never shortened yesterday at the Margaret Pyke centre in central London, as worried women tried to find out if they were at risk from their Pill.
>   Telephonists and advisers at the family planning clinic had been doubled to cope with demand; the centre stayed open late yesterday and even considered opening over the weekend to help frightened callers. (Cooper, 1995)

> The panic that followed is estimated to have led to about 3,000 abortions in Britain, while a baby boom is predicted for June and July [1996]. This week, it emerged that more than 800 extra abortions were carried out by the British Pregnancy Advisory Service alone, which also said that 41 per cent of women stopped taking the Pill immediately and 61 per cent did not finish their course as a result of the scare. (Dobson, 1996)

Figure 15.2 sets out the facts of the matter. First, the risks are tiny – typically 3 in 10,000. Second, they are greatest during pregnancy. But gradations of probability are not appreciated by ordinary people. Either the pill is "safe" or it is "risky." There is no "in between."

Extended warranties

People's inability to estimate probabilities, their profound inability, leaves them prey to a practice

> that some feel is the embodiment of "rip-off" Britain.
>   They will be persuaded to buy expensive policies insuring the item [electrical goods] for breakdowns. . . . the cost of these extended warranty policies may often be greater than the likely repair bills against which they are supposed to be

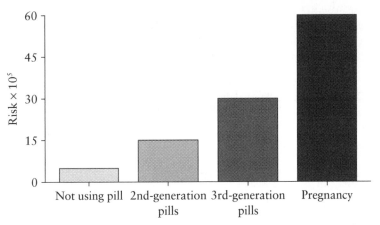

Figure 15.2 Risks of thromboembolism in women (data from Eddy & Lightfoot, 1995).

guarding. In some cases, the policy can even cost more than the gadget or appliance purchased.

In The Link, a division of the Dixon's retailing empire, the four-year warranty for a £79 mobile phone was £109. Tiny Computers, meanwhile, was asking £499 to cover a £799 computer for five years.

A five-year warranty for a £378 digital wide-screen colour TV from Currys, another Dixon's division, cost £185. Yet, according to figures from the Consumers' Association, the average cost of a TV repair is just £44. (Atherton, 2000)

The Consumers' Association has been a constant critic of extended warranties (insurance policies against breakdown) for many years.

Nearly all the profits made by Dixon's Group last year [1992], and nearly all it is expected to make this year [1993], came from the sale of extended warranties on its electrical products – an extra that has been described by the Consumers' Association as "a waste of money." (Nissé, 1993)

The possibility of making money from commission on their sale depends chiefly on customers grossly overestimating the likelihood of their purchase breaking down, assisted, of course, by the salesperson.

To summarize the argument to this point:

1   Experiment shows that people are not able to make absolute judgments of simple stimuli, nor even to make comparative judgments beyond a crude ordinal level. There is no reason to suppose that the informal estimation of probability is any more accurate, rather the contrary.

2   An important element of real gambling behavior turns on the individual's over-estimating the likelihood of winning. Bangkok has a state lottery: "one third of Thais said they expected to survive the country's economic crisis by winning the lottery" (Rooney, 2000).

In what follows I look at real gamblers staking their own real money in real casinos, and that is possible by virtue of research published by Willem Wagenaar (1988).

BLACKJACK

The two most popular games in a casino are blackjack and roulette. Blackjack is the casino version of pontoon or 21. The rules vary slightly from one casino to another; the rules applied in the Dutch casinos in which Wagenaar studied are set out in figure 15.3.

Because the dealer plays entirely mechanically, there is an optimal strategy for the gambler known as "Basic" (see Wagenaar, 1988, pp. 18–19). For each total held by

---

- Four decks of cards are shuffled and placed in a holder (the "shoe").
- A plastic card is inserted about three-quarters of the way down the shoe, at which point play stops and the cards are reshuffled.
- All cards are dealt face up, two to each player, but only one to the dealer.
- Cards count at point value, and all court cards are worth 10, except for an Ace, which may be either 1 or 11.
- The objective is to obtain a total greater than that of the dealer, but never exceeding 21.
- Ace and 10 (or court card) makes a blackjack, which beats any other hand.
- Each player may either stand or hit (that is, draw additional cards, one at a time).
- If the two cards dealt to a player have identical values, the player may split and play two hands separately.
- If a player's total is 9, 10, or 11, the player is allowed to double his/her stake and draw just one more card.
- If the dealer's card is an Ace, each player may place an additional side bet (insurance) that the dealer will complete a blackjack.
- If a player busts (exceeds 21), the stake is lost.
- When all players have finished, the dealer takes a second card. The dealer must hit at 16 or less, and must stand at 17 or more; that is, the dealer plays mechanically.

Figure 15.3   The rules of blackjack.

the player and each card turned up by the dealer, Basic identifies the most profitable action, "stand" (i.e., stay with one's existing total), "hit" (draw another card), or "double" (split one's cards and play two independent hands). To use Basic a player simply needs to memorize all the optimum combinations. It gives an expected loss equal to 0.4 percent of the stake. Basic is a better strategy than "never bust" (i.e., always stand with a total of 12 or greater, which loses 8 percent) or "mimic the dealer" (i.e., stand at 17 or greater, but hit at any lesser total; this loses 6 percent), but is not so good as "counting." Counting means keeping a count of which cards have been played (all are played face up), chiefly the proportion of 10s and court cards. In this way the card counter can distinguish situations that are favorable to the players from those that are unfavorable. Counting enables the player to win in the long run at a rate equal to somewhere between 0.5 and 2 percent of the stake. This is achieved by laying the minimum stake in unfavorable situations, and the maximum stake in favorable ones (the maximum and minimum being set by the house). But card counting is hard work, especially if one is doing it for eight hours a day, five days a week.

How Gamblers Play Blackjack

Keren and Wagenaar (1985) studied 112 players in a small casino in Amsterdam and recorded a high percentage of plays which violated Basic strategy.

> Blackjack players repeatedly explained to me that the decisions prescribed by the Basic strategy are only made by inexperienced players. (Wagenaar, 1988, p. 82)

> One player told me: "Listen, I have seen one of those card counters play. He lost his very first bet!" (Wagenaar, 1988, p. 110)

Wagenaar met a professional blackjack dealer who played blackjack during his leisure hours.

> Asked how he could hope to win both as a dealer and as a player, he explained that the whole secret is in knowing the order of the cards in the deck. He had discovered that two successive cards add up to 10, 11, or 12: after a six comes a five, after a two comes an eight. When I expressed some disbelief, he took me to the blackjack table, and indeed, his rule was confirmed frequently. A quick computation shows that about one-quarter of the possible pairs confirm the rule, whereas three-quarters do not. (Wagenaar, 1988, p. 108)

What these remarks show is that the view which habitual players of blackjack have of their game is out of kilter with reality. Indeed, many players see blackjack as a team sport. "A bad player can spoil the game for everyone" (Wagenaar, 1988, p. 107).

The illusion of a match between players and dealer is encouraged by expert dealers, who attempt to create the atmosphere of a "good fight." Many players object less to losing after they had a good fight, because it offers the excuse that the dealer was too strong. The illusion is also shared by some pit bosses. They have a tendency to change dealers rapidly when the house is losing, as if bringing in "fresh" dealers would wear out the players. (Wagenaar, 1988, p. 108)

But there are a few players who know what's what.

Ken is a professional card counter – a member of an élite band of mathematical geniuses who make a living from memorising sequences of cards.

Casinos hate Ken and will try to ban him as soon as he crosses their portals, which is why he is so secretive. In order to reach him you first have to call his mum in Birmingham, who then relays a fax to whichever casino he happens to be holed up in.

Ken switched to blackjack. He knew little about the game but worked out what is known in the US as "basic strategy": the mathematically correct way of playing. He immediately won 14 nights in a row, clocking up a £400 profit.

Then on the fifteenth night, disaster. "I lost £225, which in those days seemed like a fortune," recalls Ken. "I stayed at home and licked my wounds for a few days. But then I realised that not even the casino can win the whole time and decided to battle on."

It was not until 1978, however, that Ken began making serious money.

"I was playing Cromwell's in Birmingham and now other players were copying me. If I bet, everyone else piled on money, too. At first the casino loved it, but 16 months later when they saw how much they'd lost, they weren't so pleased and I was barred."

By now Ken was playing professionally, but he was having to travel farther and farther to get a game. Today, he cannot get a game anywhere in Britain.

Mastering the maths is only half the battle. Card counters also need nerves of steel. Most casinos keep watch for sudden swings in betting that indicate you are counting. You also have to be psychologically prepared for bad runs of luck even when your count tells you that you should be winning.

Card counting takes its toll in other ways, too. Ken rarely gets to bed before 6am and lives in constant fear of being roughed up in a casino backroom. His only companions are fellow card counters but he cannot acknowledge their presence, at least not while working, for fear of being caught. (Honigsbaum, 1992)

There are much easier ways to earn a living.

ROULETTE

The other popular casino game is roulette. Again, there are variations from one casino to another how the game is played. Figure 15.4 sets out the rules in the Dutch casinos where Wagenaar worked.

- A disc with 37 pockets numbered from 0 to 36 revolves within a bowl.
- The croupier projects a ball around the rim of the bowl in the opposite direction to the rotation of the disc. After several rotations, the ball leaves the rim of the bowl, hits one of the spoilers, and finally falls into one of the 37 pockets on the disc.
- Players may bet on single numbers, on various combinations of 2, 3, 4, 6, 12, or 18 different numbers, or on the "simple chances" (RED or BLACK, or EVEN or ODD, or HIGH or LOW).
- The expected loss is always 1/37 (2.7 percent) of the stake, no matter how it is split between different numbers (except for a special provision when betting on the "simple chances").

Figure 15.4   The game of roulette.

Betting Systems

A betting system is a plan for varying the size of one's bet from play to play. The general principle is to increase the size of one's bet after a loss in order to recoup that loss, and (in some systems) make a small profit as well. But the roulette wheel is essentially a random number generator. Every play is a statistically independent event. This means that all systems are equally good (or bad). Why then do players bother to use them? Let Ray Bowden explain.

Ray Bowden: I start low, and try to build it up. So when you start low, and try and build it up and it's not going in your section for a lot of spins, you carry on as much as you've got cash on you; and if it doesn't go, it doesn't go.

Interviewer: Why do you carry on?

Ray Bowden: To get your losses back. You get what's called the "red mist." You can't leave the table, you're frozen to the table because your mind's telling you – say you've lost a hundred pound – you're playing to get that hundred pound back. So then it goes into two hundred pound. Then it goes into three hundred pound. Then it goes into four hundred pound. Then you're telling yourself, well if they hit a number, and it goes into that section of the wheel, say, five spins out of five, you're going to get four hundred of say your nine hundred that you've lost.

	And you're telling yourself – it's called the "red mist," you can't move. You're frozen to the table.
Interviewer:	How do you feel afterwards when you've obviously lost thousands?
Ray Bowden:	Er, sick! The following morning it hits you. You think, what a schmuck! I'm never going to the casino again. You go in again, the following night. (Nelson, 1998)

As I have already explained, people (except for statisticians and actuaries in their professional capacities) have a profound inability at estimating likelihoods of occurrence. In practice, estimates are modified in light of observation of similar past events and ordinarily this learning about frequencies of events helps us to adapt to the world about us. It has given rise to folklore:

> Red sky at night,
> shepherd's delight.
> Red sky in the morning,
> shepherd's warning.

But when the events are the outcomes of games of chance, the learning is spurious. Wagenaar (1988, p. 108) mentions "the custom of displaying the numbers that have come out on a roulette table. When there is no electronic display, players are provided with forms on which they can keep their own record." The learning in the casino is the same process that works with real-world events; but because the events in the casino are random, so also is the learning. Indeed, the only (real) thing to be learned is that there is nothing to be learned, and that conclusion the natural informal learning process will never deliver! In this way continued observation of the numbers in roulette or of the cards in blackjack can lead to widely varying perceptions of the likelihood of winning on the next play or the next deal, varying quite out of accord with reality. It also means that ordinary people have a biased notion of what a random outcome would really look like and invoke the notion of "luck" to account for what actually happens in nature.

LUCK

Figure 15.5 shows sample sequences of 25 black and 25 white dots, with the proportion of repetitions (white–white and black–black) equal to 0.2, 0.3, 0.4, 0.5, 0.6, 0.7, and 0.8 in successive rows (after Wagenaar, 1988, p. 92). Now, which of those

```
A   oooo••ooo•o•oo•oo•o•o•o•oo••••o•o••o•o•o•o•o•o•o•o•o•o
B   o•o••ooo••o•o•oo••••oo•oo•••ooo•oo•o•o•ooo••oo•o•ooo•oo••
C   •o••••oo••oo•oooo•oo•••••oo•••oo•o•oo•o•o••o•o•o•oo•••
D   •o••o•oo••••o••oooo••o•o••oooo•••ooo••••o•o•oooo••••oo•o•ooo•
E   oooo••••oooo••ooo••••oooo•••oo•••oo•••ooo•••o•oo•o•o•o••o
F   o••oo•••oooooo••ooooo•••oo•••••oooo•••••••oo••••••oooo
G   ooo•••••ooooooo••••••ooo•••••ooo••••••oooooooo•••••••ooo
```

Figure 15.5 Sample sequences of white (heads) and black (tails) dots.

sequences looks the most random? Imagine that I toss a fair coin 50 times; which of those sequences looks most typical of the succession of heads (white) and tails (black) that I should generate?

A fair coin not only produces about as many heads as it does tails (average 25 in 50 tosses), but also produces as many heads as it does tails following a head (or a tail) on the preceding toss. For this reason sequence D is the correct answer; it has been constructed to have as many repetitions as it has alternations. But people tend to select sequence C (62.5 percent alternations) or even B (75 percent alternations) as typifying their notion of randomness.

Wagenaar (1970) prepared 16 different sets of strings (as in figure 15.5, but with 100 dots in each string) and asked 203 participants to select the one most likely to have been produced by tossing a coin. The median judgment of a large majority (86 percent) favored a sequence with less than 50 percent repetitions (i.e., A, B, or C in figure 15.5). Most people expect a small number of tosses of a coin, or a small number of plays at roulette, to conform more closely to the average than actually happens in nature. Consequently, a truly random sequence contains more long runs of losses or successes than people expect. Some other factor must therefore be operative to produce those long runs of repetitions. That other factor is LUCK.

Here is a gambler who believes in luck.

> *Jean Dearden:* Well I think it's 'im up there, and if 'e says it's your night, it's your night. And whatever you do, you can't lose. This is over twenty years and we've – don't we say that? – over twenty years, if it's our night, we've won a fortune on stupid things. But when it's not our night, can't do a thing. (Nelson, 1998)

> Since players do not expect long runs of wins or losses, they perceive good and bad luck as the cause of these runs. The conviction that good and bad luck last for a certain period of time changes the perceived nature of the game considerably. Instead of seeing the game as determined by fixed odds, they now feel that their task is the detection of good and bad luck. In this manner losses will be attributed to lack of skill, rather than to adverse odds. Consequently players can always assure themselves that next time they will be more alert. (Wagenaar, 1988, pp. 112–13)

Keren and Wagenaar (1985) interviewed many players about various aspects of gambling.

> We learned that one cannot force luck to happen. You should wait till luck appears, and in that sense it is much like chance. On the other hand you can lose your luck easily by using it unwisely. You can also fail to utilise it when it happens, for instance by not even noticing that this is your lucky day, or your lucky deck, or your lucky dealer. Finally, one can also ruin the effect of good luck by not noticing that it ended, thus losing everything that was won. In this sense the utilisation of luck is more like a skill. The special nature of luck explains why it is difficult to attribute the outcome of gambles to chance or skill only. When subjects were asked to divide 100% over three causal factors, chance, skill, and luck, the following results were obtained (Keren and Wagenaar, 1985): chance 18%; skill 37%; and luck 45%. (Wagenaar, 1988, p. 93)

How then can luck influence the motion of the roulette wheel? It doesn't.

> It should be realised that the outcome of a gamble is the result of a coincidence between a choice made by the gambler and a random event beyond the gambler's control. . . . From my discussions with gamblers I learned that most do not, in fact, believe that they can influence the roulette wheel. Neither that luck will influence the roulette wheel or any other randomising device. But luck may influence the player's choice. The chance outcome of the roulette wheel is the same for all players, but betting is not. Good luck may help one player to bet on the right number, whilst as a result of bad luck other players bet on the wrong number. In this manner the concept of luck does not run counter to a purely physical explanation of how randomisers like roulette wheels, dice, and cards work. But belief in luck makes all reasoning based on the physical definition of a game irrelevant. (Wagenaar, 1988, p. 101)

Personal View and Camera View

Luck is a "personal view" concept. It is a property of the outcomes as seen by the gambler who has staked the money. Each outcome is perceived against the background of previous wins and losses, whence the "learning" of random relationships between outcomes which modulates the individual's estimate of success. Contrast this with probability theory, which is a "camera view" construct and knows nothing about "luck."

A punter lays his or her bet and only then is the roulette wheel set in motion. Since the wheel is a randomizing device (and this is a matter which can be tested by experiment), the number that comes up is independent of the punter's choice. But, because people habitually view the world in personal view and adopt a camera view, if ever they do, only after long and careful education, so objective appraisal of games of chance loses out to the subjective view.

Peter lost everything through gambling 15 years ago – his house, his wife and family. He believes his problem is that he is addicted to his own adrenaline.

Peter, who has rebuilt his life with the help of Gamblers Anonymous, said: "It's nothing to do with the money. It is to do with the need to be in action. I would sit at the roulette wheel for hours with my heart pounding. I sat next to the same people for years and have no idea who they were. If I won at 4am when they close I went home totally depressed because I did not want to stop when I was winning. If the croupier tried to stop the wheel a minute before time I would be very angry."

Peter, *who has a degree in statistics* [my italics], knew all about probability but he could not believe that it was any help in winning casino games. "I could never believe that each number had an equal chance of coming up. I would notice that the ball was not falling on one part of the wheel and would believe that those numbers would come up next. So I piled my money on. I liked blackjack too because the casino would stop you if you played too skilfully. It was more important to me to play and take the risk than to play well." (Gillie, 1990a)

Barry Partridge was an accountancy student. Simple calculations with probability theory show that the expected value of a gamble in a casino is always negative. If it were not so, the casino would not be able to remain in business. Although this student was not actually studying probability, he surely should have been competent at the simple calculations involved.

An accountancy student who gambled away his loans hanged himself after losing £500 on the tables of a Leeds casino, an inquest was told.

Barry Partridge . . . was a regular customer of the city's casinos. He hanged himself after losing the loan money within three days of cashing the cheque.

Nicholas Girling, a friend and neighbour, said Mr Partridge had a gambling habit he could ill-afford. "I've been . . . with Barry on numerous occasions and he gambled quite recklessly. He was never much good with money." (*Independent*, 1991)

Why then do people gamble? Because they estimate that the combination of chance, luck, and skill is favorable. But there are others – Willem Wagenaar is one – who can see that that combination is always unfavorable. All this would matter little except for the fact that there is money involved, large sums of money. The motivational force of the large sums on offer elevates gambling into a serious social problem.

SALES PROMOTIONS

The techniques of the lottery and the casino are used in sales promotions, and in this field the market leader is The Readers' Digest Association. The advertising to sell *Readers' Digest* magazine in January 2000 included:

1   A preliminary letter (from the office of the prize draw manager) announcing that the first prize will be £250,000, accompanied by a "Notice of selection" to the effect that "MR D R LAMING" has come through to the "third and final" stage of the Reader's Digest ninety-first prize draw.
2   *Two* further letters ("Mr Laming, are you our missing winner?") with my "winner identification code" and my prize draw documents, which included:
   (a)   my "Finalist's Acceptance Document" ("MR D R LAMING is OFFICIALLY DECLARED A PRIZE DRAW FINALIST") with 6 Personal Prize Draw Numbers;
   (b)   my "Finalist's Issue Document" to be completed by finalist – which offers, in addition, a £15,000 birthday bonus and a £10,000 winner's prompt-reply bonus;
   (c)   a numbered "car key" ("gives you the opportunity to qualify for a superb SPECIAL PRIZE") – provided you subscribe within seven days;
   (d)   an offer of 100 Philips color televisions;
   (e)   a mystery gift "Star finder";
   (f)   a brief summary of all the goodies on offer;
   (g)   an advertisement for *Readers' Digest* magazine; and
   (h)   official "reply" and "no reply" envelopes.

Evidently it sells *Readers' Digest*, which has been mounting this kind of promotion for many years. Other sales promotions in my collection include:

*   Anglo-Scandinavian (foreign exchange investment managers) offering a £5,000 draw.
*   British Family Publishers (selling magazines) offering prizes up to £6,600,000.
*   Bakker Holland (selling garden plants) – a £25,000 draw.
*   Hospital Plan Insurance Services with a £30,000 first prize.
*   The *Daily Mail* "£1 MILLION RACE TO RICHES – GUARANTEE Someone Will Win £100,000 . . . It Could Be YOU."
*   Family Insurance Advisory Services Ltd.: "Six chances to win up to £15,000 in our £33,000 CASH BONANZA DRAW."

- "YOU COULD WIN THIS SPORTY NEW 'MYSTERY CAR.' PLUS A FAN-TASTIC TWO-CENTRE HOLIDAY IN KENYA AND THE SEYCHELLES AND A £1,000 SHOPPING SPREE WITH Kay's" (Kay's Mail Order of Worcester wanting to send me a copy of their catalog).

Finally, some charities have also got in on the act.

- The International Fund for Animal Welfare: "We're giving away a brand new Rover 214Si or £8,000 in cash in our SAVE THE SEALS PRIZE DRAW."
- The Association for International Cancer Research: "Have you already won a brand new Renault Clio – or £6,000 – in AICR's 'Car of the Year' Prize Draw?"

QUESTIONS FOR DISCUSSION

1 Why do people gamble and keep on gambling despite repeated losses?

2 What would be needed to enable people to estimate likelihoods with useful accuracy?

3 Why do most players of blackjack not use Basic strategy?

4 Why do roulette players pay such attention to the numbers that come up on the wheel?

16

HUMAN MOTIVATION: HOW DOES IT WORK?

Our present understanding of human motivation is, to my mind, too immature to justify the formulation of a scientific theory. We have to be content with an "approach to motivation," a framework of ideas within which the evidence might usefully be systematized and put together. There is a variety of different frameworks within which this might be attempted, and this book has been organized around three fundamental ideas that complement each other. I begin this final chapter by reviewing those ideas.

But I shall also speculate what the next 50 years of research might contribute. If it is appropriate to look on each of us as a very complicated biological machine, how might that machine work? I have in mind a theoretical architecture – not a theory in itself, but a pointer to those questions that, it seems to me, most need to be asked about what makes people tick.

THREE FUNDAMENTAL IDEAS

Personal View and Camera View

We each of us have a uniquely privileged view of our own behavior. In that view we are aware of all the internal thoughts, feelings, desires, and anxieties that accompany our behavior. No one else can access those internal experiences; they are essentially private. That is what I have called *personal view*.

Within our personal view we make observations of other people around us, what they are doing. Those observations might be shared with everyone else (except for the individual under observation). They are what a video camera might record for everyone to share, and I have accordingly called that view of things *camera view*.

We cannot see ourselves in camera view, as other people see us; we can only observe other people in that way. And we cannot see other people as they see *themselves*. While our observations of other people are a component of our personal view, we are not able to view others from *their* personal viewpoint and, for that reason, have no access to other people's internal thoughts, feelings, desires, and anxieties. We can only guess at what other people might be experiencing internally.

All this means that there are two categories of observation that need to be carefully distinguished: (1) observations of our own behavior in personal view and (2) observations of that same behavior, but by other people, in camera view. In personal view we have a free choice of what we will do; in camera view other people's behavior, and certainly that of animals, appears determinate. The question whether behavior is characterized by free will or is determinate is not a property of the behavior, but of the vantage point from which it is observed. In consequence, if the two categories of observation, personal view and camera view, are not kept distinct, there is an intellectual impasse – behavior that appears to be both determinate and free at the same time.

One might, of course, approach human motivation from either viewpoint. In everyday life people ordinarily attribute thoughts, feelings, desires, and anxieties to others around them and interact socially on that basis – a "lay" psychology. From that internal point of view "motive" means a calculation of likely costs and payoffs, as in a detective story. For example, to establish a charge of murder, it has to be proved that the defendant *intended* to kill. But an "intention" is not something one can observe from outside. It exists, if it exists at all, only in the mind of the defendant and is *essentially* unobservable by any third person, such as a witness or a juror. Lay psychology works pretty well. The intellectual impasse comes from trying to combine observations from both personal view and camera view within the one synthesis. For the purpose of understanding motivation, a choice has to be made, and I have chosen to look at other people in camera view. One compelling reason is that under especially strong motivation – terror, rage, courtship – people realize, in personal view, that they are no longer in control of their own actions, that they are doing things whether they will or no. Tracie Andrews was convicted of the *murder* of Lee Harvey, her fiancé; that is to say, the jury decided that she *intended* to kill him. Subsequently she confessed to the killing in a letter in which she wrote that she had "lost all control" (Sherwin, 1999). On that basis a personal view account of human motivation will ultimately prove inadequate.

Quasi-Mechanical Behavior

In camera view human behavior appears determinate, which is to say that it is somehow mechanical. The biological machine may be ever so complicated, but it is still a machine. In fact, human behavior appears to be extremely adaptable, and I have used the term "quasi-mechanical" to incorporate the idea that what the biological machine does may depend on a wide array of extraneous factors. If a pretty fair-haired girl walks down Great Western Road in London on a hot summer afternoon, all the young men, and some not so young, will turn their heads to watch her as she walks by, like so many rod puppets; but some other societies manage the initial stage of human courtship rather differently.

The immediate problem with this idea is that, for most of the time at least, our behavior does not seem (to us) in the least mechanical. But that is a personal-view observation, and at this point the distinction between personal and camera view becomes crucial. We need to consider the relation between the two.

If I am an amateur astronomer, I can measure the daily rotation of the fixed stars, the sun, the moon, and the planets about the earth. What I cannot measure is the rotation of the earth on its axis and its annual orbit around the sun. I cannot measure the motion of the earth because I am situated on its surface and all the measurements that I make have to be relative to the earth's motion. We know, from the work of previous astronomers, that celestial motion is most simply decomposed into a rotation of the earth about its axis coupled with orbits of all the planets about the sun. But it took humankind many hundreds of years to come to that realization and, even after Newton's discovery of the universality of the force gravitation (1677), it was a further two hundred years before the Ptolemaic view of the universe was entirely displaced in popular conception.

If in like manner I categorize my actions with respect to my personal experience, I have no way of disentangling my observations from those extraneous stimuli that actuate my behavior. Briefly, a machine cannot observe its own mechanics; it has no way of knowing that it is a machine! When I turn my head to watch the pretty fair-haired girl walking down Great Western Road, I am thinking only: "She's a very nice girl. I'd like to date her!" I am scarcely aware that I am turning my head to stare at her (because my observation of the girl is relative to the orientation of my head), nor (unless I am a professional psychologist in an analytic frame of mind) that I am turning my head, not because she is a nice girl, but because I am a heterosexual male and head-turning in such a situation is natural masculine behavior.

To put the matter succinctly, the fact that our own behavior does not seem to any of us to be mechanical is neither here nor there. There is no way, short of a professional psychological insight, in which we could see our own behavior in that light. But if human courtship was not ultimately mechanical, we should none of us be here!

Social Conventions

Human society is composed of many individuals in substantially random interaction with each other. Those interactions are sometimes forceful, violent – there are fights outside pubs and neighbor disputes, there are burglaries and homicides. In addition, groups of people come together to promote their common interests – there are political and professional associations, there are companies trading for profit, there are conspiracies to commit crime. Nevertheless, human society is for the most part peaceful, with interpersonal conflicts readily resolved. How does this happen?

It happens so because much of our social behavior is constrained by convention – we do those things that people expect of us. We seldom realize the extent to which our behavior is constrained and governed by the society within which we live, and at this point the argument set out above, about the machine being unable to observe its own mechanics, recurs with even greater force. We see ourselves in personal view as free to choose: Shall I do this or shall I do that? Both our personal experience, and that choice, are shaped by the society in which we are placed and, because social conventions inform both the viewpoint and the choice, their influence is not perceived. Only when we compare our society with some other are the cultural differences revealed. And that revelation comes at its most forceful when we make comparison with the behavior of a feral child, Victor, growing up in a society of one.

To mediate that influence there has to be some kind of instinct to respond to social signals from others around us. While it may seem to the individual that he or she chooses to respond, in reality the response is quasi-mechanical. That instinctive response underlies the development of social conventions, which evolve through the random interaction of members of society.

Money

Money is the focus of many social conventions, as chapters 7, 14, and 15 attest. Its power to motivate is necessarily acquired, and, strictly speaking, it is an incentive. But its power to energize, and also corrupt, is immense; to most people the prospect of a prodigious win from a gamble is irresistible. Money is the example above all others to demonstrate the adaptability of human behavior, with elaborate learned patterns of behavior tacked on to basic instinctive tendencies.

HOW DOES IT ALL WORK?

To this point I have presented motivated behavior as a sequence of actions that is set in motion by some trigger stimulus. The action of the trigger is ultimately instinctive, but the actual pattern of behavior thereby initiated might contain many elaborately acquired components. The acquired components do not present a problem, but the fact that different people nevertheless react differently to, say, a pretty girl walking down Great Western Road needs some comment. To put that problem simply, *homosexual* men would not be particularly interested, and interest is at its most intense in young adult men. Why these differences? I suggest that the answer is to do with hormones.

Hormones

There are 10 endocrine glands in the body that secrete chemical messengers, hormones, into the bloodstream. These messengers are transported to receptor sites where they exert their influence. There are other cells that secrete hormones over small distances only and, in some cases, entirely within the cell. Norman and Litwack (1997: Appendix A) list about 130 hormones, including the common neurotransmitters.

It has long been known that some at least of these hormones have profound effects on the body. Female reproductive physiology provides the most dramatic examples. It is also known that some environmental stimuli, especially those that impose stress on the individual, trigger the release of hormones into the bloodstream. "Getting the adrenaline flowing" has become a phrase in common parlance. What I *conjecture*,[1] in addition, is that hormones also potentiate particular kinds of behavior through their action on mechanisms within the brain.

It is accepted that mothers undergo a profound change in hormonal environment after giving birth, but Storey (2000) has demonstrated a similar, but much smaller, change in new fathers. Lower levels of testosterone in fathers after the baby's birth were associated with a more paternal style of behavior, suggesting, though not yet establishing, that the changed hormone levels are causal. Many people have discovered that listening to music can affect one's mood, and Campbell (2001) makes many claims for the power of music. Some of these effects are demonstrably mediated by the release of hormones (further examples of extraneous stimuli affecting the hormonal balance) and it is plausible that the hormones in question act, in turn, on the brain. There are many domains of motivated behavior known to involve specific areas of the brain, so potentiation could result simply from the transport of relevant hormones to receptors at the site.

I must, however, explain what I mean by "potentiation." Returning to the example of a pretty fair-haired girl walking down Great Western Road, Paddington, on a hot summer afternoon, bystanders, mostly young men, turn round to watch as she walks by. Now, it is rude to stare at someone like that – it flouts social convention – and it is especially young men who stare because of their internal hormonal balance. Their particular hormonal environment potentiates a specific range of behaviors, including watching attractive young women walking by. But – and this is the point of the example – *there also has to be a young woman to watch*. The male hormones are there all the time, but the staring happens only when there is an

---

[1] I emphasize at this point that the subject of hormones lies way, way outside my area of expertise. For any reader in a similar state of ignorance, I suggest Cornwell (1999) as a very elementary and readable entry to the subject. The conjecture that follows does so because it offers, it seems to me, a theoretical architecture rather well matched to existing knowledge.

attractive young woman to stare at. The specific pattern of behavior is elicited by the stimulus of the young woman, but the readiness with which it is elicited, and the fact that some people stare at the girl while she passes, while others do not, is a function of the potentiation of that kind of behavior by the internal balance of hormones.

Let us now look to see where scientific theory might be 50 years hence. Among other functions, the hormones selectively prime the neural mechanisms that initiate different kinds of behavior. Scientific theory will spell out which environmental stimuli cause the release of which hormones and how; and which hormones potentiate which kinds of behavior and where in the brain that potentiation takes place. There are also minor differences in endocrine function between one person and the next that can, in some cases, develop into medical disorder. Some of these differences, whether of genetic origin or whether acquired through past experience, translate into differences in propensities for this kind of behavior or that. So the theory that spells out how hormones potentiate different patterns of behavior will also explain why people differ in personality in the ways that they do; and there might also be an explanation how some kinds of drug come to interact with some kinds of mental disorder.

This is speculation about what might be discovered in the future, probably the distant future. It would, however, be tidy if personality, meaning the general characteristics of a person's behavior as opposed to specific acquired patterns of behavior, were reducible to internal factors of genetic origin. The most compelling example of the influence of hormones on human behavior, rather than just the human body, is the new mother getting up in the middle of the night to feed her baby. Caitlin Moran was on the set of the *Antiques Roadshow* television program with her 6-month-old baby.

> Dora starts making a wailing sound. A production assistant runs over. "Do you want to come outside?" she asks, kindly. "Only we've had letters. When a baby cries on the television, nursing female viewers start spontaneously lactating." (Moran, 2002)

That episode illustrates, at a simple level, the paradigm of motivated behavior that I have in mind.

REFERENCES

AbouZahr, C. & Royston, E. (1991). *Maternal Mortality: A Global Factbook*. Geneva: World Health Organization.

Agras, W. S. (1965). An investigation of the decrement of anxiety responses during systematic desensitization therapy. *Behaviour Research and Therapy*, 2, 267–70.

Aitkenhead, D. (1995). Our knight in icy armour. *Independent*, December 26, p. 14.

Allen-Mills, T. (1996). A star-maker is born. *Sunday Times*, October 20, p. 1:27.

Appleyard, B. (1997). The princes' final farewell. *Sunday Times*, September 7, p. 1.

Armstrong, L. (1991). A queen of the catwalk. *Independent on Sunday*, October 27, p. 25.

Asch, S. E. (1952). *Social Psychology*. New York: Prentice-Hall.

Asch, S. E. (1955). Opinions and social pressure. *Scientific American*, 193, November, pp. 31–5.

Asch, S. E. (1956). Studies of independence and conformity: I. A minority of one against a unanimous majority. *Psychological Monographs*, 70 (Serial No. 416).

Asch, S. E. (1958). Effects of group pressure upon the modification and distortion of judgments. In E. E. Maccoby, T. M. Newcomb, and E. L. Hartley (Eds.), *Readings in Social Psychology*, 3rd ed. New York: Holt, pp. 174–83.

Ashworth, J. (1997). Clowes denies benefit charges. *The Times*, December 19, p. 25.

Ashworth, J. (2000). Why the boardroom is still closed to women. *The Times*, November 8, *Times2*, p. 8.

Atherton, M. (2000). Beware the extended warranty trap. *The Times*, December 2, *Money*, p. 1.

Aziz, C. (1991). The untouchables of London's suburbs. *Independent*, January 10, p. 17.

Bale, J. (1997). Bloody history of a lover driven by rage. *The Times*, July 30, p. 4.

Ball, W. & Tronick, E. (1971). Infant responses to impending collisions: Optical and real. *Science*, 171, 818–20.

Bancroft, J. (1989). *Human Sexuality and its Problems*, 2nd ed. Edinburgh: Churchill Livingstone.

Barrowclough, A. (2000). A doctor's dilemma. *The Times*, June 6, *Times2*, pp. 3–4.

BBC 10 O'Clock News (2001). April 11.

Bedell, G. (1996). Virtue's reward. *Independent on Sunday*, January 14, *Review*, pp. 4–7.

Bennet, W. & MacKinnon, I. (1993). Boy, 12, in hiding as police clear him. *Independent*, February 18, p. 1.

Bennett, A. M. H. (1961). Sensory deprivation in aviation. In P. Solomon, P. E. Kubzansky, P. H. Leiderman, J. H. Mendelson, R. Trumbull, & D. Wexler (Eds.), *Sensory Deprivation.* Cambridge, MA: Harvard University Press, pp. 161–73.

Bennetto, J. & Victor, P. (1995). Rising tension erupted in conflagration. *Independent,* December 15, p. 2.

Bennetts, L. (2000). Simply unpredictable. *Vanity Fair,* August, pp. 56–61, 112–15.

Beresford, P. (1989). How bosses justify £534,000 a year. *Sunday Times,* July 23, p. B5.

Berkowitz, L. (1965). Some aspects of observed aggression. *Journal of Personality and Social Psychology,* 2, 359–69.

Berkowitz, L. (1983). Aversively stimulated aggression: Some parallels and differences in research with animals and humans. *American Psychologist,* 38, 1135–44.

Berkowitz, L. (1989). Frustration-aggression hypothesis: Examination and reformulation. *Psychological Bulletin,* 106, 59–73.

Berkowitz, L. (1993). *Aggression: Its Causes, Consequences, and Control.* New York: McGraw-Hill.

Bexton, W. H., Heron, W., & Scott, T. H. (1954). Effects of decreased variation in the sensory environment. *Canadian Journal of Psychology,* 8, 70–6.

Beynon, M. (1994). *The Human Animal: The Biology of Love.* BBC1, August 17.

Bilton, M. & Sim, K. (1989). My Lai: A half-told story. *Sunday Times Magazine,* April 23, pp. 24–35.

Bird, S. (2000). Children defy safety warnings over rails. *The Times,* August 5, p. 8.

Birkhead, M. (1997). *Tiger Crisis: Update.* BBC2, January 8.

Birtwistle, S. (1995). *Pride and Prejudice,* Episode 4. BBC1, October 15.

Bishop, J. (1981). Experts say films can prod the disturbed. *Wall Street Journal,* April 2, pp. 29, 52.

Black, J. (1993). *The Money-Spinners: How Professional Gamblers Beat Casinos at their Own Game.* London: Faber & Faber.

Blundy, A. (1998). Russia plagued by fatal wife-beatings. *The Times,* November 26, p. 17.

Böckenholt, U. (1992). Multivariate models of preference and choice. In F. G. Ashby (Ed.), *Multidimensional Models of Perception and Cognition.* Hillsdale, NJ: Lawrence Erlbaum, pp. 89–113.

Boggan, S. (1991). A law unto themselves. *Independent on Sunday,* August 11, *Review,* pp. 2–5.

Boggan, S. (1995). Angry words that ignited the tinder-box. *Independent,* December 15, p. 3.

Bombard, A. (1954). *The Voyage of the Hérétique.* New York: Simon & Schuster.

Borsellino, A., De Marco, A., Allazetta, A., Rinesi, S., & Bartolini, B. (1972). Reversal time distribution in the perception of visual ambiguous stimuli. *Kybernetik,* 10, 139–44.

Bower, T. G. R., Broughton, J. M., & Moore, M. K. (1970). Infant responses to approaching objects: An indicator of response to distal variables. *Perception and Psychophysics,* 9, 193–6.

Bradberry, G. (2001). Don't let my son die. *The Times,* January 10, *Times2,* pp. 4–5.

Breland, K. & Breland, M. (1961). The misbehaviour of organisms. *American Psychologist,* 16, 681–4.

Breuer, J. & Freud, S. (1895). *Studien über Hysterie.* Leipzig: F. Deuticke. Trans. J. Strachey (1955). *Studies on Hysteria.* London: Hogarth Press.

Bromhall, C. (1994). *The Sexual Imperative: 1. The Importance of Sex.* Channel 4, May 14.

Bronowski, J. (1973). *The Ascent of Man*. London: British Broadcasting Corporation.

Brown, C. & MacIntyre, D. (1994). Gas chief's £205,000 pay rise embarrasses ministers. *Independent*, November 22, p. 1.

Brown, D. (2002). 18-stone man hurt in 200ft bungee jump. *The Times*, August 27, p. 6.

Brownfield, C. A. (1972). *The Brain Benders*. New York: Exposition Press.

Bull, P. & Frederikson, L. (1994). Non-verbal communication. In A. M. Colman (Ed.), *Companion Encyclopedia of Psychology*, vol. 2. London: Routledge, pp. 852–72.

Burge, J. (1996). *Public Eye: Serial Rapists*. BBC2, March 19.

Burney, C. (1952). *Solitary Confinement*. London: Clerke & Cockeran.

Burt, P. (1993). Stuck outside yourself looking in. *IndependentII*, November 9, p. 22.

Buss, A. H. (1960). *The Psychology of Aggression*. New York: Wiley.

Byrd, R. E. (1938). *Alone*. London: Putnam.

Caine, N. & Davidson, H. (1997). Men still behave badly over women's salaries. *Sunday Times*, January 26, p. 5:5.

Calhoun, J. B. (1962). Population density and social pathology. *Scientific American*, 206, February, pp. 139–48.

Campbell, D. (2001). *The Mozart Effect*. London: Hodder & Stoughton.

Campbell, M. (1998). Inside Washington. *Sunday Times*, November 8, p. 1:27.

Campbell, M. (2001). Racy le Big Brother has France panting for more. *Sunday Times*, May 13, p. 1:22.

Carr, H. & Watson, J. B. (1908). Orientation in the white rat. *Journal of Comparative Neurology and Psychology*, 18, 27–44.

Carter, J. & Duriez, T. (1986). *With Child: Birth through the Ages*. Edinburgh: Mainstream.

Cash, W. (1991). Ratner's speech loses its sparkle. *The Times*, April 25, p. 2.

Catliff, N. (1997a). Can sex offenders be left in peace? *The Times*, February 4, p. 39.

Catliff, N. (1997b). *Inside Story: Megan's Law*. BBC1, February 4.

Chittenden, M., Skipworth, M., Calvert, J., & Ramesh, R. (1994). Dishonourable members? *Sunday Times*, July 17, pp. 1:11–13.

Chomsky, N. (1965). *Aspects of the Theory of Syntax*. Cambridge, MA: MIT Press.

Christie, R. & Geis, F. L. (Eds.) (1970). *Studies in Machiavellianism*. New York: Academic Press.

Clarke, F. R. (1957). Constant-ratio rule for confusion matrices in speech communication. *Journal of the Acoustical Society of America*, 29, 715–20.

Cleckley, H. (1976). *The Mask of Sanity*, 5th ed. St Louis: Mosby.

Clement, B. (1995). Mellor tops list of Tory MPs with outside jobs. *Independent*, January 6, p. 7.

Coates, S. (2001a). Gascoigne wife breaks taboo on domestic abuse. *The Times*, January 9, p. 9.

Coates, S. (2001b). Machete victim's damages "unfair." *The Times*, February 7, p. 13.

Cockburn, P. & Nolen, S. (1995). Revolt stirs over women who die of shame. *Independent on Sunday*, December 3, p. 16.

Cohen, N. (1991a). Bouncing Icke reveals cosmic mission to save the world from Lucifer. *Independent*, March 28, p. 5.

Cohen, N. (1991b). Cars are destroyed in 100 mph youth cult. *Independent*, September 1, p. 1.

Cohen, N. & Durham, M. (1993). Out of control. *Independent on Sunday*, February 14, p. 17.

Cohen, N. & Routledge, P. (1994). The revenge of the moral majority. *Independent on Sunday*, January 9, p. 15.

Coles, J. (2000). Too sexy for their seats. *The Times*, October 12, *Times2*, pp. 3–4.

Collins, J. (2000). Temper tantrums. *The Times*, May 9, *Times2*, p. 13.

Committee of Public Accounts (1986). *Twenty-Third Report (HC 56)*. London: HMSO.

Comstock, G. (1977). Types of portrayal and aggressive behaviour. *Journal of Communication*, 27(3), 189–98.

Connett, D. (1993). Tell us why the mob drove us from our corner shop. *Independent on Sunday*, July 18, p. 6.

Cooper, G. (1995). Frightened women in search of answers. *Independent*, October 21, p. 2.

Cooper, K. J. (1999). This time, copycat wave is broader. *Washington Post*, May 1, p. A6.

Cope, N. (1994). Company chief does not fit mould. *Independent*, November 22, p. 3.

Cope, N. (1995). Marshall moves into the chair at Inchcape. *Independent*, November 8, p. 21.

Cope, N. & Rodgers, P. (1996). Bonus led to fat cat having a thin time. *Independent*, February 7, p. 3.

Cornwell, J. (1999). Inside story. *Sunday Times Magazine*, December 5, pp. 18–26.

Cosgrove, S. (1994). *Walk On The Wild Side: Firebugs*. Channel 4, January 19.

Cotton, I. (1997). New model army. *Independent Magazine*, August 10, pp. 12–20.

Crace, J. (1995). Hillsborough: It's not over yet. *Independent*, April 7, *Section Two*, p. 21.

Crick, M. (1985). *Scargill and the Miners*. Harmondsworth: Penguin.

Curtiss, S. (1977). *Genie: A Psycholinguistic Study of a Modern-Day "Wild Child."* New York: Academic Press.

Cutler, J. (1999). *The Boy Who Lived with Monkeys: Living Proof*. BBC1, October 13.

Daily Mail (1995). Curb on ads that use sex to sell. January 12, p. 11.

Daly, E. (1992). The ordinary people who are capable of evil. *Independent*, August 10, p. 13.

Damasio, A. R. (1994). *Descartes' Error: Emotion, Reason, and the Human Brain*. New York: G. P. Putnam.

d'Antal, S. (2001). "That's what girls are for." *The Times*, May 9, *Times2*, pp. 2–3.

da Ponte, L. (1787/1961). *Il dissoluto punito ossia il Don Giovanni*. Trans. L. Salter. Deutsche Grammophon Gesellschaft.

Davenport, P. (1985). Passengers panic as fire races through fuselage. *The Times*, August 23, pp. 1, 2.

Davies, P. W. (1996). A copper's tale. *Independent*, July 15, p. 14.

Dawkins, R. (1976). *The Selfish Gene*. Oxford: Oxford University Press.

de Bruxelles, S. (2000). Girl, 16, beaten to death for saying "no." *The Times*, July 11, p. 9.

de Bruxelles, S. (2001). Boy knifed baby brother 17 times after family row. *The Times*, February 13, p. 14.

Defoe, D. (1719). *The Life and Strange Surprizing Adventures of Robinson Crusoe*. London: W. Taylor.

Dejevsky, M. (1989). Crushing the Beijing spring. *Sunday Times Magazine*, October 8, pp. 24–40.

Dement, W. & Wolpert, E. A. (1958). The relation of eye movements, body motility and external stimuli to dream content. *Journal of Experimental Psychology*, 55, 543–53.

Deutsch, M. & Gerard, H. B. (1955). A study of normative and informational social influences upon individual judgment. *Journal of Abnormal and Social Psychology*, 51, 629–36.

de Waal, F. B. M., Aureli, F., & Judge, P. G. (2000). Coping with crowding. *Scientific American*, 282, May, pp. 54–9.

Dickens, C. (1957). *American Notes and Pictures from Italy*. London: Oxford University Press.

Dickinson, M. (1999). Ferguson eyes up Juninho. *The Times*, May 28, p. 61.

Doane, B. K., Mahatoo, W., Heron, W., & Scott, T. H. (1959). Changes in perceptual function after isolation. *Canadian Journal of Psychology*, 13, 210–19.

Dobson, R. (1996). Why do we have to turn a scare into a crisis? *Independent*, April 16, *Section Two*, pp. 6–7.

Dodd, C. (1994). Yuck! although I rather like . . . *IndependentII*, July 11, p. 22.

Dollard, J., Doob, L. W., Miller, N. E., Mowrer, O. H., & Sears, R. R. (1939). *Frustration and Aggression*. New Haven, CT: Yale University Press.

Dowd, M., Sutcliffe, K., Lord, D., & Renn, M. (1997). *Panorama: Bridgewater – a Miscarriage of Justice*. BBC1, February 24.

Driscoll, M. (1999). Torments of a mother's tough love. *The Times*, July 18, p. 5:9.

Duce, R. (1997). Lisa Potts offered an alternative job. *The Times*, June 24, p. 9.

Durman, P. (1992a). Clowes is jailed for ten years and disqualified. *Independent*, February 12, p. 2.

Durman, P. (1992b). Clowes used cash to fund extravagant lifestyle. *Independent*, February 11, p. 3.

Ebbinghaus, H. (1911). *Grundzüge der Psychologie*, vol. 1. Leipzig: Veit.

Ebbinghaus, H. (1964). *Memory*. Trans. H. A. Ruger & C. E. Bussenius. New York: Dover. (Original work published 1885; translation first published 1913.)

Eddy, P. & Lightfoot, L. (1995). Playing safe. *Sunday Times*, October 22, p. 1:13.

Edwards-Jones, I. (1991). The college lads who don't know when to stop. *Independent*, November 20, p. 16.

Ekman, P. (1980). *The Face of Man*. New York: Garland.

Ekman, P. & Davidson, R. J. (Eds.) (1994). *The Nature of Emotion: Fundamental Questions*. New York: Oxford University Press.

Ekman, P. & Friesen, W. V. (1975). *Unmasking the Face*. Englewood Cliffs, NJ: Prentice-Hall.

Elliott, H. & Kiley, S. (1987). Private defence contractors paid back £23.5m. *The Times*, October 31, pp. 1, 22.

Emerson, R. M. (1964). Deviation and rejection: An experimental replication. *American Sociological Review*, 19, 688–93.

Encyclopaedia Britannica (1989a). Determinism. 15th ed., vol. 4. Chicago: Encyclopaedia Britannica, p. 39.

Encyclopaedia Britannica (1989b). Free will. 15th ed., vol. 4. Chicago: Encyclopaedia Britannica, p. 965.

English, S. (1997). Jeering mothers drive paedophile off council estate. *The Times*, January 11, p. 7.

English, S. & McCarra, K. (1996). Gascoignes in hiding as star tries to escape dark side of his fame. *The Times*, October 18, p. 3.

Eron, L. D., Huesman, L. R., Lefkowitz, M. M., & Walder, L. O. (1972). Does television violence cause aggression? *American Psychologist*, 27, 253–63.

Evans, M. (1991). Why *Eye Need* fails to satisfy. *Independent*, October 16, p. 15.

Exline, R. V., Thibaut, J., Hickey, C. B., & Gumpert, P. (1970). Visual interaction in relation to Machiavellianism and an unethical act. In R. Christie & F. Geis (Eds.), *Studies in Machiavellianism*. New York: Academic Press, pp. 53–75.

Farrar, S. (1999). Biologist proves animals are just as queer as folk. *Sunday Times*, June 6, p. 1:12.

Farrell, S. (1996). "Road rage" stabbing victim dies. *The Times*, December 3, p. 1.

Farrell, S. (2000). Acid thug victims find centre of hope. *The Times*, November 22, p. 19.

Fathers, M. & Higgins, A. (1989). *Tiananmen: The Rape of Peking*. London: Doubleday.

Fenton, J. (1993). Thou shalt not kill; but I may kill you. *Independent*, March 22, p. 23.

Ferguson, L. (1999). *Dispatches: Domestic Violence*. Channel 4, January 7.

Feynman, R. P. (1985). *"Surely You're Joking, Mr. Feynman!"* New York: W. W. Norton.

Fine, R. (1989). *The Ideas behind the Chess Openings*, 3rd ed. London: Batsford.

Fisher, C. D. (1993). Boredom at work: A neglected concept. *Human Relations*, 46, 395–417.

Fleck, F. & Peek, L. (2000). Bungee jumper killed as rope fails to halt fall. *The Times*, May 15, p. 3.

Fletcher, M. (1998). *Almost Heaven*. London: Little, Brown.

Ford, R. (2000). Abduction charges to halt forced marriages. *The Times*, June 30, p. 12.

Ford, R. (2001). Prisons director reads riot act over "hell holes." *The Times*, February 6, p. 2.

Ford, R. & Kennedy, D. (1998). Prison staff called in as children go on the rampage. *The Times*, November 13, p. 1.

Forna, A. (1996). For women – or for men only? *Independent on Sunday*, April 28, *Real Life*, p. 3.

Foster, J. (1993). Boys who battered James Bulger to death locked up for "very many years." *Independent*, November 25, p. 1.

Foster, P. (1997). Older bikers take the short route to casualty. *The Times*, June 28, p. 9.

Fox, S. (1999). Why am I so scared of driving? *The Times*, October 18, p. 40.

Francis, B. (Ed.) (2000). *New Earnings Survey 2000*. London: Office for National Statistics.

Franey, R. & McKee, G. (1989). *First Tuesday. The Guildford Four: Free to Speak*. Yorkshire TV, November 7.

Frean, A. (2000). Rescued from a forced marriage. *The Times*, July 17, *Times2*, pp. 6–7.

Garman, L. & Poole, C. (1994). *Horizon: Genie*. BBC2, January 31.

Garner, W. R. (1962). *Uncertainty and Structure as Psychological Concepts*. New York: Wiley.

Gazzaniga, M. S. (1995). Consciousness and the cerebral hemispheres. In M. S. Gazzaniga (Ed.), *The Cognitive Neurosciences*. Cambridge, MA: MIT Press, pp. 1391–1400.

Gazzaniga, M. S. & LeDoux, J. E. (1978). *The Integrated Mind*. New York: Plenum Press.

Geaves, W. (1994). Heaven can wait. *Radio Times*, December 10–16, pp. 29–30.

Gee, J. (1996). The ultimate roller-coaster ride. *Independent*, September 4, *Summer of Sport*, p. 11.

Geis, F. (1970). The con game and Bargaining tactics in the con game. In R. Christie & F. Geis (Eds.), *Studies in Machiavellianism*. New York: Academic Press, pp. 106–29 and 130–60.

Geis, F. L. & Moon, T. H. (1981). Machiavellianism and deception. *Journal of Personality and Social Psychology*, 41, 766–75.

Gelles, R. J. & Straus, M. A. (1988). *Intimate Violence*. New York: Simon & Schuster.

Gerard, H. B., Wilhelmy, R. A., & Conolley, E. S. (1968). Conformity and group size. *Journal of Personality and Social Psychology*, 8, 79–82.

Gibb, F. (1999). "Tragic" dispute over fence ends. *The Times*, November 19, p. 7.

Gibson, E. J. & Walk, R. D. (1960). The "visual cliff." *Scientific American*, 202, April, pp. 64–71.

Gibson, J. J. (1950). *The Perception of the Visual World*. Boston, MA: Houghton Mifflin.

Gillie, O. (1990a). Self-delusion keeps the chips going down. *Independent*, July 9, p. 4.

Gillie, O. (1990b). Teenagers "legitimise sex by being secretly engaged." *Independent*, June 12, p. 3.

Goodwin, C. & Rushe, D. (1999). Drool Britannia. *Sunday Times*, August 1, pp. 1:13 and 3:2.

Gosling, P. (1993). Pawns of the loan brokers. *Independent on Sunday*, February 14, *Business News*, p. 16.

Grose, V. L. (1989). Coping with boredom in the cockpit before it's too late. *Professional Safety*. July, pp. 24–6.

Gruenberg, G. W. (1967). Determinism, economic and geographic. *New Catholic Encyclopedia*, vol. 4. New York: McGraw-Hill, pp. 810–11.

Guest, D., Williams, R., & Dewe, P. (1978). Job design and the psychology of boredom. Paper presented at the 19th International Congress of Applied Psychology, Munich, West Germany.

Gumbel, A. (1995). After scoring 6,000, the Rimini Romeo calls time. *Independent*, August 16, p. 9.

Gutierrez, H. & Houdaille, J. (1983). La mortalité maternelle en France au XVIIIe siècle. *Population*, 38, 975–94.

Haberman, R. (1977). *Mathematical Models: Mechanical Vibrations, Population Dynamics, and Traffic Flow*. Englewood Cliffs, NJ: Prentice-Hall.

Hallam, R. S. & Rachman, S. (1983). Psychological effects of training. *Advances in Behaviour Research and Therapy*, 4, 121–5.

Halliwell, J. O. (1842). *The Nursery Rhymes of England*. London: Percy Society.

Haney, C., Banks, C., & Zimbardo, P. (1973). Interpersonal dynamics in a simulated prison. *International Journal of Criminology and Penology*, 1, 69–97.

Harvey, M. (1999). It's distressing, says wife in air "lewdness." *The Times*, October 5, p. 8.

Hawkes, N. (1999). Sponsored parachute jumps cost NHS dear. *The Times*, June 28, p. 9.

Hawthorne, P.-E. (1991). *This Week: Carry On Conning – The Rip-Off*. Thames TV, June 6.

Hayes, N. (1992). *World in Action: An MP's Business*. ITV, March 30.

Hebb, D. O. (1945). Man's frontal lobes. *Archives of Neurology and Psychiatry*, 54, 10–24.

Hebb, D. O. (1949). *The Organization of Behavior*. New York: Wiley.

Hebb, D. O. (1955). Drives and the C.N.S. (conceptual nervous system). *Psychological Review*, 62, 243–54.

Hebb, D. O. & Morton, N. W. (1943). The McGill adult comprehension examination: "Verbal situation" and "picture anomaly" series. *Journal of Educational Psychology*, 34, 16–25.

Hellen, N. (1999). Ban on gratuitous TV sex scenes angers broadcasters. *Sunday Times*, January 24, p. 1.

Hellen, N. & Barot, T. (1998). Channel 4 breaks the last sex taboo with bestiality film. *Sunday Times*, December 6, p. 1:3.

Hellier, D. & Nissé, J. (1992). The descent of Mountleigh. *Independent on Sunday*, May 31, *Business*, p. 6.

Heron, W. (1957). The pathology of boredom. *Scientific American*, 196, January, pp. 52–6.

Heron, W., Doane, B. K., & Scott, T. H. (1956). Visual disturbances after prolonged perceptual isolation. *Canadian Journal of Psychology*, 10, 13–18.

Hess, E. H. (1965). Attitude and pupil size. *Scientific American*, 212, April, pp. 46–54.

Hess, E. H. (1975). The role of pupil size in communication. *Scientific American*, 233, November, pp. 110–19.

Hetherington, T. (1988). Billed after losing the lot. *Sunday Times*, December 11, p. D10.

Hiley, C. (2000). Woman dies in Snowdonia on "canyoning" trip. *The Times*, May 1, p. 5.

Hilpern, K. (1999). "My name's David and I'm a sex addict." *The Times Magazine*, January 16, pp. 70–3.

Hilton, I. (1993). He gave himself up to the British, then they shot him. *Independent*, March 27, *Weekend*, p. 29.

Hodgkinson, T. (1993). The devil in our backyard. *Independent on Sunday*, October 3, *Review*, pp. 12–16.

Honigsbaum, M. (1992). The cautious confessions of a card counter. *Independent*, February 20, p. 16.

Hood, R. W., Jr. (1998). When the spirit maims and kills: Social psychological considerations of the history of serpent handling sects and the narrative of handlers. *International Journal for the Psychology of Religion*, 8, 71–96.

Hosking, P. (1991). Investment trick netted £8.1m for "life of luxury." *Independent*, June 4, p. 3.

Howe, M. (1999). Plumber who went berserk on jet jailed for three years. *Independent*, May 29, p. 9.

Hughes, R. (1996). Gascoigne asks forgiveness for "the rage inside me." *The Times*, November 5, p. 1.

Hunter, E. (1951). *Brainwashing in Red China. The Calculated Destruction of Men's Minds*. New York: Vanguard Press.

Independent (1990). Hillsborough families "bitter." January 2, p. 2.

Independent (1991). Student who gambled loans killed himself. November 16, p. 9.

Independent (1993). Nurse sacked "for causing distress." March 16, p. 3.

Independent (1994a). Bungee jumper hurt eyes. February 18, p. 4.

Independent (1994b). Cambridge dean resigns over student dropping trousers. April 29, p. 8.

Independent (1994c). Outlook: Making companies face their responsibilities. December 14, p. 33.

Insalaco, R. (Ed.) (2002). *Annual Abstract of Statistics*. London: The Stationery Office.

Itard, J. (1972). *The Wild Boy of Aveyron*. Trans. Anon & J. White. London: NLB.

Jebb, L. (1996). Sky high flying over the River Thames. *Independent*, July 31, *Summer of Sport*, p. 6.

Jobey, E. (1991). The major league. *Independent on Sunday*, August 18, *Review*, p. 27.

Johnson, A. M., Wadsworth, J., Wellings, K., & Field, J. (1994). *Sexual Attitudes and Lifestyles*. Oxford: Blackwell.

Joint, M. (1995). *Road Rage*. Basingstoke: The Automobile Association Group Public Policy Road Safety Unit.

Jones, S. (1985). Riot by Millwall supporters overshadows Luton win. *The Times*, March 14, p. 22.

Jones, T. & Lee, A. (1998). Rally driver jailed for double killing. *The Times*, April 3, p. 3.

Jost, A. (1897). Die Assoziationsfestigkeit in ihrer Abhängigkeit von der Verteilung der Wiederholungen. *Zeitschrift für Psychologie und Physiologie der Sinnesorgane*, 14, 436–72.

Judd, J. (1996). Schools "need lesson in teaching morals." *Independent*, January 15, p. 1.

Jury, L. (1996). Murderer with sick mind who lived out his fantasies. *Independent*, July 19, p. 8.

Kalven, H., Jr. & Zeisel, H. (1966). *The American Jury*. Boston: Little, Brown.

Kay, H. (1992). Inner city circle holds the key to top boardrooms. *Sunday Times*, June 14, p. 3:8.

Kee, R. (1986). *Trial and Error*. London: Hamish Hamilton.

Kempson, R. (1998). Di Canio cries "Foul! The ref took a dive." *The Times*, September 28, p. 1.

Kennedy, D. & Ford, R. (1998). Jail staff tell of misery inflicted by children. *The Times*, November 13, p. 6.

Keren, G. & Wagenaar, W. A. (1985). On the psychology of playing blackjack: Normative and descriptive considerations with implications for decision theory. *Journal of Experimental Psychology: General*, 114, 133–58.

Kinkead, E. (1960). *Why They Collaborated*. London: Longman.

Kinsey, A. C., Pomeroy, W. B., & Martin, C. E. (1948). *Sexual Behavior in the Human Male*. Philadelphia: W. B. Saunders.

Kinsey, A. C., Pomeroy, W. B., Martin, C. E., & Gebhard, P. H. (1953). *Sexual Behavior in the Human Female*. Philadelphia: W. B. Saunders.

Kirby, T. (1993). Burglar's nice little earners pull him in £300 an hour. *Independent on Sunday*, September 26, p. 3.

Korn, D., Radice, M., & Hawes, C. (2001). *Cannibal: The History of the People-Eaters*. London: Channel 4 Books.

Közi-Horváth, J. (1979). *Cardinal Mindszenty*. Trans. G. Lawman. Chichester: Aid to the Church in Need (UK).

Krushelnycky, A. (1986). Haunted by nightmare of disaster. *Sunday Times*, September 14, p. 9.

Lambert, A. (1995). Guilty until proven innocent. *Independent*, December 7, *Section Two*, pp. 2–3.

Laming, D. (1986). *Sensory Analysis*. London: Academic Press.

Laming, D. (1988). Précis of *Sensory Analysis*. *Behavioral and Brain Sciences*, 11, 275–96.

Laming, D. (1992). Springer's lines and Hermann's grid. *Ophthalmic and Physiological Optics*, 12, 178–82.

Laming, D. (1997). *The Measurement of Sensation*. Oxford: Oxford University Press.

Laming, D. (2004). *Human Judgment: The Eye of the Beholder*. London: Thomson Learning.

Lane, H. (1996). Interview with Jennifer Ehle. *Tatler*, August, p. 14.

Lang, A. R., Goeckner, D. J., Adesso, V. J., & Marlatt, G. A. (1975). Effect of alcohol on aggression in male social drinkers. *Journal of Abnormal Psychology*, 84, 508–18.

Lang, P. J. (1970). Stimulus control, response control and desensitisation of fear. In D. Levis (Ed.), *Learning Approaches to Therapeutic Behavior Change*. Chicago: Aldine, pp. 148–73.

Langley, C. (1988). Anti-abortion man raises baby alone. *Sunday Times*, January 17, p. A5.

Latané, B. & Davis, D. (1974). Social impact and the effect of majority influence on attitudes toward news media. Unpublished MS.

Latané, B. & Wolf, S. (1981). The social impact of majorities and minorities. *Psychological Review*, 88, 438–53.

Laurence, J. (1995). Three pill studies showed increased risk of blood clots. *The Times*, October 21, p. 7.

Leach, P. (1977). *Baby and Child*. London: Michael Joseph.

Lean, G. (1996). Bikers play safe in speeding Britain. *Independent on Sunday*, June 30, p. 2.

Leapman, M. (1996). No holds barred in battle for late-night viewers. *Independent on Sunday*, January 7, p. 8.

LeBor, A. & Boyes, R. (2000a). How did Hitler make millions follow him? *The Times*, October 16, *Times2*, pp. 10–11.

LeBor, A. & Boyes, R. (2000b). *Surviving Hitler: Choices, Corruption and Compromise in the Third Reich*. London: Simon & Schuster.

Lee, C. T., Williams, P., & Hadden, W. A. (1999). Parachuting for charity: Is it worth the money? A 5-year audit of parachute injuries in Tayside and the cost to the NHS. *Injury*, 30, 283–7.

Legrain, L. (1936). *Ur Excavations*. Vol. 3: *Archaic Seal-Impressions*. Joint expedition of the British Museum and the Museum of the University of Pennsylvania to Mesopotamia. Oxford.

Lenneberg, E. H. (1967). *Biological Foundations of Language*. New York: Wiley.

Lever, L. (1988). Hard sell million-earners "menace to the public." *The Times*, October 13, p. 1.

Lewis, J. (1985). *TV Eye: Scab*. Thames Television, May 23.

Lilly, J. C. (1956). Mental effects of reduction of ordinary levels of physical stimuli on intact, healthy persons. *Psychiatric Research Reports*, 5, 1–9.

Lindsay, P. H. & Norman, D. A. (1977). *Human Information Processing: An Introduction to Psychology*, 2nd ed. New York: Academic Press.

Lorenz, K. (1966). *On Aggression*. Trans. M. Latzke. London: Methuen.

Lumer, E. D., Friston, K. J., & Rees, G. (1998). Neural correlates of perceptual rivalry in the human brain. *Science*, 280, 1930–4.

Lumer, E. D. & Rees, G. (1999). Covariation of activity in visual and prefrontal cortex associated with subjective visual perception. *Proceedings of the National Academy of Sciences USA*, 96, 1669–73.

Lynn, M. (1988). The effects of alcohol consumption on restaurant tipping. *Personality and Social Psychology Bulletin*, 14, 87–91.

Lynn, M. & Hamilton, K. (1998). UK's most overpaid man makes an extra £19m. *Sunday Times*, October 25, p. 3:1.

Lynn, M., Hamilton, K., & Coffer, A. (1998). Which of Britain's bosses give value for their pay? *Sunday Times*, October 25, pp. 3:10–11.

McFadyean, M. (1994). Why Mandy watches Billy fight. *Independent on Sunday*, March 27, *Review*, pp. 10–13.

McGeoch, J. A. (1942). *The Psychology of Human Learning*. New York: Longman, Green.

McGilvary, M. (1999). Surfing for cybersex. *The Times*, June 29, p. 19.

McGirk, T. (1991). India discovers the lady is a vamp. *Independent*, November 8, p. 13.

McGirk, T. (1996). India bans sex tests to save "missing daughters." *Independent*, January 11, p. 9.

McHoskey, J. W., Worzel, W., & Szyarto, C. (1998). Machiavellianism and psychopathy. *Journal of Personality and Social Psychology*, 74, 192–210.

MacIntyre, D. (1994). Major rocked as payments scandal grows. *Independent*, October 21, p. 1.

MacIntyre, D. (1996). Independent body to rule on MPs' pay. *Independent*, February 1, pp. 1–2.

MacIntyre, D. & Brown, C. (1994). Hamilton forced out after fresh allegations. *Independent*, October 26, p. 1.

McKinney, F. & McGeoch, J. A. (1935). The character and extent of transfer in retroactive inhibition: Disparate serial lists. *American Journal of Psychology*, 47, 409–23.

Macrae, H. (1991). Commentary: Taming runaway pay differentials. *Independent*, April 26, p. 25.

Malinowski, B. (1929). *The Sexual Life of Savages in North-Western Melanesia. An Ethnographic Account of Courtship, Marriage and Family Life among the Natives of the Trobriand Islands, British New Guinea*. New York: Halcyon House.

Malinowski, B. (1932). *The Sexual Life of Savages in North-Western Melanesia*, 3rd ed. London: Routledge.

Malson, L. (1972). *Wolf Children*. London: NLB. (Originally published as *Les Enfants sauvages*, Union Générale d'Editions, 1964).

Malson, L. & Itard, J. (1972). *Wolf Children* and *The Wild Boy of Aveyron*. London: NLB.

Marcel, A. J. (1983a). Conscious and unconscious perception: An approach to the relations between phenomenal experience and perceptual processes. *Cognitive Psychology*, 15, 238–300.

Marcel, A. J. (1983b). Conscious and unconscious perception: Experiments on visual masking and word recognition. *Cognitive Psychology*, 15, 197–237.

Marcel, A. J. (1993). Slippage in the unity of consciousness. In G. R. Bock & J. Marsh (Eds.), *Experimental and Theoretical Studies of Consciousness*. Chichester: Wiley, pp. 168–86.

Marks, I. M. (1978). *Living with Fear*. New York: McGraw-Hill.

Marks, K. (1992). Rape. Where does it begin and seduction end? *Independent on Sunday*, February 23, p. 19.

Marnham, P. (1990). C'est la vie, c'est l'argent. *Independent*, January 25, p. 13.

Marshall, S. L. A. (1947). *Men against Fire*. New York: Morrow.

Marshall, S. L. A. (1964). *Battle at Best*. New York: Morrow.

Masters, W. H., Johnson, V. E., & Kolodny, R. C. (1995). *Human Sexuality*, 5th ed. New York: HarperCollins.

Mealey, L. (1995). The sociobiology of sociopathy: An integrated evolutionary model. *Behavioral and Brain Sciences*, 18, 523–41.

Mendelson, J., Solomon, P., & Lindemann, E. (1958). Hallucinations of poliomyelitis patients during treatment in a respirator. *Journal of Nervous and Mental Disease*, 126, 421–8.

Midgley, C. (1996). Judge praises machete heroine. *The Times*, December 10, p. 1.

Midgley, C. (1998a). TV puts on festive orgy of sex, horror and violence. *The Times*, December 19, p. 19.

Midgley, C. (1998b). TV violence has little impact on children study finds. *The Times*, January 12, p. 5.

Milgram, S. (1974). *Obedience to Authority*. London: Tavistock.

Mills, H. (1994). Men "would use force in home." *Independent*, January 18, p. 5.

Mindszenty, J. (1974). *Memoirs*. Trans. R. Winston & C. Winston. London: Weidenfeld & Nicolson.

Mirsky, N. (1996). *My Brilliant Career: Ratner, Lord of the Rings*. BBC2, January 4.

Mitchell, P. (1997). *Introduction to Theory of Mind: Children, Autism, and Apes*. London: Arnold.

Mizell, L. (1997). *Aggressive Driving*. New York: AAA Foundation for Traffic Safety.

Montagu, A. (1974). *Coming into Being among the Australian Aborigines*, 2nd ed. London: Routledge & Kegan Paul.

Mooney, J. (1994). *The Hidden Figure: Domestic Violence in North London*. Islington, London: Islington Council.

Moore, J. (1991). Boss's pay cut to £1 a second. *Independent on Sunday*, December 15, p. 1.

Moore, W. (1996). Born again, after 20 years in a dark tunnel. *Independent*, July 9, *Section Two*, p. 6.

Moran, C. (2002). I've been seduced by experts. *The Times*, March 1, *Times2*, p. 9.

Morris, D. (1994). *The Human Animal*. London: BBC Books.

Moyes, J. (1995). Bed, please, but hold the romance. *Independent*, January 23, p. 18.

Müller, W. (1997). *The Song Cycles: Miller Songs and Poems*. Trans. M. Scott & J. Roth. Woonton Almeley: Logaston Press.

Mullin, C. (1986). *Error of Judgement*. London: Chatto & Windus.

Mullin, C. S., Jr. (1960). Some psychological aspects of isolated Antarctic living. *American Journal of Psychiatry*, 117, 323–5.

Murray, C. (1984). *Losing Ground: American Social Policy, 1950–1980*. New York: Basic Books.

Murray, C. (1990). *The Emerging British Underclass*. London: IEA Health and Welfare Unit.

Murray, C. (2000). Baby beware. *Sunday Times*, February 13, *News Review*, pp. 1–2.

Murray, I. (1993). Wife seeks enquiry into killer's release. *The Times*, June 29, p. 3.

Nagel, T. (1986). *The View from Nowhere*. New York: Oxford University Press.

Nagel, T. (1995). Dualism. In T. Honderich (Ed.), *Oxford Companion to Philosophy*. Oxford: Oxford University Press, p. 206.

Naish, J. (1999a). Once is not enough. *The Times*, Special supplement on motorbiking, July 30, p. 4.

Naish, J. (1999b). Thrills and spills for the wannabe track-day racers. *The Times*, Special supplement on motorbiking, July 30, p. 8.

National Commission on the Causes and Prevention of Violence (1970). *Crimes of Violence*. Washington, DC: US Government Printing Office.

Nelson, M. (1998). *Cutting Edge: Casino*. Channel 4, February 15.

Network North (1993). *Hartlepool Mini Driver*. Tyne Tees Television, February 10.

New Earnings Survey 1997. London: The Stationery Office.

Newport, E. (1991). Contrasting conceptions of the critical period for language. In S. Carey & R. Gelman (Eds.), *The Epigenesis of Mind*. Hillsdale, NJ: Lawrence Erlbaum, pp. 111–30.

Nisbett, R. E. & Wilson, T. D. (1977). Telling more than we can know: Verbal reports on mental processes. *Psychological Review*, 84, 231–59.

Nissé, J. (1993). High-priced warranties keeping Dixons in profit. *Independent on Sunday*, January 17, *Business*, p. 1.

Nissé, J. (1998). Pay packages at SB start investor revolt. *The Times*, March 31, p. 27.

Nissé, J. & Cole, R. (1990). Dunsdale accounts showed no record of £17m client funds. *Independent*, June 30, *Business*, p. 19.

Norfolk, A. (2000). Surfing skydiver falls 15,000ft to death. *The Times*, July 24, p. 3.

Norman, A. W. & Litwack, G. (1997). *Hormones*. San Diego, CA: Academic Press.

Norman, P. (1999). Paradise of Fools, *Sunday Times Magazine*, April 11, pp. 38–43.

Opie, I. & Opie, P. (1997). *The Oxford Dictionary of Nursery Rhymes*. Oxford: Oxford University Press.

O'Reilly, J. (1997). Head tells of pure hell at the Ridings. *Sunday Times*, December 14, p. 1:5.

Orne, M. T. (1962). On the social psychology of the psychological experiment: With particular references to demand characteristics and their implications. *American Psychologist*, 17, 776–83.

Pennington, S. (1995). Debt, the old-fashioned way. *Independent on Sunday*, January 22, p. 19.

Persaud, R. (1993). Today you're bored. Tomorrow you're ill. *Independent*, March 30, p. 18.

Philbrick, N. (2000). *In the Heart of the Sea*. London: HarperCollins.

Philips, H. C. (1985). Return of fear in the treatment of a fear of vomiting. *Behaviour Research and Therapy*, 23, 45–52.

Phillips, D. P. (1974). The influence of suggestion on suicide: Substantive and theoretical implications of the Werther effect. *American Sociological Review*, 39, 340–54.

Phillips, D. P. (1983). The impact of mass media violence on U.S. homicides. *American Sociological Review*, 48, 560–8.

Pienaar, J. (1990). MP "failed duty" over $88,000 payment. *Independent*, February 20, p. 10.

Pitchford, R. (1991). Blood money. *Guardian*, August 7, p. 28.

Polanyi, M. (1967). *The Tacit Dimension*. London: Routledge & Kegan Paul.

Poole, O. (1999). Violent drunk jailed for £30,000 rampage on jumbo jet. *Daily Telegraph*, May 29, p. 11.

Popham, P. (1992). What friends are for. *Independent Magazine*, December 5, pp. 22–7.

Popham, P. (1996). The looking-glass world of Mr and Mrs Clowes. *Independent*, March 1, Section Two, p. 2.

Popplewell, O. (1986). *Committee of Inquiry into Crowd Safety and Control at Sports Grounds: Final Report*. London: HMSO, Cmnd 9710.

Powell, S. (1999). *Panorama: First Sex*. BBC1, March 8.

Prandtl, A. (1927). Über gleichsinnige Induktion und die Lichtverteilung in gitterartigen Mustern. *Zeitschrift für Sinnesphysiologie*, 58, 263–307.

Prasad, J. (1935). The psychology of rumour: A study relating to the great Indian earthquake of 1934. *British Journal of Psychology*, 26, 1–15.

Prasad, J. (1950). A comparative study of rumours and reports in different earthquakes. *British Journal of Psychology*, 41, 129–44.

Prechtl, H. (1950). Das Verhalten von Kleinkindern gegenüber Schlangen. *Wiener Zeitschrift für Philosophie, Psychologie, und Paedogogie*, 2, 68–70.

Prentice, E. A. (2000). The true cost of duck à l'orange. *The Times*, June 9, Times2, pp. 10–11.

Qualtrough, A. (1993). He is 13, has stolen 200 cars . . . and the law is powerless to stop him. *Daily Express*, February 9, p. 6.

Quétel, C. (1990). *History of Syphilis*. Trans. J. Braddock & B. Pike. Cambridge: Polity Press.

Rachlin, H. (1990). Why do people gamble and keep gambling despite heavy losses? *Psychological Science*, 1, 294–7.

Rachman, S. (1989). The return of fear: Review and prospect. *Clinical Psychology Review*, 9, 147–68.

Rachman, S. J. (1990). *Fear and Courage*, 2nd ed. New York: W. H. Freeman.

Rafferty, F. & Roy, A. (1990). Catching the gravy train at Westminster. *Sunday Times*, June 17, p. 19.

Randall, J. (1991). Golden blunder. *Sunday Times*, April 28, p. 3:1.

Read, P. P. (1974). *Alive: The Story of the Andes Survivors*. London: Alison Press/Martin Secker.

Redfern, M. (1995). Proofs of God in a photon? *Independent on Sunday Magazine*, December 24, pp. 36–7.

Reeves, P. (1993). Doctor shot in abortion feud. *Independent*, August 21, p. 10.

Reicher, S. D. (1984). The St Paul's riot: An explanation of the limits of crowd action in terms of a social identity model. *European Journal of Social Psychology*, 14, 1–21.

Reid, T. (2000). The real shame. *The Times*, August 11, Times2, pp. 3–4.

Rhoads, D. & Patterson, S. (1996). Choosing the right incentives. *Sunday Times*, November 10, p. 2:5.

Rhodes, T. (1999). Murderous revenge of the trenchcoat misfits. *Sunday Times*, April 25, pp. 1:26–7.

Rickey, M. (2001). Movers and shakers. *The Times*, August 6, Times2, pp. 12–13.

Rocco, F. (1991). Women who work too much. *Independent on Sunday*, December 22, p. 20.

Rocco, F. (1992). Mistresses of the House. *Independent on Sunday*, July 26, p. 20.

Rodgers, P. (1991). Pay and the old boy network. *Independent on Sunday*, November 24, Business, p. 8.

Rodgers, P. (1996). Did he jump or was he pushed? *Independent*, February 7, p. 1.

Rogers, L. (2002). Flatliner patients bring back evidence of life after death. *Sunday Times*, September 8, p. 1:11.

Rohrer, R. (1992). Special offer: A loan for life. *Independent*, October 30, p. 13.

Rohter, L. (1993). Doctor is slain during protest over abortions. *New York Times*, March 11, pp. A1, B10.

Rolls, E. T. (1999). *The Brain and Emotion*. Oxford: Oxford University Press.

Rooney, S. (2000). When the state lottery comes around, Thais go to bizarre lengths to hit the jackpot. *The Times Magazine*, August 5, p. 10.

Rosin, I. (1996). *Horizon: Living Death*. BBC2, November 25.

Rowlands, B. (1996). The thrill is not the kill. *Independent*, January 22, *Section Two*, p. 5.

Rumbelow, H. (1998). Suicide attempts rise to a record. *The Times*, December 3, p. 10.

Ryle, G. (1949). *The Concept of Mind*. London: Hutchinson's University Library.

Sage, A. (2000). Car-tuning craze turns French roads into deadly playground. *The Times*, December 27, p. 16.

Salaman, N. (1994). *What She Wants: Women Artists Look at Men*. London: Verso.

Sandler, J., Dare, C., & Holder, A. (1973). *The Patient and the Analyst*. London: George Allen & Unwin.

Sargent, W. (1957). *Battle for the Mind*. London: Heinemann.

Scarman, Lord (1981). *The Scarman Report*. Harmondsworth: Penguin.

Schachter, S. (1951). Deviation, rejection, and communication. *Journal of Abnormal and Social Psychology*, 46, 190–207.

Schachter, S. & Singer, J. E. (1962). Cognitive, social, and physiological determinants of emotional state. *Psychological Review*, 69, 379–99.

Schein, E. H. (1958). The Chinese indoctrination program for prisoners of war: A study of attempted "brainwashing." In E. E. Maccoby, T. M. Newcomb, & E. L. Hartley (Eds.), *Readings in Social Psychology*, 3rd ed. New York: Holt, pp. 311–34.

Schwab, R. S. (1953). Motivation in measurements of fatigue. In W. F. Floyd & A. T. Welford (Eds.), *Fatigue*. London: H. K. Lewis, pp. 143–9.

Schwartz, A. N., Campos, J. J., & Baisel, E. J., Jr. (1973). The visual cliff: Cardiac and behavioral responses on the deep and shallow sides at five and nine months of age. *Journal of Experimental Child Psychology*, 15, 86–99.

Scott, T. H., Bexton, W. H., Heron, W., & Doane, B. K. (1959). Cognitive effects of perceptual isolation. *Canadian Journal of Psychology*, 13, 200–9.

Sears, J. (1977). *The Effects of the Aggressive Behavior of Intoxicated and Non Intoxicated Subjects*. Master's thesis, Kent State University.

Seligman, M. E. P. (1970). On the generality of the laws of learning. *Psychological Review*, 77, 406–18.

Seligman, M. E. P. (1971). Phobias and preparedness. *Behavior Therapy*, 2, 307–20. Reprinted in M. E. P. Seligman & J. E. Hager (Eds.), *Biological Boundaries of Learning*. New York: Meredith, 1972, pp. 451–62.

Sereny, G. (1995). A child murdered by children. *Independent on Sunday*, April 23, *Review*, pp. 8–12.

Shattuck, R. (1980). *The Forbidden Experiment: The Story of the Wild Boy of Aveyron*. London: Secker & Warburg.

Sheffield and Rotherham Independent (1893). The rioting in West Yorkshire. Military fire on the mob. September 9.

Sherif, M. (1935). A study of some social factors in perception. *Archives of Psychology*, No. 187.

Sherif, M. (1937). An experimental approach to the study of attitudes. *Sociometry*, 1, 90–8.

Sherif, M. & Cantril, H. (1947). *The Psychology of Ego-Involvements*. New York: Wiley.

Sherwin, A. (1999). "Road rage" killer's confession dismissed by victim's family. *The Times*, April 19, p. 14.

Sherwin, A. (2001). Teacher faces the sack over Big Brother strip. *The Times*, May 30, p. 3.

Shorter, E. (1982). *History of Women's Bodies*. London: Allen Lane.

Shurley, J. T. (1963). The hydro-hypodynamic environment. *Proceedings of the Third World Congress of Psychiatry*, vol. 3. Toronto: University of Toronto Press, pp. 232–7.

Skinner, B. F. (1951). How to teach animals. *Scientific American*, 185, December, pp. 26–9.

Slocum, J. (1900). *Sailing Alone around the World*. London: Sampson Low, Marston & Co.

Smith, P. B. & Bond, M. H. (1993). *Social Psychology across Cultures*. London: Harvester Wheatsheaf.

Smith, R. J. (1978). *The Psychopath in Society*. New York: Academic Press.

Snoddy, G. S. (1920). An experimental analysis of a case of trial and error learning in the human subject. *Psychological Monographs*, 28, Whole No. 124.

Sopel, J. (2000). Violent pupils terrorise teachers. *The Times*, April 27, *Times2*, pp. 28–9.

Sperry, R. W. (1968). Hemisphere deconnection and unity in conscious awareness. *American Psychologist*, 23, 723–33.

Steele, C. M. & Josephs, R. A. (1990). Alcohol myopia: Its prized and dangerous effects. *American Psychologist*, 45, 921–33.

Steiner, R. (1998). Get down to your local Lewinsky. *Sunday Times*, September 27, pp. 3–18.

Stepney, R. (1995). You've caught it; you've got it for life. *Independent*, September 27, Section Two, p. 6.

Stevens, S. S. (1956). The direct estimation of sensory magnitudes – loudness. *American Journal of Psychology*, 69, 1–25.

Steyn, L. (2000). Why more women fear childbirth. *The Times*, July 4, *Times2*, pp. 10–11.

Storey, A. E., Walsh, C. J., Quinton, R. L. & Wynne-Edwards, K. E. (2000). Hormonal correlates of paternal responsiveness in new and expectant fathers. *Evolution and Human Behavior*, 21, 79–95.

Stouffer, S. A., Lumsdaine, A. A., Lumsdaine, M. H., Williams, R. M., Jr., Smith, M. B., Janis, I. L., Star, S. A., & Cottrell, L. S., Jr. (1949). *The American Soldier: Combat and its Aftermath*. Princeton, NJ: Princeton University Press.

Sunquist, M. E. (1981). The social organisation of tigers in Royal Chitawan National Park, Nepal. *Smithsonian Contributions to Zoology*, No. 336. Washington, DC: Smithsonian Institution Press.

Taylor, L. M. & Mitchell, P. (1996). Judgments of apparent shape contaminated by knowledge of reality: Viewing circles obliquely. Unpublished MS, University of Birmingham.

Taylor, S. P. & Gammon, C. B. (1976). Aggressive behavior of intoxicated subjects. *Journal of Studies on Alcohol*, 37, 917–30.

Taylor, S. P. & Leonard, K. E. (1983). Alcohol and human physical aggression. In R. G. Geen & E. I. Donnerstein (Eds.), *Aggression: Theoretical and Empirical Reviews*, vol. 2. New York: Academic Press, pp. 77–101.

The Times (1988). The Le Quesne Report: How the DTI licensed Clowes. October 21, pp. 28–9.

The Times (1991). Ratner's tat keeps the customers satisfied. April 24, p. 1.

The Times (1997). Mother pleads for help to trap road rage killer. October 17, p. 3.

The Times (1999a). Clowes is jailed for benefits fraud. March 2, p. 3.

The Times (1999b). Special supplement on motorbiking, July 30.

The Times (2001a). Indian lovers hanged by mob. August 9, p. 11.

The Times (2001b). Woman sentenced to death by stoning. June 26, p. 15.

Thirkell, R. (2000). *Head on the Block*. BBC2, September 14, 21, 28.

Thompson, T. (1991). Get-rich-quick hopers warned. *Independent on Sunday*, December 22, *Business News*, p. 18.

Thouless, R. H. (1931a, b). Phenomenal regression to the "real" object. *British Journal of Psychology*, (a) 21, 339–59; (b) 22, 1–30.

Thouless, R. H. (1932). Individual differences in phenomenal regression. *British Journal of Psychology*, 22, 216–41.

Thrasher, F. M. (1927). *The Gang*. Chicago: University of Chicago Press.

Thynne, J. (1987). Oxford prays for its unborn child. *Sunday Times*, March 1, p. 1.

Tinbergen, N. (1951). *The Study of Instinct*. Oxford: Oxford University Press.

Tinbergen, N. & Perdeck, A. C. (1951). On the stimulus situation releasing the begging response in the newly hatched herring gull chick (*Larus a. argetatus Pont.*). *Behaviour*, 3, 1–39.

Tomkins, R. (1987). Dilemma for the government over BP share defaulters. *Financial Times*, November 10, p. 25.

Torday, P. (1994). Coffee price soars after Brazilian frost damage. *Independent*, July 12, p. 23.

Toynbee, P. (1995). Nothing to do. No jobs. For the buzz. Dunno. Perhaps Luton's three hot nights of rioting defy reason. *Independent*, July 19, *Section Two*, pp. 2–3.

Tredre, R. (1990). Where art walks and money talks. *Independent*, January 25, p. 12.

Tredre, R. (1991). Millionaire catwalk stars waive fees. *Independent*, October 15, p. 3.

Tredre, R. (1992a). Models lead tough life as they cast about for work. *Independent*, March 24, p. 3.

Tredre, R. (1992b). The good, the bad, but not the ugly. *Independent*, February 20, p. 17.

Tredre, R. (1992c). Wannabes follow in steps of superstar models. *Independent*, July 16, p. 5.

Vallely, P. (1995). For what cause did Jill Phipps die? *Independent*, February 3, p. 17.

Vanson, Y. (1985). *People to People: The Battle for Orgreave*. Channel 4, September 25.

Varley, N. (1996). £60m spent in one day as Britain goes lottery mad. *Independent on Sunday*, January 7, p. 1.

Vernon, J. & Hoffman, J. (1956). Effect of sensory deprivation on learning rate in human beings. *Science*, 123, 1074–5.

Vernon, J., McGill, T. E., & Schiffman, H. (1958). Visual hallucinations during perceptual isolation. *Canadian Journal of Psychology*, 12, 31–4.

Vernon, P. E. (1941). Psychological effects of air-raids. *Journal of Abnormal and Social Psychology*, 36, 457–76.

Vertes, P. (1996). *Esquire* spoofs celebrity journalism. *Esquire* press release, October 15.

Waddington, D., Jones, K., & Critcher, C. (1989). *Flashpoints: Studies in Public Disorder*. London: Routledge.

Wagenaar, W. A. (1970). Subjective randomness and the capacity to generate information. In A. F. Sanders (Ed.), *Attention and Performance III, Acta Psychologica*, 33, 233–42.

Wagenaar, W. A. (1988). *Paradoxes of Gambling Behaviour*. Hove: Lawrence Erlbaum.

Wagner, H. (1999). *The Psychobiology of Human Motivation*. London: Routledge.

Warner, J. (1990). Serious Fraud Office knew company had been cleared. *Independent*, July 16, *Business*, p. 20.

Warren, R. M. (1989). Sensory magnitudes and their physical correlates. *Behavioral and Brain Sciences*, 12, 296–7.

Warren, R. M. & Warren, R. P. (1968). *Helmholtz on Perception: Its Physiology and Development*. New York: Wiley.

Waterhouse, R. (1990a). One in 10 Tory MPs linked to PR firms. *Independent on Sunday*, March 4, p. 2.

Waterhouse, R. (1990b). Tory MP "failed to tell Commons of business links." *Independent on Sunday*, February 18, p. 3.

Waterhouse, R. (1993). Clinic for sex offenders is told to close. *Independent*, October 8, p. 11.

Waterhouse, R. (2000). Confessions of a superhead. *The Times*, August 27, p. 1:13.

Weiskrantz, L. (1986). *Blindsight*. Oxford: Oxford University Press.

Westphal, C. (1871). Die Agoraphobie. *Archiv für Psychiatrie und Nervenkrankheiten*, 3, 138–61, 219–21.

Wexler, D., Mendelson, J., Leiderman, P. H., & Solomon, P. (1958). Sensory deprivation: A technique for studying psychiatric aspects of stress. *AMA Archives of Neurology and Psychiatry*, 79, 225–33.

White, L. (1999). Frisky business. *Sunday Times Magazine*, August 8, pp. 16–20.

Whitfield, M. (1994). Sex killer of boy, 7, gets life sentence. *Independent*, January 29, p. 3.

Whitworth, D. (1999a). Shakers ready to rattle and roll. *The Times*, November 6, p. 13.

Whitworth, D. (1999b). The ex files. *The Times Magazine*, December 4, pp. 43–9.

Whitworth, D. & Macintyre, B. (2000). That happens on television, says killer, 6. *The Times*, March 2, p. 5.

Wilkinson, P. (1997). Scratchcard addict is hungry for a win. *The Times*, March 22, p. 9.

Wilkinson, P. (2000). Cleared killer jailed for the lies he told. *The Times*, April 15, p. 6.

Williams, G. D., Stinson, F. S., Parker, D. A., Harford, T. C., & Noble, J. (1987). Demographic trends, alcohol abuse, and alcoholism. *Alcohol Health and Research World*, 15, 80–3.

Wilsher, P., MacIntyre, D., & Jones, M. (1985). *Strike*. London: Coronet.

Woodford, S. (1998). *Neighbours at War*. BBC1, January 5–26.

Woodworth, R. S. & Schlosberg, H. (1955). *Experimental Psychology*, 3rd ed. London: Methuen.

Wooley, A. (1990). Phobias. *Independent*, January 16, p. 15.

Young, R. (2000). Women stitched up by Henley hem rule. *The Times*, June 29, p. 6.

Zimbardo, P. G. (1972). Pathology of imprisonment. *Society*, 9, 4–8.

Zuckerman, M. (1964). Perceptual isolation as a stress situation. *Archives of General Psychiatry*, 11, 255–76.

Zuckerman, M. & Cohen, N. (1964). Sources of reports of visual and auditory sensations in perceptual-isolation experiments. *Psychological Bulletin*, 62, 1–20.

INDEX

Substantive subjects are in roman type, illustrative examples in italics. Page numbers in bold refer to figures or tables, *italic* numbers to the reference list.

aggression, 4, 5, 211, 213–14
  as feeling "out of sorts," 212
  as frustration, 212
  as instinct, 213
  as retaliation, 213
  Buss apparatus, 216
  experimental methods, 215
  instrumental and emotional, 214–15
  mean shock levels, **217**
  social constraints on, 217
  teacher's level of, 216
  validity of laboratory experiments, 217
agoraphobia, 33
  Kim Basinger, 33
  Westphal (1871), 33, *301*
alcohol, 218
  associated with crime and violence, 219
  mean reaction times, **218**
  slows reaction time, 218
"alcohol myopia," 219–20
Allegra Coleman, 130
altered states of consciousness, 42, 63
  Geoffrey Wildsmith, 64
  Nicholas Pierce, 63
  Robert Wendland, 64
anecdotal material, 3–5
  comparing with experimental findings, 217

anti-abortion campaigners, 204–5
  Operation Rescue, 204
  Rescue America, 205
Asch, S. E., 5, 173–7, 178–80, 181, 184–8, 191, 194, *284*
Asch's experiments
  awareness of majority, 179
  critical participant writes his answers, 179
  five categories of reaction, 187
  individual differences, 186, **187**
  inversion of majority and minority, 184
  method, 174, **175**
  non-unanimous majority, **181**
  planted partner, **181**, 188
  size of majority, **185**
  standard line with single comparison, **178**
  summary, 192, **193**, 194
awareness, 63, 66, 69, 75
  recall as test of, 63
  seat of, 67

behavior
  combined with basic instinctive pattern, 281
  courtship, 55, 171, 280
  other people's determinate, 279

psychological theory treats as
determinate, 13
quasi-mechanical, 2, 6, 279, 281
"substantially mechanical," 46, 51, 58, 280
Berkowitz, L., 211–12, 214, 217, 221, 235, 239, *285*
Bexton, W. H., 81, 83–5, 89, 91–5, *285*, 298
blackjack, 20, 268–9, 275
"basic" strategy, 268
how gamblers play, 269
professional card counter, 270
rules, **268**
"Blitz," the, 30
body language, 74, 223–4
enlarged pupils, 224
innate, 224
see also portrayal of emotion
boredom, 84
boredom at work, 97
airliner overflying destination, 97
as frustration of instinct, 96
boxing, 234–6
effect of watching, 235, **236**
emotional arousal, 236
heavyweight championship contests, 233
instinctive response to seeing others fight, 235
"*brainwashing*," 83, 144
Cardinal Mindszenty, 82, 145, 295
prisoners of war in Korea, 83, 145; *see also prisoners of war in Korea*
Bridgewater Three, 191
James Robinson, 192
British Gas, 138
Cedric Brown, 138
Richard Giordano, company chairman, 138
Brownfield, C. A., 85, 154, *286*
burglar, interview with, 103, 157

camera view, 275, 280
see also personal view; personal view and camera view

caste system in India, 13
brought to Britain, 114
lynching, 114
cats, 12, 211
Archy and Bella, 1, 6, 11
tigers, 47, 211
chess, 16–18, 55
predictability, 17
Sämisch vs. Nimzowitch, 1923, **17–18**
child abusers, themselves abused as children, 46, 58
childbirth, mortality in, 39
children murdered by children
George Burgess, 231
James Bulger, 230
Kayla Rolland, 232
Christie & Geis, 248–50, 254
Christie, R., 255, *286*
Columbine High School shooting, 231
commissions for financial services, 257
Barlow Clowes, **259**, 260
DPR Futures, 258
Dunsdale Securities, 260
Peter Clowes, 260
Robert Miller, 260–1
company directors
are they worth their pay?, 132
boardroom pay, 130
do they know how to do their jobs?, 133
Gerald Ratner, 133–4
how are they appointed?, 131
how is their pay determined?, 132
Mountleigh, 132
Sir Colin Marshall, 131–2
compensation for post-traumatic stress, 246
FA Cup semi-final at Hillsborough, 246
con game, 250
bargaining in, **251**
consciousness, 61–70, 75–7
different states of unconsciousness, **62**
importance to study of motivation, 79
meaning of, 62
neural signature, 65
phenomenal, 64, 68
philosophical inquiry into, 64
sectioning of the *corpus callosum*, 78

constant-ratio rule, 13, **14**
"copycat" crimes, 231–2
  President Reagan, 231
credibility when lying, 253
  relationship to Machiavellianism, **255**
"crowd," 209
  compared with "army," 205
crowd behavior
  crowd's reason for being, 205
  flashpoint, 196
  "group mind," 197
  protest against export of veal calves, 195
  random evolution of, 202; see also
    random evolution of crowd behavior
  speed of evolution of, 198; see also rapid
    evolution of crowd behavior
  the social setting, 207
crowding, 225–7
  ducks, 225
  monkeys and chimpanzees, 225, 227
  Norway rats, 225
  pigs, 226
Curtiss, S., 150, 287

David Icke, 184–5
deliberations in the jury room, 182–3, 279
  initial voting in 225 trials, **183**
  outcome of 155 trials, **184**
determinism and free will, 11–20, 69
  see also free will
Deutsch, M., 178, 180, 186, 288
Die Schöne Müllerin, 53
Doane, B. K., 85, 87–8, 93–4, 288, 291, 298
domestic violence, 219–21, 237
  example of "negative affect," 221
  in Russia, 222
  instinctive fury, 221
  one woman's testimony, 212
  Paul Gascoigne, footballer, 219
Don Giovanni, 50–1

Ebbinghaus, H., 35–7, 288
Edward L. Green letter, 255–6
Ellis Wardle, 21–2, 23, 35
Emerson, R. M., 157–8

emotion, as subjective correlate of
  motivation, 42
  differences between, 74
  two-factor theory, 213
estimation of probabilities, 265
  contraceptive pills, 265, **267**
  extended warranties, 266–7
experience of fear, 32–5
  agoraphobia, 33; see also agoraphobia
  being in control, 34
  bomb disposal in Northern Ireland, 35
  combat flying, 34
  companionship, 33
  military combat, 34
  Mima Guy's treatment for
    arachnophobia, 32
  training and skill, 35
eye contact, 253–4
  mean duration, **254**
  relationship to Machiavellianism, 253
Eye Need, 247

fashion models, 128–30, 138
fear, 21–36
  anxiety, 25
  as innate reaction, 27–8
  as instinct, 30
  compared with pain, 30–1
  components of, 25
  experience of, 33; see also experience of
    fear
  no reaction to adverse driving conditions,
    31
  origins of, 23
  "paralysis of terror," 169
  pathological, 32; see also pathological fear
  persistence of, 35–6
  recurrence of, 36
  two stages in genesis of, 27
fear in battle
  Carentan Causeway (D-Day landings in
    Normandy), 25–34, 169–70
  Kwajalein battle, 170
  of killing rather than of being killed, 170
fear reaction, 31

feral children, 147, 155
  anecdotal reports, 151
  Genie, 150, 152–3; *see also* Genie
  John, 150–1; *see also* John
  Victor, 148–53; *see also* Victor
flight KT328, 21, 37
football violence, 227
  Luton vs. Millwall, March 13, 1985, 195
  Paolo di Canio, 227–8
forgetting one's native language, 143
  Alexander Selkirk, 143, 153
  Jacob Bronowski, 153, 286
Frances Lawrence, 156, 173
free will, 17–19
  in indeterminacy of choice, 13
  see also determinism and free will
Freud, S., 23–4, *285*

gambling, 262–76
  at *Casino Club, Lytham St Anne's,* 264,
    271, 273
  Barry Partridge, 275
  National Lottery, 262, 264–5; *see also*
    National Lottery
  Peter with a degree in statistics, 275
  prevalence in Britain, 1995, 262, **263**
Gazzaniga, M. S., 76–9, 289
Geis, F. L., 250, 253, **286**, 290
  see also Christie & Geis
Genie, 150, 152–3
  abnormal brain waves, 153
  attempted rehabilitation, 151
  difference with respect to Victor, 151
Gerard, H. B., 178, 180, 186, 288, 290
Great Western Road, fair-haired girl
  walking down, 40, **41,** 42–3, 45, 51,
    279–82
Guildford Four, 189–91
  Carole Richardson, 189–1
  Gerry Conlon, 189–1

hallucinations, 85, 87, 88–9
  incidence of, 87
  when bored, 97
  with translucent and opaque masks, 88

Hebb, D. O., 83–4, 95, 169, *290–1*
Heron, W., 81, 85, 87, 93–4, *285, 288,*
    291, 298
homicides, 232
  average daily number, **233**
  following a heavyweight boxing contest,
    233
homosexuality, 56, 281
hormones, 281–2
  adrenaline, 26
  when a baby cries on TV, 3
House of Commons, 130, 134–5,
    138

Indian culture, 53
  acid attacks in Bangladesh, 171
  arranged marriages, 114–15
  caste system, 13; *see also caste system in*
    India
  cinema, 53
influence of social milieu, 241
  Medway Secure Training Centre,
    243
  The Ridings School, 241–2
  Torsten Friedag, "superhead," 242
informational and normative influences,
    177
informational influence, 178, 194
instinct, 1
  aggression, 211, 228, 237
  courtship, 55
  in prison society, 169
  interaction with others, 8
  patterns of behavior, 2, 6
  response to social signals, 281
internal thoughts and feelings, 12, 42–3,
    278–9
  essentially unobservable, 64
Internet "chat" rooms, 46
interrogation by the police, 188
  Bridgewater Three, 191; *see also*
    Bridgewater Three
  Guildford Four, 189–91; *see also*
    Guildford Four
Itard, J., 147–9, 152–3, 292, 294

John, 150–1
    acquisition of native language, 151
    difference with respect to Victor and
        Genie, 151
    instinctive care young children, 150
Jost's law, 36

Keren, G., 269, 274, 292
Kinkead, E., 83, 146, 292
Kinsey, A. C., 44, 49–50, 52–3, 56–7, 152,
        237, 292

Laming, D., 4, 65–6, 86, 265, 292–3
Lang, A. R., 4, 215–16, 218, 293
lay psychology, 43–4, 279
Leach, P., 111, 213–14, 293
Lee Harvey, 210–11
leisure activities, 98–101
    "biking," 99
    bungee jumping, 98
    fire-raising, 101
    "hotting," 100
    playing "chicken" with trains,
        100
    relationship to fear, 101
    skydiving, 99
    snake-handling, 98
Lilly, J. C., 87, 89, 155, 293
Lisa Potts, 22–3
loneliness, 140–53
    Admiral Byrd, 142–3, 286
    Alexander Selkirk, 143
    Christopher Burney, 143, 286
    comparison with sensory deprivation,
        140, 143
    Joshua Slocum, 141–2, 299
Lorenz, K., 227, 293
luck, 272–5

Machiavelli, 248–9
Machiavellianism, 248, 250
    and eye contact, 253
    con game, 250; see also con game
    relationship to psychopathic personality,
        251; see also psychopathic personality

scale of, 249
    $10 game, 249; see also $10 game
Malinowski, B., 47, 58, 294
Malson, L., 147–8, 150, 294
Marcel, A. J., 71, 74, 79, 294
marriage, 7
    and divorce, 57
Marshall, Brig. S. L. A., 25, 33–4, 169–70,
        294–5
massacres, 119
    My Lai, Vietnam, 1968, 119
    Rotherham, 1893, 120
    Tiananmen Square, Beijing, 1989, 120
maternal care, 8
memory, 36
    "false memory syndrome," 24
    persistence of, 35, 37
Milgram, S., 5, 103–5, 107–8, 110–11,
        113, 116, 118–19, 123–4, 146,
        169–70, 215–16, 295
Milgram's experiments, 104, 105
    importance of social structure, 109, 110
    predictions by psychiatrists, 104–6
    proximity of teacher and pupil, 104, 106
    relaxation of the conflict, 108
Milgram's results, understanding, 117
military obedience, 119
    Cambodia under Pol Pot, 118
    Nazi Germany, 118, 122
    Soviet Union under Stalin, 118
miners' strike 1984–5, 176–7, 181
    Chris Butcher, 181–2
    John and Joy Watson, 166
    miner going in to work alone, 176
    two rallies of miners, Sheffield, April
        1984, 206–7
money, 245–61, 281
    how much do different people earn?,
        124, 126
    people closest to the money, 125; see also
        people closest to the money
    people doing the same job, 125; see also
        people doing the same job
    people negotiating a private deal, 128;
        see also negotiating a private deal

moneylenders, 252
  credit rating, 252
  loan companies, 252
  Paul McCabe, 252–3
  pawnbroking, 252
Montagu, A., 47–8, *295*
moral constraints, 170
  subconscious, 169
moral sanction, 157, 167–8
Morris, D., 55
MPs' financial interests, 134
  "Parliamentary consultants," 136
  Parliamentary lobbying, 136
  question in Parliament in return for
    payment, 136
  Register of Members' Interests, 134–5
Mullin, C. S., Jr., 144, *295*
Murray, C., 157, 171, *295*

Nagel, T., 65, 68, *295*
National Lottery, 262, 264–5
  Beverley Miles, addicted, 262
negative affect, 212
  boy of 12 who killed his baby brother, 212
negotiating a private deal, 128
  supermodels, 128
neural correlates, 65
  binocular rivalry, 66–7, 69
  Springer's lines, 65, **66**, 68
nonverbal communication, 224
  see also body language
normative influence, 194, 179

orgasm, 39, 42
  in camera view, 42
  totals per week, 57
  women in marriage, 49, 50
Orne, M. T., 159, 217, *296*
"out-of-the-body" experiences, 91
  David Verdegaal, 91–2
  Melvyn Bragg, 91
overwintering in the Antarctic, 144
  boredom, 144
  intellectual inertia, 144
  suppressed aggression, 144

"Paper, Scissors, Stone," 14–16, 20
  and free will, 16
  internal thoughts, 16
  predictability, 16
pathological fear, 32
  agoraphobia, 33; *see also* agoraphobia
  "free-floating anxiety," 24, 26
  neurosis, 32
  phobias, 32; *see also* phobias
pedophiles, 49
  Colin Hatch, 49
  Howard Hughes, 49
  Paulsgrove estate, 163–4, 167
people closest to the money, 125
  Bill Brown, chairman of Walsham
    Brothers, 127
  Jan Leschly, chief executive, SmithKline
    Beecham, 127
  Liliane Preisler, "currency swaps"
    broker, 127
people doing the same job, 125
  earnings of men and women, 125
  House of Commons, 125
personal view, 17, 281
  see also camera view; personal view and
    camera view
personal view and camera view, 6, 14,
    40–3, **61**, 62–4, 67–9, 274–5, 278–9
  David Beckham, 6, 7
  dualism between, 68
  Manchester United vs. Bayern Munich,
    6
  see also camera view; personal view
phenomenal regression to real size, **19**,
    73
  predictability, 19
phenomenal regression to the real object,
    73
philosophical inquiry into consciousness,
    64
  dualism, 64–5, 67–8
  reduction to brain function, 64, 67
phobias, 25, 27, 32
  cats, 27
  spiders, 27, 32

pleasure principle, 47, 49
  attitudes of 16–24-year-olds, 49
  immediate pleasure of sexual intercourse, 39–40
  woman reaching orgasm, 49
pornography, 44, 51–2, 212, 238
  advertising, 52
  Big Brother, 52
  erotic magazines aimed at women, 44
  "*Lad Mags*," 52
portrayal of emotion, 74
  actress does not actually feel, 74
  body language, 74
  difference between different emotions, 74
  Pride and Prejudice, 74, 285; *see also Pride and Prejudice*
predictability, 18, 19
  of individual choice, 13
prepared fears, 27
  "*looming*," 28, **29**
  snakes, 29
  Sue Fox paralysed every time she drives, 29
  visual cliff, 27, **28**
Pride and Prejudice, 40, 45, 74, 285
  Colin Firth, 40–1, 45–6, 51
  Jennifer Ehle, 45–6, 74
prison society, 147, 168
  extrusion of sex offenders, 168
prisoners, 121–2
prisoners in solitary confinement, 140
prisoners of war in Korea, 145
  breakdown of discipline, 146
  breaking up of social structure, 146
  collaboration with communists, 83
  deaths in captivity, 146
  Turkish prisoners, 146
prisons, 8, 121–2, 168
  Birmingham jail, 122
  Charles Dickens, 154, 288
  Eastern Penitentiary in Philadelphia, 154
psychoanalysis, 23

psychopathic personality, 247
  characteristics, **248**
  relationship to Machiavellianism, 251; *see also* Machiavellianism
  unresponsive to social constraints, 247
public protest, 203
  Gracewell Clinic, 204
  pedophiles, 204
pyramid selling, 256

Rachman, S., 33, 35–6, 297
rage, 210, 212
  acute loss of self-control, 220
  "air rage," 212
  anger as the emotional counterpart, 211
  as takeover by instinctive behavior patterns, 211
  "road rage," 222, 225–7; *see also* road rage
random evolution of crowd behavior, 202
  rumor, 202–3
rape, 58
  "*date rape*," 58
  women killed for refusing intercourse, 59
  young woman at Durham University, 58
rapid evolution of crowd behavior, 198
  car drivers on the M25 motorway, 198, **199**, 200
  funeral of Diana, Princess of Wales, 200
rationality, 264
  rational man, 38–9, 264
  rational woman, 38–9
riots, 195–6, 201, 203, 205, 207–9
  Bob and Dot Dunderdale, 200–1, 203
  Brixton, April 10–12, 1981, 196
  Brixton, December 1995, 207
  Heysel Stadium, Brussels, May 29, 1985, 201
  Luton vs. Millwall, March 13, 1985, 195
  Marsh Farm estate, Luton, 208
  not predictable, 209
  St Paul's, Bristol, April 2, 1980, 196
  two rallies of miners, Sheffield, April 1984, 206–7

road rage, 222, 225–7
  example, 222
  incidence in Britain, **223**
  three principal factors, 226
roulette, 270–1, 273
  betting systems, 271
  rules, **271**
rumor, 202
  earthquakes in India, 202–3

St Francis of Assisi, 245
sales promotions, 276–7
Scarman, Lord, 196, 208, 298
Schachter, S., 26, 157–8, 213, 298
Schwab, R. S., 245, 298
  supporting one's weight, 245
Scott, T. H., 81, 85, 87, 94–5, 285, 288,
    291, 298
sensory deprivation, 84–96, 154
  cognitive deficits, 94, **95**
  difficulties in concentration, 95
  disturbance in visual perception, 85, 92,
    94
  feelings of confusion, 85
  hallucinations, 85, 87, **88**, 89
  *handwriting before and after
    confinement*, **93**
  "iron lungs," 89–90
  "out-of-the-body" experiences, 91
  sensory disorientation, 93
  water-tank chamber, **86**
  "white-out," 92
sexual behavior
  acquisition of, 47
  between strangers in an aircraft, 46
  copied from others, 46
  extraneous triggers, 51
  "falling in love," 42
  how much acquired?, 57
  match between male and female, 56
  Monica Lewinsky, 46
  number of lifetime partners, 50
  pedophiles, 49; *see also pedophiles*
  Pitcairn Island, 171
  quasi-mechanical, 45

repertoire of instinctive components, 55
sex addiction, 51
survival of the species, 54
variation in, 56
sexual intercourse, 43
  contraception, 48–9, 56
  positions during, 58
  relation with conception, 47; *Australian
    aborigines*, 47; *Trobriand islanders*,
    47
sexual license in the media, 197–8
  BBC code, 197
  Broadcasting Standards Council, 198,
    202
  Channel 4's "Red Light Evenings," 197
  Channel 5 soft-porn films, 198
  Lady Chatterley's Lover, 202
sexually transmitted diseases, 38, 48
  syphilis, 38–9
Shakers, 47
Sherif, M., 157, 177, *299*
Shurley, J. T., 85, 153, *299*
Singer, J. E., 26, 213, *298*
social cognition, 223
  identification of emotion, 223
  South Fore people, 224
social conformity, 174
  group cohesiveness, 180
social constraints, 157, 220
  modify sexual behavior, 52; *see also
    sexual behavior*
social conventions, 111–18, 123–4, 137–8,
    153, 161, 167, 171, 173–4, 192, 197,
    215, 221, 245, 280–2
  British Petroleum privatization, 111
  C. vs. S., 116
  cannibalism, 112–13
  capital punishment, 116
  caste system in India, 13
  *differ between subgroups within the one
    society*, 116
  different in different societies, 113
  *entry to the stewards' enclosure at
    Henley Regatta*, 112
  evolution, 197

social conventions (*cont'd*)
  how much do different people earn?,
    124, **126**
  kissing in public, 53
  legitimizing sex before marriage, 111
  negotiating a private deal, 128; *see also
    negotiating a private deal*
  of the larger society, 205
  people closest to the money, 125; *see also
    people closest to the money*
  people doing the same job, 125; *see also
    people doing the same job*
  positions during sexual intercourse,
    58
  sexual license in the media, 197; *see also
    sexual license in the media*
  social status of women, 114; *see also
    social status of women*
  speed limits on motorways, 112
  speed of evolution, 198
  table manners, 113
  taboos on nudity, 52; *see also taboos on
    nudity*
  women wounded in battle, 171
social extrusion, 7, 8, 140, 163, 167, 171,
    174
  Angelina Mavrides, 167
  Anne and Daniel Wiseman, 165
  as the ultimate sanction, 161
  experimental study, 157, **158**
  from community, 166
  imprisonment as punishment, 154
  interim conclusions, 167
  John and Joy Watson, 166
  Kelly Turner, 164
  Megan's Law, 163
  News of the World, "naming and
    shaming," 163
  pedophiles, 163–4; *see also pedophiles*
  revulsion at murder of James Bulger,
    167–8
  risked by critical participant, 180
  spontaneous, 167
  threat of, 194
  ultimate penalty, 157, 179

  whistleblowers, 180; *see also
    whistleblowers*
social isolation, 147, 157, 169
  anecdotal reports, 144
  conclusions, 153
  importance as a sanction, 155
  longing for companionship, 152
  overwintering in the Antarctic, 144; *see
    also overwintering in the Antarctic*
  research, 143
  toleration, 155
  unpleasant, 154
social relationship with experimenter, 4
social status of women, 114
  deaths among young Indian wives, 115
  dowry demands, 115
  in Hindu countries, 115
  in Muslim countries, 114
  ratio of men to women in India, 115
social submissiveness, 227
sociological survey, 5
solitary confinement, 143
  Christopher Burney, 143
Sperry, R. W., 76–7, 299
split brain, 75, **76**, **77**, 78
  feelings of mind, 78
  patients, 76–9
  studies, 79
Stanford County Prison Experiment, 120–2,
    124
  interviews, 122
  prison, 121
  prisoners, 121
Steele, C. M., 219–20, 299
Stouffer, S. A., 34, 299
subjective experience, 69, **71**
  auditory space, 73
  blindsight, 74–5
  foreign languages, 71
  *Leonardo da Vinci's Portrait of Cecilia
    Gallerani*, 72
  listening to speech, 71
  phenomenal regression to real size, 73
  phenomenal regression to the real object,
    73

portrayal of emotion, 74
tactile space, 74
suicides, 238–9, 246
    frequency, **239**
    influenced by media, 239
sympathetic motivation, 237
    aroused by watching other people in
        conflict, 237
    live sex shows, 237
    neighbor disputes, 236

taboos on nudity, 52
    clothes, 52
    undergraduate who dropped his trousers,
        53
tantrums, 3, 213–14, 242
    as instinctive pattern of aggression, 214
    "terrible twos," 213
$10 game, 249
$10 game, numbers in final coalition, **250**
therapy, 36, 168
    desensitization, 36
    relapse, 36
Thouless, R. H., 19, 72–3, *300*
three fundamental ideas, 6, 278
Tim Yeo, 39
Tinbergen, N., 1, *300*
torturers, 107
Tracie Andrews, 210–12, 214, 279

underclass, 171
    11-year-old joyrider, 171
    13-year-old in Sunderland, 172
    Learco Chindamo, 156, 173

Lee Ridley, 172
    own social conventions, 173

Vernon, J., 87, *300*
Victor, 148–53, 281
    attempted rehabilitation, 151
    attitude to clothes, 152
    courtship behavior, 149
    difference with respect to Genie, 151
    inability to acquire language, 152
    insensitivity to pain, 148
    powers of concentration, 148
    prior acquisition of a feral culture, 152
    repeated attempts to run away, 152
video nasties
    increase the long-term frequency of
        violence?, 239
    prompt violence, 232
violence, 3–4, 211
violence on television, 239–41
    influence of social milieu, 241
    long-term effect, **240**
    prevalence of, 240
    St Helena, 241

Wagenaar, W. A., 268–70, 272–5, 292,
    301
whistleblowers, 159
    Graham Pink, 159
    Jim Smith, 161
    PC Adrian Dart, 160–1
    Stephen Bolsin, 160

Zimbardo, P., 121–2, 290, *301*